ILLUMINATIONS FROM THE PAST

Cultural Memory
in
the
Present

Mieke Bal and Hent de Vries, Editors

ILLUMINATIONS
FROM THE PAST

*Trauma, Memory, and History
in Modern China*

Ban Wang

STANFORD UNIVERSITY PRESS

STANFORD, CALIFORNIA

2004

Stanford University Press
Stanford, California
www.sup.org

Library of Congress Cataloging-in-Publication Data
Wang, Ban, 1957–
   Illuminations from the past : trauma, memory, and history in modern China /
Ban Wang.
      p.   cm.—(Cultural memory in the present)
   Includes bibliographical references and index.
   ISBN 0-8047-4946-9 (alk. paper)—ISBN 0-8047-5099-8 (pbk : alk. paper)
   1. Popular culture—China. 2. Postmodernism—China. 3. China—
Civilization—1976– I. Title. II. Series.
HM621.W35 2004
306′.0951—dc22   2004008172

Printed in the United States of America on acid-free, archival-quality paper.

Original Printing 2004

Last figure below indicates year of this printing:
14 13 12 11 10 09 08 07 06 05

Designed and typeset at Stanford University Press in 11/13.5 Garamond.

For my mother and father

Contents

Acknowledgments   xi

Introduction: Memory and History in Globalization   1

PART I. TOWARD A CRITICAL HISTORICAL CONSCIOUSNESS

  1. Tradition, Memory, and Hope: Lu Xun and Critical
     Historical Consciousness   17
  2. Tragic Vision, Traumatic Visuality, and the Montage
     of History   58

PART 2. POSTREVOLUTIONARY TRAUMA AND
THE RECONSTRUCTION OF HISTORY

  3. Postrevolutionary History in a Traumatic Key   93
  4. Temporality, Memory, and Myth in Wang Anyi's Fiction   124
  5. Traumatic History Against Melodrama: *Blue Kite*   142
  6. From Historical Narrative to the World of Prose   163

PART 3. GLOBALIZATION, NOSTALGIA, RESISTANCE

  7. Reenchanting the Everyday in the Global City   181
  8. Love at Last Sight: Nostalgia, Memory, and Commodity
     in Contemporary Chinese Literature   212
  9. Remembering Realism: The Material Turn in Chinese
     Cinema and Street Scenes of Globalization   235

x   *Contents*

Notes   259
Chinese Names and Terms   277
Bibliography   283
Index   295

Acknowledgments

Modern history is an accelerating process of production and consumption. We are sucked into its fluid orbit, throwing to the winds memories of home, tradition, and stability. This book started out as a reflection on ruptures and traumas of this relentless trailblazing, but its coming into being has relied heavily on a community of memory. A circle of colleagues, friends, and critics kept expanding as I worked on the book. The people who have contributed to the book are so numerous and their input so valuable that an adequate recall would amount to an illustration of how the individual can do little if not submerged within a collective endeavor. I can only mention some who have been more intimately involved than others in this project. These colleagues and friends have had something important to add along the way through teaching, commenting, conferencing, administrating, requesting manuscripts, and editing. I now inscribe my deep gratitude in a firmer medium of memory. In a rough chronological order, these have steered and altered the progress of the book: E. Ann Kaplan, Leo Ou-fan Lee, David Wang, Zhang Xudong, Lydia Liu, Kirk Denton, Li Tuo, Zhang Zhen, Chen Jianhua, Martin Woesler, Liu Xinmin, Lu Jie, John Ziemer, Yomi Braester, Tang Xiaobing, Chris Berry, and Tani Barlow.

To be able to work with Muriel Bell, Carmen Borbon-Wu, Tony Hicks, and Karen Hellekson of Stanford University Press has been a blessing. I also thank the reader of the manuscript for the insightful comments and suggestions.

A summer writing stipend in 1997 and a research fellowship in 2000 from the National Endowment for the Humanities enabled me to sit down and write. I thank that great institution. My fellowship with the Center for Critical Analysis of Contemporary Culture at Rutgers in 2001 also provoked me to think more about the performative aspect of history writing and cultural memory. I thank Elin Diamond and Carolyn Williams of Rutgers University for including me in the Center's weekly seminar. The Department of Asian Languages and Cultures at Rutgers is a congenial and supportive milieu for doing research, and I thank Professor Ching-I Tu, the chair, for his unceasing support and deep understanding.

Many ideas in this book came from listening to what gradate students had to say. In various seminars I conducted over the years at SUNY–Stony Brook, Harvard, and Rutgers University, I have learned a lot from the students' views and perceptions, even as I was struggling to clarify the issues. I thank these colleagues: Michelle Huang, Li Chishe, Zhang Zhen, Wo Chingling, and Xiong Zhaohui, who were at SUNY–Stony Brook. I thank Ning Xin, Xu Lijing, Lu Yingjiu, Chen Jie, Yu-I Hsieh, Xiao Jiwei, Chang Chia-ju, and Hsu Jenyi, all of Rutgers, for their stimulating discussion on memory, history, and modernity.

Portions of Chapter 2 were published in *Trauma and Cinema: Cross-Cultural Explorations*, edited by E. Ann Kaplan and Ban Wang (Hong Kong: Hong Kong University Press, 2004). Parts of Chapter 3 were published in *American Journal of Chinese Studies* 5, no. 1 (1998). Parts of Chapter 4 were published in *Journal of Contemporary China* 12, no. 37 (2003). An earlier version of Chapter 5 was published in *Modern Chinese Literature and Culture* 11, no. 1 (1999). Chapter 6 was published in *The Modern Chinese Literary Essay*, edited by Martin Woesler (Bochum, Germany: Bochum University Press, 2000). An earlier version of Chapter 8 was published in *positions* 10, no. 3 (2002). I thank the journals and publishers for permission to reprint these portions.

ILLUMINATIONS FROM THE PAST

Memory and History in Globalization

Globalization presents two faces. Economically, it is capitalism's expanding cycle of development in the regions outside the capital concentrated metropolises. Politically, it is the continued exercise of imperial domination by the powerful capitalist nations over other nations and regions. What prompted this study of historical narrative and memory is certain historical orientations that have become more visible in the past two decades, tendencies that evolve around the fall of the Berlin Wall and the events of September 11, 2001. In the analysis of Michael Hardt and Antonio Negri, an imperial paradigm is emerging and set in motion with unprecedented acceleration, rhythm, violence, and momentum.[1] Empire refers to the sweeping idea of "a single power," a supranational sovereignty that presides over and polices conflicting powers in a unitary way. The imperial paradigm is not only about power and domination, but also projects new sets of moral authority and norms that everybody has to follow in order to live with the neighbors: it is "a new notion of right, or rather a new inscription of authority and a new design of the production of norms and legal instruments of coercion that guarantee contracts and resolve conflicts."[2]

Although it seems prematurely utopian to have high expectations for a supranational juridical apparatus and universal ethical standards capable of maintaining the world order, it is nevertheless clear that, in the ever close interdependence among regions and nations, different histories and trajectories are becoming less important in the global context.[3] The idea of universal history, fueled by the pressure to alter a culture's unique identity and to loosen the individual's local allegiance in favor of universal standards, is becoming increasingly urgent. There is a sense that the individual can no longer easily remain a member of a particular culture, a citizen of a particular nation, but has to be the citizen of the world, more in tune with universally recognized norms and rights in a global civil society. The much-celebrated difference, derived from native culture, the long durée of local history, tradition, custom, and memory, is in grave doubt. Universal history, or universal ethical orientation, seems to be an outside that no one can be protected from. As Hardt and Negri put it, "the domesticity of values, the shelters behind which they presented their moral substance, the limits that protect against the invading exteriority—all that disappears."[4] I do not think differences will disappear, and this book reconsiders local difference within global context by discussing productive tensions between memory and history.

What is troubling about the imperial paradigm, in its drive for universal norms and all-encompassing authority, is that it puts history in suspension. The emancipatory practices throughout modern history are written off in the transit to a new grand narrative. In the steady erosion of the Enlightenment narrative of emancipation, humanism, and freedom throughout the twentieth century, a new mythological narrative is triumphantly arriving on the scene. This is the narrative of capitalist modernization.[5] It tells its stories and projects everyone's future by suppressing alternative strata in vastly different historical trajectories. Under the labels of modernization, development, and democracy, this narrative was challenged for decades in the twentieth century, in a time of decolonization and independence movements. But with the recession of socialism and the accelerated spread of the capitalist economy since the late 1980s, this narrative has in recent years become the hegemonic paradigm for thinking and writing modern Chinese history both in the west and in China. In the shadows of impoverished everyday life and authoritarian politics of the past eras, the historical imagination in China has increasingly become enthralled to the glamorous prospect of global capital, the world market, middle-class prosperity, civil society, and endless economic development.[6] This narrative, as Arif Dirlik suggests, exercises its magic appeal by erasing not only memories of revolution, but also the memories of modernity's own complex and crisis-ridden vicissitudes of becoming.[7]

Earlier in the twentieth century, Walter Benjamin sought to dispel the historicist myth of technological progress, science, and rationality—the empty, homogeneous time of capitalist modernity—by brushing history against the grain. In the same spirit, I seek to brush history against the engrained historical discourse in modern China by evoking memories of alternative bypaths and substrata. A constant rearticulation of hidden memories and a vigilant awareness of alternatives are crucial to opening up diverse scenarios and prospects. Rearticulation of memory may prevent the historical imagination from hardening into some ahistorical one-way Main Street. I contend that in the era of globalization, history and memory, although at risk of being estranged into antiquated things of the museum and flattened into quaint spectacles in costume dramas, have emerged as a stronger countervailing resource. A historical consciousness that critiques the engrained historical narrative via memory will keep alive unfinished possibilities and unfulfilled dreams anticipating different lines of horizon—memories of the future. It will provide vital resources for local cultural expressions rooted in specific space-time and wage struggles in different sites against the new mythologies masquerading as History.

The creative configuration of memory seems to be one hope that cultural production will not be standardized into faceless duplicates of the transnational culture industry. But being creative does not mean creating novelties out of thin air; real creative acts are grounded in specific histories and geographies. Thus the effective response to the leveling trend of the new grand narrative is not the unquestioned embrace of progress and development, not militant resistance, nor the makeshift, stopgap hybridization, which is often a virtuoso patch-up work. Far from a shifty position or momentary tactic for survival, a coherent response must strive to make profound and meaningful connections with the past and tap local resources to stage ever-renewable cultural production in the present.

This book takes modern Chinese culture as a case but addresses the broader questions of history writing, traumatic memory, modernity, and globalization. I attempt to sketch a trajectory in which memory and history proceed in tension and unison. The historical dimension of this project focuses on the reconstruction of history and memory as mutually contradictory and complementary in Chinese culture's endeavor to become a modern nation-state. The central theme is how historical discourse—the discursive practices and imagination that reconstruct the past for the present—confronts, invokes, and uses memory.

It has been a commonplace to define memory as a structure of feeling inherent in traditional communities, as opposed to the accelerative thrust of modernity and the upsurge of historical consciousness. From Karl Marx, Max Weber, Emile Durkheim, Ferdinand Tönnies, and Walter Benjamin to numerous theorists of modernity, one finds repeated enactment of the trope memory versus history, tradition versus modernity, past versus present.[8] Pierre Nora, the influential French historian, has given this trope a subtle interpretation immediately relevant to the contemporary scene. He suggests that the memory-history distinction stems from the rupture of modern society with traditional community. Memory and history have their respective social embodiments. Societies based on memory offer the *milieux de mémoire*, settings in which memory is immanent to everyday experience, whereas history inhabits the *lieux de mémoire*. The shift from *milieux*, enveloped in affective aura, to the more impersonal *lieux* (places), is indicative of the shift in social formation, corresponding to the transit from place to space, tradition to modernity, local to global.[9] Memory ensures that culture is lived in mundane, unconscious daily life, "in the warmth of tradition, in the muteness of custom, in the repetition of the ancestral." Memory guarantees the transmission of culture from generation to generation on a personal and communal basis, without self-conscious designs to overhaul the entrenched institutions and mental habit. This memory-ensured continuity, laments Nora, is broken by the "acceleration of history," by the surge of historical sensibility, which is what modern societies make of the past "they are condemned to forget because they are driven by change."[10]

Clearly the milieu of memory still survives in obscure corners of modern society, but it is not its immediate concern. The thick aura of the milieu has thinned out into the disenchanted *lieux de mémoire*, places of memory. Memory represents a residual, enchanted form of communal life and structure of feeling. A phenomenon of "emotion and magic," memory "thrives on vague, telescoping reminiscences, on hazy general impressions or specific symbolic details." In contrast, history—modern historical discourse—calls for rational analysis and engages in demythologizing through cool-headed, "objective" critique. But history cannot divorce itself from memory or give up the need for memory. Although history belongs to the *lieux de mémoire* and eschews memory's milieu of enchanted heritage, it retains "vestiges, the ultimate embodiments of a commemorative consciousness that survives."[11] This implies that history has an unstated yearning for memory in the very act of dismantling and critiquing it. Nora's description of the tension and the link between history and memory can be used to briefly define what I call "critical historical consciousness." Historical consciousness is the ever-intensified self-conscious discourse that criticizes the "natural," embodied, inherited practice based on memory. Premised on the rupture with the past, history is forward-looking and change-driven.[12] The modern "teleological" historical narratives, be they revolutionary, capitalist, or neoliberal, fit this category. Yet memory, although subjected to historical critique, can also offer a countercritique. This critique will put a check, a "second thought," on the "change for the sake of change" kind of senseless accelerations spurred by modern history. Modern history starts as a critique of tradition and memory, but memory often has to be the critique of critique, as when nostalgia expresses not the love of the past, but a vital vision against a reigning historical narrative in the present. It is not a matter of choosing one over the other. Rather, the point is to put the two components of temporality together and set them in dynamic motion. Thus we have a critical historical consciousness, which, caught in modern acceleration, is also capable of self-critique from the vantage point of its "other" and past: the milieu of memory.

When memory becomes an issue, this usually implies an "interesting time" when historical orientation is in doubt, a time of crossroads and upheaval. In the west the disturbance of memory went along with rapid social transformation, industrialization, urbanization, and the wholesale destruction of the agrarian system.[13] At the turn of the twentieth century Bergson, Jung, Freud, and Proust delved into memory to locate some anchoring amidst the swift changes. In modern China, the period of cultural crisis may have something in common with the period of memory crisis in the west. Around the turn of the century, the drastic pressures of social change also witnessed a reinvention of an integrated cultural past by way of remembrance. For instance, the discovery of the Confucian tradition as a timeless cultural repository by the school of national essence (*guocui*) at the turn of the twentieth century was repeated by the revival of "national learning" in the 1990s. But the "memory" of Confucianism does not repeat itself exactly. In the first instance it was a defense of the crumbling tradition as it came under assault by the radical reformers; in the 1990s, the memory was recast by a neoliberal discourse as consorting with global capitalism, so that the native cultural "essence," instead of being an obstacle to modernization, is seen as having all along predestined the Chinese for capitalist development.[14] Starting from the mid-1980s, there has been a series of memory efforts to evoke some shapes of the past: the indictment of political atrocities, the search-for-roots movement, the nostalgic fever for Maoist and Red Guard legacies, and the renewed interest in memories of "warmer" days of socialist culture. In intellectual discourse and literature, one also finds a forceful turn toward personal or collective memory, serving as fragile vestiges of continuity, community, and self-identity.

For all the diversity of memory works, they seem to hint at something troubling: the difficulty of modern Chinese culture in adjusting to its past, and hence to the present, from which it needs to reenvision the future. They reveal a rupture in the collectively shared sense of time, a lack of consensus ensuring the figuration of past, present, and future. It signals a serious problem in the understanding of the past and its connection to the current reality as a living, continuous history.

I have described modern history as change driven and antitraditional. Yet this history also draws on collective memory and often it is not easy to distinguish the two. History may serve as a carrier for the preservation of the cultural past, claiming certain images of memory as its own. Historical writing in modern times selectively and arbitrarily uses and invents collective memory so as to ensure and justify the continuity of the emergent nation-state with its past.[15] In this light, history functions rather like cohesive and identity-forming cultural memory. With the help of memory, history assumes an unbroken continuity from past to present. On the other hand, history—the change-driven modern history—is by no means "friendly" to tradition and memory. Memory has its own historical unfolding, but in contrast with modern historical sensibility, it shows its tardiness and is not so prone to change. In pushing for change, history comes as a critique and revision of what cultural memory has taken for granted as natural, timeless, self-evident. In rewriting the past, history performs a critical interpretation on memory. In China historical discourse performs interpretations that are frequently antimemory and antitradition; these interpretations intervened time and again, in radical, revolutionary fashion, against the "obsolete" tradition anchored in cultural memory. The critiques of the deadweight of the past—the ossified cultural memory—in the May Fourth, socialist, and in reform periods are striking testaments.

Modern historiography, as Patrick Hutton notes, historicizes collective memory by rendering the latter into the service of the nation-state. Crucial to modern, nation-centered historiography are also ideological themes of progress, rationality, emancipation, and modernization. This grand narrative of modernity, a legacy of Europe from the eighteenth-century Enlightenment and the nineteenth-century rise of the modern state, has been called into question since the earlier twentieth century. Hutton has shown that postmodern critics and historians have intensified this critique in recent decades. No longer able to see memory as a "hidden ground of history," they tend to see memory and history as sharply opposed. Although they appeal to countermemories and counterhistories of the subaltern groups, minorities and women, postmodern historians do not set out to write another coherent historical narrative or give voice to the oppressed in traditional fashion. They do not hope to return to the "original" source of living memory repressed by History. They undertake instead to "describe the way in which the remembered past has been inscribed over time in memorial forms."[16] It seems as if what commands scholarly interest were how people were repressed, rather than how they combated repression. This entails a search for images and memory traces left from the past in their sheer materiality and an archeological attentiveness to the ways they are written into various narratives and discourses of power.

The postmodernist obsession to chase down every material sign of memory trace and inscription is exemplified by the misuse of Michel Foucault's genealogical method. This method does not project a new historical orientation. To imagine history anew and otherwise, rather than clinically examine its nitty-gritty decaying in the past, it is necessary to think of history not as a decomposable pile of arbitrary tricks, fragments, and debris, but as a source of memory and hope. In its genuine vitality, history is not an autopsy lab where a historian dissects corpses to find the predetermined causes in the anatomy of the dead. History is an imaginary horizon of what is possible. If the past is not reimagined as crisscrossed by forking paths of trajectories and road maps, intermittently shut down and reopened, both the present and future are magically sealed with death marks in the teleological end of lines culminating in liberal democracy.[17] Now, the horizon of the possible lags behind History and takes on a new name: memory. What the "science" of history has determined, Benjamin suggested, remembrance can modify and overthrow. The imaginary reconstruction of history that resorts to memory "can make the incomplete (happiness) into something complete, and the complete (suffering) into something incomplete."[18] What this "theological" history implies is nevertheless very practical and everyday: history has not ended. It has unfulfilled dreams that need to be realized, and unassuaged pains and injustices that call for continuous historical action. Thus history is not just writing and imagining on paper, much less dissection on the operating table, but more importantly doing—doing things collectively in search of a more just, livable, sustainable society.

The dialectic tension between memory and history allows us to see a constant movement between memory and history. The goal of writing history in the May Fourth and socialist eras seemed to be the construction of an imaginary continuity, amidst sharp breaks, from past to present so as to legitimate the political project in the present. Since the 1980s, there have been at least two contradictory tendencies. A strong urge to herald the coming of modernization promises to put to rest the problems of historical practice and struggle and consign these to the invisible hand of the market.[19] The new mythology of the global market is vigorously contested by a strong pull toward the pole of memory (earlier history "aged" into memory). The interplay between history and memory seems to be getting into a tension between a forward-looking acceleration and a backward drag. The speedup clearly answers to the rallying call of the new myth of global developmentalism and the magic of world markets. The backward look, suspicious of the process of globalization, tries to resurrect, nostalgically and critically, a livable past against the end-of-history mythology.

Although the myth of modernization provides a premature closure to the lingering traumas of poverty, oppression, and suffering, the nostalgic turn seeks to resist and critique the current impacts, equally traumatic, of runaway modernization. The question of trauma thus has a significant role to play in the memory-history nexus. Trauma takes two forms in modern China. One is the latent memory of past catastrophes of imperialism and colonialism as well as atrocities of the authoritarian political order. The other is the ongoing shock of the damaged older lifeworlds under the impact of transnational capital and the massive commodification of social relations. Current scholarship sees trauma as a profound blow to the individual psyche and a shattering of the culture's continuity. Traumatic events break the individual's emotional attachment to the community and the shared matrix of meaning and value that members of a culture need to "remember" in order to have a minimum sense of coherency in social and personal life. This matrix enables us to tell stories, make sense of experience, and sustain a sense of continuity from past to present in history writing.[20] Trauma underlies the crisis of history writing.

As a well-received analytical category in human and social sciences, trauma studies has given deconstruction and poststructuralism a new lease of life through its emphasis on the paralysis of the traumatized psyche and the breakdowns of the previously established categories of meaning and narrative. Associated with this approach is the fascination with cultural discontinuity, the breakdown of narrative, psychic fragmentation, contingencies, the aesthetic of the abysmal sublime, and the critique and scrambling of all received categories. Although efforts have been made to lift trauma inquiry out of the psychic and clinical closet to address the politically vital issues of history writing, community building, identity, and collective memory, the positive connection between trauma and these larger issues remains unarticulated and unclear.[21]

Confronted with the dire consequences of runaway marketization and development, Chinese critics have begun to reflect more critically on the whole trajectory of Chinese modernity as traumatic encounters with imperialism, colonialism, and, in recent decades, the new powers of global capital. The "internal" political catastrophes of the Mao era have been construed as resulting from numerous hasty modernization campaigns to catch up and surpass the west. Although trauma is undoubtedly a hidden background that continues to shape our intellectual preference and ideological orientation, it needs to be reflected on, rather than simply assumed. The historical trauma has an insidious tendency to control and limit our conceptions of alternative temporalities and social formations. In an essay entitled "Surrounded by Traumatic Memory" (Zai chuangshang jiyi de huaibao zhong), Wang Xiaoming views the embrace of the new ideology of consumption and excessive individualism as an overreaction against the traumatic memory of revolution.[22] The frenzied pursuit of individual self-interest and material gains at the cost of political consciousness masks a hidden fear of anything associated with the memory of political engagement, collectivity, public life, society, nation, and history. In this light, the unquestioned acceptance of the liberal model and the market has as its hidden backdrop the "nightmares" and the "absence of freedom" in the previous collectivity. Yet the pendulum swings too far the other way when the fresh traumas of unemployment, the polarization of the population, and the erosion of the social fabric in the recent decades appear to be shattering the hopes for the future of modernization. People begin to reminisce the better days of socialist culture and even the idyllic native village, with an equally uncritical repudiation of anything western and of anything associated with democratic society, civil rights, and individual freedom.

Fredric Jameson shows how trauma can confuse as well as enhance our historical understanding. Self-reflection on trauma may prevent the reification of a certain historical trajectory as a "natural," universal way of life. Jameson cites the example of the radical generation of the 1960s in the United States. This generation, suffering from the trauma of the "excesses of individualism" of "normal" middle-class life in the Eisenhower years—which had been an excessive reaction to the collective mobilization of World War II—asserted new social solidarity and collective imagination in radical ferments. In contrast, the former soviet population in the recent decades was tired of the catastrophic existence of "huddling together" in collectivization and was "likely to develop a horror of togetherness" and a longing for individual privacy and bourgeois private life. The traumatic memory thus needs to be interpreted in rigorous historical fashion so as to avoid the reification of one pattern of values, here individualism and the bourgeois-liberal model, as necessarily superior to the other:

The symbolic effects of such historical and generational experience need to be reckoned in specific interpretative fashion, in order to forestall the return of the kind of naturalizing ideology for which collective effort works against the grain of human nature, people are naturally prone to a regression to private life, consumption and the market are more normal and attractive to human beings than the political and so forth.[23]

Traumatic memory, in this light, can be a dead weight of the past we react to excessively and unconsciously. One the other hand, keeping a critical distance from its negative impact may enable us to have an interpretative method—indeed, a critical historical understanding. This understanding traces a certain dominant historical imaginary to a traumatic source and considers its genesis in specific circumstances. The critical history that Nietzsche spoke about suggests a similar thought. The use of history, he said, is for men to perceive "the accidental nature of the forms in which they see and insist on others seeing."[24] As survivors of trauma, a generation of historians or critics may condemn the errors of trauma and think that they have escaped them, but they cannot escape the fact that they have sprung from them. Critical history does not deny or remain captive to trauma, but makes "an attempt to gain a past *a posteriori* from which we might spring, as against that from which we do spring."[25] That is, by evoking nontraumatic visions of the past as new sources for getting over traumas, a distinction is made between the victim of trauma and the active agent of history. Defined as variable responses as well as creative redress to different traumatic situations, historical discourse would have less chances of becoming the mere repetition of the past or reified as the ultimate way to go.

Seminal research has been conducted on memory and representation of history in modern China.[26] Social scientists have gathered rich data and have provided fruitful sociological and anthropological accounts of the practices where official history comes into conflict with repressed memories. Some have focused on the ways ideological and political hegemony is linked to the mechanism of politically enforced amnesia.[27] Others have sought to write a social history of remembering by considering the popular, ritualistic practices that preserve unofficial remembrances.[28] These studies look primarily at the ritualistic and sociological aspect of memory practice. My study differs from them by taking a more humanistic approach. I examine memory practices by considering aesthetic forms of film, fiction, essays, and autobiography and by reexamining the historical imagination embedded in aesthetic discourse as psychic and narrative responses to traumatic memories.

This book is arranged in three parts and addresses three major tendencies in the interplay between history and memory. Rather than describe the historical trends in the memory-history nexus, I examine a number of resurfacing motifs and make metahistorical comments on them. The first part deals with the earlier conception of history in the new culture of May Fourth. Usually conceived in terms of the Enlightenment narrative of progress, rationality, and freedom, this narrative of national teleology came as a necessary response to colonialism, imperialism, and the decline of the traditional culture. By refusing to see its historical vision as teleologically determined and hegemonic, I seek to understand its emergence as a practical response to the urgent problems of the day. One of its political tasks is to explore the realistic historical trajectory and dispel the memory of aesthetic habit embedded in traditional fiction and theater. The critique of western modernity, the appropriation of the aesthetic category of the tragic, and the stirring of a "traumatic visuality" in the radical cinema are examples of this politically effective history. This history evokes the memories of the Enlightenment legacy as well as native folk cultural resources in envisioning China's future.

The second trend, described in Part 2, offers a critical view of history as a crisis-ridden, traumatic experience rather than an upwardly moving narrative. Most pronounced in the post–Cultural Revolution, reforms era of the 1980s, this view enabled artists and critics to grapple with the recent catastrophic history and reach deeper into the remote recesses of tradition and memory. Their probe into the past produced a series of innovative works of film and literature. Instead of writing off trauma, they retain traces of traumatic experience in their works and resist the fantasy, fueled by melodrama, catharsis, and sentimentality, that the trauma will heal soon. This critical mode of history writing fosters a constant vigilance against the plotting of a grand narrative, undercuts the urge to tell an emotionally satisfying story, and pits the traumatic against a quick, facile recovery. It challenges the established identity and the dominant structure of meaning by unearthing unclaimed experiences and memory.

Three chapters in Part 3 focus on the work of memory that arose with the advent of consumer society and globalization throughout the 1990s. This decade of market liberalization, consumption, and the influx of global capital saw a waning of historical consciousness. Under the leveling effect of global trends history has been flattened into bloodless, depthless simulacra. A powerful effort, however, has been at work in contemporary Chinese literature, cinema, and public discourse to reenergize the critical historical consciousness and reenact intimate memory, often pitching upon the mythical and nostalgic. Cultural expressions strive to "find" a sublime history and intimate community. They sought to reenchant quotidian life and human relations dominated by relations of exchange and money. Both symptom and critique of the society of consumption and simulacra, this memory work is not exempt from the logic of the spectacle and remains a nostalgia not firmly grounded in memory. On the other hand, it expresses a desire to transcend the increasingly bleached and flattened social existence.

The first chapter focuses on Lu Xun's early reflections on modernity and tradition. I offer a sympathetic reading on what is often called the teleological narrative and analyze the articulation of hope in the "negative" portrayal of Chinese reality in Lu Xun. Chapter 2 examines the way the western concept of the tragic was translated, not just into Chinese drama criticism, but also into the discourse on history. With this altered concept intellectuals were able to reconsider the writing of history and to make sense of the past in a realistic and tragic manner. The chapter further considers the link between tragedy and realism and demonstrates the use of disruptive visuality in the modern medium of film in the 1930s. The radical cinema struggled to dispel traditional and modern aesthetic mystifications and promoted a political cinema in response to a crisis-ridden reality.

The next four chapters deal with the reconstruction of history in the wake of the Cultural Revolution in the 1980s through the early 1990s. This is a period of transition that put memory and history on the agenda for intense public discussion, generating a large number of literary and film texts. Chapter 3 analyzes the ways Chinese critics read and learn from Walter Benjamin, philosopher of shock and memory, and the ways the traumatic memory of western modernity resonates with the Chinese experience. It looks at the way official history was replaced by a memory work of trauma in the post–Cultural Revolutionary "wound literature" and in the endeavor known as "searching for the roots" and its new manifestations in the 1990s. Chapter 4 addresses the tension between memory and history and, through a reading of Wang Anyi's fiction, traces a "return" to the mythical and traditional. Chapter 5 continues the theme of historical trauma by comparing films of the fourth and fifth generations. Although the Xie Jin mode, the exemplar of the fourth generation, aimed to salvage the wreckage of history through humanism and a cathartic melodramatic structure, the fifth generation retained traumatic memory in its work and created a new historical narrative. Chapter 6 discusses the changing role of the intellectual in transition from the 1980s to the 1990s. Through an analysis of Wang Anyi's novella *The Story of Our Uncle* I demonstrate the shift from the epic narrative to what I call the essayistic structure of feeling. In this process the historically engaged intellectual changes into a self-serving careerist and aesthete, but he is unable to escape the burden of memory.

With the increasing flux of global capital, the expansion of the market economy, the commodification of culture, the universal history of globalization became the triumphant keynote in the last decade. Chapters 7, 8, and 9 of Part 3 deal with the issues of globalization through a reexamination of nostalgia. The integrated global economy links the mainland with Taiwan and Hong Kong. These two regions grappled with the problems of the local and the global that the mainland is beginning to confront. The three chapters look at cultural endeavors as responses to aggressive transnational capital. As residual forms of life are crumbling and the social fabric is breaking apart under expansive capital and exchange relations, authentic experience, personal identity, and community—what is left of the *milieux de mémoire*—are becoming harder to maintain. I analyze how literature and cultural production in these three areas strive to come to terms with the lure of commodity and capital while attempting to rescue authentic experience from their reifying effects. By invoking images of nostalgia, collective memory, and residual practices of everyday life, cultural production in the mainland, Taiwan, and Hong Kong try to keep alive the longing for alternative historical narrative in a global environment detrimental to cultural memory.

PART I

TOWARD A CRITICAL HISTORICAL CONSCIOUSNESS

Tradition, Memory, and Hope

LU XUN AND CRITICAL HISTORICAL
CONSCIOUSNESS

Whether globalization is a new thing or a latter-day expansion of old-fashioned capitalism, its recent developments surely intensify the perennial divide between tradition and modernity. This divide is also manifest in the tensions between the local and the global, difference and identity, the particular and the universal, the present and the past, and the nation-state and supranational world order. Although globalization seems to pose a threat to the distinctive traditions, these tensions drive scholarly inquiry into the particular trajectory of modern China and its past, into its "unique" homegrown tradition. The integrity of "Chinese culture," hermetically sealed off in its uniqueness, is threatened and reasserted at once. The debate over what counts as tradition, how the past shapes the present, and how its burden should be borne has recurred time and again throughout twentieth-century China, but in the current climate of globalization, it is becoming more urgent.

This debate is about the relation of Chinese modernity to tradition. The discussion routinely takes its starting point in the May Fourth culture. The May Fourth quest for modernity is significantly marked by its break with the past. But in the two decades leading up to the twenty-first century, there was a shift toward modernity's troubled links with tradition. In the early 1990s the search for "traditional roots" of modernity was becoming momentous. David Wang's search for "repressed modernities" in the pre–May Fourth fiction and the intellectual debates centered on the continuity of the late Qing and May Fourth evidence this interest. Earlier, Yu Yingshi consistently argued for more intimate, hidden ties between certain traditional strata and May Fourth intellectual strains. Yu's suggestions became more important in the late 1990s.[1] This debate may imply an intellectual anxiety concerning the acceleration of a historical trend since the early 1990s: the rapid economic development, the consumer revolution of everyday life, and the expansion of a global and postmodern culture.

This chapter will address Chinese modernity's troubled relation with its past from the vantage point of history writing. History writing is not simply historiography, but a culture's discursive and aesthetic institutions that engage the past in the interest of the present. The writing of history addresses ruptures within historical continuity and offers suggestions about directions of social and political formation. I would attempt to articulate, through a brief consideration of Foucault's genealogy and an analysis of Lu Xun's earlier reflections on modernity, a "critical historical consciousness."

Fallacies in Debunking the Narrative of Enlightenment

For all its hidden linkages with the past, the May Fourth cultural movement is commonly regarded as a radical break with the Confucian ethical and political system.[2] This break goes along with a total embrace of western culture. Both rupture and embrace have been subjected to criticism. In mainland China May Fourth has long been interpreted as a preparation for a teleological unfolding of modern Chinese history. This history is projected on the model of modern revolution and premised on Marxist historiographical assumptions.[3] In recent years, this narrative has been challenged in favor of more complex strains. Attempts have been made to portray May Fourth as a liberal thread of modernity, as a hotbed of cultural controversy and contending discourses, and as a nuanced mix of tradition and modernity. Recent scholarship has moved from May Fourth's future-oriented thrust toward the persistence of the past: to the continuity, tensions, relations, and linkages between the new culture and the "premodern" tradition.[4] Questioning the legitimacy of the narrative of revolution and Enlightenment, the new interpretations cut through the historical mythologies to find the hidden strains of repressed memories, concealed traditions, and the untrodden bypaths of history. In their fascination with the "otherness" elided by mainstream historiography, the rewriting of the May Fourth culture can be attributed to the broad intellectual climate marked by the critique of the Enlightenment narrative of progress and revolution. This critique challenges the assumptions of wholesale westernization and listens to two-way negotiations between traditional and modern.

There is more than a hint of irony, however, that in resteering May Fourth away from the Enlightenment narrative toward the liberal and market model, the critique of the grand narrative is applied to the third world nationalist narratives. Nowhere is this irony more poignant than in the critique of the nationalist component of the Enlightenment narrative. The nationalist narrative arose as a response and a resistance to precisely the oppression of that grand narrative marked by imperialism, colonialism, and developmentalism.[5] Exposing the oppressive mechanism of the grand narrative sustained by the power-knowledge nexus, this critique goes from the architect of the grand narrative in the metropolitan centers to its historical victims. Nationalism bears the brunt of the critique.[6] It is true that nationalism has been rightly criticized along with various historiographical teleologies that supported the authoritarian structures in modern times. Yet the critique of nationalism is often one-sided: it tends to block a sympathetic interpretation of the modern nation as a vital political entity. Rather than simply an already full-fledged authoritarian regime, to be critiqued tout court, a specific nationalism deserves closer examination of its concrete context of formation and legitimation. Chinese nationalism is a response to a situation of colonialism and national crisis. From the mid-nineteenth to the earlier twentieth centuries China was thrown into colonial conditions, its territories invaded and carved up by the imperialist powers. Recognition of China's crisis forces one to raise the question, What it would mean, as political and ethical implications of historical scholarship, to try to retrieve an "imperial," or for that matter "hegemonic," power, in the painful emergence and struggle of a fledgling nationalist movement? The nationalist impulse was part of May Fourth culture and was a collective struggle for the Chinese to assert their right to self-determination and survival as a collectivity. Although the notion of the nation-state is imported from the Enlightenment discourse, this borrowing need not be seen as another example of the colonized being duped by a colonialist discourse. Is the nationalist desire for freedom, territorial integrity, international justice, and national autonomy, because it apparently copies the colonizer's model, necessarily misplaced? Or do the colonized have a way of altering a supposedly colonial discourse in their interest and to their advantage?[7]

Prasenjit Duara's book *Rescuing History from the Nation* is a prime example of recent attempts to challenge the rigid divide between modernity and tradition, the present and the past, historical narrative and contested memory. Duara approaches the May Fourth nationalist discourse in a Foucaultian fashion. Turning a genealogical gaze to the forces and representations marginalized by the Enlightenment history, he seeks to expose the power mechanisms, violence, and erasure inherent in the construction of a linear narrative. A unitary nationalistic subject embodies and carries out this grand scheme. Duara brings out heterogeneous elements outside the orbit of the grand narrative—forces and discourses contending with the "established" powers and with each other in the formation of a hegemonic narrative. He reminds us of the repressed historicity, the complex and dispersed moments, the "original" scenes where a new discourse emerged by going through the crucible of conflicting rivals, as it were. This is the "history" he wants to rescue from the entrapment of the Enlightenment narrative of the nation-state, which in the name of an overarching History represses histories heterogeneous to it.[8]

If we see the Enlightenment narrative against the backdrop of national crisis and anti-imperialism, however, we have to ask whether this narrative can be conceived as "hegemonic" in its formative period and already contained the seeds for all the subsequent disasters and errors of Chinese modernity. In view of the May Fourth narrative's function in response to contingencies, Duara does not seem to pay enough attention to the historical legitimacy of the emergence of the "grand narrative" itself. One needs to recall that the grand narrative was not at all grand, and in fact was quite marginal and local at its incipient moment. In the face of imperialist invasion and social crises, the new culture of May Fourth struggled to get a hearing in a state of emergency. The emergency compels an acknowledgment of the legitimacy of the Enlightenment narrative. This narrative, rather than a hegemonic structure, was actually an element in a field of contending discourses, all trying to find a way out of predicaments and crises. The need for legitimation involves delegitimation, which entails exclusion and violence. But legitimacy here cannot be prejudged, retrospectively, by an always already repressive, hegemonic structure superimposed on heterogeneous multitudes. In certain contexts, the legitimating project took on ethical as well as pragmatic priority over the claims of "other" discourses and forces. Although one needs to be sensitive to the complex, contested terrains shot through with alternative discourses, a bland pluralism and free-floating dialogue seem more suited to the multicultural, laid-back seminar room of the American university than to a situation of life-and-death struggle.

Rebecca Karl has noted a prevalent fallacy in Chinese historiography in equating the repressive power of statism with historically emergent nationalism, which is revolutionary by nature. Critiques of statism take a retrospective look at the concept of nation in the light of the nation's statist and authoritarian consequences. The nation, on the other hand, is a historically vibrant, antistatist (against imperialist and colonial states), antisystematic revolutionary movement.[9] When one is dealing with a situation in which the basic survival of every group or sector of Chinese society was in danger, transplanting the established state power back into the fledgling Chinese nationalism seems quite misplaced. In a situation of emergency, nationalism was the rallying call in the struggle for independence and freedom. Chinese nationalism in the earlier period of the twentieth century was still a long way from congealing into state power. Confusing statism with nationalism is a failure of postrevolutionary thought to remember the creative and independent spirit of the revolution. This failure, as Hannah Arendt points out, is "preceded by the failure of the revolution to provide it with a lasting institution," a form of government that "is not eternally at open or secret war with the rights of mankind." The goal of revolution is to establish a people's govenernment, a state in the interest of political freedom. Yet, as it frequently turned out, once the revolutionary or liberal democratic state was in place, "there was no space reserved, no room left for the exercise of precisely those [revolutionary or transformative] qualities which had been instrumental in building it."[10] Maurice Meisner points to a similar reversal in the Chinese state's forgetfulness of its revolutionary, nationalist spirit by quoting Robert Michels's prediction: "The socialists might conquer, but not socialism."[11] There has been much unhappy historical evidence to confirm this prediction: official doctrines and the state apparatus kill the spirit. Yet this self-deconstruction of revolution can be applied to numerous democratic movements of modern times that begin to die at the moment of triumph. The task of history writing is to separate the ossified revolutionary state from its renewable demands, aspirations, and energy forgotten by the status quo.

As in the case of nationalism, the May Fourth narrative in general sought to furnish much needed, if often hasty or ill-advised, solutions for an endangered China, but its thrust cannot, by any direct causal, linear logic, be linked to the authoritarian polity and teleological history. In critiquing the linearity of the grand narrative, one may rehearse the very same linear logic of that narrative. If the emergent, emancipatory, and revolutionary conjuncture of any struggling narrative is not set off from its subsequent authoritarian outcomes, a narrative of temporal mutation may become a closed chapter, a denouement of the powers that be. Thus a rigorous historicity is as much due to the so-called Enlightenment narrative as to the repressed alternative discourses.

The implication of this retrieval—a tracing of the hegemonic to its "marginal" and crisis-ridden stirrings—is that history is rewritten with constant renewal of memory, of the unfinished motifs and aspirations. History writing benefits from the genealogical approach, which Foucault called *countermemory*.[12] This approach enables us to uncover the hidden strata and to guard against easy assumption of an unbroken continuity underlying historical narrative. Historicist in spirit, genealogy is capable of dissecting each historical moment in its own unique dimensions, intensity, and contradictions. It eschews the notion of a telos spearheading the historical movement on a preordained track. It demystifies the sublime aura surrounding the legacy, the canons, and revered artifacts. Genealogical history is, Foucault writes, "effective" because it brings discontinuity into pretended continuity, opens up multiple, competing discourses and representations, and deprives the subject of the consoling mirror of self-recognition. Genealogically speaking, one should find it hard to recognize things in Chinese history that would readily proffer the pleasure of "Yes, that's me! That's us." Instead of a unitary consciousness taking a narcissistic backward glance at the past, we are plunged into the disorienting mess of schizophrenia. So much the better for the genealogist. For we will be so torn apart, undecided, ambiguous, and wildly dispersed among bits and pieces of the psychic rubble that there is no way we can submit to a repressive or totalitarian "millennial ending" or ground ourselves in a firm foundation.[13]

This sharp, X-ray-dissecting effectiveness is crystallized in the image of the genealogist, which is also that of an archeologist, a diagnostician, or a surgeon. The genealogist's knowledge, insists Foucault, "is not for understanding, but for cutting."[14] The problem of the genealogical approach lies, I think, with mere cutting without trying to rebuild and reconstitute. Much criticism, following the lead of Jürgen Habermas's idea of the unfinished project of modernity, has been directed at Foucault's genealogical conception. The trouble with the narrow view of genealogy, in Richard Bernstein's words, is a receding from "an ethical-political horizon."[15] Michael Roth takes issue with the suspension of "political judgment and action" in Foucault's analysis of the power-discourse nexus.[16] The genealogist aims at "effective" history, which eschews foundation, rational purpose, and continuity. The genealogist tells a story of the inescapable and ubiquitous subjugation of the individual by external power structures. Even the individual's subjective initiative to break away from the external structure is already hijacked by the subject's prior imprisonment in language, norms, and the symbolic order, and hence is self-repression. If historical inquiry traces how we have come to be what we are now—the background of identity—the genealogist is counterhistorical and is not concerned to trace the roots of our identity, but to commit himself, on the contrary, to its dissipation, thus undermining the "very foundation of our attempts to know ourselves."[17] By exposing all discourses as power-inflected constructs of repression, which preempt acts of liberation and self-expression, by treating all historical formations as instances of disciplinary, authoritarian, and instituted power, the genealogist also strips the subject of the will and ability to know and to act.

Searching for agency in his critique of pure genealogy, Michael Roth makes a distinction between the *sense de l'histoire* (sense of history) in traditional historiography and a *sense historique* (historical sense) in genealogy. The historical sense aims at a relentless genealogical dismantling of the discourse-power nexus and takes sadistic delight in parading its contingent mechanisms and arbitrary violence. The sense of history, on the other hand, is "animated by a desire to give meaning and direction to the present by finding its development in the past." This is another way of articulating the need for history writing, which is also a need for legitimation and identity. To legitimate a certain historical narrative is to validate a certain practice by making it "realistic," "reasonable," or "progressive," or serviceable to the majority, and condemns others as reactionary or regressive. Although the legitimating function has been a tool in the hand of the established powers to justify oppression in the name of History, the criticism of the repressive agenda should not take power away from those "who use history to criticize those in power."[18] No history can be written for millions of victims of the "grand history" without a workable and for that matter "interested" sense of history. A sense of history has to be based on an articulated unity, continuity, and solidarity of purpose—rearticulated in the genealogical ruins of dismantled History. Thus the retreat from the political-ethical horizon is also a withdrawal from historical discourse. If all history lies in ruins, how are historical agents supposed to write alternative histories and act alternatively to change the repressive History?

Turning to China, the genealogist would investigate the iconoclastic radical edge and the wholesale antitraditionalism in May Fourth and treat these tendencies as continuous with the nationalist, revolutionary, and communist drives for power. To push this logic further, we can also analytically cut up the socialist, Maoist legacy spanning more than half of the twentieth century. This, to be sure, has been and continues to be done in genealogical fashion. It would be unhistorical to dismiss the values and mechanism of what is often dismissively called "communist culture" and to treat a large chunk of modern history as a colossal aberration and hence irrelevant to the contemporary power relations. After the fall of the Berlin Wall, there has been a sense that with the newly discovered liberal democracy as the destiny of all human beings, all emancipatory movements could be thrown in the dustbin of history. Where one may go too far is subjecting all history to genealogical scrutiny as if all powers and hegemonies in all times are equally suspect and there is nothing positive to be gained from historical reorientation, not even from the self-empowering struggle of the oppressed, marginalized, and excluded. The possibility that the marginal and oppressed can empower themselves by taking on historical discourse, by speaking truth to power, by forging a sense of history, is very hard to be found in the vocabulary of genealogy. Would genealogy help in fostering a historical imagination and promoting struggles for just and equitable society? Would it take account of a culture's past that, as ever-renewable life resources, has shaped the way of living, seeing, and thinking of a people for centuries?

The genealogical method is effective in its deconstructionist and subversive endeavors, but it remains silent with regard to the possibility of constructing history in the hopes of transforming society and building community. Moving along with and keeping a distance from genealogy, I will look for an emergent historical consciousness and related narrative in the May Fourth culture and will examine how history and memory interplay in their construction. Writing history, in both theory and practice, is what the May Fourth culture urgently needed to do in a time of national danger. My analysis will hopefully point a way out of the genealogical "historical sense" to "the sense of history," the sense that history writing is shaped by hopes and a sense of purpose. Without hopes and visions history risks becoming a refined microscopic portrayal of existing power structures, which seem too all-encompassing to be altered. History writing is, I contend, a kind of politics—not just a political act of genealogically exposing the discourse-power nexus, but also an act of working and striving for positive historical directions. This is especially urgent in a time of globalization when we are constantly being told that history has ended, and that there is no alternative.[19]

Reconsidering Linear Historical Consciousness

When one speaks of history with reference to modernity, the very notion of history (*lishi*) takes on new dimensions not to be found in traditional dynastic historical writing. The notion of history is bound up with modernity. One cannot deny, surely, that the Chinese had been writing history all the time before the encounter with modernity. What is radically new is the assumption that history is both writing and doing, both narrative unfolding and practical reshaping of the social order. This is achieved by a people who know that they are taking their destiny into their own hands. As a modern concept, history interprets, legitimates, and projects the goal-directed, motivated movement of modern society, forging ahead independently of the authority and wisdom of tradition. Modeled on European modernity since the eighteenth century, history is much more than written records. A sovereign people, aware of themselves as a people and inspired by strong nationalistic inspirations, make history.[20] History is self-conscious and self-reflective, creating its own norms and projections from its own ongoing activity, presumably disengaged from the inherited authority or criteria of the past; it is future oriented and unfolds on a day-today basis. It is a public activity rather than a privileged domain of the elites and scribes. One can go on listing more features, but the point is that rather than a record of the past or a scholarly discipline, history is a rational, modern form of knowledge and a public practice, an instrument of ideological mobilization and reform movement.

Liang Qichao, as Edward Wang and Tang Xiaobing recently have shown, pioneered the notion of modern history. What is modern in Liang's approach is that the new historical narrative was driven by a nation-building project, premised on an understanding of political theories of government and the idea of people as citizens. History rewriting aspired to a prospectus for the new modern nation-state.[21] This view contrasts sharply with traditional historiography, in which the classics and history were identical as the repertoire of ancient wisdom and statecraft.[22] In a review of a Japanese history book about China, Liang criticizes it for merely depicting a succession of dynasties that is "without any specific structure." The reason is that the mutations of the dynasties do not fit into a historical narrative in the modern sense. The movement of modern history is self-motivated, self-transformative, and secular, and in this sense, China's past "has never been narrated historically."[23] Obviously, Liang is thrusting modern history into dynastic mutations. In his book of lectures on history, *Zhongguo lishi yanjiu fa* (Methodology in the study of Chinese history), Liang points to the autocratic and random chronology of old history and calls for a new nationalistic history, which is of the people, by the people, and for the people. Relying on this sense of history, he remarks that all dynastic histories "can no longer be called history." For Liang, modern history is also teleologically inspired while the past records are listless, antipublic, and disorganized as unstructured temporality and causality. In the light of modern, secular history, Liang urges a reform of Chinese historiography.[24]

Postcolonial historiography has alerted us to the discursive lineage of a universal history of Eurocentric provenance that underwrites the writing of nonwestern histories. The worry is that the history of a colonized culture remains mimicry of the European model of historical projects and imagination. My analysis below seeks to demonstrate that by appropriating the Enlightenment narrative, Chinese historical consciousness need not be seen as another mimicry of the European narrative. This is not simply because contradictory ideas and motifs within the Enlightenment narrative itself already call into question a uniform portrayal of the Chinese Enlightenment narrative. In its own brand of pluralism, the much-maligned "unity" of the Enlightenment is actually a straw target. I propose a rather different thesis that attends to the global interconnection of different cultures. Without a universal ethical horizon, one based on equal rights, respect for different traditions, and mutually recognized state sovereignty, the particular native history cannot be written and cannot evolve at all, because a culture's right to exist and survive in the Hobbesian world of jungles cannot guarantee itself, but must be maintained by appeal to a universal ethical demand that each and every culture in the modern world has the right to exist and an obligation to respect each other. All the international organizations in the twentieth century are premised, at least in theory, on this universalism, which is derived from the Enlightenment ideal that all human beings, regardless of geographical and cultural differences, are to be respected equally, and hence are one *in time*, as each nation or culture strives to attain equality and self-determination—the hallmarks of political freedom. That the history of those who advocated this principle might trail a wretched record, that this universalism has been constantly violated by colonial domination and imperialist violence—this does not imply that the universal principle should be thrown out. Writing a counterhistory is not to retreat to the dogmatic assertion of a hermetically sealed local culture, but to hold up the universal principle more vigorously, and to hold the violators accountable to this principle, so that both the strong and the weak are constrained by it, as one of many, as equal members of the world community. In other words, the problem with universalism in the Enlightenment narrative is not that it is universal, but not universal enough in actual historical practice. In history it has been ethnocentrism or white mythology disguised in the name of universalism while abusing it. But one needs to separate genuine universalism from ethnocentrism. If the Chinese narrative appeals to Enlightenment universalism in the pursuit of its own way of being and becoming—a modern universal narrative of freedom, can it be compatible with the evolution of a particular culture? As Lu Xun asked, does one burn down the house simply because the previous owner was a villain?[25] The newly created narratives are not another episode copied from the European masters of power, but the reenactment of the universal rules that need to be observed by the Europeans as well as "provincials."[26]

A family of modern ideas marks historical consciousness in May Fourth: evolution, progress, antitraditionalism, freedom, individualism, and so forth. We might turn to evolutionism, probably the most contested item in modern thought on world history. Critics tend to link evolutionism in May Fourth to the teleological and determinist narratives of Marxism.[27] More sympathetic readings, however, such as that of James Pusey, attempt to bring the "ethical-political horizon" back to the teleological interpretations and consider the idea of evolution as a voluntarism of the historical agent motivated by a broad notion of ethics.[28] I would further consider this point as a key component of critical historical consciousness. Evolutionism was a strong theme in May Fourth writings, and its double edge needs to be clarified. It is ironic that a theory like Darwin's has been associated with repressive teleology, determinism, and racial domination. The theory of evolutionism has the potential to undermine theological and biblical dogmas and certainties by pointing out temporal contingencies in nature and history. Stephen J. Gould, the thinker capable of combining nature with history, has this to say about the open-ended aspect of evolutionism as constant deconstruction of metaphysical certainties:

Darwin's revolution should be epitomized as the substitution of variation for essence as the central category of natural reality. . . . What can be more discombobulating than a full inversion, or "grand flip," in our concept of reality: in Plato's world, variation is accidental, while essences record a higher reality; in Darwin's reversal, we value variation as a defining (and concrete earthly) reality, while averages (our closest operational approach to "essences") become mental abstractions.[29]

Those against teleology and homogeneity supposedly embodied by Darwinism may think that this quotation comes from an advocate of multiculturalism, pluralism, and postmodernism. This quote stresses the contingent and creative aspect of Darwinism and the changeable nature of human reality as temporal zigzags and roads not taken. And this is a far cry from the official rhetoric of social Darwinism in the service of the powers that be. When evolutionism is used by the dominant powers to glorify the blind, ruthless course of history in the guise of imperial and colonial domination, its critical edge is lost.[30] Instead, the law of the jungle is recognized in human affairs as justification for imperialist aggression and colonial domination in the name of the survival of the fittest.

The inspiring force in Gould's remark on Darwinism was not lost on May Fourth thinkers. In May Fourth writings, evolutionism was one of the vantage points from which radical intellectuals critiqued the malaises of tradition and envisioned social change. In its challenge to the old ethical-political order, it carried basically the initial edge of antichurch evolutionism in the west. From the evolutionist perspective, Chinese culture should move from its traditional backwardness, stagnation, and ignorance toward a world of science, enlightenment, and democracy. In critiques of modernity in the recent decades, marred by a strong mistrust of the Enlightenment project, evolutionism is frequently discredited and is associated with the postmodern taboos of teleology, determinism, closure, and linear history. Critics have upbraided proponents of evolutionism for being misled by a determinist, quasi-scientific theory of social development, leading to social catastrophes traceable to the Hegelian-Marxist grand narrative.[31]

May Fourth evolutionist thinking, however, cannot readily be equated with notions of teleology and the linear scheme of history. Yan Fu was a case in point. In his interpretation of Herbert Spencer's social Darwinism and Thomas Huxley's *Evolution and Ethics*, Yan Fu was more attracted to the voluntaristic aspect of evolutionist history than to the depiction of history as a law-governed, inexorable process beyond human will. His approach to evolutionism is prescriptive rather than descriptive.[32] He was able to see in history an inspiring ethical imperative for China's self-strengthening and social transformation. Yan Fu deployed the familiar trope of animal versus human to "decry the deterministic implications" of social Darwinism.[33] Thus the evolution of history was driven by "the Faustian-Promethean exaltation of energy and power both over non-human nature and within human society."[34]

The manifesto of the inaugural issue of the magazine *Jinhua* (Evolution), published in January 1917, confirms Yan Fu's point. The article made an important distinction between a social Darwinism justifying the strong prevailing over the weak and a progressive, humanitarian evolutionism. The latter could inspire China's attempt to attain an equal status on the world stage with the western powers. The author, Huang Lingshuang, criticizes the moral blindness inherent in the application of the Darwinist jungle rule to human affairs and draws on anarchist theory. Anarchist theory advocates mutual cooperation and supportive community as the basis for the survival of the fittest. Cooperative animals as well as human communities exemplify this principle. It is intriguing how Huang's article suggests that animals by instinct know fairness better than human social arrangements and legal establishments. As I was writing this, a *New York Times* editorial article, "What the Monkeys Can Teach Humans About Making America Fair," cites scientific research in which capuchin monkeys proved to have a strong sense of justice when denied a fair share of food in an unfair trade-off. The editorial lesson is that the American legal system insists on the strictness of established law at the expense of general fairness.[35] The sense of fairness, we may add, is not only essential to making America fair in a time of corporate greed, the unfair bargaining of the World Trade Organization, the widening gap between north and south, and the misuse of military might, but also to making the globe a livable place. The relevance of this article to the manifesto of the *Jinhua* is obvious. Without fairness to all humans on earth, evolution means the self-destruction of humanity as a whole. But with appeal to evolution based on mutual cooperation and fairness, evolution is also reviving the oldest primal instincts of humans as a unified species.

In Huang's manifesto, the colonized and oppressed, like India and certain East European countries, were often evoked in the evolutionist discourse of May Fourth as being "unfit" for the evolutional scheme, but this habitual trope was meant to reveal and criticize, not justify, the injustice and unfairness in the blind, evolutionist history of imperialism and colonialism. Being left behind in an evolutionist scheme contrived by certain power groups actually calls for a self-conscious, self-saving endeavor to fight for freedom and quality in the international arena.[36]

The goal of evolution, in this light, is not determined by any naturally and teleologically determined trajectory, but implies an aspiration for a just and freer society based on the assumption of equality of nation-states and the rights of each for self-determination. Social evolution, Huang declares, is about "what institutions are best suited to which social conditions, about the betterment of the happiness and quality of human beings as a whole." "As a whole" is the key idea, and refers to what Huang calls the "universal principle" (*gongli*). The *gongli*, we remember, was the rallying call in the students' declaration on the morning of May 4, 1919, when they took to the streets to protest the transfer, at the Versailles conference in Paris, of the territorial sovereignty of Shandong Province from Germany to

Japan.[37] This appeal to the universal principle fueled the quest for equality and self-determination in a global context. It implies an internationalist demand binding on all nations of the world. It is clear that without a universal ethical mandate over the evolutionary scheme, the strong nations will "selectively" swallow up the particular ethnic species. Holding the imperial powers answerable to this universal principle was also meant to critique and combat their intrusion and aggression. To call this universalism naive is to be bogged down in the despair that all universalism—ethical principles that treat each human being as equals in an increasingly unequal world—is simply another trick of narrow-minded nationalism of a specific imperial state. But one should not throw out the baby of universalism with the bathwater of parochialism masquerading as universalism. The problem with universalism is not faceless homogeneity, but that it is not applied universally to all, not sufficiently generous beyond self-interests of the "civilized" nations to include everybody under the aegis of the equal right for self-determination and survival.

With more political insight, intellectuals like Lu Xun, Hu Shi, and Chen Duxiu were in sympathy with universalism in modern conceptions of history and nationhood. Instead of copying the west exactly on the latter's terms, universalism for them was a question of equality in the interstate relations. The preoccupation with global views was a political project to combat imperialism and colonialism by resorting to Enlightenment intellectual and ethical resources. The postmodern critique of universalism often misses this point: in the global context of nation-states, China must, through modernization and self-strengthening, rise to a national status to be taken seriously by the imperial powers. But this is not for China to join the imperialist club, but to enable it to be present with a voice at the bargaining table, so that the struggle against imperialism and colonialism can be waged on a fair playing field, by dint of negotiation or force. Universalism here means that China's sovereignty can be recognized and respected. This does not erase the difference embedded in cultural heritage. On the contrary, without a universalism enabling all nations to assert their own right of self-determination against external domination, the treasured cultural differences can be bombed to the ground overnight and the survival of the "culture" would not make the slightest difference, except in the museums and multicultural fairgrounds on summer holidays. A nation stripped of the universal right for self-determination and sovereignty will be a nonnation, and its nationally frustrated people would be in diaspora roaming homeless on the globe. The so-called cultural difference without the backing of a strong polity is a difference of no importance. It would be so many frills of show business and flashes of exotic diversity for the palate of the world conquerers.

Evolutionism in May Fourth was closely linked to universal aspirations and sought an open-ended vista, an array of possibilities of transition from a paralyzed tradition to a freer and more just society. In a time when the very existence of China was in jeopardy, evolutionism was not just a doctrine: it was to awaken a historical consciousness that would provide hope and purpose for practical action. Evolutional ideas were turned into a real social and intellectual practice aimed at transforming Chinese society and people, initiating a series of reform projects.

To the more pragmatic and sensitive minds in May Fourth, evolutionism and other related Enlightenment notions of history were not simply regarded as stemming from the west. It did not make a real difference if a discourse bore the signature of a Charles Darwin, a Herbert Spencer, or a Karl Marx. The borrowing of any western discourse in a time of crisis is not a matter of academic hairsplitting or semantic definition. As long as it could help release China from its dead-hand tradition and national crisis, a school of thought could be adopted and reconsidered. Beliefs in evolution of society, faith in science and democracy, and the political zeal to enlighten and transform the general population converged in an antitraditional, iconoclastic mentality and practices—all geared toward the nationalistic project of salvation. Although this is already common knowledge in Chinese scholarship, evolutionism's ethical implications and creative potential in historical narrative need to be articulated to dispel the excessive fear of its Eurocentrism and determinism.

Persistence of Tradition as Memory

The evolutionist view of history is also suspect because it denies the value of tradition and embraces western values. Yet in a time of widespread crisis, the question of what is the Chinese tradition—an essential fund of inherited cultural resources—becomes problematic. As Wang Hui shows, the rupture with tradition had occurred—irrevocably. The real difficulty

Lu Xun and his contemporaries ran into was how they could presume to critique and demystify the past when they are themselves the product of that past. They would try to stand outside the tradition, in their judgmental stance, to criticize it from a perspective of modern values. They would project a total, often dismissive view of the past without, so they thought, being framed in body or soul by it. The Enlightenment notions of individuality, freedom, and equality indeed mark a rupture with the past. The tenor of Enlightenment thought is antitraditional, antimemory and privileges modern, forward history at the expense of the cultural past. Enlightenment thinkers in the west were not inclined to appreciate tradition's persistent hold on the moderns. Antitraditionalism in historical thinking presents a self-distancing stance, the Hegelian "negativity" that embodies "a reflective sense of self-doubt about its basic norms and commitments and how that form of self-doubt was both destructive of [traditional] ways of life and also productive of new forms of *Geist*."[38] This stance of the modern historian, by which intellectuals could criticize China's obsolete past, allowed sweeping generalizations and rejection of the Chinese tradition in toto. Nowhere is this more glaring than in the madman's outcry in Lu Xun's story "Diary of a Madman." The madman's condemnation of traditional China as "man eating man" is emotional and in one breath relegates tradition to the dustbin. Less obvious are the parallels of the madman's fervor with the antitraditional stance of modern history. The image of Ah Q, who is made to bear the burden of the sum total of the benighted, degenerate attributes of the traditional persona, is another case of putting the Chinese everyman in an obsolete past. In their fury to reject the past, May Fourth intellectuals did not strive to sympathetically understand the validity of tradition and its vital possibilities. For them, terms like *tradition, Confucianism, customs, authority*, and *ritual* seemed to be devoid of any positive value; they were associated with barbarism, primitiveness, darkness, crime, errors, ignorance, lies, hypocrisy, or morbidity.[39]

But the past is not something one can throw out the window on the morning of enlightenment. Despite the acceptance of modern ideas, the past remained tenaciously alive and continued to shape the frame of existence of its critics. Current scholarship has become more attentive to the persistence of the past in the Chinese experience of modernity. Wang Hui has offered a compelling analysis of the subtle conflict and connections between modernity and tradition in Lu Xun. The intertwining of the two is the place for delineating the formation of Chinese historical consciousness in the making. Placing Lu Xun in interlocking strands of Enlightenment and modernist thoughts in the west, Wang Hui takes account of the cultural-historical needs and creative appropriation of modern Enlightenment values.

Against the historical backdrop of imperialist invasion and colonization, Wang Hui argues, China's drive for modernity, unlike western modernity, did not evolve over time naturally and internally from inside the Chinese social process. The forced "implantation" of western culture is surely inevitable, but Chinese modernity ran into the tenacious sediments of tradition. Lu Xun and his associates were torn between two cultural formations, pledging allegiance to modern ideas yet living in a traditional world scarcely touched by winds of change. Following Lu Xun's own description, Wang Hui gives the metaphor of "the thing in between" (*zhongjian wu*) for this dilemma. First noted by William Lyell and elaborated by Wang in a broader context, this in-betweenness is helpful in identifying the historical impasse experienced by May Fourth intellectuals:

> The meaning of "the thing in between" embedded in cultural fissures is this: On the one hand they [intellectuals] acquired modern values and criteria in the interaction and interweaving of China and the West. On the other hand they are embedded in the traditional structure antagonistic to the modern consciousness. As carriers of modern consciousness they were breaking out of traditional cultural structures, but nevertheless lived intimately within them. Thus they retained, consciously or unconsciously, some deep attachment to traditional culture. This attachment makes it necessary to combat both society as well as their own self. In this sense, the in-betweenness marks the split of mind among intellectuals as they were awakening to modern consciousness and distancing themselves from tradition.[40]

A familiar instance in the "Diary of a Madman" illustrates this impasse. Condemning traditional China for its cannibalistic nature, the Madman awakes to the value of individual life and dignity antagonistic to the traditional institutions. On the other hand, he also becomes conscious that he is a man-eater like everybody else and is so deeply trapped in the lethal game that there is no hope of "absolving" himself of the guilt. This guilt-laden consciousness leads to despair, but at the same time leaps to a fragile hope in the end of the story expressed through the cry, "Save the children."[41]

The idea of in-betweenness elucidates the relation of modernity and tradition only when one eschews the binary opposition of the past and present, and traces an ongoing give and take, a seesaw that marks not only the inner tension of the mind but also the historical condition that called for a provisionary synthesis, a sense of identity in nonidentity. On the discursive level, we can designate this tension in terms of "ambiguity," "paradox," "ambivalence," or "contradiction," but these are weak descriptions, for they are captive to a blockage, an irresolvable paradox, rather than suggesting an actively reconstructive agency. They sound as if modern consciousness could be disentangled from traditional elements by a sheer exercise of will or clearer thinking. When this seems impossible, a paradoxical mixture of modern and traditional comes through as oddly surprising. The rupture is thus seen as a sad consequence of modernity, not as its enabling condition. If the modern is intimately interwoven with traditional, the split lies at the very core of modernity itself. It is an inherent nature of modernity, not just its effect. As Wang Hui's study shows, it informs Lu Xun's political, social, and aesthetic views and literary practice.

I am specifically concerned here to inquire into how the "in-betweenness" relates to the May Fourth consciousness of history. We can derive from this formulation another pair of concepts conducive to an understanding of the relation of modern history to tradition. As we saw earlier, modern history denotes both a form of writing as well as practice, based on certain self-reflective, teleological assumptions about the structuring of temporality and society. But tradition is also referred to as part of history. When history "produced" intellectuals, for example, this "history" is obviously the past tradition whose temporality has left its imprints on their structure of feeling and mentality, if not in their conscious views. The past in Lu Xun's fiction not only holds sway in the present, but exerts a mythical power over the living, exhibiting a compulsion to repeat the atrocities, injustice, and ignorance of past millennia—the perpetual return of the same.

In this light, a notion of collective memory can set tradition apart from the modern, future-oriented notion of history. In current discussions of memory based on the binary of modernity and tradition, memory is perceived to be lingering remnants of the older, premodern lifeworld not yet erased by modern change. As a critique of the capitalistic abstraction of modern life, memory is associated, often nostalgically, with the village community, ensconced in its face-to-face intimacy, warmth, magic, and aura. The darker side of memory, associated with trauma and suffering, does not belong to this category but is derived from the experience of catastrophe.[42]

The relation of modernity and tradition in May Fourth points toward a rather different formulation of memory. Consider this relation in Lu Xun's fiction. Memory—the shapes of the past lingering in the present—is presented not as intermittent, heart-warming moments à la Proust of an earlier lifeworld as objects of longing, but as the obstinate, deadening hand of tradition repeating itself constantly in a mythical and cyclical way, returning as the living dead in modern events and everyday life. Despite a series of revolutions in politics, China kept repeating the old routines, enacting old remembered behaviors in the apparent ruins of tradition. Memory here echoes Marx's remark about dehumanizing traditions: "The tradition of all the dead generations weighs like a nightmare on the brain of the living and is antithetical to modernity."[43] Memory needs to be separated out from tradition as a cultural component. A different history emerges in this kind of embodied memory. This history embraces both the tradition supposedly passé and its insidious compulsion to repeat in the present. In contrast to the forward-looking, future-driven history, this brand of history refers to an unconscious strata of symbols, desires, rituals, axioms, and habit, insidiously shaping the present behavior of the moderns and running like bad blood through their bodily performance.

Memory of course has its positive side. May Fourth writers and thinkers exhibited a tendency to go back to Chinese tradition, whether official or popular, to find resources for making sense of modern ruptures. Even the most radical thinkers cannot escape connections and identification with a least some parts of tradition. Lu Xun appeared to retain not only traces of memory associated with an organic folk life and customs, but also went to great lengths to reexamine classical texts and artifacts to find resources for the present practice, rather than "points of affinity" between traditional and modern. At once enemy and partner of modernity, memory may clarify the interlocking relation of past and present.

On the other hand, history, as a rational discourse, is the rewriting of memory under the sign of modernity; it is critical of the dragging aspect of memory in its unorganized, dispersed, "embodied" state, attempting to gather it up in the hope of achieving the unity of the modern nation.

Whether understood in the rationalist or Hegelian-Marxist sense, history shapes itself up in modern times as a movement from tradition to modernity, from necessity to freedom. But this does not have to entail a complete negation of tradition or memory. Quite the contrary, one neglected thrust of the Hegelian-Marxist history is precisely the bridging of the modern ruptures between present and past—the modernized ethical life in Hegel and the unfulfilled dream of oppressed humanity in Marx.[44] This constitutes the Enlightenment critique of the instrumental aspect of the Enlightenment. To pronounce the May Fourth historical consciousness as linear and teleological, and as a complete break with the past is to ignore its inescapable, multilayered immersion in tradition. Despite its future-oriented character, a narrative of modern Chinese history would be an empty schema unless it draws on specifically Chinese accomplishments and memory, the long, material duration, so to speak, of the Chinese past. Thus an analysis of how history draws on memory can help us see the interlocking tensions, the mutual indebtedness, as it were, between tradition and modernity in the May Fourth culture.

Critical History and Memory in Lu Xun

If the apparently rigid divide between tradition and modernity is seen as a complex relation of negotiation, interweaving, and recombination of both past and present, then both history and memory would play an active role in the making of a modern historical consciousness. As a writer deeply involved in the endeavors to find his way through the entanglement of modernity and tradition, Lu Xun's work offers an occasion to explore the contradictions and views concerning history, tradition, and memory.

Lu Xun's reflection on history came in sharper focus in a number of essays written from 1908 to 1909. They are "Wenhua pianzhi lun" (On one-sidedness of cultural development), "Ren zhi lishi" (The history of mankind), "Kexue shi jiaopian" (A lesson on the history of science), and "Moluo shili shuo" (On the power of *Mara* poetry). These essays need to be read against a large context in which the Qing dynasty was coming to an end and there was much uncertainty and controversy over China's future. China's defeat in the Sino-Japanese War of 1894–95 prompted a series of reforms. In an ambitious program to modernize China on western models, the Emperor Guangxu adopted the reform proposal by Kang Youwei and Liang Qichao, only to be crushed by the conservative elements. The fall of the examination system, the social upheavals, the encroaching presence of foreign powers, the influx of western ideas, and finally a sense of the imminent collapse of the Confucian system made the first decade of the twentieth century a time of crisis and confusion. Although the "sense of history" in Michael Roth seemed to be paralyzed at the crossroads, there also arose a strong need to articulate that sense.[45]

One concern of the historical consciousness is the rethinking of Chinese tradition. Generally regarded as a radical iconoclast, Lu Xun in his work exposed the social ills and treated Chinese tradition with much bitterness and indignation. On closer reflection, however, it becomes clear that in his most reflective writings, he did not reject tradition out of hand. Through a critical, historical analysis, he indeed tried to make connections with what he thought to be energizing, life-affirming, and hence relevant elements of the past. In this pre–May Fourth period, there was no lack of conservative attempts to desperately reassert and preserve the superiority of traditional Chinese culture in the hope of restoring confidence and self-importance with regard to China's famed spiritual and cultural strength. The falsely glorified sense of tradition allowed some traditionalists to congratulate themselves by sneering at colonized countries like India and Poland, or to try to find in the Chinese tradition a forerunner for every item of western learning that happened to come to China (Lu Xun quanji [LXQJ] 1:65). Although Lu Xun saw these conservative attempts as self-delusion, he nevertheless acknowledged tradition's power on the present. Where he differed profoundly from conservatives was his modern understanding of tradition and his political agenda in writing the past into a new history for China.

I would propose that Lu Xun's work shows a strategic approach to China's cultural past. It is strategic because a discursive choice is made not in accordance with any model, past and present, but in view of the ever-flexible and ever-changing problems of survival and the common good. The strategic implies the ethical. Lu Xun did not simply pick and choose from the so-called tradition, for neither tradition as a whole nor the standards for retrieving anything from it were available or determinable in advance. In those essays, written in classical prose, Lu Xun achieves access to

China's past by a detour and makes positive connections with the past through a critique of contemporary history: capitalist modernity.

Though Lu Xun's visions of history are scattered and dramatized by his aesthetic works, the more explicit arguments are worked out in the essay mentioned above. These essays participated in the pre–May Fourth debate centered on western learning, the importation of science and technology, the values of democracy, and the fate of tradition under the pressure and exigency of change. There were strong arguments for embracing in toto western values and thoughts—indeed, western culture and institutions; there were conservative defenses of a presumed essence of Confucian tradition. There were also arguments to reconcile tradition and modern in a new combination.

In these controversies, a "tradition," such as that of science or democracy, was readily taken to be a finished thing: one either takes it or leaves it. In sharp contrast, and often in polemics against this static view of culture, Lu Xun took a second look at cultural structures not as something fixed, but as dynamically evolving and historically mutable. Instead of seeing the west as a whole, Lu Xun examined its successive historical vicissitudes. He was obviously acquainted with Ranke's historicist dictum that history should examine the past "the way it really was."[46] But Lu Xun's "historicism" is not empiricism or relativism based on the contingency of a specific historical moment. The essay "On the One-Sidedness of Cultural Development" addresses the repeated excesses or stray paths that a culture goes through time and again and attempts to approach the major events on their own terms. On the other hand, it projects a vision that rises above specific circumstances, signaling history as going in a right or wrong direction. A quick review of western history from the Roman Empire all the way to the earlier twentieth century reveals that western history has moved in twists and turns, and has gone through crooked paths of unity, disunity, and unity, unfolding a story of order, rebellion, and restructuring. The Protestant Reformation in Germany, to take a familiar instance, rebelled against and undermined the tyrannical authority of the Catholic Church, and paved the way for religious freedom and a more liberal society. The national monarchies arose to assert their independence from papal tutelage and spurred great creative, transformative energies for freedom. But monarchical orders in their turn became restrictive and their hierarchy oppressive. Then the French Revolution broke out and toppled the authori-

tarian order of the nobility, leading to greater freedom. Yet democratic society, while extending freedom and rights to the majority of the population, ran the risk of homogenizing individuals into anonymous masses. By
leveling out individuality and imposing uniform standards and norms,
modern society became in its turn repressive, resembling in many ways the
monarchical authorities it had revolted against and replaced.

We are here at the point of western modernity, which to Lu Xun
means materialism and undifferentiated, coerced mass existence. This
sketch of western history is a story of historical excesses—aberrations of
cultural development—followed by a movement that addressed and cor-
rected them. The newly established social formation in its turn fell into its
own atrophy and error, and triggered the need for a new corrective or revolutionary movement. "What I have described above," Lu Xun sums up,
"has been the major trend in recent social development, all such trends
evolve on the basis of prior developments and must be, of necessity, over-
reactions to the past, which in effect seek to reimpose a balance by rectify-
ing past excess through a process of over-compensation . . . the imbalance
is as clear as that evident on seeing a one-armed man limping on a lame
foot" (LXQJ 1:48–49).[47]

This review of western history as a story of excess alternating with re-
active redress may suggest a naively dialectical or even cyclical view. But the
cyclical view will miss the implications of Lu Xun's observations. Lu Xun
does not set out to present an objective unfolding of history for some idle
academic accuracy. Serving a polemical task, he aims against the prevalent
view advocating a total embrace of western culture. Many western-educated intellectuals and public figures at the time were promoting technology, science, and political institutions as quick fixes for saving and rebuilding a China on the verge of collapse. The embrace of the west
subscribed to an unquestioned acceptance of the narrowly evolutionist assumptions of history, dictating that China either adopt technological ex-
pertise and social institutions from the west or risk total extinction. Lu
Xun sees this view as a submission to a mythically objectified history, in
this case history of industrial capitalism. By subjecting western history, especially the period of capitalist modernity, to a critical review, he highlights
the crooked aberrations and bypaths of history and thus is able to separate
what is problematic from what is valuable. Put differently, Lu Xun re-
freshes the memory of Enlightenment notions of freedom, rationality, and

justice, which are sidetracked by the acceleration of capitalist modernity, to identify what has gone wrong and should be avoided, and to see what should be pursued in China's endeavor to learn from the west and become a modern nation in its own way.

Implicit in this essay is a critical evaluation that compares how history ought to proceed with the sorry stages through which it had been muddling along. The touchstone of this critique is the emancipatory ideals of freedom, rational consciousness, science, social justice, and individualism. Through the lens of these ideals, the story of the west is recast in terms of the unfortunate aberrations visited on human freedom. Social movements and institutional changes in the west tried to accommodate and achieve freedom, but the results are mixed at best, and dire consequences are numerous. For all its progress in science, technology, economy, and democracy, the west, in its faltering steps in modern times, did not provide a satisfactory example for the Chinese to emulate.

Lu Xun's critique of modernity not only questions the feasibility of adopting unreflectively the western institutions, but also seeks to recover what is valuable in the Enlightenment and its self-critique. From the Enlightenment he draws the idea of autonomous rationality; from the critiques of Enlightenment he takes the romantic notion of expressive individuality.

These two sources converge on a richly articulated image of the individual as an agent of history. Through this image, Lu Xun seeks to provide a form of modern subjectivity capable of promoting social transformation. This ideal individual combines the Cartesian cogito, exemplified by the quality of *zijue* (self-awareness; LXQJ 1:54), with the romantically inspired self that is predicated on a communal ethic. This all-around self is able to assert rational autonomy against external, received conventions but also possesses an enlightened inner life (*neiyao*; LXQJ 1:54) and a creative capacity to fulfill his or her own potentials. This is the individualistic part, but it is not the egoistic image of the bourgeois nomad or narrowly romantic self that draws its sustenance solely from inner resources, or a superhuman in splendid isolation from society. Rather, the ideal broadens to include every man and woman and is a goal that the whole society should strive for to become an organic community. It is a project "that will enable people to achieve a more profound understanding of the significance of life and lead them to achieve the self-awareness so critical in the development of the sort of individual potential required for the transformation of this 'country of loose sand' into a nation of human beings" (LXQJ 1:56).[48] In the same breath in which he mentions Rousseau, Hegel, and Schiller, Lu Xun portrays a self-image linking intellect and feeling in harmony. What is more, the self is also aesthetically inspired, capable of using—indeed, embodying—art and poetry as a medium for self-fulfillment and for relating organically and affectively to the whole community. "The people of a country," Lu Xun writes, "are both the repository of its poetry and the means of its literary production" (LXQJ 1:70).[49] This all-around, aesthetically grounded, and collectively based self is envisioned to play a politicorevolutionary role in changing China.

The idealized individual as ethical agent is at the core of the enduring project of "transforming the national character" (*gaizao guomin xing*) in modern Chinese history. It has been presented as a cultural, ethical, and aesthetic solution to China's problems, as opposed to what Benjamin Schwartz calls the "technological or engineering approach."[50] These two strains have persisted to this day and were once rendered into a degenerate version of "red" versus "expert." But the question remains as pressing as ever. Is Chinese history to be seen as an ethical drama that strives for justice, equality, freedom, and welfare for all, or is it simply an array of technical problems that only calls for the problem-solving experts, technicians, and legislators, relying on the efficacy of technological engineering?

The political reformers in Lu Xun's day focused their attention largely on technological engineering solutions—in redesigning political and legal institutions, economic structures, and a strong military on the basis of western models. Although these projects had the virtue of strengthening the nation, their historical vision was premised on the assumption that human society is basically a machine, which, equipped with a well-designed engine and perfect parts, can be left to run on its own. The corollary is that humans are but cogs in the machine and will change along with the changed, newly engineered environment. This mechanical understanding of history can be better characterized as teleological and determinist. It resonates with the contemporary faith in the invisible, all-powerful hand of the global market and in the power of technology that will presumably bring social and economic goods to everybody. Obviously, this notion shares the same logic with the end-of-history thesis and with the unreflective acceptance of western modernity.

In light of this broader picture, the notion of the ideal individual as ethical agent constitutes a critique of the instrumental rationality of the Enlightenment and its scientific-technical outlook. On the other hand, it puts Lu Xun's historical vision in touch with the mainstream revolutionary endeavors in modern China to transform the national character, and with the communist drive to reinvent a new society. These drives embrace both the technological powers of the west and the traditional ethic of a community-centered lifeworld—the red and the expert, rather than red against expert. Here we are on the treacherous ground of contemporary thinking on history. To avoid simplistic errors, we need to separate the traditional, communal ethic in Lu Xun and in communism as well, from its dire consequences of repressive collectivism and erasure of the individual. Whether the reassertion of a communal ethic necessarily leads to oppressive collectivism is too huge an issue to address here. But asking the question will force us to see that the "traditional elements" are posited here in Lu Xun and later in revolutionary discourse as an alternative to the engineering approach. The social engineer does not see individuals as active, self-determining ethical agents capable of making history. The question also allows us to see the rise and fall of the two strains in modern China. As we speak, it is obviously the technological engineering stance that is gaining the upper hand.

The notion of the idealized individual also places Lu Xun in another current of history related to the engineering versus ethic strain: the question of the individual's relation to community. This question asks whether the individual is compatible with or antithetical to collectivity, or whether the individual is simply an atomistic nomad of a loose aggregate. The controversy lies at the heart of the conflict between liberal and communitarian views in the west. Kirk Denton has shown how the notion of the romantic individual in Chinese literature has "fluid interaction" with the collective. Writers like Hu Feng and Lu Ling displayed a paradoxical tendency to "exalt the self and allow the self to succumb to such large totalities as History, Nation, and Epoch, or the Masses."[51] But if the individual needs to forge a "sense of history" in a time of crisis, he or she is not succumbing to the collective, but rather is trying to forge a collective solidarity that forms a united front out of loose and weak individuals. The collective at this point is what sustains, rather than takes away, individual identity. The historical, practical validity of the link between individual and collective needs to be affirmed, rather than simply left alone as "paradoxical."

The same is true with individualism. Lydia Liu's insightful study of individualism in modern China has shown that the term *individual* meant different things in different contexts, in different relations of power and political agendas in the republican era. Individualism was a critique of the Confucian tradition in the May Fourth movement, a scandal for traditionalists, a suspect term for the populists, a supreme value for anarchists and nihilists, a negotiable term for nationalists, and a dangerous ideology for socialists and communists.[52] Liu's main point is that the individual fulfilled variable discursive functions, sometimes complicit, sometimes incompatible with the varied notions of collectivity. For all her rigorous historicity underlying the term, however, we need to know more about the possible one-sidedness or excesses in the treatment of individualism. Characteristic of Foucaultian genealogy, Liu's study does not go further to ask if any one interpretation gets "right," in the sense of bringing out the validity claim of individualism, which need not always be equated with the voice of power. An awareness of its validity tied to a historical circumstance might help its proponents act in a specific situation, that is, to achieve emancipatory benefits for both individual and collective. In a time of crisis, there is a need to know what version of individualism is more useful and legitimate; otherwise, any interpretation would be just as good as another—simply another occurrence, another puppet in a pervasive, value-free game of power struggle.

To follow Lu Xun, it is necessary to identify the use and abuse of such a term historically. This question still haunts us, because the slightest suggestion of the assimilation of the individual into a collective tends to cause anxiety that it might be another episode of the erasure of the individual by hegemonic powers.[53] This is not always the case. The subtext of this anxiety runs like this: something like a coordination of individual and collective may be significant, in bouts of militant nationalism or collective war efforts, for example, but any further intimate contact between two terms will dangerously lead to the sacrifice of the individual to totalitarian power. In this light, the idea of individual fulfillment in a supportive, rewarding community remains unthinkable and undesirable in our postromantic, postmodern world, still in the shadows of totalitarianism and collectivism. Yet to even identify the excesses in the discourse of individualism, we need to posit the term as a value, and as a value compatible with the value of community.

Just as he posits freedom as a value that traversed a checkered career in the west, Lu Xun upholds the autonomous individual as the protagonist of the modern narrative, the agent of history. The idealized personality, endowed with the spirit of self-consciousness, autonomy, authenticity, vibrant creativity, and free will, is negatively directed against the foils of unfreedom embedded in the Confucian moral constraints and positively projected as the historical goal for transforming China.

Thus, instead of any overarching solution, Lu Xun recommends a project of reforming and rebuilding the character based on romantic individualism. When the Chinese become self-conscious of their potentialities for freedom and fashioned their character accordingly, they would be on their way to building a nation of free humans. The loose sand of people would then be reorganized into a nation of human beings. This principle of transforming the national character is an abiding theme in discussions of modernity in China.

In this analysis, Lu Xun evokes the Enlightenment values, which are forgotten by the material advance of modernity that he associates with nineteenth-century materialism. The Enlightenment is often associated, rather one-sidedly, with modern totalitarianism, repression, and even political catastrophes. But Lu Xun was able to see, as many of us cannot, that the modern state and liberal society had become a travesty of the Enlightenment notions of reason, freedom, justice, and equality. Although Lu Xun's valorization of the ideal character referred to Nietzsche, Stirner, and Kierkegaard, prone to a more extreme, modernist critique of the Enlightenment, his invocation of classical Enlightenment values tips the balance much more toward the memory of the Enlightenment in its more progressive and utopian moments.[54]

Lu Xun's conception of individual freedom and its realization in certain political organizations goes back to a mixture of romantic and Enlightenment traditions that count Herder, Rousseau, Hegel, and Schiller as major spokespersons. For all their differences, these thinkers attempted to provide solutions to the inner contradictions of modernity. The split between reason and sensibility, rationality and faith, intellect and imagination, theory and history, value and fact constantly finds a variant in the troubled relationship between individual autonomy and bourgeois society in which individuals are loosely aggregated without a common purpose. The notion of the individual bent on the pursuit of private interests in civil society has its political counterpart in parliamentary democracy, whose purpose is to facilitate the disparate business interests through public policy and market regulation.

In this "instrumental" or engineering relation between the state, civil society, and the individual, Charles Taylor distinguishes the expressive individual from the egoistic version. From the standpoint of the egoistic individual, society is an instrument designed to fulfill men's private needs, desires, and purposes. It is an object, not a subject that one can identify with emotionally and interact with ethically. In traditional society, men's identification with collectivity was through attachment and bonds to royalty, aristocracy, community, church, and so on. The autonomous subjectivity of the Enlightenment severed these "natural" ties from the self and condemned them as fraudulent and oppressive. Freed from these bonds, individuals were also deprived of the age-old venues of identification with the society in which they lived. But men's needs to identify with an order larger than the atomistic individual still persist in modern society. Thus the crisis of modernity is in part a constantly abortive search for grounds of identification with society as an organic, affective mirror image of oneself. Modern societies, writes Taylor, "have actually functioned with a large part of their traditional outlook intact" and modern men have constantly resorted to "some variant of the general will tradition." Modern ideologies like Jacobinism, anarchism, and Marxism, as well as myths of the frontier in America, and by extension all the collective political movements in modern China, are examples of the quest for an organic, intrinsic linkage between the individual and society.[55]

In this light, the search for history is indicative of the refusal to give up on the large structure of meaning. In Lu Xun's analysis, the crisis of modernity tackles the deformations within the individual. Problems of history are the problems of humans who make and are being made by history. Humans are alienated from their authentic self, their fellow human beings, their tradition and cultural formations, their sensibility split from intellect.[56] This deformed individual forms the weakest link in a historical transition that is nevertheless pressured to carry the burden of ensuring China's survival. So a powerful individual must be envisioned and invented to carry out, write, and enact history.

The image of the ideal character makes history by providing an aesthetic solution. By creating art and poetry, the poet/historian will enlighten and inspire the populace, who would then proceed to build a society on the model of art. Inspired by Schiller's idea of the complete, rounded personality, the individual is not understood as an egoistic entity, but envisioned as both subject and object of an aesthetic, social, and political project of self-formation and social formation. The aesthetic fashioning of subjectivity will rid Chinese of the disorientations and one-sidedness. Lu Xun's prototype of aesthetic figure is the romantic or demonic poet, whose powerful poetry is an analogy for a poetically inspired image of society. The poet's aesthetic impulse transcends the private self to make contact with and unite other men in the quest for freedom and just society. This sociohistorical concern renders radical poets, such as Byron, Shelley, and Mickiewicz, into world-historical figures like Napoleon, who, Lu Xun writes, enacted the poetry of freedom.[57] The poet is likened to the protagonist in a historical epic. Thus historical narrative is seen as driven by a dynamic, aesthetically inspired agent whose goal is the realization of his or her potentialities as a complete personality and the construction of an aesthetically reconciled culture.

This poetically inspired relation between the individual and the polity corresponds to the notion of expressive relation between individual and society as explained by Taylor. Moreover, it addresses itself to tradition and memory. As I mentioned earlier, Lu Xun has access to China's past by way of critiquing capitalist modernity. He makes a general distinction between a defunct, impotent tradition and a past that is usable for regenerating the present and anticipating the future. Specifically, the relevant past is envisioned to be a bloodline or inner voice, rather than dead letters, which animates people and keeps alive the striving, upward spirit in historical action. He constantly uses organic images in articulating the continuity of the past to the present.

The organic imagery does not entail the assumption of an unbroken continuity between present and past. That the organic continuity is broken without reprieve is amply testified to by the upheavals of history and by Lu Xun's own work. Lu Xun's "retrieval" of the past is strategic and is accompanied by a critical analysis of what is missing in the present. If there is any aspiration, it is the yearning toward an organic state for the present and future, or what comes to the same thing: an exposé of the inorganic, broken, degenerate character of the present.

The image of the individual is an image of the projected organic whole. The individual is endowed with unique, original character, which

Lu Xun often refers to as the inner light. This uniqueness underlies individual authenticity (*gexing*). Individual authenticity is further derived from
the authenticity of the life of a community or a nation. Lu Xun's conception of the individual encompasses an individualism that is radical yet anchored to the history and life-condition of a people.

In the essay "On the Power of *Mara* Poetry," the authenticity of the
poet's inner voice is traced back to the authentic voice and living tradition
in the past. The poet-historian's task is to revitalize the dormant inner
voice, suppressed and silenced by conventions and official tradition, and to
jolt the people to an awareness of their own genuine, vital past, which is in
fact self-awareness.[58] "The development of a nation of people" hinges
much on the "nostalgia for the past" (*huaigu*; LXQJ 1:56), yet the look
backward is not for judicious, even-handed preservation of some im-
mutable, valuable elements of tradition, but an act of wresting memory
from the dead hand of tradition for political purposes. The identification
with the past should be

clearly defined, so as to allow the past to function like a looking-glass, the reflection of which serves to illuminate by virtue of its lessons. A people must constantly gauge the road ahead through frequent reflection on what has gone before. While trekking the arduous path toward a brighter future, if they can retain
a certain regard for the wonders their collective past embodies, they shall be enabled to subject their new endeavors to a process of daily renovation while keeping their ancient heritage alive. (LXQJ 1:65)

The past is snatched out of its long sleep and awakened to promote self-
awareness and to unite the people into a nation. "Outside we do not lag
behind the world; inside we do not loose the inherent bloodline. Taking
from the present and retrieving from the past, we build an alternative culture" (LXQJ 1:56). In this way, the Chinese will attain self-consciousness
and fulfill their authentic potentials. The aggregate of loose sand will be reorganized into a nation of human beings.

Teleological and Active History

From this all-around individual engaged in an aesthetic project of
awakening past memory arises a utopian notion of history. As we saw earlier, May Fourth historical consciousness is characterized by evolutionism,

by a belief in progress as a teleological process of social transformation, and in the present as clean rupture and fresh beginning.[59] If this is partially true of May Fourth intellectuals and of later ideological reification of history into the iron law of progress and permanent revolution, then we need to take care not to confuse a teleological history with the utopian history envisioned by Lu Xun.

Lu Xun shares the utopian visions with many of May Fourth intellectuals and deploys the vocabulary of evolution and progress copiously in his writings. Although he views historical movement in terms of freedom, justice, and enlightenment, and although he sees science and technology as a powerful impetus for progress, he often insists that there is nothing historically guaranteed and determined about the future realization of these visions. His historical prognosis is not linear and shaped by a projected course of continuity. In the above analysis of the checkered career of freedom throughout western modernity, history is construed as a crisis-ridden process fraught with discontinuities, ruptures, and errors. The outcome of historical action is unforeseeable and unpredictable. Rarely, if ever, did Lu Xun convey the presumption that with historical goals set upon modernization, things will move and stay on a predestined course. This image of a crisis-ridden history is especially poignant in Lu Xun's literary works, suffused as they are with a tragic sense of the mythical, cyclical repetition of the past and the uncertainty of the future.

Lu Xun offers a clear theoretical formulation of this crisis view of history by addressing the privileged terms of democracy and science. In "On One-Sidedness of Cultural Development," this crisis manifests itself in the alternatively oppressive and emancipatory mutations in political institutions and cultural formations in the west. The subtext is the fate of democracy and the pursuit of freedom. Here there is no perceivable predetermined pattern or a supreme model carved in stone, dictating how freedom is to be achieved, how democracy is to be accomplished. This also applies to the history of intellectual and cultural achievement—that is, science, technology, and resultant material wealth, which were held up by Lu Xun's contemporaries as exemplary models for Chinese modernity.

In the essay "A Lesson on the History of Science" (Kexue shi jiaopian), Lu Xun again reviews the rise and fall of rational knowledge and scientific learning throughout western history, and evaluates the record according to an apparently historicist principle. The past accomplishments and failures are judged by their historical limitations and missed possibilities. It is thus ill-advised to romanticize these achievements, as some national heritage proponents did. On the other hand, identifying the limitations does not have to deny the superiority of science or rational knowledge to the practice of magic or medieval scholasticism. The pros and cons of science are estimable precisely because science is upheld as a value and is not equated with its own specific, time-bound achievement. As a value, science is not identical to scientism as an ideology. For all its historical limitations and stray paths, science is not to be overhistoricized out of its own intrinsic relevance to humanity; it should be able to transcend, not remain bogged down, in its historical limitations. By upholding this value, Lu Xun is able to perceive a series of failures as well as partial victories that science has gone through: from its inchoate beginnings in Greek times, through its suppression in medieval Europe accompanied by episodic revivals in Christendom, all the way up to its exciting restirring in the Renaissance and the reflective self-understanding in the age of Enlightenment, to its full flowering in technology and material wealth. This is progress, undoubtedly, even for those who may dread its dire effects, but there is nothing that guarantees that science will henceforth progress straightforwardly and triumphantly for the benefit of man (LXQJ 1:25–35).

From the crisis of science and its struggle against mysticism and a one-sided emphasis on normative morality in the Christian Church, Lu Xun concludes that there is no prescribed pattern of continuity in the development of intellectual culture. This crisis-ridden understanding applies to history as well: "Thus affairs of the world move forward and backward, traversing a zigzag course through different epochs. . . . It is said that the world moves in crooked paths, and is filled with discontinuities and offbeat trails, as in a spiral. There are ups and downs, and rises and falls assume myriad manifestations. But over time progress and regression will add up to some level. This is indeed true" (LXQJ 1:28).

Rather than a presumed force propelling historical progress, science is presented here as a hero who has suffered defeats, mutilation, distortion, and disasters as well as triumphs through unpredictable historical forces and misorientations. The conclusion is that although we should borrow modern science from the west, it is necessary to render it part of the project for creating a free society and for the enhancement of the all-around personality of free humans, free from the one-sidedness of rationality. Science, like freedom, is again posited as a value projected to the future as well as a guide to action. It is not envisioned as immanent to the inner dynamics of an impersonal history, teleologically and irresistibly working itself out, regardless of human agency and ethical choice.

Hope in Despair

Lu Xun's utopian impulse brings up the intricate relation of hope and despair in his works. There is a consensus that Lu Xun painted a despairing picture of Chinese society, traditional or modern. In his works, recorded history is a barbarous wilderness strewn with images of mutilated bodies and disfigured faces. It is a cannibalistic feast, with numbed figures sitting around the table, bloodthirsty and grotesque. This depository of traumatic memory seems hopelessly unredeemable and unrepresentable, rendering history into a primordial, bone-chilling landscape, exemplified in *Wild Grass* (Yecao). Hope seems illusory and self-deceptive against such a backdrop. The reforms, slogans, revolution, and other utopian urges, the ingredients of the "Golden World" (*huangjin shijie*) of history, are ghostly shadows against this all-devouring darkness.

This depressing image of history poses enormous problems for critics. Many are puzzled by the frequently arbitrary "leaps of hope" in Lu Xun from a nadir of meaninglessness to an airy epiphany in his fiction and prose poems in *Wild Grass*.[60] The problems can be answered by pointing to the lack of narrative coherence, the split in the personality, the psychological qualities of mood or biographical factors (listening to the command of the enlightened leader against one's will, for example). A better way to understand the relation of hope and despair is to place the two terms in the context of history writing. Instead of taking hope to be a private mood or psychological yearning for a better tomorrow, we need to see how it can be an integral part of the historical imagination.

The appalling record of unceasing brutality, catastrophe, and mutilation is inseparable from the recent historical traumas Lu Xun's generation had experienced. Thoughtful intellectuals went through the collapse of the Qing dynasty—China's defeat in the 1895 Sino-Japanese War, the failures of republicanism, and social upheavals under the predatory warlords. Reeling under the shocks of modern history, Lu Xun wrote narratives that carry familiar features of trauma. The traumatic narrative is marked by the breakdown of the attempt to narrate and account for a world-shattering, deeply wounding event. Instead of weaving a coherent story, the narrative reverts back, beyond the narrator's will, to the original scenes of disaster, as a traumatized patient is helplessly thrown back to the scene of injury. Yang Xiaobin's recent work on trauma and literature perceptively describes the outbreak of trauma in the rupture of literary narrative. Yang's analysis focuses on the avant-garde fiction of the 1980s, but the historical context for traumatic writing can be traced to the early modern period.[61] Lu Xun's fiction and essays show the symptoms of an insistent, repeated return to a nightmarish world. They render history into a primordial, petrified field of ruins, death, and waste. There is no history, there is nothing intended or projected for change or progress in the frozen, inhuman, antediluvian wilderness, where only wolves and cannibals roam. History—human discourse and activity in time—is rendered into timeless fate.

Yet it is precisely in the repeated, melancholy immersion in trauma that stirrings for a projected history are glimpsed. The nightmarish reality may presuppose a sleepwalker completely at the mercy of historical shocks, like a puppet pulled around by the strings of the cyclical old routine. On the other hand, it must take a desperate subject who, although inexorably trapped in the repetitive tragedy, is nevertheless able to stare into the darkness and discern something new beyond its bleakest color. Moreover, in bearing testimony to the nightmare, a sense of mastery and meaning is on the way. Writing about trauma becomes a tentative retooling of historical narrative by the imagination. Although traumatic experience shatters the culture's symbolic resources, it also points to the urgent need to reconfigure the broken representational and expressive repertoire. This involves imagining on the scale of historical narrative. Traumatic pain, as Elaine Scarry convincingly argues, is bound up with imaging. The "complete absence of referential content" of pain renders it resistant to, even destructive, of language and narrative. Lu Xun's obsession with the grim image, however, implies a huge leap of the imagination to give image to pain. Unlike unutterable, objectless pain, imaging is filled with objects. Although the body in pain suffers the gap between the self and its relation with objects and is thus passive, pain also prompts the self to actively enter into relation with the "objectifying power of the imagination: through that relation," writes Scarry, "pain will be transformed from a wholly passive and helpless occurrence into a self-modifying and, when most successful, self-eliminating one."[62]

The self-modifying act not only stems from the pained body, but also goes one step ahead of the crushing pain. If he was generally reluctant to attach any definitive role to himself, Lu Xun prided himself in being such a seer and an image-maker of darkness. By vigilantly staying with the darkness, the return to the past avoids what might have been a helpless, passive pathology and moves on to an active breakthrough in historical consciousness. Lu Xun professed that he was "in love with night" and was "endowed with the ear and eye to listen to and see the night."[63] There is always a pleasure to be gained from merging with the darkness. He held up darkness as an aesthetic quality, one preferable to the beautiful and consoling, and stuck close to the bleak images of brutality. This indicates a dual take on the tradition: a full awareness of the tradition's bankruptcy, coupled with an aesthetic impulse for depicting it in muffled indignation. The dispersed, fragmented images of darkness contain no recipe for the utopian redemption of history, but by relentlessly conjuring them up in distorted images, a narrative is launched onto history. This is the imaginary translation of traumatic memory into historical narrative.

Writing history is thus to deliver a superior insight into the degenerate conditions of the past. Sandwiched between Confucian upbringing and modern ideas, Lu Xun and May Fourth intellectuals are halfway between tradition and modernity. Lu Xun was aware that he was complicit with tradition and thus deemed himself part of the lethal burden of cultural memory. But instead of being trapped in the tradition, he turned his insider's knowledge to advantage. He understood what it was like to be dehumanized, degraded, and deprived of basic human freedom and dignity. He not only saw the darkness in tradition and history, but he also discovered traditional residues—within himself. Throughout his writing, Lu Xun turns a critical gaze on himself; he deems himself as much an object of history subjected to critique as all the inherited malaises. Yet by seeing the nightmares and registering them, by keeping a minute inventory of all those failures and disasters, he assumes an active, heroic responsibility for the victims of history and for posterity: "Carrying the burden of inheritance and tradition," as he pictured it, he "shouldered the gate of the darkness" (LXQJ 1:130). And this is to release children to a free, rational space. It is instructive to note how similar Lu Xun's way of delivering a historical message is to what Walter Benjamin characterizes as Kafka's role in literature. Kafka, Benjamin writes, is "like one who keeps afloat on a shipwreck by climbing to the top of a mast that is already crumbling. But from there he has a chance to give a signal leading to his rescue."[64]

The call for rescue from a sinking ship can be a heuristic tool to discern the negative figuration of utopia in Lu Xun's literary works. Lu Xun's stories of suffering and misery are in one sense an accurate image of society. But they are not documentary, empirical accounts; Lu Xun's narrator paints Chinese society in the most brutal, pathological hues, yet all this is done with a sideways glance to what is possible and otherwise. If the narrator only sees as much as his benighted, historically trapped characters, we would have a historical narration which is nothing but "one damned thing after another," a meaningless, random chronology. What allows him to see at all are standards of Enlightenment outside what actually exists.

Recently there have been remarkable attempts to find utopian impulses in Lu Xun's works. Wang Hui finds a positive thrust in Lu Xun's despairing picture of social reality by showing a hidden dialectic within the conflict between cherished values and wretched history. In "Diary of a Madman," for example, the cannibalistic history and hope are linked by a perception that the cannibalistic world can give rise to a self-awakened, enlightened consciousness. The distress of Wei Lian-shu in "The Loner" (Gudu zhe), to give another example, is not just traumatic and private suffering as such, "but comes from a powerful wish of the awakened to try to reform and save the masses."[65] Lu Xun's depiction of history thus is not one of simple sadness, melancholy, or darkness. It reflects an enlightened subject who feels sorrows for the wretchedness of the people and resents them for their mute acquiescence. Hope is thus deferred to a no-man's-land and is at the same time converted into a vital energy for fighting the heavy burden of tradition. Ceaselessly combating the darkness (darkness is a shorthand symbol for all the degenerate history and tradition) is for Wang Hui the overriding theme throughout Lu Xun's work of history. In a similar vein, Xu Jian analyzes Lu Xun's fictional art in terms of Adorno's negative dialectics. If the utopian impulse persists even in the darkest art, Lu Xun's depressing picture should paradoxically carry utopian hope. Both critics have shown that hope could be figured forth paradoxically and negatively within what looks like a picture of wretched reality.[66]

I would extend this valuable analysis to a utopian understanding of historical narrative. For Adorno, artworks, even the darkest ones, contain utopian hope in the form of a hidden wish: "it should be otherwise." Works of art point toward "a practice from which they abstain: the creation of a just life."[67] Now, if the utopian yearning for a just society is what art is about and seeks to achieve, why should it abstain from a frontal, full-fledged rendition of it? Two arguments are often invoked against the achievement of utopia in art. One is that aesthetic unity, the image of utopian reconciliation of social antagonism, is achieved on paper through cathartic appeal and cheap, emotional consolation. This feel-good approach belies the intractable, conflict-ridden reality. The other objection is that with the sordid, wretched reality still firmly in place, any reconciliation of historical antagonism, any materialization of hope into realized imagery, is premature and ideological, running the risk of fetishizing, mythologizing hope.

This does not mean that hope should be dropped out from historical narrative and the narrator should instead sink or swim in the darkness. Rather, it implies that the utopian impulse appears in a grim guise, "draped in black" as Adorno puts it. When history has become a stream of catastrophes, the utopian impulse "converges with the possibility of total catastrophes," as if art wanted to prevent the catastrophe by conjuring up its image.[68] Lu Xun's insistence on depicting the darkness resonates with this perception.

Without some glimmers of utopian wish for a healthy human personality, there would be no discerning of its sick condition to begin with. How could Lu Xun have defined and measured all the miseries and absurdities without some implicit aspirations? It misses the point to say that Lu Xun swings between optimism and pessimism, and it gives a poor estimate of hope to claim that Lu Xun is simply of two minds or undecided.

The much-discussed piece "My Old Home" (Guxiang) illustrates the back-and-forth movement between hope and despair. The narrator's disheartening trip to his hometown is fully matched by the desolate landscape that meets his eyes. Despite the faint attempt to evoke the fond memory of home, the narrator's remembrance is chilled by encounters with the dreary ancient custom and routines of clan connections, until the upcoming visit of his childhood friend Runtu is brought up. The intensity and quickness with which Runtu and childhood remembrances well up in the narrator's memory could be well described, à la Proust, as an epiphany of involuntary memory. Runtu is nothing less than a figure that brings back the exciting vista of a childhood dream world, virtually a small utopia in itself. We are transported to a glowing world of traditional communal festivities in the holidays, of modest and self-sufficient prosperity in material living, of temporary suspension of the hierarchy between the haves and have-nots. On top of it is an enchanted space opened up in the remembered images, of child play in the snow, the seashore, the starlit sky, the adventure in the melon field, and so on. All these wonderful dreams are in the next scenario crushed by the appearance of the real Runtu, whose life is found to be wretched, impoverished, and beastly. There also arises an impenetrable wall between the childhood friends when Runtu addresses the narrator as "sir." All is bleak and dreary until the moment the narrator departs for the city with his relatives. At this time, he finds hope resurfacing in his nephew, who yearns for future reunion with Runtu's son.

The narrator's fresh hope is the wish that children might make it out differently from the adults. Yet fear creeps up on him that any youthful hope may also turn out to be just as illusory as the adults' sour ones. On second thought, however, despair may also prove to be false, its falsity having been revealed, for example, when Runtu asks for incense burners and candlesticks for superstitious purposes. The story's equivocal ending for some critics points either to a flat affirmation of hope or its denial; others are inclined to settle on the idea of a down-to-earth, strenuous will to continue to fight, heedless of hope or despair.[69] Much can be said about this shift to the practical attitude, evidenced by the narrator's injunction to continue walking on the uncharted terrains against all odds. Lu Xun's oft-cited remark that the falsity of hope is akin to the falsity of despair seems to deny the validity of hope.

Whether hope and despair exist in reality, as Lu Xun reminds us, is beside the point. Hope, however, serves to energize historical narrative. Hope exists as a motivating force of imagination, not as something solid and empirical to be found in the real world. The materialization of hope tends to become reified, reality-conforming ideology. Hope arises, as the narrator says, as "a stretch of jade-green seashore spread itself before my eyes, and above a round golden moon hung in a deep blue sky" (LXQJ 1:485).[70] Hope is underwritten by the idyllic remembrance of earlier happiness and sustained by the yearning for a better world. Its practical historical function is to hold onto a world of possibility that, although imaginary, reveals the current conditions as wretchedly deficient and utterly in need of change. The fact that some hopes consequently turned false does not render invalid the lasting value of hoping. Hope is being kept alive in Lu Xun while being subject to demystification and disillusionment. It is hoping against hope. The principle of hope is installed at the very heart of the bleak portrayal of wretched existence.

Hope in Lu Xun thus looks like antihope. His texts raise and deflate hope in the same breath by keeping a vigil on a sordid reality, a reality apparently barren of meaning and salvation, a world of darkness and despair. On the other hand, despair is carried all the way to its extreme, until it turns into its apocalyptical opposite: enough is enough, and the whole damned world teeters on the brink of collapse under some sign of judgment or fatality. There is huge ecstasy (*da huanxi*) to be had from watching its collapse. Thus the despair is also antidespair. The despair is an energizing point of departure for getting things moving and making choice as one moves along. The same could be said of getting history started, just as the narrator muses as he moves to an unknown future:

As I dozed, a stretch of jade-green seashore spread itself before my eyes, and above a round golden moon hung in a deep blue sky. I thought: hope cannot be said to exist, nor can it be said not to exist. It is just like roads across the earth. For actually the earth had no roads to begin with, but when many men pass one way, a road is made. (LXQJ 1:485; 64)

Tragic Vision, Traumatic Visuality, and the Montage of History

In inquiries into modern China's intellectual legacy, scholars tend to look at major writers as they pronounced their views. Yet what the writers said through theoretical discourse might not be what the circumstances compelled them to say. Under pressure from social and historical contexts, they might be struggling to find a voice but still failed to do so. Our respect for the "intellectual tradition" may require us to construct a finished and coherent corpus of thought, but this reverence for wholeness may miss significant failures, which are more illuminating than the constructed whole. Just as a speaker's slip of tongue may render us more privy to his or her hidden trouble than the articulated speech, so the miscellaneous, half-spoken traces outside intellectual history may allude to the real contradictions. This consideration calls for a redrawing of boundaries of intellectual discourse and fresh attention to other disciplines.

In this chapter, I will work toward an aspect of modern Chinese historical thinking. I call it critical historical consciousness in the tragic mode. Realism in history was associated with the category of the tragic and had manifestations in literature and film. Leo Ou-fan Lee has suggested that a new mode of consciousness "began to emerge after the turn of the century and became firmly anchored in the intellectual discourse of the May Four era."[1] This consciousness imagined a certain structure of temporality. Marked by the optimism that the present epoch is special and brand new and is a radical rupture with the past, this sense of history drew on a range of intellectual resources from social Darwinism, the Enlightenment notions of democracy, science, and progress to nationalism and Marxism. In Lee's analysis, this heightened sense of history is a hallmark of modernity and modernism and carries a "unilinear time and a unilinear sense of history." It thus runs contrary to the traditional Chinese cyclical view of time.[2] Other studies also frame the emergent historical consciousness in a unilinear time of nationalism, revolution, and the ideology of progress.[3]

This upbeat anticipation of the future was weighed down with a profound sense of tragedy. In his *Modern Tragedy*, Raymond Williams notes that since the French Revolution, the ideas of tragedy have come intertwined with historical thinking and the experience of suffering. Tragedy has been seen as a response to a culture in change and crisis. The most interesting twist in this blending of tragedy into history is the perception of revolutionary change. A time of revolution, Williams says, is "a time of violence, dislocation and extended suffering that it is natural to feel it as tragedy, in the everyday sense."[4] But the revolutionaries and nationalists tend not to relate their history to tragedy. Instead, in their eyes the successful revolution becomes epic, not tragedy. The sense of tragedy as rooted in cultural crisis and its denial via an epic, redemptive narrative may be said to mark the two divergent tendencies in historical narrative in modern China. I will discuss their later manifestations throughout this book. The cultural crises were what prompted Chinese critics to warm up to the idea of tragedy. The Chinese version of tragedy was distinct from the standard interpretation in the west. I would probe the special implications of the tragic vision as it relates to history by examining not historiography per se, but literature, aesthetic discourse, and drama criticism in the first few decades of the twentieth century. I will also explore the tragic-realist strain in the disruptive visual experience in the cinema of the thirties.

Historical thinking in the May Fourth New Culture was embodied not only by the scholarly discipline of history, but also expressed in literature and theater, as well as the dynamic strains of cultural production. These spheres of culture may belong more to aesthetics than history. But when aesthetics enmeshes with history, historical narrative takes on a different function. It becomes a broad attempt to cope with the reality of the past and its traumatic effects, and to envisage a future. As a scholarly undertaking, historical discourse seeks to find truth, and the historian is trained to ascertain objectively how things were really like in certain circumstances. In contrast, aesthetically driven history makes sensory, emotional, perceptual, and psychosomatic impacts. It holds up history as an image or spectacle that one can contemplate and live with. Aesthetic history asks whether the images of the past are bearable or unbearable, beautiful or ugly, tragic or romantic. It is an ongoing shaping and reshaping of a culture's perceptual and sensuous responses, structures of feeling, and narratives and visions with respect to its past. More importantly, aesthetic history uses the past for understanding and shaping the present. The aestheticization of history, as Hayden White and many others have argued, is not simply rhetorical adornment tagged onto history proper. It is the stock-in-trade intrinsic to any representation of the past.[5] Karl Marx, in spite of his view of history as a material process, was quite ready to consider history's aesthetic dimension. Marx's well-known remark, that a historical event happened at the first time as a tragedy and the second time as a grotesque farce, is a recognition of the aesthetic configuration of historical narrative.[6]

Although White's aesthetic categories may be too much derived from the nineteenth-century European context to suit an analysis of Chinese history, his insistence on the aesthetic dimension raises the question why and how visions of the past are constantly shaped in a certain aesthetic mode in modern China. From Wang Guowei and Liang Qichao, to Hu Shi and Lu Xun, major Chinese intellectuals criticized false portrayals of the past in traditional fiction and theater. During the mid-1980s, the representation of history was again entwined with aesthetic issues. Modernism, postmodernism, and realism became the innovative means whereby writers and artists engaged the past and present. If trauma can be an aesthetic category, its use in historical discourse indicates a general willingness to confront the crisis-ridden historical reality and to eschew the received narratives that whitewash the bloody traces through melodrama or ideological catharsis.[7] Entwined with aesthetics, the historical consciousness of the 1980s once again took on a critical edge and bore some affinity with the earlier, May Fourth historical thinking.

Against the received patterns of feeling and perception, intellectuals in the earlier decades of the twentieth century saw tragedy as an antidote to self-deceptive, aesthetic representations of history in traditional literature and theater. In their writings, Wang Guowei, Hu Shi, and Lu Xun bring tragedy into historical narrative and regard it as a truthful and realistic approach to Chinese history. As a form of drama as well as a clear-eyed vision of the human condition, tragedy has a venerable tradition in the west. As this tradition came to be translated and appropriated by Chinese intellectuals at the turn of the twentieth century, it underwent alterations and contributed to the emergent Chinese historical consciousness.

Tragedy and Realism

At the turn of the century, the sense of China on the brink of collapse destroyed the age-old confidence in the moral superiority of the Middle Kingdom. China's military fiasco of the Sino-Japanese War in 1894–95, the last of long series of wars with foreign powers on the eve of the twentieth century, smashed any lingering pride in the moral strength of traditional culture. Japan's military victory lured more imperialist powers to try to carve up China for their domination. The partial colonization of China put in doubt the very survival of Chinese civilization. The pervasive doomsday mentality was well captured by the poignant phrase, the "loss of the country and extinction of the race" (*wangguo miezhong*).

In this situation of crisis, tragedy, an important idea in western drama and aesthetics, came into view for scrutiny and translation. It excited sensitive minds in the face of national emergency. In the decades before and after the May Fourth movement, the Chinese phrase *beiju* cropped up in scholarly writings, literary criticism, and theater reviews with surprising frequency. Wang Guowei, Hu Shi, and Lu Xun used the word frequently. The pioneers of modern Chinese theater, such as Chen Dabei, Guo Moruo, and Tian Han evolved their projects and aesthetics around the notion of tragedy.[8]

Given the customary perception of tragedy as unsuited to Chinese culture, this fact becomes most striking. The western idea of tragedy has been regarded as alien to the "Chinese way" of feeling and thinking. Tragedy, critics have argued, has never existed in the Chinese imagination. The Chinese are too preoccupied with earthly living and too removed from a religious or transcendental cast of mind to be thrilled by the story of grandiose heroism that thrives on suffering and death.[9] Chinese literature and art surely know sufferings, violence, misfortunes, and death, but a student of comparative literature or anthropology would be hard pressed to find in Chinese texts the kind of tragic scenarios enacted before the Athenian audience and formulated by Aristotelian theory. "All men are aware of tragedy in life," George Steiner avers. Yet "tragedy as a form of drama is not universal." "That representation of personal suffering and heroism which we call tragic drama is distinctive of the western tradition." It is not even Judeo-Christian, Steiner cautions; it is strictly Hellenic and is alien to the Judaic outlook of the world.[10]

As a concept, a figure of imagination, and an aesthetic form, tragedy would look like one of those untranslatable terms that fit awkwardly as they found their way into the Chinese language and discourse. But the notion of tragedy did get translated and stuck around with tenacity, although reconfigured beyond recognition. A glance at Chinese literature, theater, and fiction from the turn of the century up to the May Fourth period would enable us to see the word *beiju* figure prominently in public discourse. It assumed special importance in the emerging Chinese theater groups, whose members debated the concept and practiced it in their theatrical production. Writers and critics seemed to have little trouble using the term.

The Chinese translation of tragedy brings out a modern vision that was not quite apparent in the original Greek concept. In his study of the tragic vision from the standpoint of existentialism, Murray Krieger makes a crucial distinction between tragedy and what he terms the tragic vision. Tragedy as dramatic form functions as an aesthetic screen to gloss over a disturbing, demonic reality. Tragedy thus refers to a dramatic or literary form, whereas "the tragic" entails a vision of reality and history. Aristotle's formalistic theory of tragedy—action, catharsis, aesthetic contemplation, character, and plot—serves to tame and contain the irruption in tragic plots of the irrational, dangerous, and fearsome. Yet in the eyes of the modern, "less solvent generations," argues Krieger, tragedy is no longer a stabilizing redeemer and container: it has been exploded by all the carnage and catastrophes of the twentieth century. Treading the same ground as Kierkegaard, Nietzsche, and modernist novelists, Krieger characterizes the tragic vision as being "the Dionysian without the Apollonian." The tragic vision sees life as "unalleviated, endlessly and unendurably dangerous, finally destructive and self-destructive." "The tragic is like tragedy without that moment in which the play comes around and the cosmos is saved and returned to us intact." It is the tragic chaos wandering free from its "capacious," aesthetic home in classic tragic drama. "The therapy produced by catharsis, which allowed the subversive elements to be healthily exposed and aesthetically overcome, would no longer be available."[11] Krieger's analysis is a modernist translation of the Greek notion of tragedy against a backdrop of catastrophic traumas and holocausts of the twentieth century. Speaking of how a translation may be more authentic than the original, Benjamin notes that "a specific significance inherent in the original manifests itself in its translatability."[12] Krieger's interpretation tears away the Greek veil to reveal the truly tragic essence in the human condition of the twentieth century. The hidden, "modernist" tragic vision also came through sharply and was given a stronger historical dimension in its Chinese translation.

Wang Guowei was perhaps the first to have introduced the western concept of tragedy. In the time of crisis and utter despair, Wang committed suicide in the Kunming Lake in the imperial Summer Palace outside Beijing. Wang's personal tragedy, through Chen Yinque's reading, became allegorical of the imminent demise of Chinese culture. Confronted with calamities and upheavals, even the most determined guardian of culture could not but see the tragic fate of the individual crumbling with the cultural system. As "the crystallization of the spirit of this culture," wrote Chen, Wang had no choice but "join his culture in a common death."[13] This awareness of personal doom and cultural collapse seemed to be the key to Wang Guowei's understanding of the modernist tragic vision.

In his classic essay "Critique of *The Dream of the Red Chamber*" (Honglou meng pinglun, 1904) Wang analyzes Cao Xueqin's novel apparently along an Aristotelian line. The Chinese compound *beiju*, he notes, literally means "sad play," stressing theater rather than a vision of reality. Referring to Aristotle's *Poetics*, Wang recognizes "pity" and "fear" as emotional effects proper to tragic plot—distress to be purged so that the viewer's spirit may be uplifted. Yet for all his awareness of the formal properties of tragic drama, Wang does not evince any serious interest in tragedy as a genre of theater and gives short shrift to Aristotle's formalistic strictures. This deliberate neglect is illuminating and significant. Normally a discussion of tragedy would start with Aristotle's *Poetics*, for it is in this canonical text that one is supposed to find authority and consensus. Not that there was no translation of Aristotle's text in China. In the growing enthusiasm for western ideas, literary scholars had introduced the concept of tragedy in the strictly Aristotelian sense.[14] Drama critics and theorists dwelled on plot, action, and emotional effects—the prominent features of the tragic convention in the classical tradition. Wang, in contrast, seems to crave stronger, more disturbing elements of tragedy than its alleged cathartic and formalistic power. He translated and interpreted tragedy through the visions of Schopenhauer and Kant.[15]

Wang conceives tragedy as a tragic vision rather than a dramatic form. This vision stems from a historical and philosophical, rather than an aesthetic-emotive, frame of reference. In his book *Will as Representation*, Schopenhauer grounds the tragic vision on an understanding of human life riddled with incessant yet constantly frustrated desire. Following this theory of the will, Wang, in the "Critique of *The Dream of the Red Chamber*," argues for the power of the tragic/aesthetic experience in rejecting desire. There are, Wang writes, three kinds of tragedy. The first stems from the evil deeds of a wicked person. The second constitutes the tragedy of blind fate against which human capacities are powerless. The third, more tragic than the first two, arises not from wickedness or blind fate, but from the inescapable human condition where ordinary people with conflicting desires are trapped in a mutually destructive relation. The first two cases indicate the accidental character of tragic happenings, whereas the third reveals tragedy as inherent in everyday life and social relations. Tragic sufferings are intrinsic to human life because we are all slave to desire. The solution is to be found in tragic art. Tragic art constitutes a release from this wretched condition and is capable of delivering the desire-driven individual from sufferings into the zero degree of desire, a deathlike quiet or nirvana. Thus in the spirit of Schopenhauer, the tragic vision is both an eye-opening insight into the inescapable plight of human life and a defensive mindset that, fortified by tragic art, is able to keep the actual harms of tragedy at bay (4).

There is good reason to translate the frustrating human condition here into the specific historical condition of Wang's time, a time of changes, calamities, and perplexities. In the face of crises, Wang worked out a reaction-response psychic scenario consonant with the tragic vision. This vision intones that the individual needs to be tough-minded in the face of devastating events in order to survive. The sense of tragedy in Wang is thus identical to the sublime experience, which he calls *zhuangmei* (gigantic beauty). Two kinds of aesthetic experience, Wang says, can deliver us from the entrapment of desire. The experience of the beautiful quiets our agitated minds and focuses our senses on pleasing forms of objects, thus fostering disinterested contemplation and preventing us from chasing desirable things. The experience of the sublime is more effective and powerful. Terrifying and overwhelming objects wrench us forcefully from all our attachment to interests of life. "When an object directly hostile to our will confronts us and violently tears up our will and dissolves it," we are in for sublime pleasure. "We gain a penetrating insight into nature of things" (4). With its unflinching descriptions of sufferings and death, *The Dream of the Red Chamber*, Wang claims, is "the tragedy of tragedies" because it offers the experience of the sublime.[16]

It seems ironic that already subjected to the traumatic experience of historical catastrophe, Wang would resort to an equally traumatic art form, revisiting and reexperiencing destructive spectacles. His work draws a parallel between an aesthetic of tragedy and violent, catastrophic history. Although the psychic roots of this identification with the tragic may suggest an attempt to attain subjective mastery and self-control, it also points a hard-nosed, unflinching confrontation with historical reality. It fosters a tragic-realist attitude that seeks to pit a strong will of endurance against the mystifications and illusions of traditional theater and fiction.

The tragic notion thus goes along with a willingness to confront the real and with a vehement assault on emotional smugness and structural closure in the traditional theater. In "Critique of *The Dream of the Red Chamber*," Wang holds up Cao Xueqin's novel as radical departure from intellectual weakness and emotional shabbiness in the traditional Chinese aesthetic sensibility. The novel in its tragic thoroughness flies in the face of the characteristic mentality of the Chinese, declares Wang:

The Chinese mentality enjoys worldly living and always assumes that things would turn up better [literally, be content with whatever Heaven would offer, *le tian*]. So theater and fiction expressive of this mentality are everywhere tinged with this merry-go-around: what begins in sadness ends up in joy; what begins in separation will always wind up in reunion; what begins in distress ends up in prosperity. Without following this pattern it is hard to satisfy the audience's heart! (10)

This time-honored literary practice refused to stick with distressing events in their negative dimension and attempted to set the record straight. Wang charges that this self-deceptive practice turns what was incomplete and unsatisfactory in earlier texts into a palatable and appetizing story. The unfulfilled love, for instance, between the Tang Emperor Tang Xuanzong and his concubine Yang Yuhuan in Bai Juyi's poem "Song of Unending Sorrows" (Changhen ge) was fulfilled in the subsequent play *Palace of Eternal Youth* (Changsheng dian). *The Dream of the Red Chamber*, in contrast, refuses to get into the rut, and its narrative ends in catastrophe and separation. Not tough-minded enough to take this tragic ending, later writers would make the story come around to emotional satisfaction. The desire for the happy ending is not an isolated, individual preference but is present everywhere in the established repertoire of narratives and in the appreciative habit of Chinese writers and readers (10–11).

The Intellectual Agenda of the Tragic Theater

The initiatives of modern Chinese theater were also marked by a strong interest in tragedy. In the same year Wang wrote his "Critique," theater critic Jiang Guanyun published an article entitled "On the Chinese Theater" in *Xinmin congbao* (Magazine of the new people) and commented on the current state of Chinese theater. Jiang holds up Shakespeare as the exemplar for Chinese theater to emulate and privileges tragedy over comedy. He writes, "The best plays are all tragedy, not comedy. That is why there are more tragic plays in theater, and they bring good things to society."[17] Like Wang Guowei, Jiang argues that the task of the New Chinese Theater is to fortify the Chinese mind, and the way to do it is to create a tragic theater. The aim is to restore the distraught, enfeebled, degenerate mind to strength and integrity.

In theatrical circles the idea of tragedy was introduced to China by way of Japan. In 1906 a number of theater enthusiasts, professionals, fans, and overseas students in Tokyo formed the Spring Willow Society (Chunliu she), the first modern Chinese theater group. They carried out their projects under the influence and sometimes the personal guidance of the prominent members of the Japanese "New School Theater." The Japanese theater society came into being much earlier and had been engaged in translating and appropriating European and North American theatrical repertoires. Li Shutong, the best-known member of the Spring Willow Society, associated closely with Japanese theater critics and had the reputation as a meticulous reader of the complete works of William Shakespeare. In 1907 the Society staged the Chinese adaptation of Harriet Stowe's *Uncle Tom's Cabin*, and the production marked the birth of the first modern Chinese spoken drama. The production was well received and ran for three days in Tokyo.[18]

The Chinese translation of *Uncle Tom's Cabin* was known in China at the time as *Heinu yu tian lu* (A black slave's outcry to heaven), owing to Lin Shu's translation of Stowe's novel. The story is not tragic in the classical sense, but it appealed to critics and theater fans alike for its portrayal of the suffering of black slaves. Characteristically, critics and translators treated the story as an unadorned narrative of a real historical event. In the "Translator's Note" to the book, Lin Shu credits the novel with poignant and realistic descriptions of the misery and plight of black slaves, but this is not due to the author's skill in telling a good story. The fate of black slaves is simply real as historical experience, and its images might serve as a wake-up call for Chinese. The story would heighten the Chinese awareness of the danger of the "extinction of the yellow race." "In this book the miseries of black slaves are depicted in detail," writes Lin. "This is not because I am especially versed in depicting sadness; I am merely transcribing what is contained in the original work. And the prospect of the imminent demise of the yellow race has made me feel even sadder." Other commentators had similar views. Reading the story, a critic said, "one weeps for the yellow race by shedding tears over the black race, and begins to reflect on the present condition of the yellow race by reading about the past of black slaves."[19]

It was this racial sympathy that motivated the Spring Willow Society to stage the play. In their theoretical orientation, the members of the society again ignored the formalistic mechanism and subtleties of tragedy and went straight for the "real condition" that they believed tragedy was capable of representing. Thus the dominant tenet in the Society's manifesto was realism rather than tragedy in the classical sense. They were advocating, I would say, a tragic-realist approach to the representation of history.

This realism is not to be understood in the naive sense of describing the real. It involved first of all discarding traditional theatrical conventions. In the traditional theater, performance and speech were rigidly stylized and codified. Operatic singing had its fixed and shopworn rules of tone and voice. These formalistic, ritualistic features, the "conventionalization" of theater, as one critic termed it,[20] hindered the immediate depiction of real life in modern times and the spontaneous expression of feeling. The new theater, which already set itself off as spoken drama (*huaju*) in contrast to the traditional theater, was to take as its principle "the emotion charged speech and action, like what is popular in Europe and North America." This demand for real-life speech and action went along with a call for new scripts. The traditional repertoire no longer supplied any real, convincing stories. The playwrights needed to create new stories to represent the new reality. And this "new story" adequate to the reality was no other than the one that depicted the tragic suffering of black slaves, whose oppression foreshadowed the fate of the yellow race.[21]

Theater Reform and Tragic Historical Consciousness

Learning about tragedy and practicing spoken drama supplied ammunition for critiquing traditional culture. There was a growing sense that traditional theater and fiction could no longer prepare the Chinese to look crisis-ridden reality squarely in the face. Traditional theater and fiction surely depicted suffering and death, but the archetypal narrative in these popular genres was a story of self-deceptive wish fulfillment. Suffering, insanity, bloodshed, and inhumanity are depicted in the beginning or the middle of a narrative, but the carnage was always diluted and dissolved with a happy ending. Against this self-deception the disruptive tragic vision from the west could act as antidote. A new, realistic tragedy may militate against the mindset schooled in the catharsis-oriented appreciative habit, ironically a classical tragic attribute. Hu Shi called this taste for happy endings *tuanyuan zhuyi* (roundism, or belief in completeness and closure). It is an expectation for roundness and completeness in the turn-around of the protagonist's fate and in emotional gratification. Seeking to challenge this "untragic" dramatic structure in traditional Chinese theater and literature, modern theater critics turned to western discourse for radical concepts and practice in the hope of confronting the traumatic "real" of history and society. The concept of the tragic thus was more than aesthetic and became a reference point whereby the critics exposed the "weakness of the Chinese character" and its faintheartedness in the face of catastrophic events. The Chinese habit of appreciation was steeped in the insatiable appetite for emotionally satisfactory happy endings. The critics attacked this "cultural disease" of roundism, which mystified the mass audience.

Hu Shi was quick to pick up the clues in Wang Guowei's tragic critique. Hu reopened the question of the tragic vision ten years later in the journal *New Youth*, which was to become the official organ of the May Fourth movement. In October 1918 a special forum was devoted to promoting theater reform in the fourth issue of the journal. As the defining figure, Hu Shi was joined by many other critics in the debate. Prominent critics such as Chen Duxiu, Qian Xuantong, Fu Sinian, and Ouyang Yuqian pulled their intellectual training and resources together in a tirade against the traditional theater. Almost all of them agreed that western theater, especially tragic drama, should serve as the model to revitalize declining Chinese theatrical art. A list called "100 Well-Known Western Plays" was appended to the issue, "meant to be translated as exemplars for the New Chinese Drama."22

The title of Hu's contribution "The Idea of Literary Evolution and Reform of Theater" (Wenxue jinhua guannian yu xiju gailiang) frames theater art in a scheme of historical evolution. Hu rejected the view, advocated by a textbook of literary history, that the traditional theatrical form could regenerate Chinese culture and morality now in trouble. This view ignores the fact that a certain stage of historical evolution is matched by a specific development of a literary form. The age of monarchy was over and the traditional operatic form went with it. The new, modern era demanded a new theater. And this new theater was western in origin and tragic in character.23

The problem with the traditional theater, Hu asserts, is a glaring absence of tragic consciousness (beiju yishi). The Chinese have a deeply entrenched belief in things completed in happiness—the myth of roundness or roundism. The theatrical convention abounds in scenes of this happy roundness. The most common is the ritualistic appearance of a young couple happily married at the end of the play, who make a bow to the audience, so that everybody may walk away contented. Fiction and poetry also brim with similar absurdities of roundism. The many sequels to *The Dream of the Red Chamber*, such as *Postscript to the Story of the Stone* (Hou shitou ji) and *The Red Chamber Dream Come True* (Honglou yuan meng), refuse to rest content with the characters' tragic fate. They go so far as to "drag Lin Daiyu out of her coffin to be happily married with Jia Baoyu." The Tang poet Bai Juyi's well-known poem "Song of the Pipa" (Pipa xing) laments the miserable condition of the poet and the singing girl in their down-and-out encounter. Yet refusing to let them remain wretched, a Yuan writer composed a poem "that makes the Pipa girl jump over to the poet's boat to consummate in marriage." Significantly, this wish fulfillment has shaped the Chinese view of history in general and past carnages in particular. Yue Fei, although a heroic general of the Song dynasty, was put to death by the "wicked" councilor Qin Hui. This is a historical fact beyond consolation and melodramatic reversal. Yet literati of later ages took upon themselves to offer a tragic-heroic *Saga of the Yue Family* (Shuo Yue zhuan). To redress the "wrong" on behalf of Confucian morality, the new version makes the younger brother Yue Lei defeat the invading barbarians and confers on him a title of nobility, crowning this success story with the inevitable happy marriage. For Hu this myth of roundness is proof of "the weakness of the Chinese mind":

The writer knows very well that the world is either upside down or full of separation and death, yet he still wants to place every affectionate couple in marriage. He still insists that evil and good are as clear-cut as black and white, that retribution against evil is fair and balanced. He turns a blind eye to tragic dramas under Heaven, refuses to honestly describe the brutalities and irrationalities of the ways of the world. He only wants to express all-around satisfaction and joy on paper. This is a literature of deception.[24]

In his refusal to let go of brutalities and carnage in the portrayal of the past, Hu Shi comes close to the modernist tragic vision. Citing Aeschylus, Sophocles, and Euripides, he presents several major features of tragedy. In addition to the usual compelling power of the form and the viewer's empathy with fellow humans in pain, Hu moves toward an understanding of reality as riddled with tragic catastrophes, with no salvation from presumably benevolent Heaven. On the contrary, heaven and earth, the Chinese notion of transcendent power, constantly mock human will and efforts. In modern times, the sources of tragedy are the evils of society. By pointing to the destructive nature of tragedy, Hu aligns himself with the modernist tragic vision in Krieger's analysis. Modern western critics have attempted to look for the demonic, destructive forces in tragedy, and their view chimes in with the widespread uncertainties and skepticism about the power of human reason and progress of civilization after the atrocities of World War I. The tragic vision informs the existential outlook on the individual's fate and on culture and history.

Hu's tragic vision did not seem to sit well with the sanguine, May Fourth view of history as an ameliorative process of progress and emancipation. In Hu Shi's case, one may ask the question whether the tragic vision could degenerate or soften into a new cathartic roundism and whether the redemptive vision of May Fourth actually needed some versions of the aesthetic roundism Hu condemns. Surely tragic suffering and events in themselves do not raise hopes and supply meaning and purpose. If the human conditions and the course of history are tragic, how can one perceive, let alone achieve, human purpose in history? How can people go ahead and participate in the transformative project of enlightenment and progress? The redemptive value in Hu, we may argue, seems to be a cognitive gain. Something of value can be snatched from the senseless debris: by looking history squarely in the eye, one gains in consciousness and understanding. This redemptive, positive value in understanding the social conditions accords with May Fourth's generally optimistic view of historical change. It is precisely this cognitive acuteness that Hu seizes upon to make the tragic vision compatible with the sanguine historical outlook. Unlike the traditional roundism that turns a blind eye to tragic conditions of reality, the tragic vision opens one's eyes to the stark reality and constitutes a form of realism.

Realism, in imitation of real-life movements, speeches, gestures, and settings, Hu notes, was already at work in various local operas and theatrical genres. He pits this realism against the stylized conventions of the traditional theater. Realism departs from the highly stilted set of formalized acting, singing, speech, and stage setting. These obsolete devices blinded the audience to real-life situations and helped foster artificial enjoyment of mere conventional forms. Hu regards western theater as an example in realist drama, especially plays informed by the tragic vision. Chinese theater had a great deal to learn from this "advanced" realist style imbued with tragic spirit. Tragic realism could shock the Chinese into a deep insight into their wretched condition and might provoke them into reforming their society. Thus tragic theater and realism would compel the Chinese people to perceive the real historical situation. The current reality is the corrupt tradition on the one hand and the nascent trend of inevitable historical progress on the other. Tragedy, as a vision of history's inherent irrationality and meaninglessness, is here made positive and is wedded, in a rhetorical turn of redemption, to a hopeful projection of historical progress.[25]

Tragic Historical Consciousness in Lu Xun

Among the advocates of the tragic-realist approach to history, few were as persistent and thoroughgoing as Lu Xun. Although familiar with the insights of Wang Guowei and Hu Shi as well as the classical western notion of tragedy, Lu Xun infused a more unrelenting sense of the tragic into historical consciousness. In his book on Lu Xun's aesthetic thought, Liu Zaifu hails Lu Xun as the most insightful Chinese theorist on tragedy. Taking a cue from the latter's passing remark "Tragedy is to show the destruction of valuable things to viewers," Liu credits Lu Xun's insight for being consonant with the Marxist understanding of tragedy in history. Tragedy can be appreciated by historical materialism, not so much because it is a form of drama as it is an objective manifestation of historical necessity. Historical events cast in a tragic light are the results of the inevitable conflict between progressive and regressive historical forces. Tragedy figures the necessary onrush of history and thus embodies the nascent, fledgling, but inevitably triumphant forces. The progress of history may suffer temporary setbacks due to the mismatch between the emergent progressives and the entrenched reactionaries. So suffering and death are the price of history, but they reveal the potential revolutionary forces all the more poignantly as these forces struggle through momentary trials and tribulations, only to prevail at the end.[26]

Although he believed in a nondeterminist social evolutionism, Lu Xun's notion of tragedy seems much grimmer than Liu has presented. Lu Xun was sensitive to the predicaments of the modern human individual caught in the maelstrom of history. His interpretation of tragedy is quite different from the classical western notion. In a number of key works, Lu Xun held up *The Dream of the Red Chamber* as a testing stone against works of roundism—the aesthetic obsession with the completeness of happy endings and emotional catharsis in traditional drama and literature.[27] This aesthetics served as a screen against unpalatable or unthinkable catastrophes. Like Wang Guowei and Hu Shi, he also saw weakness of the Chinese character and emotional poverty embedded in the aesthetic taste for happy endings, but he broadened the meaning of the tragic to a much larger domain: the representation of history.

Lu Xun's celebrated remark, "Tragedy shows the destruction of valuable things to viewers," was made with reference to an incident in a *zawen* essay, "More Talk about the Collapse of the Tower of Leifeng" (Zai lun Leifengta de daota). Concerning the collapse of the Leifeng Tower, a historical landmark on the West Lake in the city of Hangzhou, a few old-style writers lamented the loss of what had been perfect scenery. Criticizing this taste for aesthetic perfection, Lu Xun uses "tragedy" to designate not the tower's collapse, but an unflinching acceptance of the disaster without consolation. The cries of lamentation over the fallen tower reveal a deeply ingrained, diseased mentality that craves aesthetic completeness, balance, and symmetry. Tragedy is a fatal enemy against this self-consoling aesthetic taste, against this faint-heartedness that turns a blind eye to catastrophes and disasters. Taking the fall of the tower as figurative of destruction in history, Lu Xun charges that Chinese writers and historians are always inclined to indulge themselves in the game of revising the past to make calamities appear in a more palatable light. They are ready to make catastrophes pretty, "patching up the old patterns in the midst of ruins" (*wali zhong xiubu laoli*) (LXQJ 1:193).

This last phrase points to the self-deceptive aesthetic pattern and habit that inhere in traditional and modern historical representations. Lu Xun not only critiques the popular mind-set that loves the cheaply gratifying to the exclusion of stark reality, but he also extends the tragic vision to history writing. For him, history is not just a written record of the past, not the narration or explanation of past occurrences. As Wang Hui has shown, Lu Xun looks at history from an intensely subjective stance of existential angst. This stance is not confined to the idiosyncratic or the personal but refers to a crossroads in which the individual is compelled to grapple with external forces. Lu Xun ponders the existential questions concerning the individual caught in history.[28] History is approached not on the register of narrative and generalizations, but on the level of experience, pain, and pleasure. Historical understanding hinges on how the social and cultural environment impacts, shocks, and brutalizes the individual, torturing the body and the mind. In the name of the individual's pain and sufferings, historical understanding functions as a critical, negative perspective.

In spite of all the sufferings, Lu Xun notes, one would be hard-pressed to find a straightforward record in mainstream official history. A critical historian needs to recover the body in pain in all its anguished corporeality. The madman in the story "Diary of a Madman" is a prototype of this historian, one who not only reads but also acts out the pains and nightmares of history. As a walking testimony to a trail of time replete with atrocities and violence, this historian, equipped with diagnostic acuteness, is to read between the lines of traditional records to find what is left unsaid. His approach is that of the detective, tracing the undersides and secrets of history. This is a method that Lu Xun himself practiced. Brushing history against the grain, it consists in the mistrustful probing of official history against accounts of "unofficial histories" (*ye shi*)—those loose, unsanctioned testimonials and personal memories beneath the contempt of official historians. Lu Xun played off unsavory accounts in these "wild" records against the "facts" in established history. This reading method zeroes in on the tensions and contradictions between what was lived and what has been constructed, between reality and representation.

This reading is informed by a critical historical consciousness that refuses to take history at its face value. His two related essays, "Random Remarks after Illness" (Bing hou zatan) and "More Random Remarks after Illness" ("Bing hou zatan zhi yu") bear out this strategy. In the first essay, Lu Xun begins with *Mirrors of Sichuan* (Shu guijian), a book of unofficial history that records how Zhang Xianzhong, a rebel in Sichuan Province in the Ming dynasty, mutilated and brutalized human bodies. Lu Xun focuses on an unthinkable procedure of execution that consists of peeling off the victim's skin and spreading it out on the ground. Some victims died right away, but some continued to suffer unimaginable pain for days, in full public view. Knowing the anatomy of the human body, Lu Xun is deeply shocked by the anatomic precision and exacting professionalism of this horrific procedure. He compares the rigorous execution of torture with the poverty of anatomic presentation in Chinese medical literature: "What is strange about Chinese is that pictures showing the human body's interiors are lousy and unpresentable, yet in the sadistic torture and execution it seems that the ancients already knew intimately modern [medical] science" (LXQJ, 6:165–66). The numerous gruesome practices of torture and killing are not news in Chinese history. Yet what is important is not the historical existence of these practices, but the habitual way writers and historians represent and register them.

One can either assign oneself to unthinkable "fate" or repackage brutalities by inventing interesting stories. A compelling example is the portrayal of the Emperor Yongle's execution of his two faithful councilors, Jing Qing and Tie Xuan, and the subsequent disposal of their families. The emperor decreed that one councilor's skin was to be peeled off, and the other was to be fried in oil. Tie Xuan's two daughters, well-bred and refined ladies, were sent to a whorehouse and became prostitutes. More disturbing, however, is the way writers and historians managed to rewrite the incident. They made up a happy scenario to show how good fortune befell the ladies turned prostitutes. The ladies' inborn talent, in the literati's account, allowed them to submit beautiful and melancholy poems to the interrogator. Getting wind of this, the emperor, presumably a lover of poetic talent, released the ladies and let them marry respectable scholar-officials. Their poems were published. Yet some people doubted their authenticity. Checking neglected records, Lu Xun confirms the doubt. The whorehouse at that time, Lu Xun notes, was hell, where girls were shipped from one military station to another to be raped. In such a condition, Lu Xun asked, "Could writing a poem redeem their lives?" (LXQJ 6:170–72).

This scenario of touching up pain with some poetic tricks is another example of what Lu Xun calls "playing the elegant tones in the end of opera" (*quzhong zhouya*) (LXQJ 6:171). Historians and writers put up a self-deceptive screen to cover up unthinkable atrocities and make them bearable. By contrast, wild and unofficial histories are filled with tragic sufferings. Such histories are not suited to the taste of the feeble-minded:

It is not surprising that some tenderhearted people do not like to read unofficial histories, do not want to listen to tales. Some of the things written there are really far beyond the human realm and send chills down one's spine and injure one's heart beyond cure. Brutal incidents are everywhere; better not to hear about them. Only thus can one keep one's body and soul together. This is also what is meant by "gentlemen do not go near the kitchen where animals are butchered" . . . it is only a matter of the refined taste of a serenely clear mind. (LXQJ 6:167)

For Lu Xun this refined taste marks the self-deceptive mentality of the educated elites, who sought to "find ease and delight in the pool of blood" (*cong xuepo zhong xunchu xianshi lai*) (LXQJ 6:170) or in "patching up the old patterns in the ruins":

> But some Chinese scholar-officials always liked to create something out of nothing, transplanting flowers onto trees to make up stories. They not only praised the peaceful reign but also whitewashed the dark ones. The lies about Tie Xuan's two daughters were only minor things. As to the major historical events like the burning, massacres and plundering of China by the Hu Barbarians, someone would still write poems glorying in the suicide of a heroic woman or the ravaged lady scribbling edifying poems on the walls. This legend making, this rhyming, seems more exciting and appealing than the burned down palaces in ruins and the suffering of millions. (LXQJ 6:172).

The tragic vision, in Lu Xun, aims to tear up this self-deceptive and illusionist representation, which is as much part of history's violence as the bloody events themselves. The historian with a tragic vision, in contrast, is determined to dwell truthfully on pain and suffering. For critics in the theater reform movement, the notion of tragedy was used to unmask the self-deceptive patterns inherent in traditional drama and narrative. Similarly, Lu Xun applied the tragic lens to Chinese history. His view reveals an unflinching and unsentimental confrontation with the abyss of stark reality and eschews any easy, imaginary, and cathartic resolution.

In the tragic vein, Wang Guowei argued for a sublime, inviolable mind undaunted by sufferings and misery. Hu Shi aspired to a revitalized and toughened consciousness induced by tragic spectacle and sought a mental strength for coping with crisis conditions. Both focused on a way out, a salvation out of historical predicaments. Lu Xun had profound doubts. His thoughts on the tragic nature of history and its representation point to an alternative in our relation to past catastrophes. His gaze on atrocities centers on the individual's existential fate in a history that he or she does not possess. He suggests that tarrying longer and more critically with the tragic past may help us sort out problems and predicaments in the tensions between tradition and modernity, individual and society, memory and history, before we rush on to an unknown future.

The Realist Montage of Modern History

There are links between trauma on the visual register and representation of history in film. The tragic vision as a new way of confronting history paralleled the irruption of traumatic experience in modern China. Nowhere is the traumatic visual experience more poignant than the one Lu Xun suffered in watching a newsreel in a medical school in Japan. Probably no episode in modern Chinese culture comes as close as that to a "primal scene" of well-nigh total visual and psychic collapse. This incident has triggered much speculation and controversy in literary history.[29] Rey Chow's insightful interpretation of the newsreel's visual violence in this episode has effectively introduced visuality as a factor in modern Chinese culture. The brutal scene where Chinese persons were beheaded, mediated through film and amid the roar of cheers in the classroom, launched a "projectile" at Lu Xun in his "unassuming perceptual security."[30] Chow sees the disruptive visual experience as a Chinese version of the modern disorientation and shock articulated by such critics as Martin Heidegger and Walter Benjamin. The traumatic violence stems powerfully from modern media technology and its power to disrupt the inherited perceptual pattern and structure of feeling. The shock of humiliation stripped Lu Xun of confidence in his identity as a Chinese and spurred him into a sharpened nationalist consciousness. Instead of trying to come to grips with the traumatic visual experience, however, Lu Xun and other writers, Chow claims, resorted to writing literature in an attempt to evade the trauma and to raise nationalist consciousness.

While arguing that literature is "a way to evade the shock of the visual,"[31] Chow also traces the many ways the media-induced, disruptive visuality insinuated into writing practice and gave rise to modernist, visual mutations in literature. The snapshot vignettes of Lu Xun's short stories, Mao Dun's panoramic narratives, and the documentary details of Shen Congwen, for example, revealed a filmic visuality that decentered the literary sign and fragmented the established narrative.[32] In Chow's analysis of the film *Goddess* (Shennü, 1936), directed by Wu Yonggang, traumatic visual experience also found its way into the radical Chinese films of the 1930s. Despite all these remarkable visual disturbances in literature and film, Chow's reading expresses skepticism of literary writing vis-à-vis traumatic visuality, rendering literature into a paranoiac defense or repression. She sees modern Chinese literature as part of an elitist project to exploit the "primitive passions"—the savage, the popular, and the primitive—and to assimilate them into an overarching nationalist discourse. In contrast, visuality retains its melancholy ties to the brutalities and repression of women, the oppressed, and the downtrodden.

Obviously, this reading partly resembles Lu Xun's tragic-realist conception of history. In Lu Xun's reflections, however, we have seen a closer affinity among literature, aesthetic thought, and the representation of history. I would pursue this affinity in filmmaking and film discourse. The trajectory of the tragic-realist conception of history suggests a disruption of the inherited literary and aesthetic patterns. Yet literary self-deconstruction was very much part of May Fourth culture and, as Paul Pickowicz has argued, was carried over to filmmaking.[33] The radical filmmakers of the 1930s not only dared to confront the kind of visual violence that Lu Xun experienced, but also attempted to represent collective sufferings on the screen as the population went through the war of Japanese aggression. In this context, the filmmakers were faced not only with the dead authority of the "literary sign" but the new authority of Hollywood imagery and narrative. If the dominion of Hollywood in China was a colonizing process of marketing, sentimental education, and liberal pedagogy in the interest of global capitalism, the radical filmmakers had to confront the dual burden of literary and cinematic conventions. I suggest that filmmaking in the 1930s constituted an attempt to carry over the radical potential of traumatic visuality into the screening of Chinese history. It developed its own film aesthetics that more effectively registered and engaged historical reality.

We may first backtrack the discursive shift from the tragic vision to the realist turn. In the 1918 debate on theater reform launched by the magazine *New Youth*, critics charged the traditional theater with perpetuating self-consoling, deceptive melodrama and obsolete emotional structures. The trite narrative embodying Confucian morality and yielding cheaply rounded-off emotional satisfaction, they argued, detracted attention from historical reality and blocked artistic creativity. They called for a realist theater, which would seek to cut through these obsolete narrative protocols and emotional patterns to get at the "real" stratum of history. The intellectuals seemed to be groping toward a new form that would come close to a reality "in the raw."[34] This appeal to realism was answered by what I would call the "material turn" in Chinese cinema and related film discourse.

Confronted with imperial and colonial aggression, filmmakers and critics in the 1930s were faced with a historical situation fraught with disasters and dangers. To see how they used film to engage history, we may take a look at the discussion of certain notions and film texts in the 1930s.

In a crisis situation, film production took a new turn and struggled to cope with the upheavals of war and aggression. It has become a commonplace to relate the rise of the radical cinema to the two key events of Japanese occupation of Manchuria in 1931 and the bombing of Shanghai in 1932. As a critic suggested in 1933, Chinese cinema took a drastic turn practically under the gun.[35] The two events were the immediate cause of a gathering momentum. Amid the accumulated traumas of destruction of the traditional culture, the wars, imperialist aggression, and rule by the warlords, socially engaged Chinese filmmakers and critics in the 1930s made a material turn in the way they thought films should relate to reality. The crisis was a fertile ground for a readiness to confront reality, for critiquing obsolete cultural forms, and for imagining social change.

The willingness to confront reality manifested itself in the proliferation of documentaries recording incidents of wars, disasters, and sufferings; in the critiques of Hollywood influence, and in the rejection of the remakes of traditional dramas on the screen. There was growing theoretical reflection on film as an effective medium for engaging historical experience and revealing the real.

In discussions of the cinema's capacity to engage the real, classical theater and Hollywood films were viewed as negative examples. In the debate on theater reform, the traditional theater, with its repertoire of conventional plots, its display of trite feelings, its Confucian ethical framework and happy endings, was criticized as a venue of escape from a crisis-ridden reality. On this account, what is true of classical theater is also largely true of classical Hollywood cinema. Leo Ou-fan Lee has shown the strong impact of classical Hollywood on the Chinese cinema of the 1930s and 1940s. The hallmark of this cinema, in Lee's analysis based on Miriam Hansen's work, consists in "the interweaving of multiple strands of action moving toward resolution and closure, a web of motivation centering on the psychology of individual characters, and the concomitant effect of an autonomous fictional world offered to the spectator from an ideal vantage point."[36] Hollywood surely had other faces, but for our analysis, we will have to stick with this generalization. The affinity between classical Hollywood and classical Chinese theater, it can be said, lies in a closeted world of ideological closure, stereotypical fulfillment of desire, confirmation of conservative assumptions, and the wishful smoothing down of real problems of life-and-death political struggle.

The affinity of classical Hollywood cinema with the traditional Chinese theater contributed in no small way to the formation of the mainstream Chinese cinema with a strong commercial bent. Most Chinese filmmakers struggling to build the new film industry, even including the radicals, were schooled in theater and literature and were quick to find themselves in sympathy with Hollywood before the abrupt change in the early 1930s. Simply put, the memory of traditional repertoire was filling the new bottles of Hollywood film narratives.

With the deepening of national crisis, however, there arose a strong attempt to break out of this narrative closure. Critics and filmmakers were compelled to rethink film as a medium independent of theater. Although film had for a long time been thought of as complement, if not as handmaiden, to theater—as a photographed theater art, the situation of emergency forced filmmakers and critics to see film as capable of purging the narcissistic, residual memory embedded in the conventional narrative of popular fiction and theater. Film became for them an effective medium for reflecting and engaging the external, material reality. The realization of film's affinity with textures of material reality corresponds with the notions of the photographical function of film put forth by Walter Benjamin and Kracauer.

Kracauer in his *Theory of Film* cites a passage from *The Guermantes Way* by Marcel Proust to illustrate the idea of the impersonal camera eye. The narrator enters his grandmother's room after a long absence, unannounced and unexpected. He is shocked by the eerie strangeness of her look in an unguarded moment. He sees "sitting on the sofa, beneath the lamp, red-faced, heavy and common, sick, lost in thought, following the lines of book with eyes that seemed hardly sane, a dejected old woman whom I did not know."[37] The shocking sight is registered as if by an impartial, emotionally detached camera, recalling what Benjamin suggested as the photo of a crime scene.[38] It is touched not by the loving eyes of the grandson who might well have imbued his grandmother's person with remembered tenderness. His grandmother's look, captured as if by the impersonal medium of photography, is the very image of decay and death. The sight filtered through the "camera eye" of the grandson undercuts his habitual mode of seeing, which has been charged, in Miriam Hansen's words, with "familiarity, intimacy, and memory."[39]

The impersonal camera eye, with its potential to disarm and shock, is the basis from which theorists with a material bent criticize the eye charged with "familiarity, intimacy, and memory." Critics like Kracauer and Benjamin were wary and critical of the visual habit that had been overly educated by traditional theater and armed to the teeth with all the canonized fictions of visual prototypes informing the pattern of seeing or unseeing. Modern, "inhuman" technologies like photography have a potential to strip human eyes of their false aura of romance and narcissism. Shocked out of the culturally conditioned habit, we are thrown into a headlong confrontation with "naked" reality.

Radical filmmakers and critics were evidently working toward this awareness of a shocking camera. But instead of psychic shocks, the shocking experiences in their vision were the actual devastations, misery, and life struggle in countries and cities against a backdrop of imperialism, residual feudalism, and worsening social conditions. These facts did not need a camera to be noticed, surely, but film documentation, even the staged mis-en-scène in feature films, thrust calamities and problems forcefully into public imagination and consciousness. Filmmaking, critics urged, should scan a wider social field and cover the disadvantaged, dispossessed, and downtrodden. Xia Yan, who with many others represented this radical trend, characterized the principle of filmmaking as "touching the reality" and "powerful exposé."[40] A number of powerful films were produced in the spirit of exposé and with an eye to jolting the audience out of the complacency of the urban life of consumption. They include, among many others, *Three Modern Women* (San ge moden nüxing, 1933), *The Night of the City* (Chengshi zhi ye, 1933), *Spring Silkworm* (Chun chan, 1933), and *The Torrents* (Kuangliu, 1933). These films broke with the mainstream films depicting trivial, idle matters in the daily routine of the petty urbanites, love triangles, and emotional entanglements, replete with settings of coffee shops and dance halls. Turning their exposé to poverty, oppression, and suffering in both cities and villages, filmmakers considerably widened the visual scope of China's material conditions and contributed to the formation of political consciousness in the viewing public.

It may be objected that this trend turns the "art of film" into a vehicle of ideology and propaganda. Yet in the context of the crisis situation, it was the dramatic fetishes of Hollywood, coupled with the obsolete, stereotypical traditional narratives, that proved to be ideological, for they were selling images of false consciousness concerning a bourgeois lifestyle remote from the majority audience, who tried to make ends meet in daily life. They diverted attention from rather than provoked attention to the dire consequences of imperialism and colonial modernity. The materialist turn brought film into an intensely engaged alliance with a crisis-ridden consciousness of a volatile, politically charged atmosphere. It not only registered a more complex and concrete experience of history, but also enriched the aesthetic function of film.

It is easy to ignore the vibrant aesthetic innovation in the radical films if we think that art has little to do with history. Adorno's dictum, "Art perceived strictly aesthetically is art aesthetically misperceived," should remind us how much a film's power hinges on its intimate involvement with specific sociohistorical circumstances.[41] In trying to touch history and social problems, the leftist filmmakers were working out a material aesthetic. This aesthetics derived from a camera that alienated and shocked an audience equipped with a sensibility educated by Hollywood cinema.

Although the mainstream film tended to produce images of exoticism, romantic intrigues, and self-satisfaction, the radical film sought to reveal the hidden and occluded strata of social reality: prostitutes, drifters, peasants, orphans, homeless, wanderers. . . . These people and their lives were not unknown, of course, but the film-viewing public seemed to have learned to ignore them. Although the leftist films sometimes used popular and Hollywood story lines, the camera sought to gaze at the margins of society as if in an unrelenting attempt to document them. This "naturalistic" or documentary strain in laying bare wretched everyday life conditions— what might be called a minimalist depiction of daily survival of common people—attempted to show them to be, in Raymond Williams's words, "inseparable from their real social and physical environments."[42] It was a life process under the naked eye, in a naturalist key, not prettified by the fictions of bourgeois culture, and lived by the surviving body of the downtrodden, that was captured and analyzed.

Critics have pointed to the ideological overdose in the radical film. An allegorical structure charged with nationalistic issues is said to frame the psychologically motivated character going through a narrative of interpersonal interaction. Ma Ning's pioneering study shows how, in the film *Street Angel* (Malu tianshi, 1937), journalistic writing and elements of popular culture (songs, wordplay, magic shows) form an external frame that may have the potential to steer the individualistic melodrama in the direction of a social allegory. One point of convergence between social reference and personal melodrama is woman's place in the plot as the object of sexual desire. In Ma's analysis the social reference is shown at times to outweigh the melodrama of sexual desire, so that the singing girl in the film is not only "the virgin over whom the feudal forces and the lower classes contest, but also Mother China, who is now being violated by the Japanese invaders."[43]

Social reference brings up the issue of allegory. Allegory is both an image on its own and tethered to an abstract idea for a higher meaning. An allegorical representation implies that our established signs do not refer nicely to real relations and things, yet we still have to use these corrupt signs. In Fredric Jameson's account, national allegory consists in the interpretation of the individual's psyche and life trajectory as part of the collective destiny.[44] But the link between individual and society needs not be as arbitrary as the allegorical correspondence, say, between a lion and the idea of courage. Rather, to say that the individual story should be part of the collective whole is to acknowledge the historical condition of the individual's separation from the community. Sociohistorical references in a film would appear allegorical when we accept this separation as necessary and timeless. References to external historical conditions or ideological frameworks would then seem arbitrary and extraneous to the proper individual story. Conventional wisdom has it that the individual's story should show a life trajectory of its own, its beauty untouched by unaesthetic didacticism or politicization. The allegorical severing of the individual from the community, of artworks from historical reality, can also be seen as a symptom of traumatic rupture between private experience on the one hand and cognitive and cultural resources on the other. Since the existing cognitive and cultural resources, collectively shared and hence social, are unable to integrate traumatic experience, the individual becomes atomistic and completely alone, stripped of support networks of meaning and emotion.[45]

This disconnect leads to the truncated view that the individual story in the Hollywood mode is aesthetically appealing, whereas socially engaged narratives in third world cinemas are allegorical and ideological. This is a mystification. The individual story in Hollywood film is as much part of a collective myth, as much a personalization of culturally cherished values and middle-class lifestyle, and hence of the collective destiny of capitalist modernity and "democracy." It is not too much of a stretch to claim that

Hollywood is the most powerful ideological apparatus of the United States as a nation-state and the promulgator of its national allegory of "manifest destiny." Hollywood films, especially war films of patriotism, certainly qualify as "national allegory." But even a private melodrama can be seen as an allegory, one that affirms the collective core values of liberal society. Robin Wood sees the story of the archetypal male and female in Hollywood as allegorical of "American capitalist ideology." This nationalistic ideology includes "the right of ownership, private enterprise, personal initiatives; the settling of the land."[46] In this light, Hollywood imagery is not simply national allegory; in the geopolitical context, it could be supranational or imperial allegory, as manifest in the national will to foist this narrative on the rest of the globe.

The sticky point is that a "good" Hollywood viewer is not invited to discern an allegorical leap of faith between a full-blooded, "natural" individual life and its underlying social mythologies. Furthermore, the mythologies of Hollywood are seen as real and normative, whereas third-world mythologies are seen as mythical and ideological. Yet this shutting out of the social does not prevent the individual story of Hollywood from becoming allegorical in a different way. It is an allegory that ties, arbitrarily, all the heterogeneous strands of individual, gender, class, race, and geopolitical trajectories into an overarching image of liberal individualism. This big myth—indeed, the biggest ever in capitalist modernity and in the new millennium—never tires of telling the story of romance, love, sex, family, business, overseas adventure, and prosperity. It is an allegory of the self-made, possessive individual prevailing over the social, a mythical narrative of how a self-driven individual can press his own way through tangles of personal relations and problems without support from a community, much less through public action or social dialogue.

In the national allegory of third world cinemas, on the other hand, the individual story typically aspires to merge into a unity with the social, so that it may become a part of communal or national destiny. The individual fate in this utopian vision does not merely prefigure historical imaginaries, but also points to a deferred union of society and individual, in the strong sense that my community is the objective as well as expressive shapes of myself and vice versa. This allegory would be achieved—that is, would proffer a sense of a finished symbol—if there is indeed a realized, transparent unity between individual and social, in such a way that the initial conflicts in the plot are eventually resolved in a satisfactory ending. Very few people in our postromantic, postutopian age would entertain this scenario. The problem is ours, not that of the impulse of radical art and film. This is the imaginary or formal solution to social problems expounded by Fredric Jameson, if the solution can be shown to grow immanently out of the plot.[47]

Although he addresses the role of the social in the individual story, Ma Ning does not see a formal solution arbitrarily imposed in the radical film. An implicit "material" approach in his analysis undercuts the hasty redeeming of allegory to symbol. Instead of trying to "provide the narrative with a solution in the Western sense of the word," the leftist text, writes Ma, invited the viewer to "relive those social and political contradictions unresolved by the text." This material function "is in the mode of actual social experience which the viewer relies on to form his/her critical judgment—a judgment which articulates contradictory discourses at a particular historical conjuncture. The subjective positioning of the text is a process of constant change. The set of formal contradictions that are overdetermined by social contradictions turns the text into a contradictory discursive space."[48] Social contradictions, in other words, turn up in the film as irruptions and disruptions, and remain in tension with the established discursive or generic emplotment of a smooth-running, problem-solving narrative. Thus instead of unifying contradictory elements into a satisfactory whole, instead of fetishizing an individual story as a premature symbolic solution of social problems, the radical film, in the spirit of material engagement with history, lays bare history's complexity, conflict, and myriad possibilities.

Montage and the Long Take

This material turn to history brings us to two much debated issues of montage and the long take in Chinese film discourse, which had significant uses in the films of the 1930s and 1940s. As an editing technique as well as a theoretical category, montage was introduced into China in the 1920s and 1930s. Referring to a normally fast-paced intercutting of shots assembled or "mounted" from heterogeneous space and time, montage seems to be the very opposite of the long take, which describes a stationary camera taking a prolonged look at a contiguous space. But from the perspective of the material turn to history, the two methods had much in common. In response to the historical crisis, both techniques effected an intensified, engaged relation to external reality.

In its function to effect an intensified engagement with reality, the long take is a method to immerse the viewer in an unprocessed, stripped-down piece of reality by forcing him or her to stare at it for a long time, until the material density and intensity of the space warp the viewing habit out of shape. It can also be used commercially, of course, to provide tourist sensations and cheap pleasures, which would be a different story. A materially driven montage sequence, on the other hand, places the viewer onto a shifting quicksand of interconnected or unrelated images and plunges him or her into a kaleidoscopic slice of reality. A montaged reality is one that is torn and fragmented in many contradictory directions, sometimes bordering on the schizophrenic or carnival, depending on the specific stance. But it also provokes reflection and ideas.

To see what conjoins montage and the long take in the material turn to history, we need to be clear that the brand of montage in question refers to Sergei Eisenstein, rather than to other versions. Usual discussions of montage as mere technique of intercutting gloss over its epistemological and historical potential. Chinese theorists and filmmakers started translating and writing about montage theories in the 1920s, but they seemed more inclined to accept and use Vsevolod Pudovkin's notion of montage as an editing strategy, which was aimed at the construction of a smooth continuity of shots in storytelling.[49] Pudovkin's writings on montage were close to mainstream Hollywood conventions and were indeed read for years in Hollywood as a manual—a testament to Chinese filmmakers' preference for Hollywood even in their reception of montage.[50] Eisenstein was opposed to Pudovkin's conception of montage precisely for its capacity to create a smooth continuous narrative. To Eisenstein, montage is much more than a cinematic technique. It is in a privileged position to mimic the experience of modern change. He calls Pudovkin's montage "epic" in the sense of the monistic unity and continuity of meaning and narrative.[51] This "inertia of perception" as in the customary patterns of representation should be exploded, "dynamized" by splicing common-sense reality, by yoking/cutting discrete, monadic, heterogeneous objects violently together.[52] The effect is not just emotional impact but a visceral, physical blow. Responding to Dziga Vertov's notion of a kino-eye that "faithfully" records a common-sense reality, Eisenstein declared, "It is not a kino-eye we need, but a kino-fist."[53] In this field of dialectic confrontation, new concepts and dreams will spring up. This notion chimes in with Walter Benjamin's intention to enlist montage in bringing down teleologically oriented historical narrative to contradictory elements of everyday reality. The dialectic montage is Benjamin's "now-time," which the materialist filmmaker/historian blasts out of the continuum of hegemonic historiographical paradigms. By splicing, by wrenching objects out of their reified context, the historian/filmmaker assaults the smooth, linear narrative that perpetuates existing social relations, and smashes the fetishized tableau of cinematic spectacles designed for passive contemplation. Eisensteinian montage does not present a static, alluring image; it aims to offer a crucible of suffering and becoming, and it experiments with conflicting options and ideological positions. It touches history at a moment when it is shaken with shocks, frozen into a dialectic image at a standstill. The positive elements of the past, thus far hidden or repressed, become legible and desirable in this field of dialectic confrontation.[54]

The broken mirror that montage holds up to history is a veritable experience of flux, fragmentation, destruction, and reconstruction, a history going to pieces, broken to its foundation with catastrophe, war, and revolution. In Eisenstein's most historically revealing moment, montage also corresponds with Kracauer's view of photography. Photography, Kracauer writes, is the go-for-broke game of history. The montage method contains a materialist conception of history. It sets itself the task of confronting and engaging the heterogeneous material forces at work amid the ruins of reified and idealized bourgeois culture. By presenting the jarring sequence of images that collide, contradict, and interpenetrate, Eisensteinian montage not only delivers shocks onto the viewer, but also makes him or her relive a schizophrenic life experience of modernity. The viewer not only reexperiences in the immediate sensory register the disorientations, but also the powerful transformative, utopian energy released by modern history in the making.

Although Chinese film discourse did not delve into the materialist implications of montage theory, the radical films practiced montage in stunning, innovative ways. Several critics have noted how the brilliant montage sequence in the opening of *Street Angel* "mounts" a series of images from various recesses and corners of the city of Shanghai.[55] In a sequence of fifty-two shots, images of the Shanghai skyscrapers from unusual angles cut to streets cramped with automobiles and streetcars, the neon signs of cafés and dance halls collide with the shots of the crowded surface of a canal. Scrambled together are images of folk and feudal customs of marriage ceremonies and a European-style brass band and parade. We can also find heterogeneous sequences in a number of other films. Although the montage of *Street Angel* is short, other films present a panoramic, montage view of Shanghai, like *The Night of the City* and *24 Hours of Shanghai* (Shanghai ershisi xiaoshi, 1933). These films are extended montages, montages writ large, giving a widespread exposé of the contrast and conflict in Shanghai's variegated strata of urban existence.

Rather than fascinate and mesmerize as commodified simulacra, these montage sequences scramble the viewing habit schooled in the conventional coordinates of space and time and challenge the continuity of common-sense assumptions. They send the viewer on a dizzying ride that mimics the experience of constantly living on edge and intensifies the sense of crisis-ridden modern life. Although they are fraught with grotesque contradictions between "Chinese feudalism and foreign powers,"[56] they also lack a central consciousness designed, as in goal-directed Hollywood narratives, to navigate the shifting sand of urban life and to tell an individual story of psychological development and fulfillment. The subjectivity called on by montage is a subject on trial, plunged into a "kaleidoscope with consciousness," unable to find an anchor.[57]

Ma Ning has noted the juxtaposition in *Street Angel* of the point-of-view shot, embodied by the central character of the action, with the free-floating camera movement without an anchoring position.[58] If we adhere to montage as an effective way of registering a contradictory, dialectic reality, it would be hard to claim, as Ma does, that the Hollywood point-of-view shot synthesized with Eisensteinian montage in the radical film. The "right" proportion of point-of-view shots to the "anchorless" montage reveals a tension between the narrative solution of social problems and the montage's attempt at stirring up issues and contradictions. Xia Yan, the representative of the radical film, points to the political implications in cinematic form in an essay on the film *The Night of the City*. In it he recalls a montage of Shanghai's nocturnal scene consisting of cars, skyscrapers on the Foreign Concessions, guests in dance halls, and race dogs. In contrast, there are shots capturing lives of the prostitutes, the starving, and the oppressed. This montage sequence sharpens the contrasts, discrepancies, and contradictions of city life. It is achieved largely through episodic, fragmentary cinematic exposé. Xia Yan sees montage as carrying the potential to minimize the elements of Hollywood film and traditional theater, keeping at bay their dramatic effects and emotional sensationalism.[59]

If montage traverses the tangle of lifelike fragments, the long take fixates, as if obsessed, on an opaque, unprocessed slice of reality. Critics have noted how the tragic power of the film *Plunder of Peach and Plum* (Tao li jie, 1934) derives from the use of the long take. At the outset, the film depicts the school principal's visit to his former favorite student, who is to be executed for a crime, which is more the effect of social injustice than of his own doing. The camera stares for a long time at the "dragging" trip to the prison and the impenetrable back of the student in the cell during the visit, as if to ponder why. Another scene portrays the agony and suffering of the protagonist's wife after childbirth, when she carries a bucket of water upstairs and then comes tumbling down and faints. In a prolonged shot, the immobile camera effects, in Huang Ailing's words, a "relentless siege of the downtrodden characters."[60] The long take's material connection with physical reality is striking. The camera seems to be staring into an abyss of misery and pain, seemingly unable to get on with the story; it records every detail and gesture and takes in every perceivable trace, hue, and shape. As if haunted by a dream recurrence of a shocking event, the camera cannot help bearing witness to what has been out there. The long take thus functions as a metaphor for the traumatized patient, who, when asked to tell a coherent story, is repeatedly and helplessly seized by a singular, persistent image.

For the critical historical consciousness, montage and the long take are more than cinematic devices. If treated formally, their function as signs would simply dissolve the past within a present. In this light, it does not matter whether a film engages with historical reality; it would simply be another fictional piece of entertainment without historical content. Like the category of the tragic, these two forms strive to approach the actual referent in history with the awareness that traces of the past cannot be dissolved in the present form. The past traces are the imprints of history that cannot be neatly arranged into a preconceived aesthetic pattern. I have occasion in Chapter 9 to elaborate on this indexical element in documentary and neorealism. Filmic images have been understood as bearing indexical traces of reality because the real referent is tied to the camera's "presence" at some point before our reading and appreciation of filmic images. In emphasizing the gap between past traces and the present film form, film theorist Philip Rosen articulates the tension between memory and history. The gap forces the spectator to "read pastness in the image, not only as a past as a signified . . . but also a past of the signifier, which is in turn that of a signifier-referent relation as a production." The awareness of a real referent assumes a different "when" of the productive process that cannot be immediately present. The different "when" must be inferred and filled in by the viewing subject. Thus to approach the historical referent, the film viewer must assume some ongoing productive work in the construction of film text beyond film viewing.[61] This productive work may be "memory, mental activities, subconscious investment, rational inference, the effectivity of cultural discourse," and so on. The point is to not to be fixated on a formed spectacle, but to see a spectacle being formed and produced in the murky waters of history.

PART 2

POSTREVOLUTIONARY TRAUMA AND THE RECONSTRUCTION OF HISTORY

3

Postrevolutionary History
in a Traumatic Key

For about half a century since the 1930s, the vicissitudes of wars, mass movements, political campaigns, and revolutionary transformation have brought about social changes but also traumas and calamities. There seemed to be little breathing room in all those decades of acceleration to step back and reflect on history. The end of the Cultural Revolution heralded a new but unclear beginning. The Third Plenum of the Eleventh Central Committee of the Communist Party in 1979 initiated Deng Xiaoping's reform policy. The reforms created an atmosphere of intellectual openness and gave rise to intense deliberation on China's historical reorientation. As the party negated the "Maoist excesses" and the Cultural Revolution, economic development and marketization paralleled the debate on the thesis that practice is the only test of truth. The new hopes for modernization, however, did not stop memory's retracing of the past.[1] The search-for-roots writing quickly followed the post–Cultural Revolutionary "literature of wounds." The questioning of history also manifested itself in the film works of fourth- and fifth-generation filmmakers, who probed the philosophical foundations of the official narrative. It further developed into the metafictional narratives exploring received notions of history in new wave, experimental fiction. Massive attempts were made to rewrite literary history, to preserve the painful memory of the Cultural Revolution, and to narrate personal experience. History, for a time, called for much rethinking and reconstruction. The "renaissance" of this reconstructive activity harked back to the intense discussion in the earlier decades in the May Fourth period, centering again on the tension between past and present, memory and history.

In the next four chapters, I address the interplay of memory and history in the 1980s through the early 1990s. This chapter looks at what I call the work of memory through two interrelated lenses: Benjamin's reflection on the shock of modernity and the analytical categories of current trauma studies. I begin with the Chinese appropriation of Benjamin's ideas in the reconstruction of history and move on to an examination of trauma-induced texts of literature and film.

Historical Trauma Through the Lens of Allegory

In recent years, Benjamin's insights into the widening abyss between experience and the conceptual system have come in handy in supporting the lingering poststructuralist or postmodern skepticism of the Enlightenment in the American academy. Benjamin's thinking shakes up the solidity of the signifier and historical continuity. In the growing field of cultural studies, Benjamin takes on added importance for his ability to pit histories against History and memory against the empty time line of modernity, giving impetus to a tired academy anxious to move away from the dreary closet of textual analysis into context and the real.[2]

Since the mid-1980s Walter Benjamin's work has been well received by Chinese intellectuals, with an urgency and enthusiasm rarely seen in the west. Benjamin's writing resonated with an intellectual community in search of meaning and orientation after the Cultural Revolution. Remarkably, writers and critics have been drawn to Benjamin's idea of allegory as a persuasive way of understanding history and its shocks.[3] That the notion of allegory, among others, could be so favored indicates its fecund capacity in addressing perplexities of certain historical times. In Benjamin the allegorical is less an aesthetic category or a "playful illustrative technique" than a form of epochal expression.[4] The allegorical structure is symptomatic of the mind penetrated by forces of history. To Rich Wolin, to speak about allegory apart from a particular historical time is to overlook the notion's "historico-philosophical specificity." Benjamin's allegory makes its makeshift home and strains to find an anchoring among ruins in the ages when "man's relation to the absolute has become problematic," when all culturally shared meaning has ceased to be immanent to everyday life.[5] Capturing the same point, Susan Buck-Morss argues that the allegorical is a special form of expression that "the objective world imposed upon the subject as a cognitive imperative, rather than the artist's choosing it arbitrarily as an aesthetic device." The phrase "cognitive imperative" dramatizes the urgent poignancy when it is a matter of everyday survival to cope with devastating historical traumas. In times of cultural crisis, the outlook of a whole epoch may take on the color of allegory. As Buck-Morss notes, the religious history that gave rise to the German baroque *Trauerspiel*—Benjamin's basic allegorical text—was allegorical; so was the time whenBenjamin wrote, a time when "European humanity again looked the ruins of war in the face, and knowledge of history as a desolate 'place of skulls' . . . was once more inescapable."[6]

The allegorical portrayal of historical shock found a willing ear among Chinese intellectuals after the Cultural Revolution. The Revolution and the collapse of the ideological hegemony thrust the unthinkable in the face of millions of Chinese and shattered the symbolic order by which they could "think straight" and orient themselves in history. If trauma is not simply a blow to the individual body and psyche, but rather a wholesale shattering of the symbols, affective linkages, and language that sustain the bonds of the individual with community, the post–Cultural Revolutionary period can fittingly be called posttraumatic.[7] It was a time when the collective psyche was haunted by the nightmares of the recent past while struggling to make sense of it. Xiaobin Yang's recent study of postrevolutionary trauma has shown the impact of historical violence on the psyche and narrative language. Yomi Braester has shown how traumatic experience lurks in testimonial works, reminiscences, and films in posttraumatic reflections on the past.[8] Studies like these continue the inquiry of Chinese writers and artists in tracing the causes of trauma. The turn to Benjamin helps to find a language to describe this work of memory. Smarting from the historical traumas, Chinese intellectuals turned to Benjamin with an urgency strikingly different from the contemplative calm with which the well-sheltered American professor-scholar pores through the German critic's writings.

It is no accident that the intellectuals discovered Benjamin during the mid-1980s, when sensitive minds were groping in the dark interval between the recent history of the Cultural Revolution and the pressure to make sense of that history. At that juncture to be able to say anything meaningful was nothing less than a matter of spiritual orientation and survival. In coping with the trauma and wounds, to be sure, artists have created innovative and compelling literary and artistic works that conferred aesthetic form on disorienting shocks. Although these works might have struck an intimate cord with Benjamin, the artistic explorations needed to be articulated on a discursive plane. Their undefined, unconscious strata, latent in artworks and recesses of the mind, need to be brought to critical consciousness. The following analysis addresses the ways Chinese writers and critics appropriate allegory, memory, and experience in their strenuous efforts to reformulate and rebuild culture from the ruins.

History as Catastrophe

It is no surprise that Chinese artists and writers were engaged in the imaging of history in the post–Cultural Revolutionary period. In Benjamin, imagery contributes to historical understanding. History is not merely a concept, an idea, a chain of events, or a causal structure. Benjamin envisages history as a particular kind of image. We are confronted with "history" when an element of the past flashes up as a dazzling and blinding image. This image may be macabre, morbid, and funereal, prolific with ruins, wreckage, mishaps, and death. "Theses on the Philosophy of History," the central text of Benjamin's reflection, does not offer any discursive exposition on history but lingers on image after image. Taking the image of the "Angelus Novus" (1920) from Paul Klee's painting, Benjamin envisages the individual caught in history in a helpless dilemma as "the angel of history." The angel turns toward the past and seems to be contemplating something in a daze. "Where we perceive a chain of events, he sees one single catastrophe which keeps piling wreckage upon wreckage and hurls it in front of his feet. The angel would like to stay, awaken the dead, and make whole what has been smashed." But he is helpless in the face of the raging storm of "progress." With his back turned and his body thrust forward to the future, he can only stare back at the scene of destruction where "the pile of debris before him grows skyward."[9]

What the angel is looking at seems to defy human comprehension.

He appears to be paralyzed with bewilderment and terror, unable to see anything meaningful and intelligible. Instead of looking to identify something, he only stares at the piling up of the wreckage. His body is frozen into a tense pose of helpless suspense and a readiness without a purpose (fight or flight?), with his mouth open and wings spread.

This image forms a fitting metaphor. It proffers a medium for Chinese writers to depict and envision their catastrophic history riddled with traumatic memories. One image that matches Benjamin's vision of paralysis, frequently cited in Chinese scholarship, immediately comes to mind. The Chinese writer Lu Xun's well-known depiction of a newsreel show he saw as a medical student in Sendai, Japan, has been an obsessive moment, which I discussed in Chapter 2. In it, a Chinese spying for the Russians was beheaded by the Japanese while all the Chinese onlookers rejoiced with mindless glee in the bloody spectacle, the victim's identity as Chinese completely lost on them. The numerous interpretative spin-offs show how traumatic and disgracing the image has been, even after almost a century has lapsed since Lu Xun first evoked it. For many, this is the primal scene that precipitated quick redresses and heralded more catastrophes in modern China. It is the summation of all the shames and defeats following the Opium War of the 1840s that smashed the smug confidence of the Chinese in the Middle Kingdom and in their self-image. It deals a death blow to the narcissistic self-sufficiency of the traditional culture, and prompts the desperate efforts to redress the sickness and powerlessness.[10]

The reconstructive efforts in the ruin exhibit a pattern that is different from the gaze of the angel of history. Typical responses to historical trauma stare at the bloody image for a stunned moment, and then turn away to weave a narrative in a hurry. They strive to shape nonmeaning into meaning, the absurd into the tragic, the stagnant into the progressive, the horrific into the triumphant. The historical narratives with official stamps in modern China have been of the tragic and monumental variety, underwritten by the persistent search for wealth and power on a par with the west. The revolutionary narrative is very much part of this modernization narrative. This narrative regards historical traumas as momentary hurdles and setbacks the nation must get over in the race to modernize.

In the posttraumatic period after the Cultural Revolution, however, writers and artists realized that any blind rush to a finishing line has proved disastrous and foolish. Like Benjamin, they have learned to linger on such images a bit longer, collect more fragments from the wreckage, and archive them for criticism and reflection. They are not in a hurry to resort to a cathartic, redemptive narrative, to feasible explanations to glide over the harshness of the historical real.

In her book *History and Narrative* (Lishi yu xushu), Meng Yue draws on Benjamin and uses Lu Xun's scene of newsreel watching as an allegory to present the whole traumatic history of modern China, from the Opium War to the Cultural Revolution. She focuses on the similarly unflinching, prolonged stare at the wreckage of history and comes to a Chinese imaging of history. Her views carry on a dialogue with the German critic in coming to terms with experiences of shock and suffering in turbulent times.

The pitfall of forging a historical narrative is a theme in this dialogue. In *The Origin of German Tragic Drama*, Benjamin writes that the viewer of history with an allegorical lens is "confronted with the *facies hippocratica* [death mask] of history as a petrified, primordial landscape. Everything about history that, from the very beginning, has been untimely, sorrowful, unsuccessful, is expressed in a face—or rather in a death head." Here again one is confronted with the unreadable enigma of history as incomprehensible wilderness, bereft of human interest and intention. The skull does not emit any aura: to the staring human gaze, the death head stares back, unresponsive, vague, blank.

The history of modern China can be portrayed in a similar image. The death head of history, notes Meng, has materialized in numerous literary texts and constituted a defining feature of the Chinese historical landscape and imagination. The "petrified, primordial landscape" corresponds with Benjamin's image of history as degenerating, decaying nature in all its transience, an unredeemable inertia and a cycle of repetition barely touched by human culture. One finds a corresponding image of "natural history" in the remote rural China as depicted in Xiao Hong's works. In the novellas *The Field of Life and Death* (Shengsi chang) and *Legend of Hulan River* (Hulanhe zhuang), history loses its narrative lines and crumbles into the antlike mass or mosquito swarm of humanity in a brutal, animalistic existence worse than beasts of burden. Day in and day out, there was the cycle of suffering, dehumanizing labor, illness, aging, and death. Crystallized into the image of an old, tired horse walking toward the slaughterhouse, this condition of life presents the downside of the teleological history of modernity. As Meng puts it, "History itself could be compressed into a vast inhuman will that kills off all beauty, hope and comfort and with its wheels rattling on, rains bodily sufferings and misery."[11]

This vision underlies the critique of history in the film *Yellow Earth*. A huge attempt by the fifth-generation filmmakers to reflect on history, the film bewildered the audience and struck them with images of a boundless expanse of yellow earth beneath an eternal, ancient sky, monotonous, colorless, frozen, unchanging. Time here means repetition, stagnation, or decay. It is difficult to find a starker image illustrative of Benjamin's grim vision of natural history. Floating over this huge and impersonal earth, "the course of history shrivels up and is absorbed into the setting."[12] This overwhelming deluge of yellow earth usurps the teleological function of narration and history. The film critic Dai Jinhua, a creative reader of Benjamin, puts this perception in cinematic terms. The film's true subject, she writes, is not the dramatic action that includes the soldier's collecting of folk songs for revolutionary propaganda—the female protagonist Cui Qiao's rebellion against arranged marriage and her longing for change, or even the usual sufferings and misery of the peasants. The fixed camera, the excruciating long takes, the wide span, and the symbolic framing freeze any temporal progression or goal-driven human action into an empty, ambivalent space, into a natural, stagnant setting. The typical signs of time are ones like the deep, weather-beaten furrows on the ancient face of the incredibly "old" peasant of forty years of age. In the film, space takes over time; oblique visual images render the narrating voice silent; and the burden of the historical unconscious drags down the superficial mutations of historical progression.[13]

This "natural" substratum lies dormant and undercuts the historical march to get over with traumas by making revolution, reform, and progress. As Benjamin finds catastrophes in slow motion, so Meng Yue perceives progress-engendered catastrophes in modern Chinese literature and in the real lives of millions of survivors:

Unlike Lu Xun and Xiao Hong, in the hands of many other writers, history—Chinese existence—is rather an image of catastrophic accident (*zai bian*). Either a sudden catastrophe strikes and destroys a previous social structure, or a social calamity smashes people's lives. Either a great chaos brings about drastic change in the mentalities of millions, or calamities and fate precipitate degeneration and corruption. . . . *Tea House* [by Lao She] is a site where all varieties of social catastrophes converge, and Wang Lifa [a character] is a witness. In the decades from his youth to old age Chinese existence is no more than an endless piling up of catastrophes. The ideas of nation, civilization, humanity and being linger on feebly in the midst of these accumulated catastrophes. As a witness to history, and with a sober self-elegiac clairvoyance, Wang presages the already destroyed before death—the ultimate outcome of Chinese existence.[14]

Significantly, as a painter of catastrophes, Lao She turned out to be a victim of a more grotesque and monumental catastrophe than he ever depicted, the Cultural Revolution. Like Wang Guowei and many others before him, and like Benjamin, Lao She plunged into darkness before the darkness closed in on him.

History Writing as Allegory

Through the image of history as a death mask over a primordial landscape, Benjamin seeks to tackle the question of representing history. Stressing how this image undercuts our desire to grasp that stark fact, Benjamin writes, "Death digs most deeply the jagged line of demarcation between physical nature and significance."[15] This cryptic statement implies a distinction between a "natural" stratum and culture's attempt to construct human history. The working of signs—history's process of writing and naming things—is superimposed on the realm of crude, raw nature. This signifying endeavor splits into two modes: the symbolic and the allegorical. In the symbolic the wreckage of history—destruction, death, decay, misfortune—"is idealized and the transfigured face of nature is fleetingly revealed in the light of redemption."[16] The senseless destruction in history could thus be rewritten in hindsight and become the stepping-stone toward a superior later stage. This retrospective view serves to redeem unthinkable horrors in the past. The symbolic transfiguration of meaningless destruction throws up a bridge to link the past and present, trauma and redemption, in an imaginary unity.

The allegorical mode also seeks to connect words and things, but with an unflinching side glance at the chasm. Allegory drives a wedge between history and significance. The flip side of significance is death: "The greater the significance, the greater the subjection to death, because death digs most deeply the jagged line of demarcation between physical nature and significance."[17] The allegorical hangs in a delicate balance between visual images of nature and contrived meanings of culture, between the disorienting havoc of history and sense-making schemes of historical narrative.

The experience of recent Chinese history forced the reader of history in a similar direction. The reader is hard pressed to summarize and narrate a scarred and traumatic history along the lines of the received meaning scheme. He or she is acutely aware of the tensions between our representation and the historical real. Meng Yue puts this difficulty thus:

> History will always slip through the net of our consciousness. Unless we do not look back or pretend to forget; unless we endorse what we know clearly to be the false account, the subject looking back at history, especially the history of the "ten-year calamity," is very much stranded between the positions of the psychoanalyst and psychotic patient. All he can claim is no more than the memory and the record of the fact—the primal scene that caused the illness, plus the shivers, the nightmares, the cold sweat, the stomachache he and others suffer. But the relation between the two—what constitutes meaning—has dissolved into vagueness and non-meaning beneath the threshold of consciousness.[18]

As a diagnostician of culture, the reader of history is no longer able to order a history out of joint, to rearrange the chaos, to weave a pattern of meaning. Instead, the historian/diagnostician proceeds on the assumption of the fundamental sickness and pathology of traumatic experiences. He or she tries to look past surfaces to find the latent dream thoughts that get expressed and warped in various guises. This understanding of history has provided an impetus for a new way of interpreting modern Chinese culture. Critics and scholars attempted to identify the latent impulses and desires that make the senseless history understandable. Dai Jinhua holds Foucault's motto as her principle of inquiry: what is important is not the time that a myth recounts, but the epoch that is narrating the myth.[19] This recalls one of Benjamin's goals: dissolving myth into history.

Experience: Damage and Repair

The decline of experience is crucial in Benjamin's reflection on the history of modernity. Shock effects produced by wars, technological advances, industrialization, and urbanization precipitated the withering of experience. A rich but elusive concept, experience has much to do with the sedimented layers of memory, tradition, ritual, and narrative. In Benjamin's analysis of Baudelaire's poetry, experience is that by which one yearns in vain for a seamless meshing between private sensibility and the larger patterns of perceptual and affective heritage embedded in ritual, tradition, and myth. This idea would smack much of the classical and even romantic ideal of the beautiful were it not for the marked absence of harmony and naiveté. The glaring presence of "the missing content," as Lyotard termed it, renders this experience incomplete and fumbling, which frequently degenerates into an elegiac, unreachable halo of nostalgia.[20] Experiences of fulfillment, however, are possible or can be reinvoked in a situation where "certain contents of the individual past combine with material of the collective past."[21] Benjamin does not agree with Proust that a genuine experience is necessarily a chancy affair that comes, unsolicited, in the occasional upsurge of involuntary memory. But the "atrophy" of experience was nevertheless the symptom of the psychic crisis inherent in the condition of modern accelerations that tore apart the previously unitary texture of experience embedded in community and memory.

The burden of repairing the truncated experience, for Benjamin, falls not to philosophy but to art, to the poetry of Baudelaire and the narrative of self-conscious storytellers like Leskov. One often-neglected element of Benjamin's restorative imagination is mechanical reproducibility. Although technology destroys the aura of art as well as experience, it also opens up a space for the disadvantaged class to seize on the democratized means of mechanical reproduction, such as filmmaking in Eisenstein, for collective solidarity and self-representation. Rather than turning wars of capitalistic expansion into alluring mythology, the working class would politicize aesthetic construction, yet the purpose is to achieve a new aesthetic aura for themselves as producers of history.[22]

On the psychological level, the lyrical poetry of Baudelaire was able to mimic and parry the shock effects. Although it does not really "repair" experience, it strains to do so in an attempt to gain psychic and affective mastery over the trauma. The poetry that parries trauma, even if it is shaken, forms a stay against the loss of memory. The storyteller goes further in fulfilling this duty: he is able to draw on and reproduce the repertoire of collective memories embedded in the shared heritage. Through the act of telling, he or she appeals to a community of listeners who partake of the aura of the teller's culturally loaded, charismatic personality and listen to the councils "concerning the continuation of a story" that gives directions to collective and personal life.[23]

This account of experience resonated strongly with Chinese intellectuals' understanding in the post-Mao era. "Experience" entered the vocabulary of Chinese literature, criticism, and aesthetic discourse as a prominent new concept different from the obvious Chinese term *jingyan*. Its altered usages reveal the basic Benjaminian sense: the sense of aesthetic wholeness and affective fulfillment combining present and past, individual and culture, ideal and everyday. Experience should be distinguished from the more prevalent, popular term *ganjue*, which denotes a limited sensory or sensual feeling and mood, often in the context of everyday consumption, as in the catchy phrase, *Genzhe ganjue zou* (Follow your inner sense or instincts). In his work on Benjamin, Xudong Zhang takes care to distinguish the integrated experience from the shock-induced experience. Traumatized, the mind starts scrambling to buffer the shocks, as exemplified in Baudelaire's poetry. Zhang renders the first into *jingyan*, which is close to *Erfahrung* in Benjamin. *Erfahrung* is distinguished from *Erlebnis*, which Zhang has translated as *tiyan*. Zhang locates Lu Xun's allegorical vision at the level of *tiyan* (*Erlebnis*). This points to the endeavors that strive to work from the paralyzed, traumatized state of mind toward restored, integrated experience. Allegory can be seen as a strenuous striving to move from paralyzed, traumatic *Erlebnis* to a more conscious psychic and symbolic formation, *Erfahrung*.[24]

The acute awareness of how wretched experience was in the decades of revolutionary campaigns pushed Chinese intellectuals to look into new notions of experience. Instead of industrialization, urbanization, and the mass media, the atrophy of experience in China was due to a trauma-ridden history and authoritarian political culture. In the post-Mao period a whole generation of intellectuals awoke to the fact that they had, for a good part of their life, been deprived of much life experience by the political order, by a narrow aesthetic standard that restricted the legitimate range of pleasure, emotion, and desire, by a long stream of political campaigns resulting in numerous personal calamities, and by the all-pervasive, dogmatic Maoist newspeak that drastically impoverished the means available for expression. The theme of experience is a nodal point of theoretical reflections on "alienation" within a socialist structure, the discovery of

Marx's earlier, humanistic writings, and the reassertion of a liberal notion of individual subjectivity.

Related to this discovery of experience was the elevation of sensibility and subjectivity to prominence in the mid-1980s. In a series of public lectures on aesthetics, the philosopher and aesthetician Li Zehou called for the reconstruction of a new sensibility and associated it with aesthetic subjectivity. The understanding of a new sensibility (*xin ganxing*) should, states Li, reconsider the individual as a being of flesh and blood, a creature of sensory needs, emotions, and desires, yet these creaturely aspects should also be thoroughly humanized and refined. In his new emphasis on the aesthetic sensibility, Li does not confront and look into the historically impoverished experience. Although he speaks against a backdrop of the recent experience of crisis, he is more anxious to get over it and rebuild a new form of sensibility rather than subject it to critical inquiry. He favors a socially and culturally restored, stabilized, rationalized community of sensibility, without taking into account of the contingencies of the individual experience.[25]

Nevertheless, Li's call for aesthetic sensibility based on social consensus was a strong response to the massive bleaching of experience in the past decades. It was part of the widespread humanist awakening in the 1980s and contributed to the debate about salvaging damaged experience. The damage consisted in psychic rupture, moral disintegration, and communal disconnection. One sign of this broken experience is the breakdown of the community of meaning, when one is no longer able to live and enjoy as a richly sensuous and intelligent human being, to rely on a shared source of meaning and value to make sense of the world, to connect with one's past and to form solidarity with one's neighbors and countrymen. Yet this "identity crisis" also stemmed from the homogeneous collective identity superimposed on individuals in the previous decades. In Benjamin's words, it is a question "whether an individual forms an image of himself, whether he can take hold of his experience."[26] Individual identity has to rely on a setting of civil society and traditional community rather than tight political uniformity. Its erasure was due to excessive collective identity formation, which constituted one source of the historical trauma.

The reaction in the 1980s was a return to a romantic notion of subjectivity. Yet in romanticizing the individual identity of a liberal humanist kind, the danger is to eschew the collective historical experience. In the

1980s, this was not sensed as a problem. It was in the 1990s, when private experience was becoming atomic and depoliticized, that a degenerate version of experience went hand in hand with the erasure of personal identity. Much discussion of this problem centers on private experience and sensuous pleasure at the expense of a larger community. Yet the collective experience, despite its propensity for repression, nevertheless underlies private experience. In a pithy remark about the relation of history to trauma-induced experience, Cathy Caruth says that if the trauma "must be understood as a pathological symptom, then it is not so much a symptom of the unconscious, as it is a symptom of history. The traumatized, we might say, carry an impossible history within them, or they become themselves the symptom of a history that they cannot entirely possess."[27]

This pathology is not private and individualistic, but a troubled relation between individual and collectivity. Meng Yue characterizes it as a self-deconstruction of the realistic discourse of history, an official history that buttressed the popular understanding of time; its collapse led to schizophrenia:

It is history itself that has shattered the cause-and-effect chain of realism. The frequent switch of the individual's identity and value, the massive transmutation of social scenes, the unexpected and accidental character of events taking place . . . all these constituted the experience and the shape of memory common to the majority of Chinese. Whether in actual life or in discourse, the world of things and events has long since lost its self-evident transparency of meaning presumed by realism. It can no longer regain that naturalness after all the violent, superimposed political interpretations. When the most mundane things, most familiar events, most unforgettable memory became mysterious objects and cry out for explanation; when the space linking the past and the present became blank, when the meaning of time seemed fragmented, no reassertion of realistic authenticity and "natural" authority of the visible world can cure the schizophrenia of history.[28]

Public discourse designated this prevalent mindset as the "spiritual crisis." The crisis epitomized a world out of joint, with no reliable system of ideology to sustain a livable existence and identity.

In a talk entitled "1985" the critic Li Tuo reminisces about the rise of the cultural trend known as the "search for roots." The year 1985 marked a turning point between the old and the new, a crossroads where the Maoist literature of workers, peasants, and soldiers was finally giving way to a nascent but still undefined stirring of literary and aesthetic impulses. The transition was both euphoric and traumatic, or the traumatic passing for euphoric. A general excitement and anticipation about the dawning of a new epoch was accompanied by a feeling of crisis of change and upheaval. The change required nothing less than a spiritual suicide. "You need to kill yourself bit by bit—kill the self that contains all the quests and values by which you have lived and acted in the past."[29]

In the ruins of communist ideology and collectivism, the mere programmatic assertion of a humanistic subjectivity and sensibility would not recover the experience of romantic individuality. The artists and intellectuals of the younger generation felt the need to find a spiritual home and to seek solidarity—to reestablish and reattach to new collectivities. Around 1985 there sprang up numerous artistic and intellectual communities—poetry societies, discussion groups, research centers, and reading circles. These were an embryonic form of "public sphere" in China.[30] Although Li Tuo remains skeptical of these new collectivities as a residue of Mao-style collectivism, he acknowledges the importance of the new collectivities to coping with the crisis and the broken experience. It frequently happened, recalls Li Tuo, that in these groups, a poet would write a small poem, then take a train overnight to show it to his friends and critics. They would spend all day and a night talking, arguing, shouting over the poem in smoke-filled rooms with floors strewn with wineglasses.[31]

This hysterical excitement over a poem reveals a larger distress, that of broken history and ruptured experience. The past no longer provided intelligible clues to the present; the sense of history was not available for making affective and ethical links between members of a community. Despite the radical impulse to break through the repressive political culture, it was no less disconcerting to wake up to a world collapsed into ruins. This is as much a Benjaminian problem as that of Chinese intellectuals in the 1980s. Li Tuo suggests that much was going on between the spiritual crisis and the desperate search for a spiritual mooring—now in the name of searching for the roots. Instead of embracing the craze for modernization and catching up with the west, artists and writers turned to yellow earth, to remote villages and forgotten traditions. The theorizing of the literal humanist notion of individualistic experience could not solve the spiritual crisis, because individual experience could not be set apart from collective experience.

Aesthetic Rehabilitation of Experience

The broken experience needs to be rehabilitated and enriched through constructing a meaningful sense of history, through historical narrative, through new cultural and aesthetic forms by which "certain contents of the individual past combines with elements of the collective past." This Benjaminian motif accounts for a remarkable surge of history writing, which was a potent feature of the movement of "searching for roots." China's past—first the recent past of political campaigns, then the whole traumatic stretch of modern history, finally Chinese civilization as a whole—was placed under searing scrutiny. This history writing was not carried out by historians and social scientists, but was done mainly by artists, writers, and filmmakers. The works of new wave fiction and the early films of the fifth-generation filmmakers are compelling examples.

As in Benjamin, auratic art came to the rescue of experience, so the burden of history fell to the domain of the aesthetic. The aesthetic does not simply designate the arts and literature, but refers generally to the refashioning of forms of experience with a view to readjusting the broken links between psyche and reality, individual and community, present and past. This raises the questions of what kind of history is being written, how history relates to art, and how artworks deal with spiritual crises. History writing in the 1980s did not aim to investigate or reconstruct the ways things really were, or to recall marginal or suppressed memories.[32] It was to seek a language, a form of articulation, in order to make sense of history. After a whole series of historical catastrophes, as Meng Yue observes, Chinese no longer possessed a credible language, no longer believed in the old historical scheme, were no longer able to deploy an archetypal narrative that could generate a past one can live with. Thus the simple act of telling a story itself becomes a problem. Benjamin's remark is poignantly pertinent: "the art of storytelling has come to an end. Less and less frequently do we encounter people with the ability to tell a tale properly."[33] Yet stories the Chinese needed, and they needed them badly to convince themselves that they had come from a past that they could claim as their own, and that there was a continuity between past, present, and future; they needed them to supply a credible picture of the past that feeds significance to the present; they longed to restore a sense of rootedness and belonging.

In the hands of writers and filmmakers history writing was turned into an art of memory. After the founding of the People's Republic, history writing had been crucial to the official discourse in legitimating a hegemonic culture and national identity. But in the post-Mao period, no grand history could designate collective missions and direct personal life experience. Instead, memory, often private and marginal, was explored as a source of meaning and identity. This was a strong feature of the "subjective turn" in criticism, literature, film, and the arts. The outpouring of fiction works that address the remembrance of things past—personal incidents, family sagas, local traditions, and regional lore—testified to memory as a way to fill up the gaps left by the official history. These works opened new ways of recovering and recreating alternative, livable histories. Among writers noted for their achievement in this regard, notably Su Tong, Mo Yan, Zhaxi Dawa, and Ge Fei, Han Shaogong is the most interesting and exemplary. In his work he provides several elements that may tell us how Benjamin's idea of experience resonates with the Chinese experience.

Han Shaogong's fiction is marked by a grotesque and often mythical evocation of the defunct ways of life embedded in the primitive setting in a remote area and distant past. This fascination with the primordial may serve the cultural critique by holding up contemporary Chinese society in a microcosm of self-image steeped in backwardness. But the past for Han is not simply a tool for cultural criticism. He is keen on exploring how the past persists in the present, how a present entwined with the past may enhance experience. Playing with the Bergsonian theme of the primitive unconscious as the infantile stage of the culture, Han believes that the artistic mind exercises intuitive thinking, a mental function close to Proust's involuntary memory. Intuitive thinking takes elements of primitive culture as its specimens, writes Han; buried deep in unconscious memory, these can be recaptured in dream, in madness, in drunkenness, or in the infantile state of mind.[34] In contrast to the atrophy of experience, the primordial data intuited in the present constitute a genuine experience. Because this experience occurs through the inspired state of the artist, the intuitive mind in Han's account confirms Benjamin's belief that "only a poet can be the adequate subject of such an experience."[35]

Han's reflection shows how experience is possible only in a certain relation with the past, a relation that does not keep apart the primordial, the political, and the private. The intuitive function of the mind resonates with the ideas of voluntary and involuntary memory by emphasizing the importance of historical change. In Benjamin involuntary memory names the spontaneous upsurge of emotionally charged memories of past events that elude deliberate conscious recall. Voluntary memory, by contrast, consists in the activity of a managerial ego that selectively absorbs external stimuli under the guidance of the intellect. In arbitrary accelerations of life's rhythm, the divorce of involuntary from voluntary memory becomes a symptom of disintegration of historical time, a time out of joint between present and past. Involuntary memories are imprints of past events that have been pushed back into the unconscious. These unconscious residues are not accessible to consciousness except at the moment when they suddenly surge up at the prompting of certain cues, the classical case being the celebrated madeleine in Proust's *A la recherche du temps perdu*. The widening gulf between two forms of memory in Benjamin accounts for the atrophy of experience. In China, this gulf would correspond to the historical tension between the culture's relentless drive to modernize and its increasingly neglected traditions.

It is at this crossroads between memory and history that Han's story "Gui qu lai" (Return) comes through as a compelling instance of rewriting history as memory. It is a strenuous aesthetic gesture to remember and contain the flux in a "crisis-proof" form. Although the story's title in Chinese mimics the fifth-century poet Tao Qian's longing for a timeless, pristine world, it is more a mockery of nostalgia than a celebration of the rejuvenating power of primordial culture. In "Bababa" (Father, father, father), another of Han's stories best known for its search for roots, Han depicts the primitive scene and undercuts both the stagnant primitive culture and the progressive modern endeavors. "Return" moves away from the palpable description of the "real" scene to a narration of pure sensory impressions floating apart from memory. Memory in the story is presented as both crucial to and unreliable in assuring self-identity and the sense of historical continuity.

The story begins with the protagonist's experience of identity crisis when he finds himself in a remote village that appears at once familiar and foreign. Endowed with a supersensitive capacity to relate to the objects along the way, he feels that everything signals a meaning, an intention, yet the objects remain mysterious and "magical"; their sense scintillates darkly between intelligibility and darkness. There is much out there, Ma seems to be telling himself, but not for me. He meets, talks, and hangs around with villagers, who obviously remember him well enough, yet are constantly taking him to be someone else. As he gets more involved with the villagers, Ma is thrown back to two strata of "history," both in danger of eluding the grasp of his memory. The detailed reminiscences with the villagers remind him that he was unmistakably among them for a time and was indeed actively involved in the maelstrom of modern, revolutionary history, in all those campaigns and epochal changes that had descended upon this backwater "tribal" village. Yet this recent history has already crumbled into dusty traces like prehistoric relics. One of the folk has kept the textbooks Ma once used to teach the peasants and tries to show one to him:

He shuffles up the stairs. It is quite a while before he re-emerges with threads of spiders' web in his hair, patting a few pages of a small, mimeographed book. It is probably a character-learning textbook. The cover has already been ripped off, and it smells of mold and *tung* oil. Crudely printed inside are an old night-school song, miscellaneous characters used by the peasants, the 1911 Revolution, Marx's discussion on peasant movements and a certain map. Each character is very big, with blobs of printing ink. There is nothing strange about these characters: I could indeed have written them.[36]

On the other hand, Ma is fascinated by the "magical," primitive aspects of village life—the traces of a prehistory that persist and intersect with modern political history. He is invited as a friend to join the villagers in their ancient rituals of eating, entertaining, bathing, talking, visiting, and so on. Assuming these rituals are from time immemorial, he plays along until this immersion in the "savage mind" and the primordial landscape brings him to face his own forgotten "savage" deeds in the past: He had an innocent, fairy-tale love relationship with a village girl, a relation that was later spoiled by his modern attitude. And he killed a man for something he does not remember.

The author takes care to focus on the physical caress of a scar on Ma's leg that brings back, against his conscious will, the memory of his killing. By emphasizing the bodily and sensuous experience of Ma's involvement with primitive life, the story begins to suggest that the "involuntary memory" of prehistory lives in the characters and the villagers and "enriches" the sense of time emptied out by modern, political history. Indeed the story moves from discursive memory, the embodiment of homogeneous, empty political history, to something like involuntary memory, which brings the character to the "real" of his personal past. Yet this involuntary upsurge of the past is only the tip of the iceberg that encompasses the archaic, collective unconscious and the phylogenetic stratum of the human race. Requested to take a "ritual" bath in a huge tub in which a woman pours hot water, and in a room where women come and go, Ma suddenly reaches an epiphany when left alone:

The lard lamp above my head, shining through the steam, creates a bluish mist and tinges my flesh blue. Before putting my shoes on I look at my blue body. I suddenly feel very strange as though it is someone else's. . . . There are no clothes or accessories here, no strangers, so there is no one to hide anything from or to pretend to. There is only bare, exposed me. The real me. I have hands and feet, so I can do things. I have a gallbladder and a stomach, so I have to eat. I have genitals to reproduce. . . . Our ancestors came into existence only by the coincidence of a sperm joining with an ovum. Not until this ancestor coincidentally met with another was there a fertilized ovum and a latter-day "I" in existence. I am one of many coincidentally fertilized blue eggs. What am I in this world for? What can I do?[37]

Memory now returns to the naked basics of nature; it is on the embodied memory and bodily sensations that one falls back; memory is turned into an aesthetic experience of a "self" swimming in bodily and primordial sensations.

If Han Shaogong exemplifies the cultural attempt to rehabilitate experience by searching for its roots, he did not, at least in this story, find any workable resources to fix the impaired experience and provide any viable mode of making meaning. To demand such an achievement would make him larger than an artist. He is indeed successful on another account. His writing portrays sharply the work of memory in its strenuous, risky endeavor to rescue experience, and proves symptomatic of the memory's crisis-ridden journey into the past and the deep interior of the primal unconscious. It is expressive of the subterranean ruptures of memory by which his fiction is shaken. He has succeeded in creating an aesthetic image that, to quote Benjamin again, "holds in his hands the scattered fragments of genuine historical experience" of posttraumatic China.[38]

Learning from Walter Benjamin did not provide satisfactory solutions to the problems of the 1980s, but it surely shed much light on the crucial problems in a time of historical ruptures. The question of historical narrative, memory, experience, aura, and the reconnection of the individual with community would continue to be asked as China moved on to the world market and political reforms. The move toward the global market creates the widespread illusions of a postideological, posthistorical social landscape. But the old questions of history, community, and memory deepened and spread to various spheres of cultural production. The persistence of these questions acts as an antidote to the thesis of the end of history.

The Trauma of the Cultural Revolution and Memory Work

In the decades since the founding of the People's Republic, the preoccupation with history was often less about the past than about the present, or less about the present than about the future direction of the nation. A blueprint of Marxist historical materialism underlay historical inquiry and discourses about social change. Writing history was frequently an arbitrary unearthing of certain past events, based on an exclusive principle of political selection, to find the inchoate clues that foreshadowed and hence justified the present move toward a preordained future. The reconstruction of history was more an attempt to confirm the status quo than a serious, scientific inquiry into the records and residues of history. Harnessed to an illusion of the thriving present and an even brighter future, it glided blithely over too many bloody ruptures in the past and the unresolved predicaments of old. As Mao's all-too-antihistorical dicta declared, "Put down the burden and get the machine running," and "Use the past for the present." But it is one thing to say that all history is contemporary history and another to believe that the past can simply be manipulated at will. The notion of history in Mao's remarks does not adequately respect the past and refuses to see the present moment as coming, secondarily and humbly, in the wake of it. It is not accidental that when madness carried the day during the Cultural Revolution, the age-old temples were smashed and the relics were swept away with perfect ease and fanfare.

The "unprecedented" consequences of the Cultural Revolution awoke the Chinese to an intractable, tenacious past. At the end of the day, when no brave new world emerged on the horizon, the revolution-weary Chinese realized that the past was not something to toy with and to manipulate at will. The recent catastrophic past was still hurting, and the diagnosis of cultural pathologies pushed a radical inquiry further backward in time. First the political history of victimization, then the "feudal legacy," and finally the entire way of living, feeling, thinking—the Chinese culture in its entirety, dating back thousands of years, came under investigation, all done with a renewed historical consciousness. The search-for-roots drive traversed many areas of cultural production: literature, art, film, theater, history, and social theory. Significantly, filmmakers, humanistic scholars, critics, and writers of avant-garde fiction spearheaded this radical historical inquiry. In their hands Chinese history broke down into incoherent images and phantasmagoric scenarios. These historical investigators ransacked and laid bare the oppressive and dehumanizing strata of the Chinese tradition still lurking in the present. The search-for-roots drive did not find any continuous roots, but fueled a widespread, demystifying scrutiny into the burden of the past that had time and again sneaked up on us from behind.[39]

Apparently a "return" to memory, the search-for-roots ethos was fueled by a renewed historical consciousness. It arose when the official mode of history writing was losing ground. For a long time this official discourse designated the collective destiny and gave the individual a sense of orientation, however illusionary that was. The decline of this "master narrative" since the 1980s gave rise to an urgent need to redefine China's relation to the past and to rewrite history. Yet for lack of a totalized notion concerning the relation to the past, of some explanation about how change takes place, history writing became multiple attempts to debunk the legacy of the official historical discourse on the one hand, and to create numerous personal life histories and autobiographies on the other. Monumental historical narratives and sweeping statements gave way to personal, incoherent accounts of past experiences and encounters. One thinks of the numerous memoirs of the "educated youth," the family sagas and regional lore by Mo Yan, Jia Pingwa, Zhang Wei and others, the biographical sketches of scholarly careers, the reminiscences of colleagues and friends, and the thriving cottage industry in personal essays.

One crucial reason why memory came on the scene as a mode of finding connections to the past can be traced to the traumatic experiences of a long sequence of sociopolitical catastrophes. As a devastating blow to the individual and community, the trauma shatters a culture's repertoire of representational and expressive means. These means are the virtual lifeline by which we live, perceive, and understand the world around us. Through these vital resources we are able to tell stories, make sense of experience, sustain cultural continuity, and, above all, write history.[40] Traumatic events not only break the individual's emotional attachment to the community, but also, more importantly, cripple the shared, collective matrix of meaning that keeps alive cultural continuity and personal identity. More a persisting condition than the violent quality of a one-time occurrence, trauma remains active as the haunting impact of a catastrophic event on the mental functioning of victims.[41]

Trauma constitutes the biggest stumbling block and the greatest challenge to rewriting and making sense of the past in modern China. It is also a powerful cataclysm for the shift from history to memory. Although no consensual symbolic resources were available by which a historical narrative can be reconstructed, the need to reorder and rearticulate past experience was daily getting urgent. The plethora of history writing since the mid-1980s testified to this urgency. In the face of a confusing array of multiple personal, family, and regional histories, the best one could do was to engage in the elaboration of the lived nuances and complexities in the act of remembering a crisis-ridden experience. This was memory remembering and enamored of itself in all its life-affirming or death-bearing immediacy and authenticity. It was memory fascinated with its own self-reflection. It is also history, done on experiential level, complementing and commenting on the act of writing history.

The work of memory staged a deconstruction of history without abandoning the impulse to weave historical narrative. Against the axiom that time always heals, works remembering the traumas of the Cultural Revolution sought to preserve the wounds and to keep a vigilance against repetition of past calamities. When history is infected with trauma, its temporal scheme is put out of order. Normal history writing flounders on traumatic memory. Traumatic shocks crash into the psyche and paralyze consciousness buttressed by the defensive framework of meaning and emotion. The shocks bypass normal consciousness and perception and fail to be remembered in the sense of being consciously absorbed and assimilated into narrative and history, of being assigned a time slot and a location. The overwhelming impacts are simply "deposited" in the deep psyche and will return and haunt the victim in a later time, in the form of repetitive images, thoughts, and hallucinations.[42] The traumatic memory is memory in wreckage; it is, as Shoshana Felman puts it, "composed of bits and pieces of a memory that has been overwhelmed by occurrences that have not settled into understanding or remembrance, acts that cannot be construed as knowledge nor assimilated into full cognition, events in excess of our frames of reference."[43]

Trauma is thus what shatters the received repertoire of language, narrative, and meaning, which constitutes a source for writing history. As such, it cannot be placed in any schema of time and in space, but cuts across historical time to haunt and possess the victim. The traumatic memory is the case par excellence of the "present past," the past that refuses to pass away. Yet the less the trauma is understood the more desperate and fervent the attempt to make sense in remembrance. Since the mid-1980s a body of literature has come out in response to the inadequately understood traumatic experience of the Cultural Revolution. It ranged widely from simple chronologies, memoirs, and personal testimonies to more artistic treatments of psychic wounds in literature and film.

The contemporary writer Lin Jinlan has offered a compelling literary representation of traumatic memory. His ten pieces of reminiscence of the Cultural Revolution have been widely read and commented on. In 1996, on the twentieth anniversary of the Cultural Revolution, he wrote another ten, this time with a more pointed motive to combat growing forgetfulness. Yet his remembering act ran into various cases of madness, hysteria, and schizophrenia, his conscious effort of retrieving the past overrun by madness. His reminiscences do not observe the distinction between real and fictional, yet are able to convey the poignant intensity of psychic suffering. The hysteric's pathological response to historical experiences feels fantastic and surreal, but nevertheless carries the traces of external, "real" history. Lin's reminiscences listen closely to the symptoms and read rather like a collection of recorded case histories yet to be sorted out by explanation. An objective, coldly clinical element marks these grueling, grotesque stories.

In his preface to these stories Lin focuses on symptomatic manifestations of history by analyzing the ideological and social connotations of hysteria. In classical Chinese, he notes, the layman's term for mental distress is *yi*, which the modern dictionary equates with hysteria. Although in the new era people are hopeful for the future, many are suffering from hysteria. The concept of hysteria is one of those western terms that found their way into the Chinese language in the May Fourth era. In the pre-communist period the concept denoted symptoms of hypersensitivity, an outpouring of emotion, mood swings, incoherent raving, and so on. These were primarily confined to individual idiosyncrasy and limited in incidence. The hysteria that Lin finds in the decades after the Cultural Revolution is a social epidemic and plagues a large segment of the population. The victims are mostly in their middle or old age, and became sick during those catastrophic years. Passage of time does not cure it, nor is there any cure.

Lin stresses that mass hysteria displays a bewildering array of unexplained symptoms beyond diagnosis. The classical Chinese term *yi* (craziness, mental problem) already hints at this elusiveness. Rather than denote *bing* (sickness), it designates undefined symptoms, signs, traces, or proof of an unknown pathology. Yet these traces are too elusive to pin down in terms of medical science. They "are present at one time and absent at the next, like black holes, and all unreliable."[44]

If symptoms defy medical or psychological diagnosis, they may be regarded as traces of an impossible history, riddled with a memory that each victim carries within him- or herself. It is mostly hidden, yet poised at any time to possess the individual and inflict debilitating pain. The story "Trembling" (Duosuo) describes this effect. It narrates three instances where the characters collapse in fear and trembling under the paralyzing effect of political power and oppression. The protagonist, the director of an education department in a work unit, is criticized by the Red Guards as a "capitalist-roader" and severely beaten. Convinced that he has been a genuine revolutionary, he writes a self-statement in a big-character poster to vindicate himself, claiming a consistent red thread and a credential as a true veteran soldier and cadre. Yet in order not to lose him as the "trophy" of the campaign, one Red Guard changes a Chinese word in "Long Live Chairman Mao" in the poster so that the slogan is turned into a condemnation of the Great Leader. As he is pushed by the angry mob to face his "crime," he trembles and collapses. The reason for his breakdown, as he confesses later, is not the pressure of the Red Guards but the haunting power of another traumatic encounter. The fear was implanted by a story told by his former superior. A veteran soldier who fought countless battles, this man of heroic courage was summoned to Mao's residence to see the Great Leader. As he waited in the solemn, immaculate hall, he saw on the wall the shadow of a giant figure approaching. The soldier, who had fought bloody battles and never trembled in the face of death, began to shake and went out of control. This incident was so contagious as to be deeply lodged in the protagonist's mind. It resurfaces to haunt and destroy him at a fateful moment in his life. Even ten years after the Cultural Revolution he would shake uncontrollably when someone unexpectedly knocked at the door.

As reminiscences, Lin's stories do not shape up into full-fledged narratives. They consist of bits and pieces of memory, anecdotal, unassimilated, incoherent, constantly punctuated by the irruption of a latent trauma. But the impulse to shape these pathological cases signals the need to work through the trauma in hopes of healing. Thus the reconstruction of history also evinced a tendency to get over traumatic memory in the very act of remembering and repeating it. In Lin Jinlan's writing, the historical catastrophes ravaged the mind and shattered the psychocultural resources for writing narrative. But rather than shut down the impulse to write history, trauma compelled writers like Lin to forge a new literary discourse. The loss of language, or aphasia, forced writers to generate a shaky and risky language that keeps representation and history constantly in tension. This constitutes a critique of history writing itself. The very act of telling a story, as Meng Yue notes, "became a matter calling for a whole different way of connecting present and past, a whole different mode of interpretation and perception. And these different interpretations and visions were bound to generate new a discourse and language."[45]

Lin Jinlan's anecdotes of "clinical" cases suggest a schizophrenic textuality in history writing. The family sagas of Su Tong, Mo Yan, and the regional histories by Zhaxi Dawa, Jia Pingwa, Zhang Wei, and others also probe into a new way of making connections with the past. The cinema of the fifth generation was most active in this regard. It represents an audacious, self-conscious search for a new image, a new language, a new visual medium for articulating the traumatic past (see Chapter 5). The fifth-generation cinema presents a refined art of memory. It turns its focus to other places and other times that the filmmakers themselves have encountered through their earlier experience in the countryside. In the ruins of official discourse, the filmmakers strive to dig through the wreckage to find a "pristine" ground that might redeem the lost experience as well as mock the bankrupt, still coercive ideology. This memory work, as Xudong

Zhang notes, takes itself to "the marginal or residual realms of nature"—
into the Yellow River, the Tibetan Plateau, the Mongolian grassland, the
mountain village near the border in Yunnan, into all those real and invented customs and rituals lost to memory. On the edges of culture the
cinematic imagery confronts the high-flown, word-clogged official discourse with the mute, wordless physicality of raw nature, a nature unen-
cumbered by culture. The imagery of the primordial, silent landscape appears ambivalent. It defies the official historical discourse, narrative, and
language, but the defiance is premised on a posture of eloquent silence.
Still in the grip of trauma, the fifth generation gropes for a language of its
own. Thus the stark imagery reveals in the cinematic medium the crisis of
cultural resources: it is a dire symptom of the shortage in expressive and
representational means in posttraumatic China. "The Fifth Generation
landscape," Zhang writes, "constantly returns your gaze, in Benjamin's
words, and thus establishes itself as a source of knowledge, of meaning, of
the aura in which a faint childhood memory, a failed love, or a wasted
youth can be preserved in full."[46] It returns the gaze, not in full, but in the
incomplete, unassimilated fragments that unceasingly aggravate the ache
of longing.

Chen Kaige, Zhang Yimou, Tian Zhuangzhuang, and others are lan-
guage-conscious filmmakers. Their works strain at the limits of language
and narrative. Intent on purging the overload of official culture, they
crafted the imagery of mute nature as antilanguage and antinarrative. This
undertaking was timely and politically effective in posttraumatic China.
Along with the prevalent intellectual climate that affirmed the value of the
individual, the fifth generation also had recourse to a new language of sexuality and desire. The personal story of traumatic memory often masked a
larger story of sexual frustration under the heavy-handed constraints of political culture. The film *Army Nurse* (Nüer lou, directed by Hu Mei, 1984)
skillfully infuses sexual desire into a collective traumatic experience. Set
against the turbulent backdrop of the Cultural Revolution, the story tells
of troubled love between an army nurse and a soldier patient. The nurse
and man constrain mounting but fearful passions by distancing themselves
from each other. The need to dress the patient's wound throws the nurse
with the patient together, alone in a room. With a series of soundless close-
ups that stresses the increasing intensity of emotion and desire, the mise-
en-scène lingers on the bare bodily parts, the blood of the wound, the

painfully slow-moving bandaging, the uncontrollable but muffled utter-ances—all this is building up to the breaking point of erotic explosion. E. Ann Kaplan rightly points out that this episode is central to a new insis-tence on sexual desire in a period of political opening.[47] Yet remarkably, sexual arousal happens in the agonizing act of dressing a wound. The nurse and the patient share a background of wounds: their fathers both were ca-sualties of political persecution and mass atrocity. An apparently loose strand in the narrative enforces this shared wound: An elderly patient of their fathers' age, unable to endure the persecution, makes an abortive at-tempt at suicide and is rushed to hospital and put under intensive care. The soldier patient goes out of his way to care for this fatherly person and plays a mournful tune on the harmonica hours before his death. Deeply in love with the soldier, the nurse secretly listens to and watches him playing the tune beside the dying old man. The mournful tune dominates the en-tire film as the leitmotif and is the key element in the nurse's memory of the soldier. Clearly the lovers are united in feeling as well as in a shared ex-perience of pain. As she dresses the soldier's wounds, the nurse is also ex-posing and dressing her own. Their love fails to consummate because of the self-censorship of the soldier and the unreasonable demands of the girl's career. As she quits an arranged "date," the unloved fiancé, in the end of the film, she revolves to come back to her hospital, as a "bird of hope," to dress more wounds and serve more patients.

Sexuality in the film appears to be a potential cure for the wounds, a transient soothing balm for personal frustration as well as the larger collec-tive trauma. Yet the language of sexuality does not and cannot dress the wound. On the contrary, it reveals unfulfilled sexuality to be as much part of the wound of those inflicted by political repression.

Nostalgia and Utopia

If the post–Cultural Revolutionary period confronted the Chinese with the painful reality of lingering, haunting trauma, the roaring 1990s brutalized the mind with new anxiety, distress, and uncertainty. The new shock stemmed from the large-scale influx of global capital and the mas-sive commercialization of all aspects of life. Reverence for highbrow cul-ture—in the sense of the best that has been thought and written in the past—was cast to the wayside. Artists, writers, filmmakers, and scholars gladly joined the profit-making culture industry. Emotional and personal links in the community were thinning out, giving way to cold, calculating business relations. Along with transnational capitalism, the belief in individualism of a reckless kind and the worship of money and pleasure created a new spiritual void. The mood of the day was captured by the two slogans "Have great fun and die!" (*guo ba yin jiu si*) and "Play for thrills" (*wan de jiu shi xintiao*). Both are titles of works by the best-selling writer Wang Shuo, who had become a cultural icon.

Among such bewildering historical change, nostalgia raised its head (see Part 3 for a full discussion). In the works of memory of the 1980s writers searched the past for earlier signs of cultural malaise and subjected them to scrutiny. The purpose was to use the past to understand and critique the current state of affairs. These writers might depict the past as surreal, grotesque, and distorted, but they tried to make connections with the past in earnest, interrogating it in order to find answers for the present. The nostalgia in the 1990s stood in a different relation to the past. It looked backward to find whatever there was that might soothe the soul and give the mind peace, seeking consolations missing in the present. As a form of memory, nostalgia in this mode lacks the critical sense of history in the 1980s that recognized both the pastness of the past and the persistence of the past in the present. The new nostalgia refused to accept the changing times but sentimentalized a fond memory of a golden age. It was more about desire than a rational historical inquiry. Whether in the renewed Mao's cult among large segments of the populace, in the ex–Red Guards' reminiscences glorifying a purer, more idealistic and flamboyant youth or in artistic representations, memory searched its dusty recesses to find an old image, an old myth, an old story, by which one could claim a spot as home in a time of spiritual homelessness. As symptoms of real history, nostalgia also expressed an urgent desire for the intimacy of social relations when the individual was left on his or her fragile self, without trustworthy communal connections and support.

Xie Fei's film *A Mongolian Tale* (Ai zai caoyuan, 1995) offers a reflection on nostalgia and its implications in contemporary history. The film was adapted from Zhang Chengzhi's 1982 novella *The Black Steed* (Hei junma), itself a nostalgic portrayal of childhood and youth in a Mongolian herdsmen's community. Although the novella was eagerly read and won a prize at the time of publication, it deviated from the main current of search-for-roots writing marked by a radical, demystifying, antiromantic cutting edge. The fact that in the 1990s Zhang Chengzhi was asked to rewrite his novella into a film script, later shot with spectacular cinematography, speaks to the urgent need for new romantic, nostalgic images.

The film expresses nostalgia for home and a way of life that does not exist in China and in the Han culture. It seeks to evoke a mythical world of grassland, horses, and tents that lie outside the modern progression of time. The unusual production of the film already aims at the unfamiliar and exotic attributes of a world apart. The director and filmmakers are Chinese, and the story is about herdsmen in Inner Mongolia, which is under Chinese sovereignty. Yet in the film all characters speak the Mongolian language, and Chinese subtitles are supplied so the audience can understand this "foreign" film. Schoolchildren in the narrative also learn to read and write the Mongolian language, to the exclusion of Chinese. To enhance the "tribal authenticity," actors and actresses from the Republic of Mongolia were hired to play the roles, and many outside scenes were shot in that country, with temples and scared sites of the real Mongolian culture unavailable in Inner Mongolia.

The search for home begins with the protagonist's return from the outside modern world to his childhood home in order to find his love, a Mongolian girl. As he travels up and down the grassland, he also travels down memory lane to remember and indeed reinvent the beautiful and enchanting story of his childhood. Through his monologue the film portrays the grassland as a timeless, romanticized fairyland. The vast, magnificent grassland, the solid, sturdy, but exotic Mongolian tent, the caring and nurturing grandmother who has raised numerous children, the strong, honest, and hard-drinking herdsmen, the affection and love among the people, and the magnificent steed that incarnates the spirit of the land— all these converge into a mythical, unspoiled paradise of purity and harmony. This place—a milieu of memory conjured up for nostalgia—is evidently a repository of meaning, value, and wisdom, a source of life and vitality. The protagonist's love of the Mongolian girl Somiya is the culmination of all the best things that the Mongolian paradise can offer. The two play and sleep together, and they entertain what the Chinese call an "unsuspecting, childlike affection" (*liangxiao wucai*) for each other. But the serene and innocent grassland is intruded upon by signs from the outside, modern world. In a transition scene, the teenage boy gazes at the sky after reading books about technology and sees an airplane shooting across the blue. As a logical sequence, he jumps at the first opportunity to study in a far-away vocational school and then prolongs his study in college.

Meanwhile, Somiya is raped by a Mongolian man and has his baby. Yet the loss of purity is nothing more than a passing cloud in the bright, clear Mongolian sky. Here even the patriarchal degradation of women is made a virtue: that the woman proves to be fertile is cause for celebration. With the support of her grandmother and an honest man, Somiya comes through as strong as her grandmother. She survives the worst when her grandmother dies, and she becomes the surrogate mother for all school-children, assuming the role of the all-powerful, nurturing grandmother. The main character eventually meets his girl, only to find how much he has missed by leaving home to seek modern life. As they part in the end, Somiya pleads with him to send his children, if he has any, to her to be nurtured. Paradise is lost for him, but there is still hope for the children.

Nostalgia is a striking element in the historical imagination in con-temporary China. Interestingly, the nostalgic does not travel in time through Chinese history to find a home. In the wake of waves of destruc-tion and demystification of the age-old, "bankrupt" tradition, China's past seems so run down and broken—at least to the nostalgia of Zhang Chengzhi's type—that little can be used to fire the imagination, to elevate the soul and arouse longing. The Mao cult and the restaurants of Educated Youth seem too kitschy, too playfully ironic to cultivate serious attach-ment. So the nostalgic reinvents what Svetlana Boym calls an "imaginary affective geography that does not coincide with any scientific map."[48] In commenting on the postcommunist situation in Russia, Boym writes that in the deadwood of communist ideology nationalism tends to fill the gap and becomes a rallying call. Nationalism "modifies capitalist individualism and gives people an imaginary sense of community, a mythical map of rewritten history."[49] Mythical nostalgia in *A Mongolian Tale* corresponds to the rising nationalistic sentiment in China in the earlier 1990s. Its heart-warming spectacles offer the seduction of homecoming, the caring tender-ness of the mother, the affection of brothers and sisters, the nurturing, en-chanted land, the supportive community, the consoling myth of blood and soil—all liable to nationalist and xenophobic sentiments. It apparently looks to an earlier time or another place, but the real trip is back to the future, for nostalgia entertains the hope that in the Chinese streets things need not be dictated by MacDonald's and Coca-Cola. It is a utopian desire against the postindustrial, global "history" aggressively pushing its way around the world.

Temporality, Memory, and Myth in Wang Anyi's Fiction

Lived Experience and Lived History

The mythical strain in nostalgia was a response to the effects of modernization and the stress of modernity. In the 1980s, the work of memory reflected on the past traumas of political history with a vision of modernization. With the visible outline of "millennial capitalism"[1] on the horizon in the 1990s, memory can be placed in a broader context of global modernity.

The history of global modernity implies a universal time line. Historians and social scientists have used this time line to measure widely divergent histories and geographies by a homogeneous yardstick of progress, modernization, and development. Derived from the universalist conceptions of human civilization, this time line, in Agnes Heller's apt description, "has no relation to men, nor to the single exister, nor to people; it is a speculative concept of time with no practical relevance."[2] It seems erroneous to discard this universal time line in a hurry because it has served the imperial interest of some groups. Although in actual history the homogeneous time has proved a lethal instrument of domination against those incapable of toeing the line, its universalist assumptions could be an important aspiration supporting the notions of equal right and global justice. In addition to its scientific relevance in space physics or industrial time management, this time line also has the radical, revolutionary function of pushing inherited authority embodied by the monarchy and modern states into the fluid process of civil society based on public spheres and democratic participation. On its dubious side, it also renders any overarching structure vulnerable to divergent pursuits of the atomistic individual. "God is dead" can be a metaphor for the disintegration of culture and history in the moment of transition in China from the 1980s to the 1990s. With the previously godlike terms of history, revolution, and ideology in shambles, what used to carry meaning and authority is retreating from state institutions and the public sphere to the private experience of the individual.

Memory may be an attempt to recover a nugget of meaning when the providential foundations are not available for anchoring experience. Memory seeks to recuperate "life-time" from the impersonal flow of homogeneous, empty time. Marcel Proust's *mémoire involuntaire* is the classical testament to this rescue effort. In *A la recherche du temps perdu* the well-known scenario of memory stems from the restorative power of the pastry, the madeleine. The taste transports the narrator to a past moment redolent with experience and joy, an enactment of unconscious connections to beloved persons and enchanted places. Walter Benjamin suggested that Proust's whole novel is a desperate attempt to reinstall the storyteller, a figure of collective memory, by resurrecting childhood experience.[3] Chinese writers in the 1990s also took such an approach to childhood or adolescent memory. Wang Anyi, Chen Ran, Su Tong, Li Rui, and many others sought to resurrect memories of childhood experience. Intimate, subjective, and precious, this memory is linked to the controversial phenomenon of individualistic writing (*geren hua xiezou*).[4] In these new forms of literature, lived experience is distanced and even disengaged from history as shared, public experience.

Taking personal memory as the depository of meaningful experience, however, has its limitations. By rescuing some modicum of private experience from history, memory may turn its back on history. In her analysis of modern temporality, Heller makes a very useful distinction between life *as* history and life *in* history. Subjective lifetime—lived minutiae of the individual sunk in his or her private needs and drives, may still be inauthentic, for all its sensory immediacy and personal worth. Single-minded insistence on the pleasure and pain of living as such is decadent in the Nietzschean sense, premised on a consumptive, atomistic notion of free-floating individuality as the solitary ground of existence. On the other hand, the experience of Heideggerian *Dasein* opens up the possibilities of returning subjective experience to history, to a shared experience. "History," Heller asserts, "is always shared. One remembers an experience regarding one's relation to others, and one remembers along with others."[5] Thus we make or share "lived history" rather than hearing about each other's interiorized experience. Lived history is "the great blessing (and luckiest thing) in life":

Lived history happens if two (perhaps a few, but not many) men or women live together so that they share experiences, mutually work on their past, and become transparent for one another so that their bygone experience is not endangered. They do not feel the lack of time; they do not say that time goes too fast or crawls too slowly. They do not complain that something came too early or something came too late, for they do not notice time, since they are living history.[6]

Heller seems rather cautious in saying that only a few, not many—not numerous enough to be a community—can live a life worthy of history. But hers are prescriptive remarks, not descriptions of reality. Her notion of lived history projects an ideal relation between memory and history, subjective lifetime and historical time line. Clearly, it is also this intimate link between memory and history that allows Benjamin to see a hint of despair in Proust. Proust thought that one could take hold of one's experience only by chance—through occasional flashes of involuntary memory. To Benjamin this is too limited and does not touch upon the real problem of memory. Sheer involuntary memory is, Benjamin cautions, "part of the inventory of the individual who is isolated in many ways," and who is unable to define himself by relating to his social environment and neighbors. Lived experience, in order to be authentic, must not simply be private, fragmented experience. It has to rely on the combination of the individual past with the collective past. Traditional rituals and festivals or similar collective activities, will combine personal memory with collective experience over and over again, so that involuntary memory will lose its stain of isolation and decadence, and become reconciled with voluntary memory, which is conscious, rational efforts in shaping life experience.[7] The conscious shaping of life experience in collective, concerted efforts have an old name: history.

History in a Mythical Key

It is in the spirit of lived history premised on a merger of subjective memory and shared tradition that we will look at the contemporary writer Wang Anyi. Her works address the memory/history nexus and correspond to the changes from the 1980s to 1990s. They simultaneously present a subjective time endemic to personal memory and a discontent with the narrow individualistic closet of that time. This discontent compels Wang to go beyond autobiographical narrative and family genealogy and to look for scenarios capable of combining personal memory and collective experience.

Some additional comments are needed regarding the ambivalence of modern history writing, an institution of the nation-state in its relation to collective memory.[8] The nation-state follows the linear, universal narrative of modernity in its portrayal of history and tends to cut its links from the traditional past. The nation and its past have been figured as modern versus tradition, progress versus backwardness, and capitalist versus feudal (in Chinese history, the last pair is cast as socialist versus feudal). Under these binaries, modern China has been marked by continuous revolutionary breaks with its past. It is a commonplace to say that this homogeneous, futuristic narrative suppresses differences of local custom and tradition and has been an instrument of imperial and colonial domination.[9] Yet even this futuristic history does not reject the notion of lived, shared pasts: the modern nation-state constantly rewrites history by drawing on its collective past so as to become organic with it. The official historical narrative mobilizes elements and motifs from the past in the name of nationalism and socialist reconstruction. These elements belong to collective memory that may be antihistorical (nonlinear), antimodern, or anticapitalist, even though the "anti" here already involves affinities with the modern. Thus history stands in an ambivalent relation of continuity and break with cultural memory. In building and legitimating the modern state, history and cultural memory fulfill each other's function, complementing and conflicting with each other in giving shape to a new time line. History may serve as a vehicle for the preservation of the cultural past, claiming certain images of cultural memory as its own. I mentioned in the Introduction the two revivals of Confucianism in China, one at the beginning of the twentieth century and the other in the 1990s. In these revivals historical writing

selectively uses and invents collective memory so as to ensure and justify
the new political structure's relation with its past.[10] From the perspective of
continuity history would look like coherently assembled cultural memories
under the aegis of national unity and embedded in an unbroken stream
from past to present. On the other hand, the modern history of nationalism is by no means "friendly" to tradition and memory. The modern aspiration, with its demands for change and innovation, treats the traditional
world of memory with suspicion and outright hostility. In the eyes of
modern nationalists, the ritual, myths, superstitions, and axiomatic wisdom belong to a benighted past, and its enduring residues need to be kept
at bay or simply swept away.

The acceleration of modernity, however, is haunted by constant returns to the mythical. Since the early 1990s, and in the widening scope of
market forces, the erosion of the social fabric accompanied the quickening
pace of economic development and drastic transformation of social relations. The modernization process has broken "the threads which in the
past had woven human beings into social textures," as Eric Hobsbawm
puts it so aptly. These textures are fabrics of memory, which encompass not
only human relations and their forms of political organization, but also
contain prescribed roles of behavior toward each other.[11] Increasingly abstracted into economic, administrative, and exchange processes, the matrix
of meaning and values that used to connect individuals to society and the
past to the present has lost its self-evidence. In the emergent society of consumption and mass media, the older Marxian notion of history as social
and political practice is receding from public purview, and the past is being dissolved into spectacle. In the cultural reflection of the 1980s, as intellectuals attempted to deconstruct the dominant history of revolution and
nation, they still relied on the notion of history as an unfolding narrative
of political praxis, which paradoxically supported the hegemonic discourse
of revolution. This critique of the grand narrative did not throw the baby
out with the bathwater: intellectuals needed the basic premises of Marxist
historiography to critique the errors of Maoist extremes. Yet in the 1990s
this deconstruction was taken over by the liberal-consumerist tendency
that suspends history under the spell of global capital. Cultural production
has exhibited a downturn to the immediate and the everyday and to pro-
fane and consumptive practices and pleasure. In opposition to this turn
there also arose a renewed engagement with history, an intensified impulse

to seek unfulfilled possibilities in the past for understanding and charting epochal changes. Wang Anyi, in spite of her varied, changing profiles as a writer in the maelstrom of change, epitomizes a serious engagement with history. In the waning of history, she attempts to revamp historical consciousness by conferring on history a mythical aura. A look at her two works may shed light on this interesting combination of history and myth.

Wang Anyi's novel *Reality and Fiction* (Jishi yu xugou) represents a poignant attempt to recover an alternative memory so as to reconstruct a meaningful historical narrative. It seeks to rescue history as a continuous source of meaning when the sense of the past is flattened out into images of entertainment and drained out of public consciousness. As in *Song of Unending Sorrow* (Changhen ge, 1995) and *Fu Ping* (2000), Wang displaces the experience of global modernity of the 1990s into the nationalist modernization of the republican period and revolutionary modernity in the socialist era. This displacement sees a continuous identity in the project of modernization, be it nationalist, communist, or socialist, culminating in the current drive of globalization. It reads all these seemingly different strains as riddled with problems of alienation, rationalization, bureaucratization, psychic fragmentation, and the sense of homelessness in the midst of swift change.[12]

This temporal displacement, embodying an overview of a continuous stream of Chinese modernity over a century, allows us to see how a "homogeneous history" encompasses two apparently incompatible trends of capitalist modernity and nationalist/socialist modernization. The history of modernity has imposed a crude alternative between two teleological paths. Modernity is supposed to thread through not only revolutionary historical transformations, but also through the liberal-humanist, technocratic history of capitalism in its worldwide expansion. Whether under the rubric of capitalism or socialism, this narrative of modernity tends not to recognize other possibilities. The search for a different history by way of memory or nostalgia, in this light, is a quest for alternatives beyond this reified, black-and-white narrative. In the context of the 1990s the quest projects a different social imaginary that seeks to break out of the uniform march of production, commodity, exchange, spectacle, and consumption.

The novel *Reality and Fiction* uses "preglobal" and premodern materials to critique the global trends. In an autobiographical form, the narrator strives to evoke the experience of initiation and socialization in childhood in Shanghai's urban setting. On the other hand, she also traces the genealogy of her own family on a different, "mythological" track. Despite its search for a unity between past and present, the novel is less a continuous, coherent narrative than a mélange of unconnected scenarios, speculations, remembrances, philosophical comments, and philological investigations of facts and names. The lyricism over intensely mythical events of the remote tribal past calls into question the novel's apparent status as autobiographical or historical narrative. To ask whether the novel is fiction or history is to raise a wrong question. The more interesting question would be to see how fictional and imaginative elements are implicated in a historical imagination, which is itself a response to China's current situation.[13]

It is important to consider why the historical imagination needs to take the form of autobiography. Following George Lukács, we may treat the autobiographical form as a symptom of lost history. Lukács suggests that the collapse of historical totality leads to the emergence of the modern novel. The loss of history opens up an abyss that yawns between "a conceptual system which can never completely capture life and a life complex which can never attain completeness because completeness is immanently utopian."[14] Lukács's organic concept of history assumes that the individual, in his or her joint venture with others, should be the agent of history, its mover and maker. History is a collective movement propelled by organized individuals carrying out a drama of social transformation. Clearly, this is similar to Heller's notion of lived history, but on a grander scale. In the emergent market atmosphere, however, the individual is not living a life of history, but a life away from history. The individual is becoming narrowly individualistic and atomistic in the single-minded pursuit of self-interest and consumption. As middle-class lifestyle and moneyed success are becoming the buzzwords of the day, the notion of history as public activity and collective project is losing its appeal. Yet one cannot arbitrarily cut oneself loose from the past and community; some kind of shared history still needs to be imagined and written. The need for history, in the absence of shared memory (or common history), Pierre Nora notes, compels each group to "redefine its identity by dredging up its past."[15] Thus the waning of public history leads to a proliferation of discrete histories of minority and marginal groups. Likewise, the individual has to seek his or her roots and sources of identity by way of genealogy and personal trajectory.

This is why the form that strives to bridge the gap between the individual and community turns out to be biographical or autobiographical.[16] We may recall the classical bourgeois novel of the nineteenth century, which was preoccupied with the painful socialization of the individual into the uncharted terrains of modern society. This attempt to find something of history within the individual, a seeming contradiction in terms, may be partially confirmed by the contemporary interest in the testimonial in the American academy.[17] The testimonial, with all its torn, splintered inner life, seems to confer a form and hence a structure of meaning, however idiosyncratic, onto a routinized, treadmill existence. The biography or autobiography form is able to give a semblance of organic form, a personal imaginary of plenitude and fulfillment. It implies a longing for community in one's private personal trajectories, as if an individual can be self-sufficient, a community onto oneself. Its aesthetic aim is the forging of a semblance of meaning through varied patterns of individual trajectory. It is a reaction formation against the loss of the larger meaning of community and history.

In *Reality and Fiction* the waning of community is linked to the portrayal of the individual's body in search of intimate experience of contact with other bodies and authentic origins. This search is set against a backdrop of the transnational economy and its abstracting trends. The new socioeconomic conditions threaten to turn human relations into the impersonal relations of exchange and money. The body, its feelings, anchoring in community, and emotional attachment, is at risk but defiantly tries to reconnect. The narrative describes characters who live in the socialist periods of the 1950s and 1960s but who have to grapple with the "modern," "postsocialist" problems of rootlessness, loneliness, spiritual homelessness, and, ironically, lack of community in Mao's communist China.

This displacement of proverbial "modernist" elements into socialist life should not be viewed as an anachronistic scrambling of temporality. Socialism, theoretically, is a phase of modernity that arose both as a departure from as well as in continuity with capitalism. Many massive projects of social engineering in China since the founding of the People's Republic absorbed the liberal and rational components of capitalism, in terms of the Enlightenment ideology of technological betterment of society, industrialization and high productivity, the division of labor, and the rationalization of the bureaucratic and administrative apparatus. More importantly, state power in Chinese socialism has much in common with the technology of power that Adorno and Foucault find so pervasive in modern society in the west.[18] Thus the institutional forms of capitalist modernity for social production, in the sense of Weberian rationalization and streamlining of administrative and social structures, were at work in China's revolutionary drive and socialist modernization. This trend of social engineering was apparent during Mao's days as both a goal and a target of revolution. In Wang's novel, capitalist modernity, which is of course an urgent problem in the 1990s, is displaced and pushed further back into an earlier time of socialist modernity in the 1950s and 1960s. This explains why the main character could experience problems of identity, the thinning out of history and community as if she lived in an environment in which someone like Baudelaire might have felt uncomfortable and which Marcel Proust would have written about.

The search for identity goes on two seemingly unrelated narratives: the narrator's childhood in Shanghai, and her clan's genealogy through centuries in the Mongolian steppes. The Shanghai memory depicts the child's loneliness, her constant yearning for playmates and her distress of isolation, the euphoria of children's play, the sour taste of unfulfilled love, and the plunge into the fateful events of history. Apparently this evocation of past experiences resembles the "search-for-roots" tendency most vibrant in the mid-1980s. But the search-for-roots writing was fundamentally a critical exposure of the lingering malaises of tradition and culture. The novel's narrative of search, in contrast, does not "retrieve" anything "back then," but wrestles with the distress of memory that severs the links between now and then, a temporal blank left by China's modernization and change.

The narrator/character's own family provides an instance of the revolutionary disruption within the entrenched terrain of old Shanghai's urban, "alley" culture. Her parents entered the city in 1948 as members of the liberation army and are the outsiders to the native city dwellers. The family belongs to the "comrades" circle, opposed to the "petty city dwellers" (*xiao shimin*). She grows up speaking Mandarin Chinese instead of Shanghai dialect, and she has no clue about all the residual, traditional customs, life forms, and rituals, which seem to her richer and more colorful than the modern standardized lifestyle of her revolutionary parents. The narrator's nostalgic remembrance displays the symptoms of a lost, alienated individual deprived of memory by two homogeneous registers of time: the time of revolution and the time of global economic expansion that further ruptures the already weakened sense of historical continuity. The official historical time renders the individual spiritually homeless. At present, the narrator notes, no one, indeed, is native to Shanghai. This vast metropolis has "the powerful capacity to erase memory." "The city is the gathering place for drifters: we are exiled and condemned to live here."[19]

The novel thus addresses the classic questions of modernity: Where did I come from? Who am I? How do I come to this? The nostalgic play of Shanghai remembrance is exercised in Proustian fashion, but it is a conscious, willful invention rather than involuntary upsurges of past memory. In its intermittent, short-lived, and tear-filled fragments, the childhood memory is insufficient as an energizing resource for coping with the problems of identity. It falls to the other part of the novel to shore up the fragile image of the makeshift self. The quasi-historical account of family genealogy weighs in with a laborious researching of the narrator's ethnic background going back fourteen hundred years. In an attempt to reenchant the quotidian life of urban neighborhoods with the sublime aura of myth, this genealogy strives to bring a sense of continuity to one's truncated, nameless existence. City dwellers are homeless drifters cut off from family myth, writes Wang Anyi. "Without family myth, we are all orphans, restless and anxious. Our life is plunged into utter darkness on one side and obscured in misty remoteness on the other" (75). Walter Benjamin observed that "to live means to leave traces."[20] Wang echoes this desire for self-retaining traces. In a vast city like Shanghai, our names are ironically traces of us having never lived; they are empty signs marking anonymous, atomic, transient individuals on the move to the administrative statistics. Every homeless person, the narrator observes, must feel the full weight of the question "whose child are you?" for it reminds her that behind an individual "there stood a great, affectionate community" (76).

The search for the family origin focuses exclusively on the maternal line—an instance of mythical thinking. Through a double procedure of philological exegesis of her mother's surname "ru" and a willful poeticization of whatever is associated with that name, the narrator arbitrarily chooses a Mongolian nomadic tribe that might have borne that name. It is the mythical, heroic, and poetic potential, rather than historical fact, that draws the narrator to the Mongolians. Wang writes that a Japanese scholar reminds her of the meaning of her maternal name as "earth." This sacred symbol inspires her with a procedure for the quest: "this search is actually a method of transfiguring symbolic meaning into reality" (77). This principle informs Wang Anyi's mythologization of history. "The rise and fall" of the narrator's maternal Mongolian tribe

Bring me back to the vast and magnificent grassland of the northern steppes [*mobei caoyuan*]. There the soil is rich and water plenty; sunrise and sunset are sublime and majestic; the clanking and clashing of swords and spears and the galloping of the horses give a tragic grandeur to the backdrop of my life. Searching for the roots is more often a selection and a spiritual roaming. Now I have decided to name my family myth and I will call it "ru." (77)

This is history writing in a mythical key, a spectacular gesture toward finding remote resources for one's identity. The birth of a small nomadic tribe of her family is absorbed into the famed nations of Tamerlane and Genghis Khan. The defeats and conquests in tribal feuds, the lightning steeds, and the breathtaking primordial landscape of the northern steppes evoke a world of miracles, omens, oracles, and horoscopes. Lyrical exuberance muses over the sublime fatality and miraculous turns of events and superhuman deeds, a wild and untamed space far removed from degraded urban existence.

Reality and Fiction represents a reversal of the major literary trend of the 1980s. Deconstruction of history as myth was at that time a salint feature of the new wave, avant-garde literature. In this novel we see a shift from the previous historicization of myth to a remythologization of history. The radical dismantling of the grand narrative in the 1980s freed writers from the official mode of history and opened up possibilities for unearthing the suppressed strata of the past. But this radical trend also helped open the floodgate for the invasion of consumer lifestyle, the market, and imported discourses. Blinding varieties of the past barely conceal the void. The greatest sustaining myth for modern China is, by default, history. For all the ruptures and catastrophes in the twentieth century, history, the conscious process of shaping and transforming social reality, is what fuels and empowers cultural production and political reforms. Under the leveling impact of consumer culture and the market, history is in danger of becoming bloodless, painless images. As Eileen Chang put it half a century ago, it is like a butterfly nailed to the board. Caught in shopping malls and bombarded by images of advertisement, Chinese writers find they are stripped of history and are hungry for meaningful myth. Wang Anyi's work represents both a symptom and a response to the decline of history.

Rescuing Traces of Memory from Modernity

Fiction and Reality is a melancholy attempt to mourn the decline of history by reawakening myth. The quickening pace of the market economy and globalization, on the other hand, is daily imposing a new myth. This new myth of economic development, technological utopia, and consumer paradise is illusory and destructive. It rehearses the empty, homogeneous time of both the Great Leap–style modernization and capitalistic global expansion. The historical shocks resulting from it can be measured in terms of the daily traumas of lived experience with regard to the sense of time. The feeling of time is no longer draped with religious, symbolic, or ritualistic elements that used to endow time with quality and value, hope and desire, ensuring meaningful connections between past, present, and future. Time is splintered into discrete units measurable with reference to efficiency, productivity, and profit. This instrumental time is accompanied, on the other hand, by an emptying process that strips time of its intrinsic meaning, reducing it to sheer trivial externalities and leisured boredom, like the sheer ticking of the clock. The meaningless, empty time without affect gives rise to the classical modern symptom of spleen or ennui, which, alongside the time of productive labor, sees little more than an unending series of trivialities and absurdities, or simply an endless flux. It is a melancholy gaze that reveals "the passing moment in its nakedness."[21]

Lest I turn Chinese literary figures into a Baudelaire stricken with ennui, there is good reason to say that the gaze into an empty space or a melancholy feeling of empty time is a leitmotif in Wang Anyi's fiction. It has become a recognizable feature of modern experience in her works. In the story I will discuss below, the village chief, a peasant, comes under a strong spell of ennui when he finds that an official of the provincial government will take away the village's symbol of hope embedded in tradition and ritual. This hope consists in the memory of a girl who is the village's beloved daughter. Anticipating the loss, this peasant suddenly perceives starkly, as if for the first time, the familiar outlines of the hills, the sun, and the village scene as sheer senseless materiality, sheer inert, brute things.

Nothing seems to be left, and time seems to be floating over ghostly things. In Wang's novel *Song of Unending Sorrow*, one also encounters those recurrent lethargic winter afternoons, with lengthening shadows of the yellowish, aging sun, with its naked moments of drowsy inactivity and hopeless drag, the purposeless stare into empty space, the sinking of the heart that the bottom has dropped out altogether.

Wang Anyi is particularly remarkable in taking a turn from history to memory. In her works in the 1990s we witness another turnaround from the search for mythical historical continuity and sources of identity to an exposition of the abyss in time opened up by modernity. In the 1980s she burst upon the literary scene with her novella *Little Bao Village* (Xiaobaozhuang). As an instant classic of the search-for-roots writing, the novella belongs to the mode of tracing political nightmares in a genealogical account of primitive myths. In the 1990s, however, Wang showed a propensity to look at the past with nostalgia and tenderness. But the nostalgia in Wang is not a romantic idealization of the past and outright rejection of modernity. We will read another story and see how the portrayal of memory traces of the past performs a critique of modernity.

The short story "Tianxian pei" (Marriage of the fairies) cuts into the entangled problem of tradition and modernity in a startling way by introducing a genuinely mythical dimension. In an isolated village in a mountainous area, a young man is left buried in a well that the villagers have just dug and constructed. The heartbroken parents, having lost their only son and hope, attempt to take their own lives. The urgent problem for the village chief is how to keep the suicidal parents from despair by supplying hope. His solution is to open up the grave of a young woman long dead, remove her remains, and have the dead young man marry her in a new grave. This, of course, is the traditional ritual of marriage of the dead.

This traditional solution works well psychologically to sustain the parents' hope and belief in their son's well-being. Complications arise, however, when a retired government official, who used to be the young woman's sweetheart during their college and then revolutionary years, comes looking for her remains. If her remains are taken away from the village, it will mean much more than just another loss for the bereaved parents. For behind the young woman there has accumulated a solid fund of collective memory. She is virtually the legendary daughter of the whole village community. A soldier in the revolutionary army, she was fatally wounded and wandered away from the troops during the nationalist attack on Yan'an's revolutionary base in 1942. She ran into the village Xia Jia Yao and lay beside a haystack to die. The villagers surrounded her and watched her bleed, unable to help. As they watched,

> She only had a slight lingering breath, which refused to go away. The villagers were weeping. . . . Everybody pitched in to build a hut above her to shelter her from the night dew. They stacked a few quilts around her, so that the little girl seemed tinier, like a baby. Thus it is, that by the seventh night, she breathed her last. Before that, she uttered a sound "Mommy," crisp and clear, as if she were well. . . . Hearing this the villagers wondered if her mommy was missing her somewhere, not knowing her daughter was here. With this cry for mommy, she might as well take Xia Jia Yao to be her home.[22]

The girl's legendary status is enshrined in the collective memory of the village as an image of tenderness and an enduring symbol of intimacy, home, and human warmth. But by the time our modern story begins, no one, except a very old man, is old enough to have seen the young woman in person. Yet her image is firmly deposited in the collective mind and transmitted by word of mouth from generation to generation. She stays forever young and ageless. When visiting the village, the government official, the girl's former boyfriend and comrade, passes around her photo, and everybody is able to "recognize" her, as if they had long known her personally and intimately. Her ageless image is the reason why the village can erase the age gap and have her marry the dead young man, and why the parents accept her readily as their daughter-in-law who would care for their son in the afterlife.

One may object to the ritual of marriage of the dead and the related beliefs as feudalistic and superstitious. The belief in historical materialism and modernization would quickly dismiss these as obsolete residues of traditional culture. But it is far from the purpose of the story to privilege the modern over the traditional. By raising the memory of the girl to a legend and folklore, indeed to a life-sustaining myth, it raises issues that the development of modernity—itself a deadening myth and a process of abstraction, tends to ignore and suppress. These questions include the claims of the past on the present, the memory that still informs and animates daily living and shapes the habits of the body, human intimacy embedded in a local setting and face-to-face contact, and the need for hope and

meaning. It should also be noted that this local myth is not strictly traditional. Although the frame of ritual that adopts the girl, a stranger, into the
"maternal" fold of the village appears to be traditional in form, her acceptance is an updating of tradition by embedding relations of intimate kinship in a new context.

As the retired official starts searching for the girl's remains, he represents an external threat to the mythical memory surrounding the girl. The
official comes from a modern world engaged in the revolutionary drive to
transform society and maintain the modern nation-state. A cadre in the
provincial government, he starts writing a memoir in retirement and is
looking for evidence of revolutionary history and the intimate memory of
his beloved in his student days. Through the modern bureaucratic system,
and with the help of a local historian, he finally locates the whereabouts of
the girl's remains. As the girl's biographical information is being passed
around to the villagers, a modern, "official" image emerges and proves to
be alien to her mythical status long nurtured by the villagers. Among the
peasants, she is named Feng Feng (phoenix), a local, folksy-sounding
name, when she is married to the dead young man. Now she turns out to
be Li Shuyu (literally, book and jade). This mandarin, discursive-sounding
name is associated with a typical career path of many educated young people involved in the modern revolution. As the aged cadre and his associates
tell the "official" story of Li Shuyi, the chief feels that

He can never relate the little girl soldier to the name Li Shuyu. The girl soldier
in the haystack—what a pitiable, suffering maiden. Several scores of years have
passed since she died, and few remain in the villages that have ever seen her, yet
she is very much alive. With her recent marriage with Xi Xi [the dead young
man] she comes up right in front of you when you close your eyes . . . but who
on earth is Li Shuyu, and what does Li Shuyi have to do with all this? The name
sounds, as Lao Yang says, like a female martyr, to be written about in books and
newspapers, and belongs to a great figure.[23]

Indeed, what does Li Shuyu, a modern revolutionary, have to do with her
mythical, local image, burdened with all the obsolete beliefs, rituals, and
superstitions?

The legend, the ritualistic marriage of the dead, and the communal
memory are traces of the past. They belong to tradition. The tradition
here, however, is not the dead weight of the past. For the village caught up

in the modern process, tradition is still vital to the villagers' survival. Tradition, as Anthony Giddens says, is routine that is intrinsically meaningful, rather than merely empty habit for habit's sake.[24] Tradition is a way of organizing time and space to give both meaning. With the development of modernity, time and space become empty and abstract and can be filled with random elements and arbitrary meaning. The story suggests a backdrop of modernity, with its wars and casualties, catastrophe, rational organization, random encounters of people, and the rise of consumer society. In a landscape increasingly empty of meaning, the function of tradition and memory reembeds time and space in a contextually implicated setting, one that offers emotional aura in the ritual of bodily activity and in the security of lived experience. "Tradition," asserts Giddens, "contributes in basic fashion to ontological security in so far as it sustains trust in the continuity of past, present, and future, and connects such trust to routinised social practices."[25]

The intrinsic meaning of tradition in the story is that the traditional ritual keeps memory alive, supplies hope and consolation, and sustains intimate human relationships. Even the official of the modern state cannot dispense with this traditional value. Though married and with many children, he wants to have intimate, direct access to the physical remains of his former girlfriend by placing her in a memorial park. Yet even with that "traditional" value in mind, the official rejects the village's superstition and speaks proudly of his atheism and faith in a rational ideology of materialism.

Tradition in this story persists not in itself, but rather fills in the void left by modern life. Taking away the girl's remains, although justified, can be seen as an act of stripping away, an act of disenchantment. It will dash the parents' hope and dispel the comforting aura enveloping the girl, who is the common daughter of the village, and destroy what remains of human trust in a faithless world. Despite the village chief's attempt to block his search, the government official finally tracks down the girl's remains. As he hands over the girl's remains to the official, the chief feels that the girl has aged instantly, just like the old official. This is a sure sign that the timeless myth is historicized and disenchanted. Yet the chief is under no illusions that a mere ritual will make the bare landscape pretty or meaningful. With the girl's remains gone, he has to invent another myth to save the newly wrecked parents of the deceased young man. His solution is again traditional and mythical. Through the recounting of a dream, he convinces the parents that their daughter-in-law's departure has been decreed by the Jade Emperor in heaven so that the young couple will have a better life elsewhere. The daughter will go first, accompanied by the government official, who has been sent by the emperor, and then their son will follow.

This solution again works nicely, and the departure is accomplished with an elaborate ritual. Through evocation of myth and enactment of ritual, this recourse to inherited collective memory and practice intensifies the contradiction between tradition and modernity. The village chief is fully aware that he is using a "superstitious" method to deal with a potentially fatal psychic trauma, but what else can he do in a world stripped of consoling fictions? His method is self-consciously expedient and ad hoc. But it helps where modern progress continues to strip the village of the last remnant of hope. His justification of superstition reveals a double consciousness and is worth pondering: "After all, he has been educated, and is a believer in historical materialism. But then, when you come to think of it, it is idealism that is actually better, for it eases one's distress. It enables you to have hope and desire wherever you go. Materialism cuts off one's hope and desire. Thoroughgoing materialism cuts off one's hope and desire thoroughly."[26] Educated in historical materialism, the chief is "enlightened," and would not regress into mythical, prerational ways of dealing with social and psychic problems. This strand is in line with the materialistic, secular rejection of tradition and superstitions and is part of the revolutionary break with the past. In this light, whatever modernity and progress we may achieve is a result of relentless historicization, and human self-fashioning is based on rational design, on demythologizing myths, and on leaving memory behind in anticipation of the "poetry" of the future. The arrow of our endeavors is directed to an endlessly renewed future, without substantial connections with the past. The retired Marxist official in the story keeps faith with this belief. The poetry of the future heralded by progress and development may be part of the village chief's education, but it is not attractive to this peasant, whose village is more a casualty of modernization than a beneficiary. More importantly, the incessant remaking of history threatens to strip the local community of the familiar and enduring anchorage of trust, relation, and security. The chief knows very well the distinction between the potential emptiness of thoroughgoing historicization and the antihistorical, mythical values of memory. On the

cusp between modernity and tradition, between objective time line and
"subjective," mythically lived experience, the chief is a self-reflective believer in myth and superstitions. His is a useful, if not naive and intrinsic,
approach to myth. He is enlightened, but he sees no reason to be so enlightened as to be orphaned from the "false" consciousness of collective
memory, myth, and tradition. In his reasoning, we arrive at a pragmatic articulation of modernity to tradition. Memory represents human beings' vital connection to a particular space in a particular time, which, despite the
flux of the homogeneous time line, will always resurface as a functional
myth.

5

Traumatic History Against Melodrama

BLUE KITE

Historians who care to look closely at how history is written in China have often noted therein a strong moral element.[1] Ethical principles, more than any other methods of temporal ordering, dominated the interpretation and recounting of historical data for a long time. History written strictly within a moral framework often functions as an evaluative assessment of the praise and blame of past events and figures. As a result, the historical consciousness that motivates history writing in a spirit of critical inquiry gives way to an ahistorical mind-set or an equally ahistorical desire to turn away from history. In twentieth-century China, history writing—historiography and other discursive activities and visual production dealing with the past—has undergone revisions to meet the challenge of political and cultural circumstances. One thinks of the renewed attempts in the May Fourth, socialist, and post–Cultural Revolutionary periods at rethinking Chinese history and tradition. Yet it is not clear how these "radical" changes have fundamentally shaken the tenacious moral, ideological, and teleological underpinnings of history writing and the attendant historical narrative and perspectives. Historical raw data itself, to be sure, does not automatically tell a story that makes more historical sense than morally or ideologically conditioned narratives. But it certainly does not help with the understanding of the past when, in depicting it, one persistently adheres to a preconceived outline of history grounded in moral imperatives, in the Enlightenment narrative of progress and emancipation, in an uncritical form of historical materialism, and more recently, in the universal history of postmodernism and globalization.[2]

The post-Mao period saw a serious attempt to rethink history, culture, and tradition. But as scholars have noted, this critical reawakening was enmeshed in a rigid set of terms not exactly conducive to a critical historical consciousness: tradition versus modernization, past versus present, political errors versus enlightenment, east versus west, stagnation versus progress. These terms reflect a strong desire to shake off the nightmare of recent history, particularly the trauma of the Cultural Revolution, and to envisage the possibility of a more meaningful, hopeful future. The self-reflective (*fansi*) movement, wound literature, and the search-for-roots drive in the 1980s were the major manifestations of this historical desire. Meng Yue's analysis of Liu Xinwu's story "Ban zhuren" (The head teacher), a key work in wound literature, points to the prototype of the narrative embodying this desire. In Meng Yue's analysis this story attempts to overcome the pain of the recent past and rushes to find hopes, eliding the complex and hard lessons of history. What is elided indeed constitutes the several decades' worth of contemporary Chinese history: "the massive catastrophe, the barrenness of existential meaning, the ruins of value, as well as the contingency and senselessness in collective and individual life." These dire experiences are quickly "absorbed into a narrative of hope and redemption, so that a story of the inevitable triumph of justice in wresting value from evil" would be a widely accepted scenario and a palatable summing up of historical experience.[3]

To complicate the picture further, Chinese cinema from the early to late 1980s joined the enterprise of historical representation with a stunning array of images that galvanized the population and further intensified the desire to achieve a quick therapeutic treatment of past wounds. As a medium for public dissemination of images and narratives, film seems more effective in this regard. To understand the past by way of cinematic images and narratives is to run into film's particular way of appropriating historical data in the service of entertainment, often in the form of cathartic release of emotion. Consider the historical films made in the 1950s and 1960s, which not only followed preconceived patterns, but also evolved their own cinematic storytelling conventions for producing emotional impact. This genre depicted the history of the communist revolution, with its anguish and suffering, triumph and joy. Strictly speaking it is not "historical." Its narration is predetermined from hindsight, which is a teleological unfolding of the victory of the communist revolution over traditional and regressive forces. Such a narrative is well poised to cultivate uplifting emotion and triumphant sentiment, but in its single-minded and total vision, it suppresses myriad possibilities, dense complexity, ruptures, offbeat paths, and unspeakable, sorrowful moments in history. It is both edification and entertainment, but it does not encourage the audience to confront historical experience.

The films made after the Cultural Revolution were slow to break out of this edification and entertainment mode. Xie Jin's work could be taken as exemplary because it brought the narrative of desire and emotion to a new cinematic extreme. Along with the preconceived moral and ideological patterns mentioned above, Xie Jin succeeded in bringing exuberance of emotion into historical narrative. It is worth some thinking how emotion can become a historical element and add to morally and ideologically conceived history. Critics like Ma Ning, Paul Pickowicz, and Nick Browne consider melodrama as the hallmark of Xie Jin's films.[4] In 1986 a debate was launched in the newspaper *Wenhui bao* (Assembly of writings) in Shanghai about what was generally recognized as the Xie Jin phenomenon. The debate centered mostly on the emotional and melodramatic effect of Xie Jin's films concerning political victimization in the past.[5] Several elements have been identified as contributing to the melodrama's emotional power, which tends to smooth over a rugged historical terrain. The personalization of historical and social forces, the privileged site of the family as the microcosm of historical crisis, the portrayal of a beautiful, piteous woman as the victim of injustice, the clear-cut moral polarization of good and evil, the dramatically inflated scene and sound—all this works to play on the senses and the hearts of the audience and to produce catharsis.

Because Xie Jin's films draw on both Hollywood and Chinese melodrama, the historian Robert Rosenstone's question about the emotional effect of Hollywood historical film speaks directly to our concern. Rosenstone asks, "Does history gain something by becoming emphatic? Does film, in short, add to our understanding of the past by making us feel immediately and deeply about particular historical people, events, and situations?"[6] This question becomes more poignant with regard to Xie Jin's work, for what we have there is not just historical people, nor an audience seeking to understand its distant past, but a people and an audience having to reckon with their own recent, trauma-ridden history. This painful moment in the early to mid-1980s compelled the filmmaker and the audience to look back at the past. But it is not clear whether the gaze backward was also a looking away from that horrendous experience. The dramatized history seemed to contribute to this turning away. It met emotional needs and served an ideological agenda, rather than sharpened the historical consciousness. Paul Pickowicz, another historian wary of melodrama in the guise of history, has noted emotion-cum-ideology in Xie Jin's films. Taking cues from Peter Brooks, Pickowicz points out that the ideological function of melodrama is to respond to a time of historical transition and social crisis. As the previously cohesive values and order are in trouble, the melodrama comes in as a "symbolic act" to appease anxiety and give a semblance of order. Pickowicz's remark on the melodrama of Xie Jin's *Hibiscus Town* (Furong zhen, 1986) reveals a historian's deep suspicion of the genre's value in representing history:

> A deeply rooted system of melodramatic signification is used by Xie Jin to identify the difference between darkness and light and thereby ease the anxieties of a mass audience that has been severely shaken and thrown into profound moral confusion by various cultural calamities. The melodramatic mode provides easy and comforting answers to difficult and complex questions. It offers moral clarity at a time when nothing seems clear. But by personalizing evil, the film leaves the impression that everything would be fine if only the "evil" people were removed from power and replaced by people of "virtue."[7]

Although the melodrama may have strong expressive and emancipatory dimensions in the western tradition, it may also be used to derail a sober, critical sense of history. A critical historical consciousness is necessary for coming to terms with the traumatic memory of the past. To suggest, on the other hand, that film can indeed contribute to a critical historical consciousness, I turn to Tian Zhuangzhuang's *Blue Kite* (Lan fengzheng). The works of the fifth generation are generally imbued with a reflective historical consciousness. *Blue Kite* was made in 1993, when the fifth generation had already grown out its historically reflective vein and ideological agenda, but Tian's film pushes further the critical historical consciousness so remarkable in the earlier phase of the fifth generation. By comparing Xie Jin's melodramatic films with the trauma-ridden *Blue Kite*, we will be able to bring to sharper relief the ways Chinese cinema works in the broad context of rewriting history in order to come to terms with traumatic memory. For this purpose I intend to demonstrate how Xie Jin's films obscure and smooth down a traumatic, complex history, and how Tian Zhuangzhuang's work engages and questions preconceived, cherished historical narratives.

In the Shadow of Trauma

Contemporary Chinese cinema has consistently infused a strong sense of history into film narrative. For Xie Jin and the fifth generation, the historical consciousness derived from the traumas of the Cultural Revolution. Xie Jin's depiction of the revolution and its earlier political precedents on the screen is already a familiar story. The fifth-generation filmmakers were just as interested as Xie Jin in putting the Cultural Revolution on the screen as they were eager to revolt against his mode. But the fifth generation addressed not so much the Cultural Revolution as its dire implications in the culture in general.[8] Although in the early 1990s prominent directors diverged in their artistic pursuits, they continued in the exploration of a crisis-ridden history. Works like *Farewell My Concubine* (Bawang bieji, directed by Chen Kaige, 1992), *Blue Kite* (1993), and *To Live* (Huozhe, directed by Zhang Yimou, 1994) all attest to a concern with a sociopolitical history that culminated in the Cultural Revolution.

Even when they do not deploy the Cultural Revolution as subject matter, works by the fifth generation show a tendency to depict the revolution's disaster at the climatic moment or allude to it as a backdrop. Those works marked by the attempts to "search for roots" in the rural areas and in the cultures of ethnic minority seem to concern another space and another time. *Sacrificed Youth* (Qingchun ji, directed by Zhang Nuanxin, 1985) could be cited as a compelling example. But it is not difficult to sense the Cultural Revolution as a vast background. The Cultural Revolution is the indispensable framework crucial to understanding the works of the fifth-generation filmmakers, whether in the earlier or "post" phase.

The repeated cinematic enactment of the Cultural Revolution implies a compulsion to return to the scene of injury and loss, to dwell on and reexperience the wounds. This psychic feature has been made familiar by studies of traumatic memories of the horrendous historical events in the twentieth century. I invoke the notion of trauma not only to designate a psychic disorder, but a social and cultural situation and a collective pathology. Premised on a metaphor of cultural health and illness, trauma is seen as a blow that destroys one's relation to the cultural fabric of meaning and value. A traumatic occurrence is a profound damage to the psyche and a shattering of a culture's continuity. Traumatic events break the individual's emotional attachment to the community and the cultural matrix of meaning that ties individuals and society together and keeps both afloat. As has been noted by scholars, the power of trauma consists in the belated reexperience of the overwhelming event. It is not so much the original moment as it is the structure of its experience or reception, at a later time, of the traumatic event that is crucial to an analysis of its pathological manifestations in cultural and symbolic expressions. As Cathy Caruth has summed up from numerous case studies: "the event is not assimilated or experienced fully at the time, but only belatedly, in its repeated possession of the one who experiences it. To be traumatized is precisely to be possessed by an image or event." To be possessed by trauma also means being unable to possess or grasp it: the traumatic scenario remains unknown to consciousness or inadequately understood by its victims, although it was registered as unconscious memory. Yet the lack of understanding is not due to the individual's failure in understanding. As the ability to understand history is part of one's cultural equipment, the traumatic symptom needs to be referred to history. If trauma must be understood as a "pathological symptom," says Caruth, "then it is not so much a symptom of the unconscious, as it is a symptom of history. The traumatized, we might say, carry an impossible history within them, or they become themselves the symptom of a history that they cannot entirely possess."[9]

It seems that it is this lack of understanding and the urgent need to take account of the trauma that has driven the filmmakers, time and again, to reenact the traumatic scene. The primal traumatic scene is, of course, the Cultural Revolution, which exerts a tight grip on the mind of fifth-generation directors and uncannily repeats itself. In conceiving the plot of *To Live* Zhang Yimou expressed displeasure about Tian Zhuangzhuang's obsession with historical traumas in *Blue Kite*. Not wanting to dispel the trauma himself, Zhang intended to infuse humor into misery to imply a more "philosophical" outlook of a seasoned survivor. Zhang's film was to suggest a familiar version of Chinese stoicism—a sheer will to live on, even in a subhuman existence, against all odds. One of Zhang's collaborators pointed out, however, that each major segment of *To Live* was invariably geared to culminate in someone's tragic death.[10] In spite of the ingenious addition of comic elements to lighten up the suffocating atmosphere, the work as a whole maintains a sense of constant calamity. The trauma catches up with the humor and overshadows it. Despite his conscious efforts, *To Live* repeats what Zhang wanted to avoid in *Blue Kite*. No amount of humor and farce in the climatic hospital episode (the starving doctor is taken out of the cow hut to help with the delivery of the baby and, having devoured seven water-filled buns, is unable to help the hemorrhaging woman in labor) can brush away the profuse blood, the hysterical rush from room to room, and the end-of-the-world sense of doom. In another film by Zhang, *Shanghai Triad*, shock and trauma are also a hidden motif. Beneath the sleek surface of nightclubs and showgirls lurk intrigues, hidden conspiracies, murders and bloodshed, deception, a scheming gang, and live burial in the dead of night. The country boy acts as a receptacle of these shocks, unwittingly bumping into them again and again. As the camera eye for the unfolding narrative, the boy's constant visual disturbances and shock experiences seem to be a mirror of millions of boys and girls who were enthused and shocked in the maelstrom of historical upheaval and violence.

Out of the Darkness of History: The Xie Jin Approach

In the face of unthinkable horror the cherished schemes of representation can be quite resilient and can still be made to function. The received historical narrative, even in disrepair, can be tapped to cover up the traumatic experience, if only as a makeshift defense against psychic distress. Earlier attempts to represent the Cultural Revolution relied on the conventional narrative to make sense and to redeem the abyssal darkness of history. Xie Jin's films are a compelling example.

One way to get over the trauma and to squeeze a modicum of meaning is to cultivate an unquestioned trust in the "justice" of history. One invests history with moral sensibility and a juridical power to punish the evil and reward the good. An anecdote about Ba Jin may illustrate this view. Ba

Jin clung to the justice of history in adverse circumstances. He was condemned to hard labor and subjected to daily criticism, his works being branded as poisonous weeds. His friend wondered if he was able or whether it was even worthwhile to continue to live. His answer was laconic and confident: "I believe in history."[11] This answer epitomizes a blind trust in a "judicious" history that has been prevalent in the PRC. "History," it assumes, is dozing off at the dead hours of night, but the day will come when it wakes up and opens its eyes, and the grand jury will surely pass down the verdict "not guilty." This article of faith is the premium that Ba Jin paid for his trust in history; it sustained him, as it did many others, through humiliation, torture, and dehumanized existence; it sustained him with hopes of future compensation or payoffs. Sometimes it is precisely in the very nadir of insanity that some sort of meaning is wrenched out: by enduring the plight as a necessary price or "tuition" one atones for one's "guilt." The agent capable of carrying out the just will of history is the communist party. The party is assigned the ability for self-understanding and a readiness for correcting its mistakes. Thus as soon as the party realizes that the course of history is going awry under its erratic policies and ideologies, it will wisely reject the old lines and adopt new policies that promise to put lives of millions back on the right track.

In Xie Jin's work, the party's rectification is built into the narrative logic itself. In the endings of his three most important films about political victimization, *The Legend of Tianyun Mountain* (Tianyunshan chuanqi, 1980), *The Herdsman* (Muma ren, 1982), and *Hibiscus Town*, invariably it is the party's rehabilitation policy that precipitates the turnaround in the victim's fate. *The Legend of Tianyun Mountain* revolves around the conflict between the rehabilitation of a rightist and the attempt to block it. The main female character, Song Wei, tries to restitute Luo Qun, the rightist, her former lover, who was severed from her when he was condemned as counterrevolutionary. Her husband, who had incriminated Luo and who is still in power, tries to suppress Luo's case. The film traces Song's recollection of her traumatic relationship with Luo and her anguished attempt to atone for her "betrayal." But she does not succeed until she appeals to a higher authority, the party secretary of the region. *The Herdsman* portrays how kindly and generously the common folk of a remote region protect the condemned rightist Xu Lingjun, yet it is a decree from the higher authorities that restores him to his normal status and confers on him the legitimate job of elementary school teacher. *Hibiscus Town* repeats this pattern. After all the misery and suffering, the victim Hu Yuyin's plea is "Give me back my man!" In granting her request, the party reunites the broken "family." In these endings a traumatic and senseless history is written off by a balance sheet of right and wrong. Injustice is attributed to the temporary mistakes of the party, but also on different levels in the official hierarchy: the higher the official ranks, the wiser the party. It is only those unrepentant, benighted, local, lower-ranking officials who mess everything up. These endings also have a clear temporal demarcation: they are a cutoff point between darkness and light, a signpost of transition from the unthinkable past toward the secure present, a transcendence from meaninglessness toward the enjoyment of a happy ever after.

In depicting the party's self-corrective adjustment, Xie Jin's historical work also has to confront the deep trauma, which can hardly be erased by a redemptive narrative of rehabilitation. To criticize the ideological excess of the party system is one thing; to cope with the traumatic, deeply personal memory of the past is much more challenging. Xie Jin's melodrama seems to have a way around the trauma. It converts the politicohistorical question of understanding the trauma to an aesthetic matter: the obsessive burden of the past is lightened up by an emotional roller-coaster ride.

Xie Jin's melodramatic film centers on the vicissitude of personal relations and on the dissolution and reunion of the family. For the film critic Dai Jinhua, Xie Jin's work converts a catastrophic and crisis-ridden history into an emotional story of personal happiness and misery.[12] Drawing on the staple of traditional melodrama, it places an aesthetic distance between history and traumatic memory by tirelessly depicting love, sexual union, family, and individual happiness. This melodramatic narrative functions as a safe haven that keeps threats of history at bay.

It is true that all three films mentioned above not only share a similar ending, but also confront deeply traumatic moments. Yet the traumatic moment is quickly glossed over through recourse to the humanistic values capable of saving the characters from sinking into the abyss.[13] In *The Herdsman*, the traumatic moment is turned around by a portrayal of a profound attachment to the grassland, to the vitality of animals, and to meaningful work. In the warm embrace of the local people, in the cradle of the magnificent and nurturing grassland, the political victim Xu Lingjun finds a refuge. He is first seen in a dark stable, down and out as a newly condemned rightist, visually on a par with the beasts of burden. The film dramatizes his intention to commit suicide through a number of quick zoom shots between his gaze and a hanging rope. Suddenly, a horse whinnies and brings him to an awareness of the tenacity of animals' lives. This sense of animal vitality is interwoven with the images, in the subsequent segments, of vast nurturing grassland (this motif is stressed by the lyrics taken from an ancient Chinese folk song–poem). His marriage to Li Xiuzhi, a woman who embodies fertility, productivity, and motherhood, crystallizes his "salvation" from historical disaster. Twice cast out, by his family and the party, Xu Lingjun finds a new home, a new father and mother in the caring herdsmen, and a new self.

The Legend of Tianyun Mountain gets over the traumatic moment through the spectacular self-sacrifice of the female character Feng Qinglan. The rightist Luo Qun is charged with a counterrevolutionary crime and banished in exile. Yet this moment of despair also signals the beginning of his salvation through his union with Feng Qinglan, his female coworker. The film makes a point of depicting their union as both tragic and grandly poetic. Sick with fever in bed, his broken hut penetrated from all sides by a blizzard, Luo is blessed by the arrival of Feng, who has quit her government job to become an underpaid village teacher in order to be with him. Feng's saintly kindness is elevated to a tragic proportion when she pulls Luo in a rundown cart, through the raging blizzard and over the winding, rugged path, to their new home. Their married life provides a safe haven against political storms, yet it is Feng's body that bears the blunt. Beaten by the Red Guards for preserving Luo's manuscripts, Feng is dying of unhealed wounds. As a woman's bodily experience, her sacrifice receives scanty attention in the film; instead, it is depicted as a hidden source for her husband's redemption. The film presents her injured body and impending death as the potential catalyst for political change. Her misery is narrated as something that happened in the past, but also as a necessary sacrifice for a meaningful end. She redeems senseless suffering by telling her story in her letter to Song Wei, in which she anticipates a bright future. Shouldering the curse of history, she "erases" her own traumatic experience.

Hibiscus Town delves much more into the cruelest moments of the Cultural Revolution. Calamities fall fast and furious on the main female character Hu Yuyin. In one scene, Hu wanders to the graveyard in search of her husband, recently put to death by the public security forces. The grotesque and ghoulish shapes looming around, the sound track that plays an absurd, jarring music, the agonized state of the character and the quasi-fantastic rejoinder between a shadowy figure and Hu about whether he is a man or ghost—all this gives the scene a surrealistic and nightmarish aura.

Scenes of this intensity make up the film's heart-wrenching, compelling effect. Although the Cultural Revolution is its backdrop, the film recasts historical forces in interpersonal relationships, displacing the wounds of history into a more manageable narrative of interpersonal conflict. Li Guoxiang, the party secretary, and Wang Qiushe, the local cadre, are portrayed as major culprits who perpetrate a violent political outrage against the tranquil life of the town. They embody evil, and their evil traits are amply depicted. Li Guoxiang deals in political and sexual prostitution, and Wang Qiushe is simply a good-for-nothing ready to jump at any opportunity for selfish gain. By identifying and portraying these "evil" characters as responsible for catastrophe, the film turns away from history even when it strives to engage it. It becomes a story of how the evil characters persecute innocent victims, and how the victims are eventually vindicated by a retributive history.

By blaming the catastrophic history on certain "wicked" individuals, the film on the other hand invokes humanistic values embodied by the good characters. This thins out historical complexity into a clear-cut drama of good and evil. It is as if armed with notions such as beauty, kindness, love, human sympathy, and the intrinsic goodness of human nature, one is able to survive the worst and see the light at the end of the tunnel. This set of notions is often coupled with the popular Chinese belief in the harmony of the family, cozy and stable daily living, economic prosperity, affective attachment to the community (the masses in the contemporary sense), and continuity through generations. These beliefs indeed are the mental support that sustains victims, yet by calling forth a heroics of victimhood in adverse circumstances, we console ourselves by turning away from a history where precisely heroic virtues were of little use, where we are as much victims as victimizers.

Humanistic values are best dramatized by love and marriage between the rightist Qin Shutian and Hu Yuyin, the newly condemned "bourgeois element." Both are condemned to a wretched life of sweeping the streets as punishment. Yet it is precisely here that a silver lining appears. Their "romance" is a story of quasi-romantic love in adversity. Gu Yanshan, the "good" official criticized during the Cultural Revolution, proclaims as he presides over their secret wedding that it is the streets and a pair of brooms that served as their matchmaker, not him. This remark sums up the development of their relationship from love to marriage, dramatized in the film by several close-ups of the brooms touching or nestling, followed by shots of the two exchanging gazes, and finally of physical intimacy in bed.

The film sets up a contrast between the victims' genuine, free love and political-sexual prostitution between Li Guoxiang and Wang Qiushe. Li uses her position to get sexual favors from Wang, while he licks her boots in order to get political advantages. The discovery of the "dirty" clandestine affair between the couple (the target of Qin's pranks) also strongly affirms Qin and Hu's mutual affection. Their love is presented as a force that redeems other values discredited by the Cultural Revolution. The scenes of their secret family life (the restoration of the broken family), of eating the long-missed rice bean curd (anticipating the new economic policy), their marriage presided over by Gu Yanshan (restoration by the right leader), and the birth of a boy all emphasize the healing power of their love.

The most emblematic, hence problematic, instance of redeeming history through humanistic value is the intensely lyrical depiction of the couple's street life as sweepers. Immersed in a misty, bluish light, their hard and degrading labor is turned into a ritual of romance and courtship. In one scene Qin Shutian turns the debasing drudgery of street sweeping into a graceful dance. With a demonstration, Qin teaches Hu how to dance while wielding the broom, and Hu, unwilling at first, attempts to swerve gracefully. The film presents this act as a ritual by setting it apart from the narrative flow as a habitual occurrence. Accompanied by melodious music, the act celebrates the triumph of beauty against darkness. One might well characterize this as a sugar-coating of history's bitter pills.

The ending of the film has been praised for its cautious, skeptical tone. Here Wang Qiushe, gone mad from vicissitudes of fortune, keeps shouting the slogan "Another movement!" Whether this is a warning or an assurance hinges on the interpretation of the last sequence of shots. A cut from Wang reveals the newly united family, with Qin in the middle of the frame, accompanied by his wife and son. Moreover, the family shot emerges out of the shots of the masses, who watch as the crazy man walks out of the frame. All stand vigilant and attentive, as if on guard against another disaster. This seems more of an assurance than warning in the context of the previous narrative episode. The episode begins with Qin Shutian's return home; he has been released from prison and rehabilitated. As he runs into the party secretary, Li Guoxiang, he speaks with more authority and confidence, as he warns her against meddling with ordinary people's lives. The shots of his actual arrival in the village are breezy, colorful, and sprightly, set in the springtime against a blooming field. The family reunion is tearful and emotional. In light of this sequence, the final series of shots presents the image of the newly united family as a bulwark of stability and future happiness, enfolded in a protective community of the now sober-minded masses. Against this newly acquired strength, Wang's shouts for another Cultural Revolution appear to sound "crazy." This assurance of reborn social order invokes the consoling logic, already rehearsed in the practice of recalling the past and savoring the happiness of the present (*Yiku sitian*). The point is now that the past is past, we should go on to appreciate our present safety and prosperity and never let the past repeat itself.

Blue Kite: Tarrying with Trauma

Rather than gloss over the trauma with a redemptive narrative and a satisfying sense of emotional release, the historically conscious films by the fifth generation question the cherished ways of interpreting the past. In this regard Tian Zhuangzhuang's *Blue Kite* is exemplary. Tian's approach to history attends to those private, unsettled, unabsorbed experiences. This does not mean that collective memory is not important, but rather that the collective experience at its traumatic core takes the form of individual memory. Public remembrance, in taking stock of a political event like the Cultural Revolution, tends to pass over private memories of bodily suffering and mental anguish. Although public remembrance frequently congeals into generally accepted discursive forms under the rubric of historical knowledge, private memory remains obstinately testimonial and can hardly be reduced to a formula. In the testimony a first-person narrator recalls bits and pieces of impressions that affected him or her as an eyewitness to an event. By calling forth memory fragments, by exploring the unresolved tensions between the import of the event and the witness's capacity to grasp it, the testimony gives due weight to the singularity of traumatic shocks. Surely testimonial memory cannot be a reliable "historical" account of the Cultural Revolution. Yet it is precisely private memory's settled and unsettling quality that makes it more profoundly historical than historical knowledge. Comprehensive understandings of history that serve to tame the flux of traumatic experience have been far too plentiful. Testimonial memory, on the other hand, encourages a skepticism that has the potential to keep historical knowledge unstable and uncertain, so that one can live "on edge" against the all-too-hasty ordering of history.[14] It is through the exposition of the unhealed wounds, unsolved mysteries, and unresolved tensions in the individual's relation to history that the historically sensitive films of the fifth generation register the trauma of Chinese culture and history. Through its questioning and predicament, they undercut the hasty attempt to tell a reassuring, total history of the Cultural Revolution and of trauma in modern China.

In his interview with the independent filmmaker Wu Wenguang, Tian Zhuangzhuang recalled the childhood experience of bewilderment and searching that partially motivated him to make *Blue Kite*. Tian's was a filmmaker's family: before the Cultural Revolution, his father was the director of the Beijing Film Studio. His happy and carefree childhood gave way to misery and disillusionment at the age of fourteen, when his parents were condemned as bad elements by the Red Guards and he was forced to shout slogans against them at public gatherings. Pushed to the margins of society, Tian began to suspect that grown-ups had been building a false atmosphere all along and that the world was unreal. He learned to see through that falseness to the harsh and conflict-ridden reality of Mao's China. Obviously these earlier unsettled perceptions, as impressions of "witnessing," creep into the conception of *Blue Kite*. The film offers the perspective of a keen yet baffled observer trying to get at the bottom of things and situations.[15]

Nowhere is this perception more evident in the narrator's position, which contrasts sharply with that of Xie Jin. Xie Jin's three films, discussed above, rely on an omniscient narrative position; the camera mostly stands outside the narrative, never allied with the viewpoint of a character to any significant degree. This enunciative position in Xie Jin's films tells something about a bygone past. It assumes the stance of a survivor on this side of the abyss, looking back at the past with a cold sweat, yet confident of his present security. The narrator of *Blue Kite* does not boast such a déjà vu, and still remains hostage to history. The past weighs heavily on his narration and refuses to yield to a meaningful order. The film's highly enigmatic, allegorical beginning suggests the haunting, obsessive presence of the past and the difficulty of surveying and recalling history. The first image that appears on the screen is a blue kite, fluttering, solitary, in the wind. Then comes the title, handwritten with a quaint simplicity. The shape of the kite is hardly visible at first, and the background is a bare space awash in white, without any trace of a definable object. The wistful music and the singing of a crow song (an ominous song constantly sung by the child) evoke a sense of indefinable loss and yearning. The memory of a past life, this series of images seems to suggest metaphorically, is obscured in the outline and feebly fluttering in the wind, barely visible in the void of time. Then, in the voice-over, an adolescent narrator begins to mumble his life story. He speaks in a strong nasal tone, as if suffering from a bad cold. Ominously, he begins his life story in a neighborhood called "Dry Well Lane," in which nobody has ever found water. The inauspicious and enigmatic beginning highlights the awkwardness and difficulty of recalling the past.

In the film, the adolescent narrator/character does not have a superior perception and is constantly groping as he "witnesses" the victims' lives around him. A sustained bewilderment at incomprehensible, mysterious happenings of the adult world marks the unfolding of the narrative through his vision. The same puzzlement and confrontation with traumatic shocks also informs or disfigures the adult experience.

The emphasis on shocks as historical experience may account for the film's narrative structure, which corresponds to the major periods in contemporary Chinese history. Although the film, as Tian Zhuangzhuang intended, is very much about the Cultural Revolution, the episode of the Red Guards' rampage comes only at the end of a long string of political campaigns. Yet the film by no means gives short shrift to the revolution. The pre–Cultural Revolution campaigns are depicted as surging with an unstoppable momentum toward a disastrous apex in the 1960s. From the viewpoint of an individual caught in these sometimes euphoric, often traumatic, campaigns, the experience is almost indistinguishable from, if not more sinister than, the final violent rampage and riots. Thus, to depict the individual surviving one shock after another is tantamount to describing the Cultural Revolution. And to understand the fate of the characters is to grasp a human condition embedded in a period of contemporary Chinese history that came to catastrophic proportions in the Cultural Revolution. This narrative strategy is also used by other directors of the fifth generation, with less intensity, in Zhang Yimou's *To Live* and Chen Kaige's *Farewell My Concubine*, whose major time span also traverses roughly the same period of historical upheaval.

Blue Kite dwells on traumatic experience without trying to dissolve it. A comparison with Xie Jin's film again may make this clear. In Xie Jin's films the devastation of history is kept out of the safe haven of the family, the atrocity warded off or countered by human sympathy, love, and sexual union, political oppression mitigated by a caring community of the folk, the stigma lifted by the final act of rehabilitation. *Blue Kite* also casts the massive sweep of history in a melodramatic family narrative. But it departs drastically from the Xie Jin mode. Polemically *Blue Kite* depicts how families, everyday pleasure, marriage, sexual union, mundane daily living—staples of melodrama—are steadily ravaged by historical events. The film's three components, entitled "Father," "Uncle," and "Stepfather," depict three failed attempts to establish and sustain a family. The main female character, Chen Shujuan, marries three times, yet all these are violently cut short—in the death of a "father" and violent separation. *Blue Kite* offers numerous family scenes: weddings, taking care of children, visiting, cooking, eating, talking, gathering, celebrating, and so on. But in contrast to the Xie Jin mode, a family dinner around the table is frequently poisoned by conversations about politics or news of victimization and campaigns, or simply disrupted by sharp disagreement over party policy among family members.

Xie Jin's films suggest that a traumatic history can be turned into a bittersweet drama and that historical experience can be capsulated in a melodramatic mode. *Blue Kite* seems to point to the contrary: a melodrama is untellable and unsustainable in the face of ceaseless historical upheavals. The melodramatic motifs of everyday living and pleasure, affection, family, sexual relations, and so on are indeed the tenacious and lingering undercurrent of the narrative. They represent a strong need for spatial and temporal anchoring in everyday life against a world of sudden calamity and destruction, a desire for survival, for moderate, decent earthly existence beneath the blinding ideological storms. (In the film, blinding is a striking metaphor for history's overwhelming force, as in the increasing blindness of Chen Shusheng.) Yet it is precisely this desire, and the melo-dramatic narrative as a vehicle of this desire, that are constantly disrupted, aborted, truncated, and deconstructed. At an ominous moment of the storm looming in the horizon, a flood of diffuse sunlight dazzles Chen Shusheng. The film immediately cuts away to a play-within-a-play scene to highlight the illusion of a crisis-proof melodrama. In a rehearsal, Zhu Ying, the army actress, plays the role of a peasant woman in a drama in which, after the murder of her father by a landlord, her husband flees and vows to take revenge. She urges her son to wait patiently for the return of his fa-ther. This narrative epitomizes the revolutionary melodrama of the Chi-nese revolution. The plotline is typical: the murder of a peasant by the bloodsucking landlord, the fleeing of the peasant's son to the revolutionary army, the finale of the soldier's return and revenge, and the triumphant closure in the reckoning of the "debt of blood." Ironically, the rehearsal in the film stops at the moment when the peasant woman says, hoping against hope, that a long wait for the father's return is worthwhile, leaving the future hanging in the air. This rehearsal piece allegorically rehearses what will be the norm in the film. The narrative of melodramatic fulfill-ment is cut short, and the wait is endless: He who flees never comes back, the parted do not unite, the wrong is not righted, the wedded will separate, and the death will go unavenged. The case of Zhu Ying is most acute and ironic. Her "future" union with her fiancé Shusheng is hopeless, because she is jailed for refusing to give in to her superior's sexual advances; yet she is unexpectedly released right at the beginning of the Cultural Revolution.

The film establishes quite early that the narrator's family and others have to live under constant threat, under unexpected shocks. The first mar-riage, supposedly a happy event, is cast in deep shadows. In it, the new couple, Lin Shaolong and Chen Shujuan, move into their new apartment with the help of their colleagues. Although the mood is festive, mourning music suddenly begins to play offscreen, and the guests stand silent, lis-tening to the news broadcast of Joseph Stalin's death. With national mourning for the soviet leader, the political realm intrudes into the private domain: the wedding date is postponed, as is Tietou's (the narrator's) birth. Despite a comic touch in the old lady's question about Big Lin (Stalin) and the narrator's complaint of his belated birth, the film stresses the enigmatic and haphazard nature of ordinary people's lives constantly threatened and disrupted by an intrusive history.

As the film proceeds, the lives of the characters are increasingly threatened and enigmatic. The film refrains from locating the source of political victimization: no villain embodies evil, no erratic party policy can be identified, no cause for redress is found. What confronts the characters is some incomprehensible, bewildering force working against everybody's well-being and chronically inflicting pain and death. Reality is mystery, and history is something to be deciphered. In this sense, the film unsettles historical discourses that seek to grasp decades of traumatic history with a hasty diagnosis. It represents a radical shift from the overt political criticism of the mistakes of Maoism to an existential exploration of the human experience under an invisible, opaque authoritarian order.

Unlike Xie Jin's moral clarity, which elicits an equally clear-cut response to its melodramatic portrayal of suffering, *Blue Kite* depicts the political event as a series of enigmas and shocks. Interpreting party policy and political messages is a constant necessity for survival. In the domestic setting, over the dinner table, discussion and haggling over how to interpret and react to the events frequently occurs. Mrs. Lan, the business owner who struggles to change her degraded status, is at a loss what to make of her son's letter, which wonders why one's merit can never change one's negative political background. Does the party then mean what it says when it insists on one's good behavior? The film emphasizes the bewilderment by having Mrs. Lan and Lin Shaolong puzzle over the letter, struggling to fathom its ominous import.

Lin Shaolong's puzzlement and anxiety at the outset of the Antirightist Campaign are depicted through a series of tension-ridden mise-en-scènes with psychic depths, and through unusual shooting angles. The scene begins in the morning, when Lin is seen squatting outside his room in the courtyard; the air is tense with the blaring of the broadcast about someone who has revealed his "true color" in criticizing the party. The blaring loudspeaker is a favorite prop to indicate the charged atmosphere of the Cultural Revolution, as in *To Live* or *Farewell My Concubine*. But here it is more psychological than circumstantial. Close-ups reveal the puzzled expression of Lin Shaolong. In the next shot, his wife is seen inside the room, looking with anxiety from an oblique angle toward the door. Looking with her, we see Lin's bending back as if he is listening alertly and anxiously. The shot frames his back between both sides of the door frame, as if he were being squeezed, making his image off-center and tightly hemmed in.

The film indicates the enigmatic nature of the campaigns through an ecliptic crosscutting technique that shows only bits and pieces of an extended event, not trying to capture the whole. To show the branding of rightists during the Antirightist Campaign, for example, the film cuts quickly between disparate scenes of meetings and condemnations. In this "slow" film, this technique makes things happen too quickly to catch and thus adds significantly to the sense of bedazzlement. Chen Shusheng, who suffers from worsening eyesight as the campaign escalates, seems to be an ironic figure for this rapid bedazzlement. His eye problem starts on the eve of the Antirightist Campaign, during which a blinding light symbolically bedazzles him as he emerges outside from a dimly lit room. Yet the worse his eyesight becomes, the sharper his criticism of the political campaigns. Fearing he may soon go blind, he travels to a remote prison to see his fiancée, Zhu Ying, who responds to his anxiety by stating that it matters little if one can or cannot see, as if to imply that political victims are already psychologically blinded by shocks and outrages.

The way Lin Shaolong is condemned a rightist also points to the haphazard and random nature of history. This most absurd and grotesque episode begins when the staff of the library, Lin's workplace, convenes and the director asks whether they should pick one more rightist, or they may fail to fill the quota. There is dead silence for an agonized stretch of time. Then Lin leisurely gets up, opens the door and goes to the men's room. The next shot reveals his hand opening the door, with the sound of a toilet flushing offscreen. The door's narrow opening reveals two long rows of heads at both sides of a long table and all eyes staring at him, the toilet still flushing and the sound grating on the nerves. It is clear that something horrible is happening. Lin steps inside, looks are exchanged; the look and the rows of heads seem fraught with significance, yet painfully indecipherable. What has happened while Lin was in the restroom seems completely beyond his comprehension and remains a poignant mystery for the viewer. He has, of course, been condemned as a rightist. If he had not chosen that moment to go away, it might not have been him. The absurdity of history consists in the futility of asking "Why me?" This Kafkaesque incident recalls Milan Kundera's principle of writing history. In his novel *The Joke*, the character Ludvic sees all his friends and colleagues vote, with perfect ease, for his expulsion from the university and hence his ruin. He is certain that they would do the same for his hanging. For Kundera, this "revelatory, existential" moment offers Ludvic the insight that man should be defined as "an animal capable of consigning his neighbor to death."[16] In *Blue Kite*, as in Kundera, it is not the social, political, or even moral-emotional narration of history, but history at its most existential, enigmatic, and traumatic core that flashes a profoundly historical truth.

The film's ending is most revealing in its striking contrast with *Hibiscus Town* in temporal sequence. In *Hibiscus Town*, the historical sequence is marked by a series of dates 1963, 1965, and 1979. These road signs of political periods signify a redemptive historical progression, a forward movement of increasing enlightenment and self-adjustment. Led by the self-corrective party, the nation is steadily climbing back from the historical abyss. By this logic the narrative must end in the post–Cultural Revolution period, known as the New Period (*Xin shiqi*), with all its rehabilitation of past wrongs and its forward-looking gaze. Dai Jinhua rightly remarks that Xie Jin's films are always narrated in the present perfect tense, implying a visit of the living to the dead and yielding therapeutically an affirmative sense of the validity of the present and an anticipation of better things to come.[16] In contrast, *Blue Kite* eschews this reassuring pattern of political periodization. In its abrupt ending, Tietou lies flat on the ground, bruised and wounded all over, gazing at the broken kite dangling in the tree branches. His voice-over narrates the destruction of his makeshift family: his stepfather's death and his mother's imprisonment. His announcement of the date of death, "September 7, 1968," exudes a deadly finality and singularity, and sounds both full and hollow. Time here becomes a full stop or simply a bleeding wound (visually analogous to the wounded boy lying on the ground gazing up at the broken kite). This moment is not measured by a new value-laden mark replacing a previous mistaken one, by an anticipation of purposeful progression. The temporal flow has suddenly frozen into a standstill, a moment of unspeakable shock that does not connect with any other moment. The narrative comes to a screeching halt in the Cultural Revolution, right in the midst of its most catastrophic events. It turns the revolution into a traumatic encounter with death and trauma. This "ending" does not offer a cathartic wrap-up but rather poses challenging questions for the audience to ponder. The film begins with the image of the blue kite and the nursery song of the old crow and ends with the same song accompanying the torn kite stuck in the tree branches. History seems to come full circle. The narrator, Tietou, comes all the way from his past, only to gaze at a gaping, bleeding wound, the Cultural Revolution.

Blue Kite presents the Cultural Revolution and other political events as historical trauma. The film implies a new historical consciousness in representing traumatic history. To know the present one needs to remember the past. Xie Jin's work offers a way of connecting with the painful past by retrieving redemptive values so that the audience can get on with life, strengthened and reassured. Through melodrama it offers a form of memory that forgets more than it remembers. In heralding the new era, it turns away from the trauma of the past and manages to write, blithely and quickly, a clean bill of health. By confronting the trauma of political oppression, *Blue Kite* offers a more critical way of understanding our relation to the past. It treats the historical wounds not as something we have left behind and recovered from in our craze to build a modern and postmodern society. It treats them as something still corroding the supposedly healthy fabric of contemporary Chinese culture, something troubling our narrative and meaning-making schemes, something that may make an uncanny, cyclical comeback. The film makes it difficult to draw a clear line between past and present. And in contemporary China, those eager to draw the line may well be engaged in a political business of forgetting. *Blue Kite* does not hasten to heal the wounds or prescribe a quick therapy. It refuses to let go of the singular, complex individual experience of wounds and shocks. Confronting the wounds is a sobering way of remembering the Cultural Revolution and other historical events, and hence a way of better understanding ourselves. It constitutes an antidote to the self-congratulatory assumption that we are finally done with pains and traumas of the past.

6

From Historical Narrative
to the World of Prose

The comparison between the fourth and fifth generations reveals the divergence between dramatization of history and critical historical consciousness. This split parallels another divergence: the rise of the personal essay and the decline of the epic-style novel in the 1990s. In this chapter I would treat this generic shift in terms of a structure of feeling I venture to call *essayistic*. A comparison between the philosophical-historical agenda of the novel and the essay may illustrate this shift. The novel of revolutionary realism has been the literary paradigm of historical narrative in modern China. For many decades this genre served as an ideological apparatus and literary medium for providing coherent temporal structures linking past, present, and future. The realist novel's underlying assumption is historical in the sense described by Georg Lukács, who construed the historical novel as a narrative depicting conscious human activity steering the temporal direction of society and human existence.[1] The realist novel in modern China represents a strenuous but eventually triumphant realization of the harmony of utopian ideals and social reality.[2] The flourishing of the personal essay in recent decades, however, indicates the turn of literature from the epic coherence of ideals and experience to dispersed and fragmented sensual pleasures and sheer appreciation of images or anecdotes. Enjoyment and display of private and random memory have replaced coherent history writing. A sign of retreat from historical consciousness, the essay, or rather the "essayistic structure of feeling," responds lightheartedly to the

advent of consumer culture. It satisfies the modest needs of the urban consumer whose sensibility is becoming "essayistic" and everyday, preoccupied
with the most immediate, intimate, and quotidian matters. It envisages a
life form that is life cut off from history, but not life of history. I would
consider the shift from the historical narrative inherent in the novel to the
essayistic structure of feeling epitomized by the essay. This shift also parallels the changing role of the public intellectual. I will take a look back at
Eileen Chang's thinking on the essay and trace the link between the modern essay and the rise of urban consumer culture. Then, through an analysis of Wang Anyi's novella *The Story of Our Uncle* (Shushu de gushi), I
demonstrate how the retreat from historical consciousness to the essayistic
structure of feeling is dramatized as well as subject to an immanent critique
by Wang's groping, explorative essay/fiction. The career of the main character, Uncle, illustrates the waning of historical consciousness. Recalling
Heller's distinction between life in history and life of history in Chapter 4,
I seek to understand the degrees of engagement with history in generic
mutations. My contention is that the shift from historical consciousness to
the essayistic is ambivalent in its political implications. The pursuit of the
essayistic signals a space of freedom from the constraints of the grand narrative, but in its excessive obsession with the quotidian, the fragmentary,
and the personal, it also contributes to the withering of critical historical
consciousness in contemporary China.

The Essay and the Novel

The essay as a cultural form can be grasped in its relation to the
novel. In twentieth-century China, the novel in the epic, realist mode had
been the dominant form of literature and a pivotal ideological apparatus—
probably up to the mid-1980s. The novel of socialist realism is both epic
and historical. Its epic characteristics lie in the historical scope and teleology, the engagement with social and political issues, the intertwining of the
individual's fate with collective projects, the aesthetics of the exemplary
hero, and the striving for transcendence within everyday immanence. The
novel in the Mao era and in the post–Cultural Revolution period, often
dubbed the New Period, strives to achieve an imaginary unity of transcendent ideals and quotidian reality. It depicts a universe in which the world

and the self "never become permanent strangers to one another" and the individual's growth is of one piece with communal destiny.[3] It is true that the 1980s saw the emphatic upsurge of interest in the subjectivity of the autonomous individual, but far from the atomistic individual of appetitive self-interest and self-pleasure, the main fictional character was still figured as the agent of history. For all its seeming revolt against the dominant mode, the image of the newly awakened modern self in the fiction of the New Period goes hand in hand with the sociohistorical process of socialist modernization, fictional characters serving as protagonists of this new narrative. Thus, Fredric Jameson's concept of national allegory, in which the individual's fate tells a larger story of collective destiny, can apply equally well to the realist novel of the Mao era as well as those written in the reform era.[4]

If this view of the novel sounds anachronistic to contemporary China, it remains a useful reminder of the striven-for unity of revolutionary ideals and social reality, of theory and practice. This projected unity is a prominent tenet in the utopian legacy of Marxism and is probably the strongest antidote against the dissolution of history into simulacra. As a literary medium that strives for this unity, the Chinese realist novel features a mythical and epic structure in which dream and history, individual and collective become one. The realist novel is supposed to be more than a text you read, curled up on your couch in a snowy winter night in solitary comfort. It is ideological, educational, edifying, its grand narrative projecting material praxis. It aims to instigate you to go out into the streets or impoverished villages and get organized with other fellow humans to change the status quo and make history.

The rise of the essay in contemporary China is a sign that the novel in the epic mode has become an endangered species. This is not merely a problem of genre, nor am I suggesting that readers are flocking to essays and abandoning novels. My point is that the novel as a medium of envisioning the totality of social life and registering experiences of temporality is giving way to the essay, or more broadly to the essayistic structure of sensibility. I play with the idea of the essayistic in order to refer to the essay as a canonical, identifiable textual form as well as those discursive moments in literary texts embodying an "essayistic" quality or structure of feeling. This emotional structure consorts with the everyday sensibility of a city

dweller and consumer. This new form of writing and sensibility is inseparable from the new literary culture of an emergent consumer society.

The Hegelian Marxist perspective is helpful here for understanding
the shift from the novel to the essay. For Hegel art is necessary because it
strives for a seamless, organic apotheosis of transcendent spirit and mundane reality. This view, although historical, can lead to two contradictory
conclusions. Art is historical because it is a stage on the journey of human
self-consciousness to its realization in social institutions. As art evolves as
historically transitory forms of this reflective consciousness, the movement
of history leads to the abolition of certain forms of art and even to the demise of art altogether. On this account the novel would be a casualty of
historical movement of the consciousness.[5] For Hegel art becomes problematic and obsolete because the "world of prose" has attained the empirical form erstwhile aspired to by ideal driven art. In the world of prose, human self-consciousness has realized itself in the unfolding of social agenda
and political praxis, exemplified by the institutions of the modern nation-
state. The polity embodied by the modern state is for Hegel the epitome of
theory put into practice, a real image of realized art. As Lukács puts it, "art
becomes problematic precisely because reality has become non-problem-
atic."[6]

Lukács, however, draws a contrary lesson from this historical or more
precisely the end-of-history, end-of-art thesis. Taking issue with Hegel's
view of art as "aestheticized" body politic, he argues that the problem of
the novel is a mirror image of a world gone out of joint. In modern times
the novel is still alive and effective, as the impulse of art is still refreshing
and pressing. The novel is aesthetically and epistemologically vital not because the established reality has achieved what art, driven by self-consciousness, can only dream of. On the contrary, the novel is a desperate attempt to patch up a broken reality and to inject little doses of meaning
into a world emptied of spontaneous and totalizable significance. Therein
lies its irony, the irony of dreaming the perfection of the world while
knowing acutely the impossibility of perfection.

Interestingly, Lukács's insight into the ironic, self-reflexive nature of
the novel provides a glimpse, not into the novel but into the inner structure of the essay. In the Chinese realist novel, to be sure, the historical totality of communist utopia emerging out of a degenerate reality is a shining symbol of inspiration, bearing a superficial resemblance to the

Hegelian realization of human self-consciousness in the nation-state. But the faith in the final triumph of communist utopia and the attainment of a fully emancipated society is presumed by the novelistic discourse as law-like, and hence realistic and inevitable. Thus the decline of the novel, the novel in the epic mode, can be read as the decline of the grand Marxist narrative endowed with historical teleology. In contrast, the rise of the essay harbingers a more fragmentary, disjoint, and individualistic form of signifying practice that is springing up in the cracks of the mighty narrative and pointing to a world out of joint.

The world out of joint offers a compelling image of today's China going commercialized, globalized, and fragmented in all aspects of life. The phrase "out of joint" denotes the explosive vitality as well as disorienting chaos, the drama and trauma, of the Chinese scene unfolding in the last two decades. To grasp China as a vast marketplace, a rising consumer society, an emergent culture of mass media and spectacle, I refer the reader to numerous reports by journalists, economists, and essays written by writers who have recently turned to the personal essay as a forum. Literature, as a historical vision and ideological medium, is evidently losing ground. Like many other spheres of culture, it has become commodified and entered the marketplace, being packaged into one more item in the mass media and entertainment industry. This altered social context is crucial to understanding the essay as a literary form and a cultural medium of expression. But this link between the culture of commodity and the essayistic mode of writing is not a brand-new phenomenon.

To take a historical perspective, we may turn to the earlier period in modern literary history. Eileen Chang's essays and her reflection on the essay offer an interesting instance of the marriage between essay and urban culture in the 1940s. This marriage finds its contemporary manifestations in the work of Wang Anyi. An analysis of Eileen Chang's thinking on the essay will help us understand Wang's work, which has pushed Chang's literary imagination in a new direction. Eileen Chang's views give the essay a clear shape as it emerged in conjunction with urban and consumer culture. Wang Anyi's essays and especially the essayistic moments in her fiction mark the return of this consumer-oriented genre under new historical circumstances.

Eileen Chang and the Essay in the Urban Setting

The story and essay writer Eileen Chang can be identified as one source for Wang Anyi's work. Although Eileen Chang wrote fictions of urban life set in Shanghai and Hong Kong in a mixture of traditional and modernist styles, her writing is a departure from the grand narrative of the May Fourth Enlightenment and revolution in modern Chinese literature. Her stories relish the irrelevancies, minor manias, trivia, and anxieties of the modern individual adrift in random episodes of urban existence. The intriguing depiction of the narrow romance and personality of the petty urbanites, *xiaoshimin,* is her forte and attraction. The prose of life in a squeezed and congested milieu is not only the hallmark of her fiction, but also constitutes the major themes of her essays. Although her essays correspond to and illuminate her fiction, her thoughts on essay writing serve to highlight the aesthetic quality of the essayistic in modern Chinese literature.

Eileen Chang's essay collection *Floating Words* (Liu yan) is a compelling example of the essay as it emerged in China's urban culture. In the opening essay entitled "The Child Utters His Words Without Constraints" (Tongyan wuji), she equates her essays to the chatty, whimsical, and willful airing of pent-up feelings whenever and wherever she can, like an unrestrained child. Writers like her, she says, have little to do with earthquaking, epoch-making historical events and should also drop the dream of immortality characteristic of the self-portrayal of best-selling autobiographies. The satisfaction and salvation for a writer are writing "bits and pieces about matters concerning oneself."[7] The matters concerning the self, as Chang continues, include money, dress, eating, important personages and their grotesque undersides, and family relations. Within a few pages of this first essay we have a range of sundry themes expressing interest in consumer habit, survival in the city, and personal and social relations in an increasingly compartmentalized urban culture. Running down the table of contents of Chang's essay collection, we have trouble classifying what the essays focus on, except to say that they essay opinions and play with perceptions and feelings of just about anything in city life. They touch on whatever flickers through the mind, passes into view, appeals to the senses—any stereotypical or routine scenes or acts in the urban setting. To give a taste of their randomness and miscellany, we encounter short pieces about living in an apartment, beating up people, private and intimate words, shallow impressions about art, changing dresses, woman, rain, umbrellas, even the routine act of going upstairs.

Although it is surely impossible to box these essays into a general category and extract from them a unifying principle, Eileen Chang points beyond this charmed collection of casual essays to the grand historical narrative and thus provides a reference point for what the essay refuses to do. If it is unclear what the essay is, Chang shows what it is not. She sees the essay in its withdrawal from and rejection of historical discourse and in its all-consuming absorption in the mundane, fragmented, individualized urban scenes. The nature of the essay seems to lie in its irrelevance to history as a literary principle:

> I have no desire to write history, nor am I qualified to make judgement on the historian's perceptions. But privately I hope they would say more things that are irrelevant. Reality as such is not systematic; it is like seven or eight chatterboxes sounding simultaneously, creating confusion. But amidst this incomprehensible sound and fury there occur moments of illumination, poignant and bright, enabling us to hear the tune and understand a bit, only to be swallowed up by the thickening darkness. Painters, writers, and composers connect these chancy, fragmented discoveries and create artistic wholes. (*Liuyan*, 41)

As a writer Chang does not believe in artistic perfection. She creates "imperfect" and flawed characters in her fiction, as she repeatedly claims. In her essays she holds it important to write about irrelevancies, for, as she proclaims, all life's charms are to be found in the irrelevancies (*Liuyan*, 42).

Eileen Chang's views on the essay reflect certain aspects of Chinese modernity that provide a condition of possibility for the essay to emerge as a prominent cultural medium. The essay for her is a writing practice that militates against the historically oriented and politically charged literature, the teleological historical narrative, and the monumental work of art. Formally, the essay is random, self-contradictory, narrowly expressive, and therapeutic. Eileen Chang's essays are a radical departure from Lu Xun's *zawen* (the occasional essay of mélange). Despite its similarly disjoint, personal, and casual form, the *zawen* à la Lu Xun is polemic, militant, acid, socially and political engaged. It seizes on the small and transitory, but its gaze shoots past them to the culturally and historically significant. This engaged ethos puts the *zawen* in a close lineage with the didactic tradition of May Fourth literature aimed at raising readers' consciousness or jolting them out of the half-sleep of tradition and convention. Eileen Chang's essays, by contrast, were pitched perfectly at the leisurely tone of the feuilleton, or literary supplement section (*Fukan*), of newspaper and leisure magazines.[8] They cater to the consumer's need for entertainment and even pander to his or her modest, if not philistine, literary sensibility, providing a small measure of satisfaction to demands of the urbanites for a little self-image and self-recognition. The rise of consumer mentality, urban culture, and the new role of the writer as a professional thrust to prominence the values of entertainment, charm, taste, performance, charisma, and glamor—values of urban culture with a good appetite for entertainment, images, and spectacle. This emergent sociohistorical context was marginalized by the dominant political ideology and historical movement in the decades after Eileen Chang's short-lived popularity.

In the 1990s, and in Wang Anyi's work, urban, commercial culture reemerged with a vengeance. The fate of the essay or the aesthetic quality of the essayistic cannot be understood without considering the revival of urban and consumer culture and its increasing detachment from historical consciousness.

The City Without a Story

Wang Anyi's work in the 1990s shows how deeply urban commercial culture has penetrated and transformed literature. The novel in the epic mode depends on a preconceived story pattern that delivers ideological and historical convictions about temporal perceptions of past, present, and future. One symptom of the shift from the novel to the essay is the acute sense of lack of story, the sense that the archetypal stories that writers used to rely on to generate their narratives are no longer convincing. For Wang the dearth of stories is directly linked to fragmented life in the urban milieu. The title of one of her essays on literature, "The City Has No Story to Tell" (Chengshi wu gushi), highlights the disappearance of sharable, communicable narratives in the city's amorphous atmosphere and in the anonymous urban crowd. This essay clearly describes the sociological transformations that have given rise to the generic shift from story to nonstory, or from narrative fiction to the essayistic mode. In it Wang sets up a contrast between village community and urban social organization. The tightly knit rural communities, such as villages and small towns, are the nurturing ground for stories. As the social relations are largely those of family, kinship, or clan, human contact and communication are more intimate and primarily face to face. Individuals act out their life stories in accordance with a pregiven trajectory and within a received social network of work, authority, and hierarchy. The stories are told over and again against a backdrop of tradition and self-evident custom. Traditional values and age-old customs shape the stories people tell each other and assure their intelligibility and guarantee cultural continuity. In short, temporal and spatial perceptions deposited in the sharable stories are part of collective memory, inherited and sedimented over time and repeatable in new stories.[9]

This argument brings to mind Walter Benjamin's critique of the modern novel and reevaluation of the communal storyteller. The village community is embedded in an inexhaustible fund of stories and exemplified by the culturally cohesive role of the storyteller.[10] Benjamin's familiar argument takes on new significance when the difference between village and city is construed as a metaphoric tension between the epic mode of the realist novel and the disappearance of the sharable story in the city. More importantly, this tension foregrounds the accelerated modernization process that has rendered obsolete, in little more than a decade, the relatively habitual and time-honored sociopsychic infrastructure. It brings into sharp focus the market-oriented, amorphous urban setting where the individual threatens to become atomic, cut loose from the social moorings of kinship, community, and family, from lineage and history. Thrown into the competitive marketplace and evanescent impersonal relations, the individual has to rely on his or her own ingenuity and resources on the spur of the moment. Because they come from different areas and are isolated from each other in the compartmentalized life spheres and specialized work, urban dwellers only have their own vastly different and incompatible stories to tell, stories that are narrowly biographical and not readily meaningful to other people. Thus the apparent proliferation of stories implies the lack of a communicable story. This endlessly varied confusion and lack of common interest leads to the disjointed, fragmentary, anecdotal, performance-driven form of writing whose typical form is the essay, a form that caters to the consumer's essayistic structure of feeling, a relaxed state of mind, or mindlessness after a nice dinner.

The Essayistic in Fiction

Wang Anyi's novella *The Story of Our Uncle* illustrates the transition
from the historically oriented literature to a form that could be characterized as essayistic. The novella was written in 1990, a time of drastic change
for Chinese society and culture as a whole. From a culture dominated by
an ideologically oriented and centralized state, China was moving quickly
into a brave new world of frenzied economic development, investment,
consumerism, and pop culture. The rapid change drastically shook the basic fabric of Chinese society. *The Story of Our Uncle* registers a sensitive aspect of the epoch-making transition. Tang Xiaobing notes in this novella a
new way of writing that is "concentrated on capturing and gauging a
mood," on registering the experiential pathos of longing, sorrow, and nostalgia.[11] These psychic, generic elements imply a deeper problem: the disintegration of the organic connection of the artist with the narrative resources he or she commands in telling a coherent story. Hence the
abundance of metafictional reflection on the procedure of writing Tang has
described.[12] I would see this novella as a document tracing a shift in literary and social history. Focusing on a novelist's career, it delineates the shift
in the value and function of literature in a time when ideology and politics
were giving way to the market, to economic development, and to consumerism—all under the rubric of modernization. Through the vicissitudes of a writer it shows how the novel as a cultural form loses its ground
and how literary sensibility shifts to the essayistic. This generic shift provides a glimpse into the fundamental social transformations in the 1990s.

Critics have noticed the presence of essayistic quality in Wang's writing, especially in her fiction.[13] In *The Story of Our Uncle*, one finds the essayistic prevailing over narrative. The novella reads more like an essay—
rambling, random, analytical, disjointed, gossipy, chatty—than a straight
narration, a fact acknowledged by both critics and the author herself. In
this narrative-essay a young writer, on behalf of his generation, attempts
make a biographical assessment of an older writer they call Uncle. One
would be disappointed if one expects engaging actions or a dramatic story.
Although the text retains the outward shape of a novella, it is a hybrid
composed of diverse genres, with literary and art criticism, gossip, conjecture, history, philosophizing, anecdotes, and stories all rolled into one. The
narrator suggests that this novella is an essay in the double sense of textual

form and playful, explorative literary exercise. He proclaims in the opening paragraph that this story of Uncle has been assembled out of a hodgepodge of elements, and there is no way to distinguish truth from falsehood. "Many blanks need to be filled up with imagination and inference," and the story is filled with "subjective coloring." The subjective, arbitrary, even whimsical character of the text is associated with the mode of production that writers have adopted as they are geared toward an emergent literary market. Writers, the narrator says, are people who spend their time making up stories. One day "we started circulating his [Uncle's] maxims. To the laborers like us, the maxims are significant, for they are capital in commodity production and can produce surplus value, which can put back to expanded reproduction."[14] *The Story of Our Uncle* is thus premised on fragmentary axioms, an arbitrary principle of composition, random fantasy, and the form of commodity.

Wang's text resonates with the usual comments and generalizations about the essay as a literary form. In Theodor Adorno's well-known essay "The Essay as Form," we find numerous descriptions well suited to an analysis of the essay in the Chinese context. Adorno pits the essay against the institutionalized discourse of philosophy, the doctrine of scientific positivism, and its attendant sociocultural condition of reification. The essay is envisaged as an *enfant terrible* or a serious playboy seeking the utopian space of the pleasure principle. Thus the essay turns up its nose at the notions of totality, completeness, systematicity, and the universal and the eternal. It is marked by fragments, excessive fantasy, interpretation, exploration, and experimentation. Its supposed form is actually formlessness. Abandoning the rigid conceptual schemata, it seeks and engages the object in its historical specificity and quotidian trivia.[15] Although Adorno's comments are apt and in tune with much of Eileen Chang and Wang Anyi's musings on the essay, the philosophical framework that the essay runs up against is different: the essay is up against the high-minded tyranny of western philosophical tradition. In the Chinese literary convention the essay is not so clearly defined against something so established. Its polemic pole, as already dimly suggested by Eileen Chang's reflection, is to be identified as the Enlightenment and Marxist paradigm of teleological history and its literary counterpart: the novel of revolutionary realism.

The essay is a literary exploration trying to break out of the conceptual and discursive straitjacket. Quoting Max Bense, Adorno goes on to say that the essay is distinguished from a treatise: "The person who writes essayistically is the one who composes as he experiments, who turns his object around, questions it, feels it, tests it, reflects on it, who attacks it from different sides and assembles what he sees in his mind's eye and puts into words what the object allows one to see under the condition created in the course of writing."[16] The dropping of a grand, complete vision and opting for the incomplete, trivial, and experimental are what makes for the essay. The German word *Versuch*, attempt or essay, Adorno writes, is the place where "thought's utopian vision of hitting the bullseye is united with the consciousness of its own fallibility and provisional character." This "indicates . . . something about the form, something to be taken all the more seriously in that it takes place not systematically but rather as a characteristic of an intention groping its way."[17]

An intention groping its way into the mysteries of Uncle's life aptly describes the essayistic quality of *The Story of Our Uncle*. As a text assembled out of disparate materials—hearsay, gossip, guesswork, fantasy, and conjecture, the narrative enacts a wide array of pregiven discourses and narrative patterns to grope at the "real" life of Uncle. These discourses and narratives are in their own turn commented on as objects of inquiry and are critiqued on a "meta" level and treated as options in an experimental writing. As an intellectual, Uncle is typical of hundreds of thousands of others persecuted in the political campaigns whose suffering and reinstatement in the post–Cultural Revolution period is now a familiar story. But at the very outset, the novella unpacks the myth of the suffering intellectual into forking paths of narrative. One can make up a narrative of Uncle on his way to the place of exile, for instance, by recourse to a tragic-sublime scenario of political victims echoing Dostoevsky. Riding in a beat-up truck through the vast, snowy Siberian landscape in the northwest plateau, the victim-hero would ponder the significance of life and fate with an elderly wise man. One could also cast Uncle in a lackluster, comic, or even grotesque light, reduced to a mere creature of survival, trapped in narrow village life and a sexual entanglement. Like thousands of other writers, Uncle was persecuted and exiled because of his writing. But this fabled story of the tragic-heroic writer is again playfully retouched into three different versions by Uncle's own retelling after the fact. In the first telling, his persecution is a political story, indicting the oppression of the political system. Then it is redone as an existential story, intimating the individual's difficult choice in the mysterious and ironical workings of fate. Third, it translates into a prophetic story, in the fashion of Aesop's fables, full of prescience and tidings of catastrophe.

This intention groping its way into Uncle's life draws on various types of narrative patterns and aesthetic resources. This is by no means a literary embellishment for pure rhetorical variety or pleasure. The narration is saddled with difficulties of understanding and getting Uncle's life straight. The difficulty is not due to the usual generational gap, but rather reflects different historical experiences and memory that separate the young from the old. This difference not only drives a wedge into the writers as a group, but also gives rise to the divergence of generic practice and aesthetics. This divergence is the key to understanding the essay and the essayistic.

The older generation, having experienced political persecution and historical traumas at first hand, is deeply grounded in historical consciousness and the teleological narrative. The generation of Uncle is intensely committed to writing literature as praxis for social change. Uncle's meteoric rise to the leading writer in the aftermath of the Cultural Revolution indicates that what Gramsci called the "organic" intellectual remains strong, even thrives. The popularity of his novels shows that a work of literature can be a tremendous hit and can be an effective medium for criticizing the flaws of the system and raising the social and political consciousness of readers. It revives the legacy of the New Literature of May Fourth and is rightly rebaptized as the embodiment of a zeitgeist, the "Literature of the New Period" (*xin shiqi wenxue*). It is the voice of the farsighted and the vanguard in China's modernization drive. Despite all his traumas and sufferings, Uncle's generation remains firm in their belief in the organic totality of sociohistorical process and the people's capacity to steer the course of history. Literature is simply one vehicle that carries this historical mission.

The historical consciousness embodied by Uncle is to find its corresponding form in an epic mode of writing: the realist novel. Uncle's general outlook on the world is epic in the Lukácsian sense. The young narrator captures this *Weltanschauung* very accurately:

The political life of the past few decades has filled up his experience and life. This enables Uncle to keep his worldview firmly anchored to reality and politics. The state and government encompass the whole world for him and form the vast backdrop for human activity. Patterns of people's behavior and conduct are but representatives of social life. The concept of culture sounds very abstract and empty to him. Art to him also should perform real and political functions.[18]

The young generation, in contrast, is not so firmly grounded. Growing up in a period when the dominant ideology is in decline, they are left floating in the winds of various imported ideologies and newfangled -isms. They are creatures of the newly emergent market and players of nihilistic intellectual fashions. For them writing literature no longer carries a sociohistorical mission, but is a playful, aesthetic game unburdened with any responsibility and weighty purposes. Art has become an artful, artsy activity, floating free of sociohistorical grounding. Literary activity to them means attending pen conferences, pursuing hot fashions, innovating fresh forms and tastes, brandishing new theories, making up sensational and marketable stories. All this also leads to the enhancement of a writer's charisma and even sexual appeal. Indeed, to the young generation, it is old-fashioned to believe that literature contains historical or social significance; literature becomes instead sexy and commercial.

Retreat of Literature from History

Uncle's writing career is an allegory of withdrawal from history and the dangers involved in doing so, exemplified in his crisis-ridden metamorphosis from a historically grounded writer to a playful artist, from novelist to essay writer. Uncle's earlier success thrusts him to the status of literary celebrity and stardom: he becomes a prominent figure in the media. As the younger writers pursue fashions and cater to new consumers with playful, entertaining, artsy literary goods, Uncle feels the need to catch up. His new position as a glamorous writer allows him to become a globe-trotter. At the invitation of literary and academic circles and institutions around the world eager to know a newly opened China, he journeys from country to country, giving talks and socializing at literary cocktail parties. Increasingly, sightseeing and superficial impressions of exotic foreign countries become the only materials he can summon: he becomes a tourist and a writer of travelogues.

Going along with the role of a player in an increasingly cosmopolitan, global, and consumer-oriented literary market is a new philosophy of writing, which favors a showy, playful, essayistic quality at the expense of the epic, social, and historical. Uncle is reborn, the younger narrator rightly observes, into a new life, and into an enclosed new realm of pure artistic creativity. He addresses serious social problems playfully, in the style of black humor and through the use of narrative techniques that mix past and present. He becomes more and more detached from the grave political issues of the day. His new outlook is derived from a purely aesthetic principle:

Aesthetic and artistic activity has become a way of life, realizes Uncle with extreme excitement. He is not only an artist shaped by life experience, but one who shapes life experience through artistic creation. Uncle finally perceives that he has become a new man, an artist. The past sufferings were preparation for this artistic goal, as if nurturing certain qualities. From now on real life is no longer real, but provides raw material for fiction. (47–48)

Emptied of historical substance and filled up with fragmentary and rambling impressions in his global trips, both life and writing of Uncle thin out into personal, irrelevant, discontinuous fragments. His writing begins to take on an essayistic quality, bordering on sheer images or simulacra, getting closer and closer to that of the younger generation. Real human relations are "only a literary conceit" (52). Within the aesthetic shelter, "Uncle can no longer become excited or moved and is immune to suffering." Tragic suffering is now only a literary category, and "the awareness of this is the hallmark of Uncle's becoming a pure writer" (50). Parallel with this essayistic quality is Uncle's changed lifestyle. He is obsessed with things he in the past would have considered vulgar, low, or quotidian; he becomes more listless and yuppyish. He is interested in women and sexual intrigues and conquests; he indulges in vulgarity and trivial pursuits, exulting in money and showy, exotic collectibles. In short, he metamorphoses from an image of the epic novelist and organic intellectual to a middle-class professional writer.

The transformation in Uncle reflects the retreat of literature from a historically grounded medium to a form of light-hearted, playful entertainment. The problem with this change, as the novella's ending suggests, is that it is self-deceptive. Despite Uncle's willful creation of an aesthetic cocoon, history manages to intrude in the end as a return of the repressed, in the person of his vengeful, murderous son. His son embodies all the painful memory and disgraceful experience of Uncle's past life, unfit for the epic treatment in his novels and repressed in his ethereal, airtight, essayistic experiments. The son's attempted murder of his father signifies the revenge of a history that Uncle is trying to shut off from the serene, trouble-free aesthetic realm.

Our concern, however, is not with the interpretation of the story itself, but with the way Uncle's fate indicates the shift in literary form. If Uncle's story apparently traces the trajectory of a novelist to a writer who not only writes travelogues and essays but also is imbued with essayistic sensibility, then the essay in contemporary China is a release from the epic form of writing and historical discourse. It is a release into the literary market and consumer taste, a response to the pervasive secularization of life and rising consumerism. It comes as an image of a loosening up of ideologically conditioned life and as a shift to a life that is becoming more private, more disjointed and fragmented, more removed from the totalistic social and political process. Yet history has not become a simulacrum to play with, as envisioned by the younger narrator or Uncle himself. In contemporary China, reality does not correspond to the essayistic playfulness one may wish for. Thus the essay as a cultural form is caught in a tension between withdrawal from the burden of history and the ever-present danger of the return of the repressed.

PART 3

GLOBALIZATION, NOSTALGIA, RESISTANCE

7

Reenchanting the Everyday
in the Global City

When one moves quickly from modernity to postmodernity to globalization, the shady sides of modernization are not questioned. The heavy
toll of "progress" and "development" on many societies unprepared for
rapid capitalist transformation renders some of modernization's accomplishments dubious and problematic. "Modernity," the discursive counterpart to technological and social modernization, is a double-edged sword.
Its visions of the future may hold out the promise of progress, emancipation, freedom, and universal prosperity. Yet all too often this sanguine vision is little more than a euphemism to conceal the injustices of the global
expansion of capital and the maintenance of the asymmetry of resource
and power. Globalization, trumped up before its real benefits are felt, is often a new trick on the part of corporate executives and their hired economists to revamp the earlier modernization project and to rationalize the
aggressive advance of capital around the world. The dire consequences of
modernization for underdeveloped societies become overwhelming as soon
as one switches from those sunny smiles and inexhaustible abundance on
TV commercials to the unforgettable disasters in the twentieth century:
social and political upheavals, civil wars, military interventions and mas-
sacres, depletion of natural resources, and the deepening of uneven development.[1]

The psychocultural trauma of the global condition is less obvious.
The spread of global capital produced a disenchanting effect on previously

"organic" communities buttressed by tradition, collective memory, folk-lore, and kinship relations. In the rush to embrace economic development, consumer goods, and a uniform mass culture, many societies risk losing their cultural heritage and history. The lifeworlds constituted by relatively stable associations, by shared collective memory and commitments, by time-honored attachments and structure of feeling, are fading from the horizon. If they are still around, these "relics" of the older lifeworld are fre-quently packaged into one more exotic item in tour books or in theme parks or museums. The attempt to preserve the valuables of these life-worlds—the communities of imagination and memory that have endured longer than global trade, consumptive frenzy, and stock fluctuation—is in-creasingly becoming a bitter struggle. Some may offer consolation by ar-guing that local and native cultures will adopt new forms, the electronic media for instance, to repackage and hence preserve their cultural identity in a new bottle. Arjun Appadurai speaks of "context-producing" virtual neighborhoods and "translocalities" as a flexible way to assimilate the global while recreating the local.[2] Others place a premium on the much-touted hybridity, whereby floating around as a cosmopolitan chameleon or adaptable émigré is favored over place-bound rootedness. People who yearn for a home away from home have indeed tried these makeshift strategies. But the road to the merger between global and local, metropo-lis and village is all too treacherous for a theatrics of hybridity to handle. And the prices for changing one's identity and inventing one's history every few minutes have not been calculated.

National literature, written in a time-honored language and tied to a sedimented tradition, is both vexed and privileged in addressing the dilemma of living under the global condition. This challenge, new to mainland writers in the 1990s, was a déjà vu for Taiwan and Hong Kong writers and filmmakers. Taiwan writers have addressed the nexus of the lo-cal and global in response to the chasing speed of modernization and de-velopment. Part 3 discusses the issues of memory, nostalgia, and everyday experience in the face of expansive global capital and the reifying trend in Taiwan, Hong Kong, and the mainland. The new challenge brings three regions together for a general perspective on their commonality. This chap-ter will examine the effects of the global process in Taiwan and Hong Kong in two related aspects. One is the reifying, homogenizing trend in everyday life, and the other is capital-driven immigration and the consequent deval-

uation of memory and home in Hong Kong. The works by Taiwan writer
Zhu Tianwen and Hong Kong filmmaker Clara Law evince a tenacious
hold on memory in the practice of everyday life, an insistence that can be
a viable strategy amid swift, blinding change. The analysis of Taiwan and
Hong Kong will provide a preliminary historical analogy by which we understand the perils and opportunities for mainland China.

Literature as Witness to Alienation

In the 1980s through the 1990s, Taiwan literature registered the profound social changes resulting from the island's rapid economic development and entry into the global financial and economic orbit. Whether referred to as modern or postmodern, Taiwan literature testifies to a
condition of life marked by a disjuncture between the traditional lifeworld
and the new global environment. Although one cannot step into the same
river of modernity twice, the change in Taiwan certainly bears some analytical resemblance to the condition of large-scale industrialization and urbanization in nineteenth-century western Europe. Industrialization, technology, and urbanization—prime movers of modern history—created a
radically new environment that severed huge populations from the traditional way of life and plunged "free" laborers into the impersonal process
of machine manufacturing and urban existence. Ferdinand Tönnies's classical study of the transformation from *Gemeinschaft* to *Gesellschaft* represents an exemplary attempt to grasp this change. It was nothing less than
an epochal transformation from a mode of social organization based on
the traditional family and village to new socioeconomic structures embedded in urban existence, in the anonymous market, and in the rule-bound
and abstract relations of civil society. With the advent of the modern age
came the opposition between town and village, urban society and organic
community. Critics of modernity and capitalism—Marx, Max Weber,
Lukács, Adorno, Benjamin, Henri Lefebvre, and many others—have characterized the new condition as alienating, abstracting, traumatic, or catastrophic. For them the overriding image of technological progress and
alienation is the metropolis: the urban environment is monstrous in its
widespread, impersonal administrative structure, its regulative power, and
its economic operation. The economy based strictly on the production of

commodities has a tendency to turn individuals into anonymous, random things and particles. Caught in this alien setting, the operations of which remain invisible to the naked eye, the individual slips away from the supportive, intimate milieu of memory—the village, the network of kinship, the communal setting of handicraft work and pleasure. Walter Benjamin diagnosed this as "the decline of aura" in the blinding industrial age: the aura of authentic experience embedded in tradition, ritualistic festivals, artworks, collective memory, and history. The fading of aura also resulted from the loss of intimate and integrated contact with one's body and creative activity.[3]

Although the classic critique of modernity is premised upon a nostalgic appeal to an Edenlike village, its implicit impulse for striking out alternative, livable byways beyond the uniformly boring expressway of capitalism still bears a critical edge. What looks like a withdrawal from the status quo is actually a head-on confrontation with it. Without an imagined Eden, the world ruled by the market would be too much "the way it is," rooted in the reality principle, reified in its corporate raison d'être, sanctified in the megamall bearing the logo of the "End of History." Thus the utopian impulse for alternatives is waning daily but is at the same time becoming urgent.

Alienation, abstraction, and reification are notions descriptive of an epochal transition from the agrarian to industrial mode of production. They take on renewed intensity in the face of the current changes and ruptures in China, more massive and abrupt than those in the industrial nineteenth century. What was confined to a few metropolises is now sweeping through the big cities and rural areas in less developed countries, so rapidly that one begins to wonder if any green pastures still remain on the planet Earth. Yet it is precisely the trauma of these changes outside the metropolitan centers that evokes the enduring descriptive and analytical power of the concepts of reification and commodification.

Reification, as expounded by Georg Lukács, functions as a key metaphor for understanding the human condition in advanced market societies. It points to a cultural environment penetrated by pervasive commodity exchange. The relation of exchange stamps the individual, mentally and bodily, as an exchangeable item, turning a person into one faceless thing as any other. Because labor no longer produces use value for personal survival and pleasure, it becomes abstract and deprived of its empirical, experiential value. Reification thus means "the progressive elimination of the qualitative, human and individual attributes of the worker."[4] For Benjamin this would mean the degrading and withering of authentic human experience. Human experience and value, not instantly negotiable or exchangeable, are now blowing in the economic, profit-driven winds of the day.

The process of commodification and reification is becoming ubiquitous and is especially rampant in Asian countries. Taiwan, with its speedy economic takeoff in the 1970s into the circuit of global capital and the world market, has virtually compressed some 200 years of industrial modernity in the west into a few decades. Contemporary Taiwan literature keeps a detailed paper trail for damaged life under this condition. Zhu Tianwen's writing can be better understood in the context of this epochal change. Criticism of Zhu's works tends to valorize their belletrist aspect and may have obscured their intensely sociohistorical stratum.[5] Zhu's works illustrate the way Taiwan literature actively engages with the psychocultural issues of globalization, despite their seemingly aesthetic detachment. The aesthetic expression of literary writing needs to be considered as a response to globalization. Zhu Tianwen's writing represents an acute response to and a critique of the sociocultural condition as part of the expansion of global capital in the late twentieth century. It is true that her portrayal of the situation is literary and marked with a rarified sense of artworks. I would argue, however, that social and political in its unconscious implications, Zhu's critiques of the global come in those unlikely places of the aesthetic-body: crafting images, perceiving everyday objects, and experimenting with sexuality.

Critics and scholars have discussed Zhu Tianwen's exquisite literary style, her exquisitely crafted images and texts. This style, along with a delicate sensibility, is also aligned with a feminine tradition of writing marked by a penchant for freezing a stunning image as a symbol of timelessness against the chaos of change. David Wang has captured this well by designating this style a "verbal alchemy," a style of writing with a magic ring.[6] We may project a historical and "global" dimension to this style if we regard it not simply as a stylistic innovation of a writer, but also as a social and symbolic act carrying collective imports. It is a gesture of an individual trying to articulate deeply felt human needs, needs that are being eroded by the pervasive trend of commodification and reification.

Reification and Disenchantment

In Zhu Tianwen's works one is confronted with the typical cityscape of global trade, transnational capital, and flows of media images. The city of Taipei seems stifled by high-rise office and apartment buildings competing for shrinking space and depriving the residents of breathing room. In this furnace of a metropolis, glitzy shops line the streets through which goods from all around the world flow. Media-suffused information and communication is the very air that people breathe. The newest fashions in Paris or New York cause overnight sensations and frenzy among Taiwan consumers. The whimsical behavior of the superstars and celebrities in the metropolitan centers in the west, through media dissemination and advertising, can launch a tidal wave of imitation, instantly create a new lifestyle, and alter people's bearing, looks, and aesthetic taste. The cityscape here constitutes a complete shakeup of the traditional way of life. What drives this place is not government, politics, kinship, or morality. The engine of society, population movement, and economy is money, advertising, the insatiable desire for consumer goods, and the ubiquitous media.

This global scene has radically transformed the individual's relation to the immediate world of objects and his or her perception and imagination. This estrangement can be traced to the process of reification and commodification. Reification strips objects of their value and meaning, which are an extension of human attributes. Stripped-down objects appear to have no other value than marketability: they are up for sale and consumption. In transforming the object from its use value to its exchange value, from experience-enriched production to passive, experience-bleached consumption, commodification blocks and wrecks the culture's living memory and history. It erases the remembrance of how objects and life environments are made by humans, over a long period of time, often with their hands, and how people have come to be what they are through interaction with their life settings, how society has moved from then to now. As Richard Terdiman writes:

The experience of commodification and the process of reification cut entities off from their own history. They veil the memory of their production from the consumers, as from the very people who produced them. The process, in Theodor Adorno's terms, created an unprecedented and uncanny field of "hollowed-out" objects, available for investment by any meaning whatever, but organically connected with none at all. Moreover, as Benjamin glossed Adorno's description, the rhythm—we might say the efficiency—of such "hollowing-out" of the elements of social and material life increased ceaselessly over the course of the nineteenth century.[7]

We may also add that the rhythm of such hollowing-out of everyday social life has accelerated into a blinding speed in the last two decades in Taiwan and in the 1990s in mainland China.

The experience of reification affects sensory and perceptual activity in two ways in Zhu's fiction. On the one hand, perception is sucked into the whirlwind of media-bound and advertised images. Because the reception of media images is mostly passive and contemplative, I venture to call it the consumerist mode.[8] The consumer absorbs whatever the media have to offer, which is mostly evanescent and sheer sensory stimuli. A very different kind, implying a discontent or resistance, may be termed the nostalgic mode. This is a state of mind that imaginatively searches for the lost horizon among and beyond the sanitized, hollowed-out images. Active and defying at times, it starts from a refusal to accept the present as it is. It dreams and yearns for things, feelings, relations, stories, and myths—the green grass beyond the dreary and monotonous cityscape. It strives to reawaken objects and images to their magic charms and mythical aura, intensifying the utopian desire for alternatives. These two modes provide a key to Zhu's treatment of images and perceptive activity.

Images in the consumerist mode are fundamentally the afterimage of abstracted objects in reality. Before these free-floating objects, the characters of Zhu's fiction are spectators, eager to be hooked. Mia, the female protagonist in "Fin de Siècle Splendor" (Shiji mo de huali), is an insatiable image-watcher in this mode. "Mia is an individual who fervently believes in the sense of smell. She lives on memories evoked by different smells."[9] Yet a specific fragrance does not bring back anything like Proustian involuntary memory that dredges up a fondly remembered past experience or emotion. It only echoes a very recent impression of a short-lived event, such as an advertising campaign, a promotion of a new product, a fashion show, a cycle of new style, and the like. An unending stream of shades of color, brands of fabrics and texture, and stylistic variation of dress fashions envelopes Mia's perception and consciousness. She is very much into a hundred and one things of multicultural origins, from India, Japan, and

Paris to Taipei—all in one swoop, yet the origin is precisely what is missing, erased by a sheer flatness in her impression. What the images evoke is
brightly colored, nuanced texture, a kaleidoscope without depth, a euphoria of weightlessness, a perpetually dazzling present.

Mia and her lover Lao Duan may be aesthetes of sorts as they contemplate the multicolored palette of the skyline at sunset. But their sensibility is modeled on Monet's impressionistic painting at its extreme visual.
The sublime outbreak of sunshine has a pure rococo effect on Mia, but the
rococo quality is emptied of its cultural memory. Rather, its extravagant
glory stems from the Hollywood movie *Amadeus*, which has recently
boosted the sales of classical music in Taiwan. The lovers' emotional response to scenes of beauty seems to be shock-induced thrills. Classic aesthetic sensibility has no place here. That they are addicted to sensation and
thrills is clear from this description: "They indulge themselves too much in
beautiful things. They spend their energy in long hours of admiration and
contemplation or allow themselves be shocked to pieces by strange spectacles, such that they forget what they are supposed to do as lovers" (203).
This self-indulgence of sensations, often little more than an echo of commercialized images, is less aesthetic than consumerist: it is symptomatic of
consumerist fetishism.

Nostalgia and Mourning

In the society of media-induced consumption the individual is compelled to experience the phenomenal world at second hand. The lived experience, involving the whole body and sensory perception, whittles away
in such a heavily mediated, spectacle-suffused setting. Thus the search for
authentic experience, the experience of intimate contact with one's own
body, with other bodies and objects, becomes critical. In Zhu Tianwen's
writing the flattening of perception is countered by a nostalgic narrative of
yearning.

This nostalgic mode recalls a strong tradition of Taiwan literature
that expresses a longing for the lost world of the traditional village, the
family, childhood, and the network of intimate friends. The "village of
yearning," *juan cun*, is a constant setting in Zhu's fiction and embodies its
rich ambivalence. The village refers to a government housing project built

for dependents of military personnel after the nationalists' retreat from the mainland.[10] More than a residence, the village speaks symbolically to the hopes of returning to and recovering the lost mainland and is thus concomitant with a sense of loss. Yet the loss is doubled, as the village in time became a venerable image, frequently portrayed in literary works. In the cultural imaginary it became a favorite haven, resonating to a general nostalgic desire for authentic experience, whether or not tied to the mainland. This image of the village, doubly removed from the real referent, can be attributed to an intensified loss of authenticity and innocence in more accelerated socioeconomic development. This longing for a pristine village has wide collective resonance in the capitalist sociocultural changes that occurred in Taiwan in the decades since the 1960s.

The image of the village contains an ambivalence that characterizes the power of nostalgia. A nostalgic seizes upon traces of the past, as Susan Stewart puts it, as "the now-distanced experience, an experience which the object can only evoke and resonate to, and can never entirely recoup."[11] Out of reach and yet constantly made available, inviting yearning and caress, the object of nostalgia works to tantalize and to appease. Aware of the impossibility of reuniting with the past, the nostalgic still yearns for and keeps on telling stories about it. The real paradise, as Marcel Proust famously said, is the one that is lost. What is real is the narrative that is being woven around the void. The village is the lost origin that both originates and spins off narration, encouraging the yearning for an elusive, purer past.

Zhu Tianwen's story "Eden No More" (Yidian bu zai) poignantly illustrates this nostalgic mode through the short life of Zhen Sulan. Zhen's story is one of progressive alienation in her career as a media personality, countered by her fruitless search for the lost world of home. She is known by three names, which constitute a token of this progressive estrangement. The name most alien and hateful to her belongs to the character she plays in a hit TV drama. The less hateful name is Zhen Li, which is given to her by her lover and which marks her affair with him, the director of the drama. Both are media-related. Zhen Sulan is the name that she was given at birth and remains on her identity card. The last name harks back to a period of her life in the *juan cun* village she can call her own.

Not that her childhood life in the village is an Edenlike paradise. On the contrary, it is portrayed as lost even when she was living it as a child.

Narrated in retrospect, without a sentimental halo, her childhood is one of trivia, squalor, and mind-numbing daily routines and frustrations. Her tender years bear a heart-wrenching witness to the deterioration of her mother and the enduring stupidity of her father. Yet despite its ugliness, it is her life, offering "real" if painful experience. Sometimes she misses the "solid reassuring tit-tat sound of the sewing machine" (118). She enjoys playing the role of caring "mother" to her ailing mother. Even as a child she already cultivated a habit of nostalgic mood, and she would gaze with fascination into the photos reminiscent of the family's happy moments in still earlier times. Before she commits suicide toward the end of the story, the vision of the village comes back to her: "She recalls the long-gone days in the *juan cun* village, many of them, which were not that happy and sweet, yet all are her own. No matter how bad, how unpleasant, how sad the tears she wept, they are her own" (132).

As an actress, Zhen Sulan is a media image, packaged for mass consumption, and she has little control over her identity and her own body. The fate of the female character she plays in the hit TV series corresponds to her own: "a rootless person in the wide world. Even if she could make decisions, things could not be placed under control" (123). The director of the TV series, her lover, also directs her bodily movement. She is instructed to watch herself, to be self-conscious of what she is doing, in order to follow the script and the demands of the story. In one episode of the play she is drawing a baby face, which has eyes, nose, and mouth, yet is without the couture of the face. The director rightly comments that she has "no sense of boundaries separating her from external objects" (133). As she is being transformed into things, she also feels that "the strangers often send their shadows to visit me" (133). The strangers, in their dreamy, surreal shapes, seem to come from another world, one other than the present. They seem to be the shadows that her present self is beckoning.

In a constantly nostalgic mood, Zhen Sulan yearns for shadowy figures of the past she knows little about. Her stellar rise in the entertainment industry is a rupture with her already fractured life. The nostalgic mood aims at fixing the rupture, at least emotionally. Not having a pure past, but one that was no less distressing than the present, she turns her past into a melancholy, bittersweet picture she can come back to again and again. She displays a rare ability to frame the past of her reveries in a still picture. As a nostalgic object, the family photo, which she never tires of gazing at, proffers the memory of an age of innocence and happiness, yet it is also frozen by her gaze into a timeless tableau, purged of its lived, unpleasant reality. The danger, she muses, is for the figures in the photo to fly out of the frame (118). Zhen extends this photographic or "painterly" perception to her present life. A true nostalgic, she seeks to awaken the object for her own enjoyment. In distress, she has a way of suddenly pulling up short and will begin to frame an object, a landscape, a view into a still picture: "Looking backward at the long, dark road she has come running, she collects, reclaims and patches up the chaotic fragments of self" (120). Zhen Sulan is a fervent nostalgic with little past resources; she is more in love with nostalgia itself. Her consolation comes from an intensely contrived aesthetic relation with an imagined past. The story of her life is both a losing battle against emotional estrangement and a poignant reminder of what is missing in the media-dominated society.

Sailing to Utopia

Zhu Tianwen's fiction portrays a world of commodity exchange, advertising, commercial spectacle, and mass media. This machinery works effectively at the bidding of the global market to make sure that everyone behaves as a functional, productive citizen. In a society saturated with media infomercials and image blitz, the individual's thoughts and feelings become administered and managed; yet it is extremely difficult to detect the hand that does the controlling. Administrative control blends invisibly into the bodily experience of discipline and work. Thus, as a functional member of modern, rational society, the individual is required to inscribe the rules of society on his or her mind and body, and thereby act as a self-disciplined person.

In his or her self-disciplined and self-regulative bearing, the consumer of "cultural goods" is less a subject, possessing complex internal life and rich experience, than a particle adrift with the fashions of the moment and the whims of circumstance. The inner, integrated consciousness is under erasure. This evaporation of subjectivity renders obsolete the classical expectation of fictional character as a multifaceted, full-blooded individual. Indeed, the idea of "characterization," dependent on a notion of the whole personality with a biographical past and ethical evaluation, is out of place. Most of Zhu Tianwen's characters have one-dimensional, flat traits. Figures of sensualists, aesthetes, voyeurs, artist-craftsmen, and role players populate her works. These figures constantly indulge in sensory, sensual, and sexual pleasures and thrills. They nevertheless feel helplessly trapped, flattened into impoverished experience and abstract creatures. This one-dimensional trait is to be attributed to the logic of commodity and consumable spectacles. In a highly commodified culture, individual life loses its nonnegotiable aura of uniqueness and begins to be defined by its exchangeability and consumability. The personality is simply another commodity in circulation, lodged in its abstract, quantitative value equitable to other things of equivalent value. In Zhu's fiction even the characters' escapism or defiance simulates the way the commercial society operates. The celebrated novel *Notes of a Desolate Man* (Huangren shouji) is a case in point. The conflict between discipline and deviation, a major motif in this novel, plays out in the testimony of the desolate man in an increasingly desolate world.

At the outset, the narrator draws a picture of a subtle power structure by discussing at length Michel Foucault and Levi-Strauss. The discussion arises from a scene of a huge mass congregation celebrating a national event.[12] The mass gathering represents the crowd's ecstasy in beholding the leader and their blind confidence in the political order. Retrospectively, however, it was the happy age of innocence, when only faith prevailed, with everyone free from doubts. But that reassuring "authoritarianism" may be less passé than it seems. A new, benign, and invisible control is taking over the old power of the political regime. It is the administration of the mind and the body in the economically developed, globalized society, where not the leader but money is holding sway. The previously collective, centralized control seems obsolete and gone, yet the mind and the body are in thrall to new rules that are felt as pleasure and enjoyment.

The Bachlike harmony in the political festivities, capsulated in the national celebration, shares an impulse that motivates Levi-Strauss's lifetime work, as the narrator goes on with discursive savvy. Levi-Strauss aims at uncovering an underlying order beneath seemingly heterogeneous ethnographic data. On the other hand, Michel Foucault posits not so much resistance to the order as its insidious fine-tuning and dressing up. Foucault detects the fine prints of the microtechniques employed by the repressive structure of power. For the narrator, Foucault, in his homosexuality as well as in his relentless scrutiny of the small, imperceptible disciplinary technology, offers a lesson in how not to be assimilated and absorbed into the system.

The invocation of Foucault reads like a statement of purpose for the desolate, superfluous man/narrator in his attempt to evade and resist disciplinary power on the body and mind. Through his analysis of disciplinary technology Foucault reveals a form of control extending to the whole urban, postindustrial society, which appears benign and democratic yet is no less totalitarian and restrictive. Power, in its control of sexuality as well as of consciousness, takes on a scientific, clinical, "humane" face: it functions in terms of rational explanation, scientific management, and therapeutic adjustment. It uses experts, doctors, and psychiatrists to smooth out its hidden constraints over its subjects. Power is so subtle and pervasive that it insinuates itself into the deepest recesses of our being. The individual is made euphoric in his or her happiness (false happiness, as Herbert Marcuse would have said), not unlike the joy of the cheering crowd on a national holiday. It makes us enjoy the control of our sexuality and "convinces us deeply that we are liberated in sexual openness and transparency, and gain freedom in sexual enjoyment" (63). The figure of the desolate man is a study of the difficulty of breaking out of this minuscule management of the body through a utopia of libidinal fulfillment.

It is a mistake, however, to read sexual fulfillment in this work as offering license for sexual abandonment. Excessive sexuality in this novel has been viewed by critics as vitally redemptive in a world where little remains but broken vestiges of beliefs and communal bonds. It has also been noted that the sexual pursuit in the novel is consonant with an art for art's sake tendency, coupled with an extreme oriental aestheticism. This aestheticism is further regarded as a principle that strains to derive value and meaning in a postindustrial world going broke. Thus wanton sexuality and its wistful aestheticization are almost indistinguishable, and each in its different way serves the need to redeem lost cultural meaning.[13]

To collapse excessive sexuality into aesthetics and to elevate it into a redemptive shrine, however, risks assigning too much "spiritual" and emancipatory value to sexual abandon. This view overlooks sexual life's embeddedness within a libidinal economy with ties to the dominant political economy. The single-minded pursuit of sex is in fact a by-product of the reified exchange economy that separates libidinal pleasure from other, more productive activities. Sex here is an afterimage of the requisite specialization of work and pleasure in a life penetrated by commodity. The system of commodity production and advertising compartmentalizes libidinal energy and bodily pleasure in a realm sequestered from active production. Hence the illusion of the newly won freedom and autonomy of sexuality. Sex, or libidinal life in general, is actually degraded and discounted in its splendid isolation and useless disassociation from the totality of life.

In the novel the human body, as it is uprooted from creative, libidinally productive work and experience, is set adrift on a consumerist spree of "cultural and historical goods." The body travels around the world as a tourist, seeking exotic, outlandish sights, strange sensations, fresh thrills. Floating in a cosmopolitan sea of unrelated humans, it looks for an all-consuming arousal from evanescent and intense intimacy with other bodies. For the homosexual lovers, to give one example, the monuments of civilization in Rome do not evoke historical consciousness and cultural memory. One does not see Rome and die, as the saying goes, but instead, one sees Rome and has sex. Cultural monuments are valued only when they are flattened into tourist postcards, to be sent to friends, made available for consumption. For the desolate man, there is hardly any distinction between the sublime beauty of Michelangelo's painting *The Creation of Adam* and his mundane enjoyment of the seductive sleeping position of his homosexual partner, which provokes "aesthetic" contemplation indistinguishable from sexual desire. We are told that multinational corporations are cashing in on historical sites: NHK of Japan is financing the renovation of the Sistene Chapel while making documentaries of tourist sites. The couple, emotionally ardent yet street-conventional, will take the designated, well-advertised route running from one country to another and will of course take photos and write postcards.

Their "honeymoon" travels seek new sights and sensations that serve as an aphrodisiac. Excessive sexuality, even of the kind that defies convention, does not necessarily mean sexy or libidinal freedom. On the contrary, pursued solely for its own sake, sexual excitement is desexualized rather than life-enhancing. Sexual orgies are pursued as an end in itself, something narrowed down and flattened out into a single-minded, one-dimensional activity. In other words, sex is abstracted and thus impoverished, on a par with a consumable, disposable commodity.

The utopia of the alleged libidinal fulfillment is in fact a sexual no-man's-land, as far as the sheer intensity of sexual activity is what is sought after to fill the emotional void. Yet a sense of utopia indeed comes through when the protagonists engage in a fruitful tension between a consumerist mind-set and a consciousness informed by nostalgia, memory, and history. There is a tug between endless enjoyment of dazzling surfaces and sporadic yearnings for the depths hidden in the past. At one time the desolate man thinks of marrying his lover in St. Peter's Cathedral after the bored repetition of sensual abandon. This is indicative of their search for the solemn aura of authority and authenticity offered by civilization's past. Much depiction is given to the indoor gatherings in which friends are invited to appreciate a collection of the couple's Italian friend Mo Mo. Mo Mo used to study as an international student in China and has assembled a collection of tapes, scripts, bric-a-brac, and artifacts. The guests' appreciation and reaction concerning the collection suggest that nostalgia and memory can be both consumerist and utopian. Mo Mo invites his Chinese friends to appreciate a disorienting array of collected items—tea, poems, music, scripts, handiwork, artworks, craft, and so forth—so miscellaneous and disparate as to seem incongruous. The items range from the sacred icon of the Dharma, traditional embroideries from Guizhou Province in China, classical bamboo paintings and engravings, artworks from Suzhou, small donkey figurines, and even posters of ideological films made in the 1950s.

This array of collected objects does not hark back to the specific histories and concrete contexts from which the objects originated. Context-bound and history-ridden objects may serve as souvenirs as they turn attention to the past and fuel nostalgia—a utopian desire for firsthand and authentic experience. Yet the eclectic collection here plays up the exhibition value of the ensemble instead of serving as a strong reminder of each object's origin or context of acquisition.[14] As such it functions as an entertainment or a showcase of exotica. This transformation of history into exotica is precisely what strikes the narrator with a sense of incongruity and irrelevance. But this social gathering for exotica gradually gives way to a more serious communal activity and historical consciousness: the narrator is irresistibly drawn into the appreciative circle and thrown back to concrete memories of the past. One small detail is quite significant: he looks at a photo that captures Mo Mo's experience as a foreign student in China.

A faded black-and-white photo reveals Mo Mo in a vegetable field, dressed in a Mao-style suit: the scene was 1974 at Liaoning University. Photographs in Zhu's fiction frequently authenticate nostalgic desire. As a screenwriter, Zhu Tianwen sometimes inserts photos into the film's flow of images. Thus, although the eclectic collection may be entertainment that caters to a consumerist sensibility, the nostalgic mind resurrects the object as souvenir expressive of a yearning for the innocent, and perhaps purer, youth, for the firsthand, lived experience. Mo Mo's interest in showing his collection may also serve a double purpose. He is nostalgic not so much for a specific memory of a certain place, as for his pure, probably more exciting experience in China. The collection is thus not only looking backward, but also provokes anticipation. Mo Mo is looking to stage a portrait of the self to his audience and to himself by way of collected fragments of his past. The emphasis is on "now" rather than on "then." The narrator senses this and finally catches on to the fragility as well as the necessity of self-fashioning through nostalgia: "As I watched all this I felt as if I were witnessing the broken pieces of my own youth, strewn everywhere on the ground" (75). Mo Mo's Chinese memory serves as a source of identity. For the desolate man the collection reminds him of the need to collect his past and record what is trailing behind him. The gravity of the marriage may be a sign of this impulse to find a stay against endless, superficial consumer items and sensual, transient pleasures.

Reenchantment of Objects

This utopian yearning for an auratic object also characterizes the female character Mia in "Fin de Siècle Splendor" (Shiji mo de huali).[15] Mia is a tireless seeker of magic aura. Walter Benjamin considered auras to be mental associations of memory that cluster around an object.[16] In a socioeconomic environment that constantly severs the links to the past and to the lived body, Mia seeks residual connections to a time when the body was more intimately and fully involved with things endowed with aura. This is best dramatized in her creation of a floral shrine and her homemade paper.

After a number of fashionable whirlwinds, Mia becomes self-conscious about herself as mannequin, and she cannot relate to and warm up to this self-image. In pursuing one fashion after another, she feels that there is no authentic experience to be gained. She begins to play along with ever-changing rhythms of fashion and trends with ironic distance. Her relationship with her lover Lao Duan at this conjuncture begins to suggest an occasional suspension of the endless consumerist activity and reified human relations. What binds them together seems an earnest search for authentic experience absent from the ongoing world of commodities.

This search marks Mia and Lao Duan as nostalgic of a different kind. In this story nostalgia does not simply designate a longing for the past, as poignantly portrayed in "Eden No More." Yet as the latter story already shows, nostalgia does not necessarily need a real object that actually existed before. The nostalgic mood, in Susan Stewart's phrase, is "sadness without objects" and is a longing for the context of origin and contact, for a realm of firsthand, lived experience, its unreality notwithstanding.[17] It is a mood that is not happy with the impoverished present. That Mia and Lao Duan are nostalgic for "the present" is evident in their shared interest in souvenirs. Lao Duan's many souvenir gifts to Mia bespeak his ability to treasure lived experience in the recent past and to preserve the aura stemming from his once being in the locale of the souvenirs. Mia admires and loves Lao Duan most intensely when he is able to trace her five carefully picked floor cushions to the respective stores where she purchased them. This implies he knows the context of origin intimately.

All this may be dismissed as another aping of commercial fashion, à la Martha Stewart. But the urge for authenticity can still be channeled through commodities and "new age" fashions. The problem is how to read it beyond the individual act. The nostalgic mode is at its most poetic when, toward the end of the story and after the repetitive cycle of fashion shows, Mia retreats from the fashion model to what may be called a "floral alchemist." It is quite revealing that Lao Duan feels, as he sees Mia in her abode, as if he were in the company of a medieval monk, or better, a sorceress. Mia assembles a collection of exotic plants, of dry flowers and weeds, handmade, colorful oil and soap, homemade herbal tea—a multilayered array of colors and shapes that seem to be an extension of her body. The collection constitutes an enchanted refuge and aura-filled enclave set apart from the marketplace. It is a magic circle where objects are transformed from mere short-lived items of consumption to a context of production and aesthetic appreciation. The disenchanted objects are reenchanted, rescued from commercial circulation into the innermost space of privacy. What could be more privately sacred than her bathroom, now made into a virtual shrine, continuous with intimate lived experience of body and contact? Her bathroom / shrine gives an authentic feel of naked, unadvertised, unfashioned sensuous existence. The objects are reendowed with the magic of creative efforts imbued with pleasure because they are handmade and created by Mia herself for her own enjoyment and contemplation.

Even these enchanted and enshrined objects will fade and their authentic aura will vanish. Thus Mia's next move, more drastic, is making paper with her own hands, with fruit juice added so that the paper retains the fragrance. Is this another instance of the do-it-yourself lifestyle fashion, or is it to be appraised as a creative enactment of utopian dreams? The interpretation again turns on what purpose this activity serves. For Mia, this is a vigorous reenchantment of objects deprived of their use value—their use for personal and aesthetic enrichment. Creating a floral shrine and making paper are only two sides of the same project. Both can be seen as an allegory of handwriting against vast reification. Throughout Zhu Tianwen's work the project of reenchantment is envisioned as writing, a style of literature that snatches moments of charm and fulfillment from a disorienting flux. Parallel to Mia's pursuit, Zhu's writing is a project of rewriting and reenchanting the object in an increasingly stripped-down, disenchanted world.

The flattening trends of globalization are rendering native cultures a disenchanted land, and transnational capital is increasingly turning human beings into commodities. Yet in Zhu Tianwen's fiction this trend is not a seamless and all-consuming worldwide web. There are many possibilities for the individual to work through and against this homogenizing process. Although the magic of memory and nostalgia is wearing thin, Zhu tries to invoke the power of these resources and reenchant the objects and images with a new aura. The attempt to reenchant the world is private, limited, and haphazard. The individual's search for fulfillment does not have collective resonance and is not extendable to collective solidarity. But it seems necessary to keep trying. Thus Zhu's fiction, in many ways similar to Wang Anyi's work of nostalgia, constitutes a poignant response to the loss of history and memory in the era of globalization.

Hong Kong: Its Political Ambivalence
with the Mainland

As a global city, the image of Hong Kong raises the issues of historical consciousness, modernity, and memory. Clara Law's film *Autumn Moon* (Qiuyue, 1992) offers an occasion to see these problems intersect and evolve. Directed by a well-known Hong Kong director, this film is set in Hong Kong, portrays its cityscape and urban environment, delves into the anxiety of immigration, and depicts characters very much embedded in Hong Kong culture and language. On closer inspection, however, it is hard to name anything beyond these to get a firmer picture of Hong Kong. This intuitive impression may simply be uninteresting to pursue. Why should anyone begin to talk about the Hong Kong "characteristics" when we are constantly told that the city, after its return to Chinese sovereignty, has everything the "world" has to offer? Why should we ask about anything precise and specific about Hong Kong at all, when it is allegedly so cosmopolitan, hybrid, multiethnic, multicultural, and global? But if we are to analyze Hong Kong as a geopolitical, social, and cultural entity the question of identity, or lack thereof, immediately presents a challenge: why a pregiven identity of Hong Kong in its own terms cannot be easily recognized, as in mainland China or even Taiwan (whose identity is also unclear, but not so drastically ambiguous)?

Critics have no difficulty in analyzing China both as a nation-state in the classic sense and as a member of the precarious structure of global governance. As a sovereign state China exercises self-determination in regulating and shaping its internal and external affairs. For all the signs of its increasingly flexible international relations, mainland China still keeps to itself as a sovereign political body. Despite the rise of the market economy, integration into the global circuit of capital, and the decline of the national-state; despite the emergent associations and strata roughly called "the new middle class" and the growth of a society more "civil" than political, the power structure of China is still firmly embedded in the framework of nation-state sovereignty.

Hong Kong does not quite fit into this picture. Despite its return to China, Hong Kong is not fully embraced within China's state power. Hong Kong is constituted as an entity under one state astride two societies, a fact that needs to be taken more seriously as a point of departure for analysis. Hong Kong is protected by the Chinese state if it is involved in international disputes and if it has trouble in geopolitical relations with the rest of the world. If a foreign army intrudes into Hong Kong, it is surely the PLA that must defend it, not a UN peacekeeping force. Yet much of Hong Kong's estates, investment, and interests are not the wealth of the Chinese nation. The assets of Hong Kong are transnational and multinational. Hong Kong is a trading port, a center for global finance, and the supreme nodal point for multiple flows of transnational capital, service, goods, and labor. If we define China and the Chinese identity in terms of nation-state, Hong Kong, in its ambivalent relations with the mainland and cozy intimacy with multinational business interests, seems to be a political no-man's-land or everyone's adventure land.

From the vantage point of postcolonialism Hong Kong's current status goes back in part to its colonial history. Postcolonial critics charge that the colonizers' imperialist narrative has distorted and suppressed local trajectories in different geographies. The injustice of colonial historiography to the "other" needs to be redressed through rearticulating layers of subaltern culture embedded in rituals, customs, everyday life, and traditional worldviews. In Rey Chow's account, this nativist approach seeks to "argue for the autonomy of a historiography by the 'natives' themselves, so that the past that has been usurped from them can become available and accessible once again in 'native' language."[18] But Hong Kong's history and culture have too many diverse backgrounds to constitute an identity. More importantly, there was not an independent state to preside over its society. Since most Hong Kong people are ethnic Chinese, the nativist retrieval of its history would deepen itself to link up with traditional Chinese culture and further with the history of Chinese modernity. It may also link up with other non-Chinese cultures in Asia. A nativism assertive of cultural particularism may become indistinguishable from Chinese nationalism, which has ironically attempted to dominate and colonize Hong Kong. Yet nativism and nationalism could be allies in resistance to colonial western domination. In the eyes of Hong Kong natives, mainland Chinese nationalism is suspect and threatening; for it harbors chauvinist intent toward the former British territory and shows a dismissive attitude to the latter's culture as decadent, commercial, and inauthentic. Thus for Hong Kong to assert its own autonomy by resorting to the nationalist or nativist discourse would run the risk of compromising its democratic process and liberal way of life, its own project of self-representation and self-determination.

Chow's view suggests a separatist aspiration for Hong Kong, casting it in a dual victimhood under the imperialist or colonial domination of both China and the British colonial legacy.[19]

By situating Hong Kong between China and Britain, Chow argues for a third space "that cannot simply be collapsed into the dominant native culture or the western colonizer." Hong Kong's culture is thus a matter of negotiation between two potential aggressors, Britain and China, carving out a space where it is neither simply the puppet of British colonialism nor of Chinese authoritarianism.[20]

This understanding of Hong Kong does not take into account the more sinister situation, in which globalization, allied with an imperial agenda, is turning "free trade" into economic domination. This tendency is threatening both China and Hong Kong. How China can respond effectively to the potential threats of globalization is a huge challenge. The rising tide of neoliberal views exalts the value of the free market and turns a blind eye to the dire costs of globalization. The drastic polarization of the rich and poor, worsened inequality and poverty, political chaos, the erosion of social fabrics, military conflict, economic violence, environmental disasters, the disintegration of community, and human sufferings—all this seems to be the necessary price in the rush to become global. The new trend has been touted as the new telos of world history. Resistance to this myth and process is as relevant to China as it is to Hong Kong. It is true that Hong Kong might evolve a different trajectory of culture and polity, but isn't this also true for a lot of other local regions and cities within China? Local people in China, like those in Hong Kong, will continue to produce vibrant forms of life, culture, and political associations distinct from any imposed structure from outside. In the globalization process, however, Hong Kong, armed to the teeth with global capital, information technology, and the modern trappings of liberal institutions, is edging north to influence many regions and to dominate the public consciousness.[21] Indeed, in the official neoliberal discourse of development and globalization, Hong Kong has been upheld as a shining example of what's to come: it is the bridgehead to the future. In mainland China, the image of Hong Kong has without question become a hegemonic discourse rather than a marginal phenomenon.

The more urgent question, therefore, is not about Hong Kong being under the threat of China, even though this is an issue in public discourse of civil society. China, along with Hong Kong, is confronted with a global process that is posing a bigger threat and that has inflicted much pain and injustice. Hong Kong needs to be viewed together with China in a context of globalization and related consequences. This shift of emphasis sees the two regions in light of a continuing process of Chinese modernity since the late nineteenth century. Although Hong Kong went through colonial modernity while China sought a varied modernity of nationalist, revolutionary, and socialist stripes, in this age of global interdependence, and under the threat of neoimperialism and neocolonialism, the priority is not whether Hong Kong can carve out a space for a more democratic polity and autonomous community; it is how China and Hong Kong can do it together and carve out a more livable space and achieve sustainable development in the broad context of global geopolitics.

Between the lingering influence of Britain and sovereign mainland China, Hong Kong apparently enjoys a disengaged, freestanding status as a port and a center of capital flow. This makes the identity of Hong Kong culture dubious. Observers are onto something when they are not prepared to attach "culture" to this former British colony. If the concept of culture is limited to a coherent, sanctified set of aesthetic, discursive, and symbolic forms legitimizing a modern nation-state over extended time, the absence of culture was the birthmark of Hong Kong's colonial condition from day one. Before it was ceded to Britain after the Opium War, Hong Kong was a fishing village. The British were not interested in Hong Kong as a territorial trophy to be ruled by its sovereignty. Hong Kong was set up as a headquarters for British trade and equipped with the necessary organs of law and order and administration, so that it would serve as a convenient port of entry into the Far East.[22] As a mere entity of trade and commerce far from the centralized political power, Hong Kong did not get much chance to develop, accumulate, and build up a cultural edifice, complete with monuments, institutions, treasures, classic canons, and the continuous transmission of memory adequate to the territorial sovereignty and history of a modern nation-state. The city of Hong Kong does not boast the monumental cityscape, the seat of political power, that marks Paris, Beijing, or Shanghai. Hong Kong's "orphaned" status has given rise to that dismissive epitaph "cultural desert," even if some critics want to uncover something like refined culture from popular culture in Hong Kong.

But if Hong Kong does not have a state-sponsored, state-supporting culture as envisioned by Matthew Arnold, it certainly has cultural practices as anthropologists would see it, encompassing everyday tradition, customs, and rituals—in short, a distinct way of life.²³ It has a culture that in its creative energy is indistinguishable from a homegrown livelihood within the global economy. The Arnoldian notion of culture, as Masao Miyoshi reminds us, is an "apologia for the state" and buttresses the framework and exterior order of the state: "Culture was to serve as an agency for law and order."²⁴ This modernist notion of culture implies an integral, vertical relation between culture and state hegemony. In this light, it seems ill-advised to look for a state-sponsored cultural "heritage" in Hong Kong; but it is very timely to ask whether China can retain its national culture these days, for it is embracing the western cultural industry at the risk of losing its distinct culture heritage and tradition. Just like Hong Kong, cultural production in the mainland is becoming increasingly indistinguishable from economic activity and market operation. The need to keep alive the local community and its homegrown culture is as urgent a problem in China as it has long been recognized in Hong Kong.

Immigration, Nostalgia, and Poetic Justice

Hong Kong needs to be grasped as a brand-new phase of global capitalism that continues the same traumatic process that we saw in Taiwan. As a global city, Hong Kong could be interpreted through David Harvey's diagnosis of capitalist geography as "time-space compression." The history of capitalism has been marked by a "speed-up in the pace of life" on the one hand and the overcoming of spatial barriers on the other. This shrinking process is so "overwhelming that the world sometimes seems to collapse inward upon us." Space shrinks to the global village, and time is shortened to "the point where the present is all there is (the world of schizophrenic)."²⁵ Space-time compression is a decentralizing force that accelerates the process of production, exchange, and consumption and is a sign of capital accumulation in its most dispersed, global phase. Note the tinge of violence and trauma in Harvey's description of space-time compression.

The current project of Hong Kong Disney is a concrete example of this telescoping of time and squeezing of space. As Michelle Huang's study shows, Disney was attracted to Hong Kong because of the city's convenient infrastructure, transnational and multiethnic diversity, and closeness to the Asian market.[26] But a deeper metaphorical affinity obtains between Hong Kong and Disney: each mirrors the other as a composite, flattened image blithely indifferent to the depth of heterogeneous histories and geographies. If the world's divergent geographies and the varieties of culture can be compressed together for the viewer to fetishize on a roller-coaster ride, this spectacle might well be Hong Kong or Disney. The project to build a Disney theme park in Hong Kong, expected to start in 2005 and to be fully completed in 2020, has behind it the driving force of global capital that is becoming more and more the production and consumption of simulacra.

Time-space compression is related to another phenomenon: the mobility of people and labor. A horizontal movement of labor goes hand in hand with the global flow of capital. The new communications technology is turning former industrial production into flexible, piecemeal production around the globe, into the virtual production of information and image. Instead of the centralized control, production and consumption are flexible, instant, and dispersed. For the laborers, "this all implied an intensification (speed[ing] up) in labor processes and acceleration in the de-skilling and reskilling" required to meet the new labor needs.[27] The laborers have to be constantly on the move, dictated by the accelerative thrust of ever-mobile capital. This is one reason immigration has become a universal experience in the late twentieth century. For people on the move against their will, immigration may be uprooting, and relocation is a word of denial for dislocation.

The phenomenon of immigration and labor flows, whose victims are millions of hapless migrant workers and professionals, is particularly poignant in Hong Kong. Human labor follows the circulation of transnational capital, and people migrate to wherever jobs and opportunities are. Hong Kong sees more arrivals and departures, comings and goings, than any other city in the world. If there is still romance attached to the globe-trotting, frequent-flying, and cosmopolitan business managers or intellectuals, one needs to be wary about the daily traumas of uprooting and the stress of making a new home every few years, never having a chance to warm up to the milieu of memory: home, school, community, kin, and friends. Remarking on these daily traumas, Ackbar Abbas writes that Hong Kong history is one of shock and radical changes.[28]

The accelerated turnaround and turnover of labor power, products, and services are attended by a sense of always living in the present. There is no sense of depth and embeddedness associated with memory and history. In order to train themselves to adapt stoically to dislocations and disorientation, people need to develop a blasé attitude, a staunch defense through willed forgetfulness. Abbas rightly observes "Hong Kong people have little memory and no sentiments for the past. The general attitude to everything, sometimes indistinguishable from the spirit of enterprise, is cancel out and pass on." The memory traces, residues of having lived in a particular juncture of time-space as part of one's life intertwined with many other lives, tend to become indistinguishable from the swift turnover of products designed for planned obsolesce. Even if we may find traces of the past, says Abbas, "in the jostling anachronisms and spatial juxtapositions that are seen on every street," one wonders if this "history," flattened out into spatial mosaics, is not already hijacked by the global drive of enterprise or developers.[29] These powerful manipulators are all too happy to throw history into the proverbial dustbin and repackage whatever remains of the past through the Disneyfication of everything for the spectacle.

Turning history into spectacle is not just a selling pitch of the transnational corporations. For people unable to go with the flow, becoming accustomed to the transient and ephemeral trends through media saturation is a symptom of blasé defense. Hong Kong cinema is a medium that trains desensitized sensibilities. It is quick to register painful dislocations and discontinuities and tries to come to terms with the scrambling and compressing of historical trajectories and geographies. From Abbas's description, one gets a dispiriting sense of the utter elusiveness of history, played out over and again on the screen. The screening of history drives out the emotion-soaked memory related to particular places and pasts:

Related to the question of space is that of affectivity. In a dislocated space, affectivity in turn becomes problematic. It is as if all the ways of relating have somehow shifted, the bonds that join us to others as friends and lovers, as daughters and sons blurring like the lines on a television screen that is not tracking properly. It is not just a question of traditional responses versus modern indifference: the opposition between tradition and modernity is already too stable and predictable. Rather, what we find represented now are emotions that do not belong to anybody or to any situation—affective intensities with no name.[30]

Thus we shift from memory to empty images: from human emotion to sheer affectivity, from lived relations of family and community to show-time relationships, from genuine response and communication to talk show evanescence, from tradition to modernity, and from the ethical subject of responsibility to a thing without a name and without a heart.[31] Captains of global corporations would be pleased to see people as buyers without names, devoid of emotions, connections, and love, denuded of the burdensome entanglement of local and national belongings, just a clean slate and market niche for the marketing and consumption of goods and images. Without irony, Abbas's description of Hong Kong's simulacra and fluid mentality would seem the good news to the CEOs of Disney or Hollywood whose dream is to turn the globe into Planet Hollywood.

Cinema, not just Hong Kong cinema, is an appropriate site for analyzing the issues of globalization and its discontents. The danger is that with the tendency to transform lived experience into cinematic images on a massive scale, cinema works easily as a symbol of the contemporary global regime of simulacra rather than its critique. The tendency to mimic and register the glow and flow of the global city marks Hong Kong cinema, whose aesthetics have been linked to the raciness, fluidity, and rootlessness of the transnational cityscape in East Asia. It is only fitting that Esther Yao names a recent anthology of Hong Kong film criticism *At Full Speed*, as if Hong Kong cinema were a high-tech propelling device.[32] In this light Clara Law's film *Autumn Moon* is a bold attempt to question, critique, and expose this blinding velocity of time and space compression.

Transnational, cross-cultural migration has been celebrated together with the waning of the nation-state, the crossing and breakdown of boundaries, and the abundance of opportunities elsewhere. In the neoliberal vision of global civil society based on free markets, "free" flows of people are signs of freedom and democracy. Yet "thrown into a vast open sea with no navigation charts and all the marker buoys sunk and barely visible," as Zygmunt Bauman warns, "we only have two choices left: we may rejoice in the breath-taking vistas of new discoveries—or we may tremble out of fear of drowning."[33] The film *Autumn Moon* (1992) tells the stories of people—tourists, perennial drifters, and would-be immigrants—who suffer from the fear of drowning in the uncharted scene of transience, uncertainty, and death, trying to hold onto some markers or signposts. In a situation where everything or everybody is on the threshold of being somewhere else, destined to disappear and die without trace, the film evokes hidden memories beneath the flat cement and simulacra of the city. These nostalgic memories, of how we once lived, are shockingly brought to the surface and cast a critical light on the devastating daily condition of deprivation and dislocation.

The film offers a threadbare narrative of how a young Japanese tourist meets and develops a deepening friendship with a fifteen-year-old Hong Kong girl. The girl is fretful over the prospect of immigrating to Canada. Although immigration before 1997 was driven by a fear of Hong Kong's return to China, the issue can now be put in the perspective of global modernity. The Japanese young man comes to Hong Kong to escape boredom and to taste "real" Chinese food, while the young girl is suffering from the stress of having to immigrate. Although barely able to communicate in English, the two come together through the evocation of common places and activities of the traditional family, a form of life in the process of being erased from urban space. The major figure embodying the remainders of the threatened life is the girl's grandmother. On the immigration papers, the grandmother is pronounced "dead," for the immigration visa cannot be granted if the grandmother, a nonlabor power and hence a nonperson, comes with the family to Canada.

The immigration paper's death verdict, along with the grandmother's impending death, is not only the condition of Hong Kong writ large, but also the fate of the older, change-resistant social relations and experiences. These relations are becoming a phenomenon of the imminent past. With the anticipated death as the vanishing point of everything "traditional," however, the grandmother emerges as a figure that provides a sanctuary and holds the ground amid acceleration, departure, and planned death, bringing real life within the atrophy of urban space.

The film's portrayal of Hong Kong's cityscape presents an image of vast cement blocks drained of life, an image of urbanized and manufactured death. Against this alienating space, the narrative expresses a desire to cling to something that does not quickly die, evoking permanence in the ephemeral. The film produces its most striking visual effect of the cityscape through a deliberate use of long takes and long shots aimed at the huge blocks of beehivelike, depressively functional apartment buildings, some from a low angle to highlight their towering magnitude, others from a bird's-eye view to look down on the utterly desolate and uniform building tops. Whenever we stare at these faceless buildings through the prolonged gaze of a static or moving camera, we are thrown up against the wall of the overpowering, suffocating presence of a monstrous space, a space that makes a travesty of the "human habitat." Indeed, the long shots and long takes of the cityscape amount to a visual as well as visceral violence that assaults the longing of human self-affirmation within the immediate milieu of habitat. The huge cement blocks seem to dominate and crush tiny human figures, who are often squeezed into the corner of the frame. At the first moment when the Japanese tourist arrives, up in the sky is the roaring jumbo jet, and down on the ground is the truncated view of a taxi. With a video camera in hand, and against the backdrop of an industrial metal fence, the tourist tries to fish for some images of touristy interest, but with all the blocks of high-rises and superhighway ramps rushing at him as he rides in the taxi, all he can do is turn the camera onto himself as reflected in the window of the taxi, shoot the faceless blocks, and then film everything he has just purchased in his tiny, cheap apartment. Trying to film all the footprints and traces of his trip, the tourist ends up filming himself filming—a complete, self-referential, and empty circle.

The Hong Kong girl is also faced with the same homeless, traceless, and makeshift existence. A profound melancholy hangs over the girl as she and her friends suffer the uncertainty of having to marry foreigners and move elsewhere when they grow up. Still a child, the girl returns again and again to her "past," cherishing the childhood memory of her yearly birthday celebrations in a corner of a McDonald's, which, as the Japanese reminds her, is "the same the world over." But the girl's constant remembrance of her past points to the truncated, transient temporality of life: she reminisces as if she were a grandmother. The vanishing without trace intensifies the search for the time lost.

Meanwhile, the Japanese tourist discovers, to his delight, the "authentic" food that the grandmother cooks for the family's dinner. In her sickness and dying, the grandmother stands out as a figure embedded in rituals, custom, and tradition. One unforgettable scene dramatizes how this life of the past is violently reduced yet tenaciously alive. With her grandmother in the hospital, the tourist and girl try to cook by themselves; they find the refrigerator fully stocked, with bottles of soy sauce, ingredients, vegetables, condiments, and so on—a bundle of life frozen and squeezed to a corner. But as a life that is lived with working hands and with the family, it is a life as complicated, as the Japanese tourist says, as the building of an atomic bomb, and just as worth remembering. The cinematography captures the force of the outburst of memory. In a slightly panning close-up long take, the sundry things in the refrigerator burst out as the "return of the repressed." This discovery leads the Japanese to another revelation. As he films the grandmother when she makes her wish in the hospital in anticipation of death, he records a wish embedded in past life. It is a wish that secures its self-image against time and materializes itself in ritualistic burial and other customs. It signifies human beings' return to nature and to a full-blooded afterworld that would continue the meaningful intimacy between the living and the dead.

The past is not a temporal category here. It sinks its roots in an organic, "traditional," "natural" life form, sedimented in the local practices that intertwine ways of living with culture. Planners, immigration officers, experts, and proponents of globalization hastily pronounce the past obsolete. Another trick to dismiss the past in favor of the ever-changing present is to laugh off memories as nostalgia. The film's approach to the past, it is important to note, is more melancholy than nostalgic. The sense of melancholy comes from the inability to mourn and disengage from the lost or dead loved ones, a psychic structure characterized by immersion in the pastness of the past without trying to get out of it and to move on. A melancholy response to the vanishing things comes about "when the object was loved not as separate and distinct from oneself, but rather as a mirror of one's own self and power."[34] This immersion in the past may be narcissistic, regressive, and self-defeating, but in the context of swift change, the "getting stuck with the old" may be a source of renewal and self-empowerment. It is a resource of resistance against fast acceleration and deracination. This self-renewing nostalgia refuses to accept the view embodied by the immigration paper that pronounces the grandmother dead. This change-driven view dismisses nostalgia and says, the past is really past, so why bother fantasizing about it?

The melancholy understanding of the past, however, cannot make a clean break, because the very identity of the subject in the present is constituted inescapably by the past and needs constantly to maintain ties with it. This understanding does not believe that the past is really passé, but it lives a submerged, half-forgotten life beneath the swift flow of the present and often bursts through its surface. Toward the end, the film evokes classical poetry that mourns sad autumn and separation. It once again dwells on the details of past life through visits by the tourist and the girl to the fishing village, now in ruins. It strikes a celebratory note when the two friends, bound in memory, stage a poetic recreation of Midautumn Festival. The film thus casts a melancholy eye on the past, on the premodern, "natural" life, on the ruins and remains deemed irrelevant to modern change. If there is a romantic nostalgia here, it is not to be read as another advertising gimmick or tourist attraction derived from an aesthetic that treats history as a spectacle. It is a nostalgia that is still able to imagine a past that refuses to succumb to the change-crazy present.

In this light what Adorno says of romantic nostalgia comes as a critique of the complacent dismissal of nostalgia. Nostalgia, in its melancholy form, reveals a guilty conscience that is nonetheless mixed with pleasure in looking at the old walls and a cluster of medieval houses. But our pleasure of nostalgia may survive the "insight that makes it suspicious." What makes nostalgia "suspicious" is the dogmatic conviction of a change-driven historical sensibility that embraces everything new and downgrades everything old. Yet this view is suspect from the standpoint of nostalgia's desire. Adorno makes this point clear: "So long as progress, deformed by utilitarianism, does violence to the surface of the earth, it will be impossible—in spite all proof to the contrary—completely to counter the perception that what antedates the trend is in its backwardness better and more humane." Globalization along the lines of development, rationality, and change has not transformed the human condition into "living life." On the contrary, it is stripping humans of their particular context, belongings, geography, and experience. The global process is part of modern history on a utilitarian and instrumental track and has wrought havoc on human bodies and the environment. It is a record of shock and catastrophe. In the context of abstraction and simulation, and under the pressure to pass on quickly to somewhere else, nostalgia "endows the traces of immediacy, however dubious and antiquated, with an element of justice."[35]

On this view, nostalgia is not another fanciful play, but embodies a consciousness that "incorporates nature's wounds" and is etched by the real suffering of the past.[36] This is a form of poetic justice that seeks to right the wrongs of history. The ending of *Autumn Moon* suggests a registering of the destruction and mutilation of Hong Kong's past by going over the ruins of what used to be a fishing village, which might well be the home of the Hong Kong girl's grandmother. It also evokes the celebration of the tradition of Midautumn Festival. With the remembrance of past sufferings, the film brings out the imagination of an alternative. This nostalgia is ancient, uncertain, and fragile, but refuses to submit to the current trend of globalization.

Love at Last Sight

NOSTALGIA, MEMORY, AND COMMODITY IN
CONTEMPORARY CHINESE LITERATURE

The rise of nostalgia in China in the 1990s was symptomatic of epochal changes in the preceding two decades. Expressions of nostalgia retraced what had already occurred and is still going on in Taiwan and Hong Kong. They can be understood in terms of the overlapping strains of modernization and modernity. If modernization was only a vague aspiration in the mid-1980s, heralded by material goods such as TV sets and refrigerators as well as waves of western ideas, the enthusiasm began to wear thin in the 1990s. The large-scale influx of global capital and the unleashing of market forces have accelerated the modernization process with staggering yet uneven results. Although the centralized political structure remains in place, the basic fabric of everyday life and social relations are undergoing drastic, frequently traumatic changes. The acute sense that all that is solid melts into air is indeed very much apparent.

Nostalgia has seeped into many quarters of cultural production and threatens to become a pervasive structure of feeling. Some anecdotal instances suffice to offer a glimpse of the tremendous drive to preserve the oldies. Demolition of old city blocks for residential and business high-rises is accompanied by desperate rescue efforts to document in film, video, and photography the last vanishing vestiges of a receding era. Memoirs, reminiscences, reproduction of old artifacts, new releases on video of films of the 1930s and 1940s as well as of revolutionary history, new films bent on romanticizing the village tucked away in a purer past, and thriving nostalgic restaurants—all these and more seem to be evidence of nostalgia as a mass mentality.

Nostalgia needs to be understood against the acceleration and shocks of modern experience that, for all its excitement and adventure, also brings trauma and loss. The ferment of nostalgia in the 1990s stemmed from the dire consequences of the blinding speed of the market economy, the rise of consumer society, and the overhaul of the administrative structure stumbling on the corruption of inherited power. The consequences of modernity as a process of rationally restructuring society in little more than a single decade brutalize consciousness and daily life with violence and anxiety. The sharp increase in unemployment, the disappearance of trust and security, the thinning of the communal network, and above all the loss of a cohesive ideology prompted the disenfranchised populace to yearn for better images of life in the past. All of a sudden the prerevolutionary times, and even Mao's years, are glowing in their simplicity and solidarity, in their inexhaustible hopes and common destiny, their poverty and cruelty conveniently forgotten.

Nostalgia provides a buffer not only for victims of modern distress but also for the proponents of globalization. The drastic social transformation along the lines of Weberian rationalization and the embrace of the global market cut short the lingering legacy of socialism that shaped the outlook and lifeways of millions. Yet jumping on the bandwagon of global capital by no means guarantees smooth sailing. Although one can don the hat of a transnational businessman or a globe-trotting intellectual overnight, to have a "cosmopolitan" identity thrust upon the self is not without pain and struggle. There arises the need to find the seeds of continuity in the past that anticipated a future that seems to have suddenly arrived. Thus we have a nostalgia that does not look beyond the current state of affairs to challenge it, but seeks to find images of lineage, to cloak the fast-paced development with the enchanted mantle from the past. This is the nostalgia that imagines a strain of modernity that had supposedly been repressed by socialist practice but is said to enjoy a renaissance in recent years, promising to deliver China from its revolutionary "deviations" to global capital. The neoliberal embrace of the global market is inclined toward this version of nostalgia.[1]

From a historiographical perspective nostalgia can be construed as a resistance to the homogeneous narrative of globalization. In his recent study of Wang Anyi's works, Zhang Xudong sees nostalgia as invocations of substrata of unofficial histories, intimate lifeworlds, and memories of long duration beneath a homogeneous history. This history includes revolutionary modernity, with its radical transformations and developmentalist agenda, as well as more recent trends of capitalist globalization. The undocumented, lived, "natural history" that Zhang uncovers from beneath the uniform history comes in the multilayered images of the city of Shanghai, of residual middle-class lifestyle, the lingering habit of consumption, and the aura of communal living and aesthetic experience.[2] I share Zhang's intention to discover the "other" of history and to explore alternative horizons of temporality in a critique of the homogeneous narratives of revolution and capitalism. In this chapter, however, I will focus on the looming phenomenon of commodity and its cultural and literary implications. My point of departure is that the different, often incommensurable uses of the commodity, whether as a "thing," a mental image, or a network of relations, offer a key to understanding the forking paths of historical imagination. For this purpose I shift from a cultural and literary analysis to one based more on political economy, political theory, and the politics of difference.

Commodity, Homogeneous History, and Abstract Labor

The blanket term *homogeneous history* encompasses two trends of capitalist modernity and socialist modernization. If modern history on the global scale since the late nineteenth century to the end of the cold war is a crude alternative between these two distinct paths, the narrative of teleology, whether of Enlightenment or utopian communism, is one of worldwide accumulation of capital in the name of imperialism and colonialism, as well as China's socialist modernization. Locked in this Manichean polarity, the teleological plot does not recognize other possibilities. Nostalgia, in this light, seems to be fueling the search for alternatives beyond this reified, black-and-white narrative. Thus it may be seen as a projection of a different social imaginary that seeks to break out of the uniform march of production, commodity, exchange, spectacle, and consumption—a process that is shaping different cultures with imperial momentum. In this regard Karl Marx's analysis of the commodity form becomes useful in unlocking the inner contradictions within a homogeneous history of globalization, and, paradoxically, "Marxist"-oriented socialist development.

In *Capital* Marx analyzes how the vastly extended relations of commodity exchange affect human productive activity: labor. In laboring to produce goods to satisfy the individual's needs and wants, the producer engages in real labor and produces concrete use values. But under the all-encompassing relations of commodity exchange, labor becomes abstract because its sole purpose is to produce commodities for exchange. Manufactured to realize only exchange value, "products of labor acquire, as values, one uniform social status, distinct from their varied forms of existence as objects of utility."[3] Thus real labor as a necessary human activity to produce things of individual use is taken over (not completely, because its incompleteness is what I want to insist on) by abstract labor in the massive social production of commodities for profit.

Abstract labor also affects the producer's subjectivity and his or her relations with other human beings. Real labor is real because it shapes the individual's unique existence, personality, and trajectory. But commodity exchange melts unique individuality and concrete relations into an abstract, formal relation. Developing Marx's theory of labor and value in the era of high capitalism, Theodor Adorno compares the process of commodity exchange to a mathematical model that relies on pure formal properties and on the reciprocal equivalence of "the like-for-like accounts that match and that leave no remainder."[4] The "remainders" here refer to the specific qualities of "unalienated" labor and its anchoring in specific time and place. Bodily experience and sensuous particulars are reflected in the producer's work. Not tethered to streamline commodity production, such work is associated with concrete experience, aesthetic aura, and emotional resonance. Marx's 1844 *Economic and Philosophic Manuscripts* is devoted to rearticulating the aesthetically fulfilling and hence human qualities of work. The disappearance of the "remainders" is what prompts nostalgia to retain past traces. Given the loss of traces, the classical notion of history as human labor is in jeopardy. Without real labor, it becomes difficult to see history as a praxis enacted on the present, an ongoing human activity in articulating and reproducing the material condition of human life.

For Adorno and Benjamin the system of exchange threatens to strip history of concrete experience of collective self-creation and choice, replacing it with a uniform time of industrial production and an atomistic, libidinal time of consumption. This means "nothing less than that recollection, time, memory are being liquidated by advancing bourgeois society itself."[5] Nostalgia, in this bleaching abstraction, arises as a reaction against the homogenization of time. It is a defiant attempt to find the remainders of history beyond or within the world of commodity.

Abstract labor is rightly dubbed homogeneous because it flattens myriad, infinitely heterogeneous forms of individuals' activity and experience into identical entities, measurable in money and interchangeable in the market. This abstracting process runs parallel to Weberian rationalization. The "empty, homogeneous history" designates a process that strips real human activity of its concrete contents of labor and sensuous existence. It bleaches infinitely varied human practices into a uniform process of production and consumption. This is a transition (the period of transition, *zhuanxing qi*, is a keyword in talking about China's changes) from many different, disparate temporal horizons into a synchronic rhythm of abstract labor. The talk of the end of history signals the "final" conquest of the commodity (capital) form. No wonder very few people these days would bother to critique the commodity from a humanist perspective, because it is the very air we breathe.

The commodity form, however, cannot erase real labor and use value completely, just as globalization cannot globalize local communities and traditions out of existence. In the production of use values, real labor is also implicated in the network of commodity exchange, but as Dipesh Chakrabarty puts it, there remains "that which cannot be enclosed by the sign 'commodity.'"[6] The tension between real labor and abstract labor, use value and exchange value; between the triumphant march of homogeneous history and local difference implies that a memory (or nostalgia) tenaciously clings to the experience of real labor in the commodity. This memory may cling to the residual mode of production of the old, yearn for the traditional lifeworld, critique the current abstracting process, and anticipate different horizons of the future. This is how, as a form of memory, nostalgia exerts its political function and invokes historical difference right at the heart of the commodity.

The commodity form, on the other hand, has positive dimensions that Chinese intellectuals can ill afford to throw out the window. The commodity implies a social relation: it is not a thing. We need to remind ourselves that there were commodities before high and global capitalism; the commodity needs to be disengaged from capitalism per se for strategic purposes. Economic development, a thriving market, and the abundance of commodities are still the dream of the larger population and provide an important, if not necessary, precondition for achieving a better, more open society and polity. From the perspective of political theory, abstract labor has its related juridical framework of the "equal rights" of the abstract individual, which, for all its "bourgeois" legacy and distortions, underlies the notions of democracy, freedom, and political reform. Marx describes dialectically how the exchange relation can be conducive to freedom and difference. Exchange relations "can satisfy the manifold wants of the individual producer himself, only insofar as the mutual exchangeability of all kinds of useful private labor is an established social fact, and therefore the private useful labor of each producer ranks on an equality with that of all others."[7] This remark recasts the "homogeneous" and "uniform" condition of equal rights of all individuals in more democratic terms. It says that only in a social environment of equality can one be free to be different. This condition does not erase but is in fact necessary for maintaining difference in unique individual trajectories.[8]

With this sketch of the dual character of the commodity form—its negative homogeneity and its potential political and economic benefits for China—it is easier to see why Wang Anyi, of many active Chinese writers, commands wide attention, both critical and popular. In her works since the early 1990s, Wang has proved to be most sensitive to the possibilities inherent in the aggressive commodity form and open-minded as well as critical in laying out different historical trajectories and temporalities in the context of globalization.

Apparently Wang's turn toward memory and nostalgia can be explained as a mourning for a familiar lifeworld fast receding from view. Her work corresponds to a prevalent understanding of how modernization dismantles traditional ways of life. We may describe the consequences of modernization as going in three directions. The first is the abstraction of the entrenched social relations of trust and intimacy into a fluid, bloodless cash nexus. Emotionally and ethically charged social relations are reduced to the bare bone of money relations. Second, the subject of critical thinking and autonomy, a mindset in the 1980s redolent of the intellectual fervor of the May Fourth enlightenment, is now being dissolved into bits and pieces of consumer items and momentary thrills, into decentered, free-floating "subjectivity" or its schizophrenic abandon. The vibrant reflective consciousness of history that seemed to be the tenor of the 1980s is now disappearing into the glittering fascination of advertised images. Third, the experience of time is abstracted into a homogeneous time of repetitive production, reproduction, and consumption.

These developments spawn the themes of memory in contemporary literature. In the period of Maoism, the function of memory was to evoke a past that confirmed the present and anticipated the future. When social life is now stripped of its unified community and communication, memory arises to replace the official historical structuring of lived time. Memory comes to its own, cutting loose from its previously organic anchor in the continuum of life. If collectively shared and maintained, memory "automatically" conserves traditional relations of trust and intimacy in the close contact of family, community, and larger social associations. Memory ensures identity and relates the individual to a past, personal and collective, that feeds relevance and identity to the present. Memory, in other words, makes connections, but these connections are lived spontaneously and do not need to be continuously reinvented; there is no need for memory to do a heavy-duty job. The strong need for memory at present is a sign of the severing of vital connections under commodity exchange.[9]

Making connections to the past is premised upon the notion of history, which is being jeopardized by the advanced form of commodity production. Thus an intriguing factor in Wang Anyi's work is its resonance with the theme of the society of the spectacle that engulfs substantive reality into thin air, turning it into a plane of images. As the dominant feature of late capitalism, the spectacle fascinates many critics. Guy Debord, Jean Baudrillard, and Fredric Jameson have developed Marx's idea of the commodity as a "fantastic form of a relation between things" into an all-encompassing screen that not only transfigures the real, but also maps out and constitutes the real itself.[10] For Baudrillard, the era of the simulacrum coincides with a process whereby all goods, commodities, and labor are rendered equivalent and become consumable images and items of affective intensity. The classical distinction between being and appearance, between a solid substratum of nature, labor, and experience on the one hand, and the figurative superstructure on the other no longer holds and is actually preceded by overarching simulacra.[11] Baudrillard quotes a fable from Jorge L. Borges to describe the total collapsing of the map (figurative) into the territory (the real). In the fable, the cartographers of the empire draw up a map "so detailed that it ends up covering the territory exactly." In this global, imagistic subsumption of all social fields, the simulacrum substitutes "the signs of the real for the real" and short-circuits all historical vicissitudes and concrete references.[12] To what extent this hyperreal is true of present-day China, which is indeed sliding on a similar slope, is not an irrelevant question and deserves critical attention. We remember that the spectacle for political mobilization of the masses was a repeated phenomenon and practice in revolutionary movements and political culture.[13] Recently, the revolution-inspired spectacle has turned commercial; the public has turned to sheer publicity. Some of Wang Anyi's works already display flows of simulacra that are little more than a stream of self-generating intensities and pleasures. One can also mention the stellar rise of Wei Hui, the young Shanghai writer whose works very much bank on performative theatrics and simulacra. What is more interesting in this hyperreal, however, is the imaginary resurrection of the sense of authenticity and lived experience of an unrecoverable real. Nostalgia is another name for this resurrection.

In the pervasive flow of images as commodity and capital, the question no longer pertains to a return to the lost reality, but displaces the search for reality to the search for difference. Nostalgia is a quest for difference and is carried out not through bypassing the images but creatively swimming, if not dancing, with them. The consumer's creativity is the place where Walter Benjamin, Michel de Certeau, and David Harvey attempt to project an active politics of difference. Like these writers Wang Anyi does not reject the commodity out of hand. She looks into the ferment of memory, nostalgia, and commodity but tries to read past the fantastic forms to uncover the hidden memories. This entails an ambiguous or dialectic approach to the commodity form as well as a mixed attitude to the socialist legacy. The general wind of intellectual and aesthetic trends in contemporary China tends either toward an uncritical embrace of globalization and the commodity form, or toward a moralistic rejection of westernization in a nostalgic throwback to the socialist good old days. Wang Anyi is walking a tightrope between these rigid historical trajectories. And her invocation of hidden memories of the past, frequently nestled within the commodity itself, proves most critical and open-ended in asserting a form of historical imagination under the pressure of globalization.

Historical Mutations of Commodity and Literature

Wang Anyi's engagement with the commodity form and its residual memory becomes clear in a longer perspective of history. For clarity of analysis, we may distinguish a literature produced mainly for entertainment and consumption from one that is committed to educating the audience about weighty social issues. Commodified literature is different from literature of commitment. Although these two categories overlap at certain conjunctures (a didactic novel needs to be marketed before it can educate; a text of pleasure may teach didactic lessons about how to live against ascetic ideology), the literature of commitment had until the late 1980s appeared to be mainstream. For literature of consumption, we may recall the Mandarin Duck and Butterfly fiction, film literature written for commercial cinema in Shanghai in the republican era, and most remarkably, the Shanghai style (*haipai*) as opposed to the Beijing style (*jingpai*). These commercial strains fell outside the established canon of modern culture for a long time. The distinction between the two is helpful in underscoring the way the commodity stood in sharp tension to the modern historical narrative. For instance, Shanghai style refers to a form of writing and an aesthetic taste geared toward the market and urban consumers, a literature of amusement and entertainment.[14] In contrast, Beijing style is intensely preoccupied with historical issues and committed to raising social consciousness under the aegis of the May Fourth ideology. Ironically, by repackaging traditional literary repertoire, the "commodified" Mandarin Duck and Butterfly form of culture catered to a population of fans who were mostly modern urbanites schooled in modern ways of life. Meanwhile, the Beijing style, or literature of commitment, is "elitist" and radical, equipped with modern western notions of historical progress.[15] Although the two trends operated side by side in the republican era, after 1949, the Shanghai style was very much marginalized. Not until the late 1980s and early 1990s, with the expansion of market economy and the rise of consumer society, did something akin to Shanghai style begin to revive and even take center stage.

This brief outline shows the vicissitudes of commodified literature. The notion of literature as commodity is inimical to the canon of modern Chinese literature—and for that matter, to almost the whole century of the emancipatory project in China's quest for modernity. This project is to find a Chinese road to the status of the modern nation-state, an undertaking aimed at self-consciously reshaping society. It engages practical, collective action in a process of transforming a people and their inherited ways of life. The familiar charge from this quarter against commodified literature is that the latter tends to divert attention and energy from this "real" revolutionary movement and praxis. Literature as commodity and entertainment turns active participation in history into a petty bourgeois, self-indulgent immersion in images for consumption. The active historical agent is turned into a passive recipient of spectacles.

The ahistorical nature of commodified literature is what prompted many historically minded humanists to vehemently turn against it when it resurfaced with a vengeance in the early 1990s. The anger against the close alliance of literature and commodity gave rise to a heated debate about the loss of the humanist spirit.[16] For defenders of humanism and hence guardians of historical consciousness, commodified literature is suspect and degenerate.

The humanists are right in laying their finger on the ahistoricism of commodified literature. Yet the positive side of commodified literature in relation to the mainstream of Chinese modernity needs to be spelled out in a more dialectical fashion. Commodified literature presupposes a social practice of the commodity, which is premised upon a cluster of assumptions about individual rights, equality, self-fulfillment, and a market-oriented civil society. These belong to the legacy of the Enlightenment and the eighteenth-century bourgeoisie in Europe, which exerted great influence on May Fourth discourse. To the extent that Chinese socialism is a continuation of some of the May Fourth themes, personal happiness, material welfare, and universal prosperity within civil society are still unfulfilled, attractive motifs that appeal to a liberal mind-set. Socialism, as classical Marxism reminds us, has to work through bourgeois, liberal, and Enlightenment values rather than reject or bypass them. Yet the dialectic of history always pulls tricks on the supposedly good values. Just as the commodity may flatten the real history of labor and production into seemingly timeless images, communist history, all too often and without the help of the commodity, turned into its opposite: the fetishized symbol of utopia in the here and now. Revolutionary history, originating as a dynamic, transformative force, became reified into some mythical, "objective" laws or elevated into a theodicy. It takes on the abstract currency of the commodity without being a commodity. Given the propensity of history to turn into myth, the rise of commodified literature in the last two decades or so, to the extent that it asserts private freedom and enjoyment, is a sharp reminder to the communist project that it has not acted upon its original, emancipatory potentialities. Now the Chinese government or the dominant "liberal" discourse seems to have taken cues from this reminder all too well, and the pendulum has swung drastically from a mythologized history to a fetishized market. What seems to be calling the shots now is an all-out embrace of commodified literature, or commodified anything.

In this light it would be a mistake to condemn or embrace commodified literature tout court. When commodified literature, or literature written for pleasure, is able to reveal what is missing in the hegemonic discourse that abandons individual autonomy and freedom, it recalls not only the memory of private enjoyment based on the use of the commodity and the related "civil," democratic connotations, but also the memory of the emancipatory potentials of the utopian, revolutionary project. Yet when it embraces the market with open arms, it shoots itself in the foot and once again falls into self-indulgent, private closure, lapsing into a premature belief in the end of history.

The Nostalgic Spectacle of Shanghai

The literature of nostalgia reveals an anxiety about the general, runaway commodified atmosphere of the early 1990s. By evoking a past more idyllic than the present, nostalgia points to what is lacking in the current state of affairs. On the other hand, there are also attempts to come to terms with the emerging social relations derived from the system of commodity production. The market, after all, has become a historical given and has created a new culture ruled, willy-nilly, by exchange relations. Artists and writers confront a new reality and the new challenge of engaging history via commodity images, for which Wang Anyi's work offers an exemplary case.

The quickly consumed literature in China offers itself as a product of the rising culture of commodity. The popular romances from Taiwan and Hong Kong, Jin Yong's works of *kongfu*, the sensational phenomenon of "Shanghai Babe," and many other forms of commodified literature are very much at home in the market and proudly offer themselves as entertainment. Those works that still claim to be "serious literature" through a strong nostalgic return to the past are more difficult to categorize. Since the late 1980s critics have hailed two remarkable styles of "serious" writing: new historicism and neorealism.[17] Both could be seen as edging toward the new commercial culture. Among many other features, they show a strong turn toward the everyday life of an isolated individual. Neorealism places a premium on mundane, trivial life. With a magnifying glass, it creates a narrative, in soap opera fashion, of distress, anxiety, pleasure, and ennui of the quotidian. Collective activity and reflective history no longer exist here; what is left is sheer survival, *huozhe*, the bare facts of living, day after day, month after month, year after year. The fiction of new historicism, on the other hand, plays a variation on mundane realism with historical trappings. For all its apparent interest in fragments, contingencies, and submerged memory, new historicism remains a pseudohistory. It does not focus on significant historical events and refuses to comprehend the reason and movement of history. Like neorealism, it dwells on the pure survival aspects of the individual. The individual acts not as a responsible agent seeking to understand and shape history, but as a street-smart survival creature trying to cope with whatever falls into his or her lap or whatever fate inflicts on the body. Historical flow here is a chronology, a time of living from moment to moment, a succession of "one damn thing after another." As long as you are a monk, you need to ring the bell every day, to use one of Mao's favorite phrases. If modern history now seems to be an "empty, homogeneous time," "telling the sequence of events like the beads of a rosary," then a chronology of an individual's survival, not in historical praxis but in the comfort or distress of his or her living room supplied with TV and soft drinks, is a clock ticking away empty hours.[18] The historical moment is now drugged with the everyday and becomes indistinguishable from the self-indulgent present.

Wang Anyi's works of the 1990s also edged toward a fascination with images of commercial culture, but whether they submit to the ideology of the market is yet to be analyzed case by case. The novel *Changhen ge* (Song of unending sorrow, 1995) offers a good example of how the narrative of nostalgia both affirms and critiques the rush to the market. It does so, ironically, not by resisting the commodity but by working through it. It depicts the commercial culture in Shanghai in its halcyon days before 1949, which tenaciously persisted in a submerged existence through the Mao era, and finally resurfaced in the post-Mao period. By evoking its prehistory the novel attempts to infuse an aura of authentic experience and lend a historical dimension to the commodity. In Wang's hands, the timeless mirage of the commodity is transformed into a thoroughly historical trajectory overlaid with intimate depositories of time and memory.

The three parts of the novel correspond to the three significant historical periods in modern China: the republican, socialist, and post-Mao. In the first part, the novel proffers a total spectacle of the society of commodity in preliberation Shanghai. On the surface this glamorous society resonates with the world analyzed by Guy Debord in his book *The Society of the Spectacle*. The whole society—human relations, consciousness, desire, interests, and needs—seem to be penetrated by the commodity and its ubiquitous images. This commercial paradise, fitted with fashion shows, department stores, movie theaters, leisure magazines, society people, nightlife, and beauty pageants, is made complete with all the modern capitalist paraphernalia of mass media and highly sophisticated visual technology.

The principle protagonist Wang Qiyao figures as an image of the triumphant commodity in the first part of the novel. Wang is a symbol of Shanghai's material culture—but only in part. Her ascent to the stardom of Miss Shanghai in a beauty pageant is orchestrated by effective mechanisms of mass media, visual technology, and market strategies, involving filmmakers, photographers, journalists, designers, the PR or "campaign manager" for the beauty contest, and so on. Indeed, that Wang, who looks only a notch better than other girls in the *longtang* neighborhoods and lacks stunning beauty and financial means, could be crowned Miss Shanghai indicates that her success is a happy result of the image production of mass consumer culture. Her winsome "beauty" presupposes an aesthetic of the commodity distinct from classical western notions or traditional Chinese criteria. She is "discovered" by a film director who notices her resemblance to the film star Ruan Lingyu, whose image is etched into the memory of millions of fans.[19] Yet far from being a starlike luxury item, her charm comes through as that of the domestic, demure "Nice Girl of Shanghai"(*hushang shuyuan*)—the title for her inside cover photo in a popular magazine. Her photo, the narrator tells us, is "good looking" (*haokan,* or pretty; 38), not "beautiful"; it can be used in advertisements only for everyday things like laundry detergent or MSG, not for French perfume or expensive watches (38). Her beauty is, in short, an everyday commodity: domestic, accessible, next-door, democratic, and fully circulatable, so everybody can have a share. It is very much in tune with Shanghai's commercial culture and popular taste, for it combines the qualities of a traditional boudoir-bound lady (Chinese) and the street-smart, fashionable modern girl (western). Indeed, that a Guomindang military bureaucrat buys her to be his mistress is proof of her commodity status and indicates the bureaucrat's taste for a mixture of traditional and modern.

The combination of traditional and modern is an index of a hybrid style that caters to commercial interests. The evocation of the glamorous scenes of commercial Shanghai is softened by a narrative convention suggestive of the Mandarin Duck and Butterfly fiction and *The Dream of the Red Chamber.* Eileen Chang becomes widely popular in Shanghai nostalgia in the 1990s, in part because of her ability to blend traditional style into the everyday modern life of Shanghai urbanites. Wang Anyi seems to have inherited this strain but extends it much further, into a broader historical dimension traversing three social formations. The total representation of a glamorous society, incarnate in the lovable figure of Wang Qiyao, projects aspirations to the global market in the guise of nostalgia. The frantic pace of the market needs legitimacy and prior "tradition," for which the Shanghai spectacle supplies a bridge across time and a mirror for self-recognition and self-affirmation. In this mirror, postsocialist consumers, liberal theorists enamored of the market, as well as modern businesspeople and technological leaders, will find something that they can call their own, something that was around before but is now being carried on with renewed intensity and fanfare.

But the rush to the market comes at a price: the loss of another tradition that is felt to be deeper and more intimate, distinctly "Chinese." After all, the Shanghai spectacle smacks of the "Paradise for the Adventurous" (*maoxianjia de leyuan*) from the west and of "the ten-mile foreign business strip" (*shili yangchang*). The traditional motifs and style come in here to fill the void, so that the reading public could not only claim that the Shanghai culture is ours in the high commercial age even though it was supported by foreign capital, but also that this culture has been around for a long time, subsisting in obscure customs of life and stories embedded in the literary memory of Mandarin Duck and Butterfly fiction or *The Dream of the Red Chamber*.

Love at Last Sight

It would be a mistake, however, to claim that *Song of Unending Sorrow* is a celebration of the commodity. The most important contribution of the novel is its active reflection on history within a new social framework, at once threatening and exciting, of commodity production and exchange. It is necessary here to distinguish what kind of historical trajectories the novel engages. The three-part structure evidently points to a history of modernity, in the forms of national capitalism and semicolonialism, the socialist period up to the Cultural Revolution, and the "rebirth" of the free market in the 1980s. In the eyes of the market-oriented nostalgics, the commercial glory of the first part would be a mirror of the now more aggressive market. The enigma is the middle, "interrupted" period. How does this chunk of history link with the other two?

If Mao's China can be understood in terms of modernity by other means and with strong antimodern impulses—a transformative project of reshaping social relations, bureaucratic structure, and utopian revolutionary culture—there seems to be an affinity that traverses all three periods. Wang's novel has as its backdrop this sweeping historical awareness. It is true that the communist revolution abruptly cuts short Shanghai's glamorous stream of commercial spectacles, and the new socialist society would banish Wang Qiyao and the likes of her into the proverbial dustbin. The question becomes, How does the commercial world manage to live through the obscure tunnel of history until it sees the light of day again in the reform era? What are the implications of narrating the persistence of life forms left over from the old Shanghai?

When the city that never sleeps falls into the hands of the revolutionaries, nostalgia arises. Wang Qiyao and her world become a charming memory overnight. This does not mean that the memory of old Shanghai is fanciful and has no place in historical reality. Quite the contrary, it is this memory that heals the wound of historical rupture and sustains the lingering breath of the past. Wang Qiyao retreats to her grandmother's home in the country after her lover dies in a plane crash. Her lover's death and the collapse of the nationalist regime signify the downfall of the whole edifice of a bureaucratic structure coupled with commercial culture. The return to the grandmother's home is a return to a primal village, a maternal haven where one is protected from the traumatic, "alien" times. But instead of finding a refuge in the "timeless" village, instead of settling down in her own home, Wang returns to the city, the scene of trauma, and envelops herself in the afterglow of her former self and in the lingering halo of the vanished Shanghai. Her return to Shanghai is in fact a real homecoming, and the city is seen through a veil of tears. Even in the very heart of the city, another prior city is missed with a deep sense of melancholy. As she looks out the window as the train is entering Shanghai, she sees "reflected on the window pane the shadows, all of old figures, one on top of another, and her eyes are filled with tears" (147).

Not only is Wang in love with her lost self, but she also becomes an object of erotic yearning, a legend, and a living memory that presides over the lives of a group of old-fashioned acquaintances. She is the sad moon around which a residual small world revolves. She exudes an aura of faded glory. Owing to the auratic nature of her image, "suffusing and coloring the air around her" (190), she is never portrayed as a consummate sexual partner for the various men she has affairs with. Indeed, as the past incarnate on the margins of a future-oriented, homogeneous history, her image is intermittently captured, a brief eternity in the fleeting. It is the tension between an incomprehensible, external historical time and the perception of momentary flashes of her past beauty that gives rise to the never-to-be-fulfilled yearning and poetry of melancholy. Kang Mingxun, the man burdened with Shanghai memory, falls in love with her, not at first but at last sight, treasuring the vanishing traces of the beauty queen. The search for her "identity" as Miss Shanghai by Kang, a close confidant of her old-fashioned world, illustrates the overlapping of layered temporalities and the eternal in the fleeting. Kang "has lived through the junctures of the two epochs and knows intimately the secret of this city" (190). He knows that Peace and Safety *longtang* (where Wang lives) is but a crack of the city and conceals a lot of broken and piecemeal lives.

He seems to detect the light and color behind Wang Qiyao, like mirages in the desert, but upfront, she looks almost an image in the hall of a nunnery in the shadow of fading candlelight. When playing mah-jong, the light from above casts shadows upon her face, but her eyes shine in the darkness, suggestive of some remote profundity. All of a sudden she raises her eyebrows, and smiles. . . . The smile reminds him of a person, who is none other than the movie star Ruan Lingyu in the 1930s. In Wang Qiyao's simplicity, he perceives elegant colors, which suffuse and taint the air around her with a haze. . . . All this city has left is some nostalgic sentiment and you can hear it ring in the bells of the electric streetcars. (190)

For Kang, Wang Qiyao bestows a "soul" hovering over the city that is also recognized as his own, as his lost possession. The soul represents the fantasy of spectacles, pleasure, and nightly carnivals believed to be the essence of Shanghai. This fantasy world collapses overnight as the history of socialism takes over and begins to chart a course of violent transformation and rapid modernization. The historical trajectory dimly heralded by the short-lived consumer culture is replaced by a homogeneous, empty time of revolutionary history. Does this mean, from the hindsight of the 1990s, that the "genuine" possibility of modern Chinese history is disrupted by the decades of political "errors" and "aberrations," until history picks up the half-buried thread again in opening up to globalization?

The novel's historical sharpness stems from its ability to open up time to alternative versions of temporality. Wang Qiyao and her confidants live in the interstices of two kinds of temporality: one of constant revolutionary change, and the other of the residual way of living previously based on a market economy. The glamorous commercial world is indeed in the midst of ruins and does not continue in a submerged half-life, waiting in the wings teleologically for its future comeback, as many market nostalgics would have it. Yet the relics of the commodity are being recollected as memory, which opens onto a noncommercial stratum of time. It is this time, the lived temporality of the ordinary people in their daily life, nourished on the memory of a prior commodified world, that cuts through both the ever-changing time of revolution and the frantic, teleological time of triumphant capitalism (which is believed to be the future unfolding before us). Wang and her Shanghai urbanites continue, in spite of the drastic historical changes, to live a kind of existence that has its own interests and pleasures apart from the pressures of mainstream official time, whether revolutionary or capitalist.

This culture of the average city dwellers—what is often referred to as "plebian culture" (*shimin wenhua*)—is symbolized by another image of Wang Qiyao, not as a success story of the spectacle, but as a girl next door, as a figure indistinguishable from common urbanites who live in the cramped space of the *longtang*. Zhang Xudong approaches this stratum as "nature" entangled with the history of modernity.[20] Derived from the Marxist distinction of history as culture acting upon nature, this notion points to a layer of temporality "unrationalized" below the Lukácsian second nature of reification. At the same time it dialectically refers to the frequently "naturalized," fossilized cultural process as a premature and often violent actualization, hence travesty, of vital, dynamic revolutionary projections. Constant change becomes mythical and reduces human dreams to the objective iron law of historical progress or ever-expansive capital.[21] It allows us to perceive residues from the older lifeworld persisting in its ruins alongside the blazing trail of modernization. The natural stratum does not "continue" its prior forms, but is recollected and lived by way of memory, through the inherited ways of living and feeling taken from an undefined, even immemorial past. It specifically addresses the realms of bodily experience embedded in everyday living, in the family, neighborhoods, community, sexuality, and unconscious dreams.

As a residual form of urban commercial Shanghai, the *longtang* life, if we are allowed this shorthand, is tied indirectly to the exchange relation that infiltrates human relations and structure of feeling, giving rise to the "false consciousness" of the commodity in theories of commodity culture. But as Michel de Certeau has shown, consumers do not have to behave as dupes in the grip of false consciousness and as docile bodies at the bidding of commodity and advertisement.[22] They can appropriate, employ, and recreate consumer goods to pursue their own needs, interests, and pleasure. Recalling the earlier distinction between exchange value and use value, we can say that what is meant to reap exchange value through the market can be transformed by ingenious consumers into genuine life-enhancing use value. It is not the consumers who have to succumb to mirages of the commodity, but the commodity that has to be taken into possession, made use of, and turned into a vehicle of life.

Admittedly, in the socialist epoch where the commodity's exchange value was minimized and scarcity upheld as a virtue, resistance to the mirage of commodity is not an issue, or not as important as in the current situation when the commodity threatens to reign supreme. The question then becomes, What role does the commodity play in a political economy ruled by central planning? This is a complex question beyond the scope of this chapter. One thing that can be confidently said, however, is that the socialist economy still leaves a considerable residue of exchange relation that allows the worker to exchange his or her labor power for commodities. The presence of commodities opens a limited space for desire, enjoyment, and hence use value, even though this is vigilantly guarded against by the dominant ideology. Thus, instead of being a corrupting lure or mirage, the use of the commodity has the potential to assert the basics of life against a more pervasive, mythical mirage: the colorless, disembodied ideology of production and efficiency for collective, utopian goals. Thus already in the earlier days of the socialist era, there is a lesson to be drawn about the creative use of the commodity.[23]

In the socialist period, Wang Qiyao and her associates are no longer consumers in a strict sense. But the commodity's images live on in their life, as something not governed by exchange value, but as a basic resource for survival and for a reasonably decent human existence. In the numerous scenarios of ritualized living and consumption in the *longtang*, the commodity in its downfall paradoxically rises to a more elevated status as an everyday cult around which the aura of a vanished life is imagined, savored, or even enacted. The people who share the same "background" memory as Wang cluster around her as a cult figure, which embodies the lost world as a tableau vivant. The aura of art, in Walter Benjamin's account, is fully the aura of the art of everyday living, sustained by bodily life and embedded in the accumulated experience nourished by a specific time and place—a particularized, personalized, immediately embodied temporality. The aura is "inseparable from its being imbedded in the fabric of tradition."[24] The aura plays upon the distance between remote intimations of significance and physical closeness that are held in suspense by the auratic figure. Hence Wang Qiyao is both far and near, elusive and accessible, so is the image of old Shanghai. The aura also acts as a channel of communication and emotional intimacy, linking correspondences and responsiveness among the urbanites.

In the spell of aura, the commodity shifts from spectacle to use value. With this, the characters relate to the lost image of commodity as an authentic experience. The cult and authentic experience find their nurturing ground in daily ritual. Wang Qiyao and her associates invent a ritual or a tradition in the cramped space of the *longtang*, which derives not from any inherited traditional Chinese custom and habit but from the memory of Shanghai's commercial, material culture. This is not a culture lived on the register of the beauty queen or movie star or fancy ballrooms, but at the grass roots, in the obscure lanes and alleys of the *longtang* and romanticized avenues covered with French maples, the shop fronts, the oldies, and the streetcars. The cultural imaginary of the grassroots, of course, includes the undying charms of the movie star and beauty queen and combines high and low. Ritualistic activities of reminiscing about the past, chatting, buying groceries, eating, discovering new friends and bonding, and recruiting new members of the club—all this forms the bulk of the novel's narration of the socialist epoch, which is the most significant and compelling part of the book.

The ritualistic rounds of conversations, eating together, and reminiscing inside the cramped yet neat space of Wang's apartment are set against an external time of dislocation and uncertainty. The intimate scene of bonding, solidarity, and conviviality is a moment of eternity snatched from fleeting time. "This moment is a mood, a scene wrested from the forever fleeting" (165). There is mutual consolation in the chats, "the boiling pot is whispering a warm inner voice" (165). The novel devotes long passages to two related rituals of communal bonding and conviviality in two separate chapters: "The Afternoon Tea" and "The Fireside Chat at Night" (literally, the night chat around a hot stove, *weilu yehua*). These nocturnal get-togethers create family-like intimacy and affective bonding, the warming of the hearts that flow together, and mutual dependence. "All desire becomes a need to lean on each other; the rest is of no concern" (184). This community of affect and memory is maintained by a fine art of material living that refines cooking and eating together to a craft of sensuousness, an aesthetic, as if, amidst the humdrum existence, some moments of redemption could be captured from the exquisitely perfected artistry of savoring every passing moment. The cultic overtone is unmistakable: they act as if they "are waiting for the New Year to arrive" or "keeping wake for the dead ancestors" (185). Against a raging history outside, the characters indulge themselves in trivialities and mundane details. But it is precisely the trifles and details that form the building blocks of a livable life, a tiny strain of temporality that survives in the storm.

This reliving of the past through nostalgia and memory, by attending to bodily needs and private desire, defies the homogeneous current of revolutionary history that seeks to suture the individual into the identity of the nation-state and to unify heterogeneous social life into a homogeneous continuum. The novel thus recovers an important legacy of commercial culture. Moreover, it also evokes the recent memory of the 1980s, whose enthusiasm toward the market, material life, democratization, and individual self-realization seemed consonant with an "inevitable" historical necessity. It is no wonder that after hiding in an obscure corner for three decades, Wang Qiyao has made a huge "comeback" in the reform era as a classical figure of commercial culture, a forgotten legend, and a model of authenticity that make all copies pale in comparison. I put "comeback" in quotation marks to keep at bay the assumption of an unbroken line of continuity between the old Shanghai and its alleged revival. It is the ideological need of the reform era as well of the 1990s that seeks to find the prehistory of the present in the image of a romanticized, commercial Shanghai.

Although the nostalgia for material culture may provide a livable space in the revolutionary era and heralds a bright future for the new period of reforms, it also punctures the historical continuum of the present, which is now felt by many to be falling short of the enthused expectations of the 1980s. The market, endowed with an aura and a human face in nostalgic memory, has a tendency to dwindle into the blind and heartless pursuit of profit and disintegrate into social chaos. There is the danger that the multicolored layers of lived temporality, promised in the aesthetic enjoyment of the commodity's use value and premised on material prosperity for all, are being reduced to a crass developmentalism, an obsession for sheer growth, a society of mere spectacles, an unquestioned acceptance of global capital and the transnational cultural industry. In nostalgia and memory, history is opened to different time frames and versions of life form. Now the current history is being flattened into a single-minded, teleological continuum, which is also the alleged demise of history. The end of history thesis prematurely sounds the death toll for the modern understanding of history as conscious, rational human decision and collective self-fashioning.

The novel's critique of the new myth of commercial culture is a criticism of the current social condition that drugs itself on the fantasies of endless development and globalization. Toward the end of the novel, the author sets up a contrast between the old city and the surrounding suburbs, where the roaring from the construction of high-rises dispels residual romance along with dust and chaos. No sooner does the city get a chance to revive its auratic past than it is endangered by a new commercialism and money-grubbing. Against the city's romantic image, the noisy construction sites and monotonous high-rise apartments epitomize mindless progress and the pursuit of profit. By extension, the younger generation is also engaged in a frenzied chase for the new, shining surfaces. The description of the typical party in this "new zone of development" (*xinqu*) characterizes the general atmosphere.

People of all colors attend and enjoy themselves; there is an air of celebration for all. Especially in Christmas parties, when they sing Christmas songs, you do not know if you are in China or a foreign country. This kind of party immediately strikes you as a place devoid of heart and soul. It has not accumulated any memory and carries an empty head on its shoulder, unable to use remembrance. This is the mentality of the new zone of development. . . . In droves and groups, bouquets and wine in hand, pouring in and out of the elevator, are mostly strangers, of all shapes and colors. (331)

This new mentality also affects the nostalgia of the younger generation for the faded world of Wang Qiyao. Their nostalgia attempts to recover and appreciate the decorative and simulacral surfaces—nostalgia for nostalgia's sake, a fascination with the faded spectacle without a deep sense of history.

If we regard Wang Qiyao as a figure that, through the memory of commercial culture, opens up possibilities of multilayered temporality in history, then her murder at the end of the novel foretells the consequence of a frenzied commercial culture going awry. A member of the profit-driven younger generation murders her for her gold, which, as a gift from the old Shanghai days, is never used as capital for profit but is preserved as security. The scene of the murder corresponds to the mise-en-scène in the film studio Wang Qiyao saw in her first trip there: a gorgeous woman in her nightgown lies dead in her bed in a bedroom cast in shadows by a shaded lamp. This hackneyed movie scene is both familiar and enigmatic. The cause of the woman's death is not clear. In the moment of her murder, Wang in a flashback realizes that the enigmatic woman is no other than herself: death by homicide. This looping back to the beginning seems to allude to the fated, doomed trajectory of Wang's commercially conditioned image as Miss Shanghai, the icon and legend of the old commercial Shang-

hai. The novel begins with a clichéd mise-en-scène and ends with a dramatically trite murder that would probably be just another item in the
evening newspaper for the jaded reader. But this final glimpse may be a
love at last sight from the standpoint of the novel and its reader, an infatu-
ation substantiated by an experience rescued from the mainstream historical continuum of both revolutionary change and the brave new world of
global developmentalism. Between these two points, we are offered the
salutary imaginary of a genuine and authentic history, which is regrettably
becoming a vanishing point. We are made to see the forking paths and
jagged stories of modern individuals in deep and troubled involvement
with the beloved object of modern life: the commodity.

9

Remembering Realism

THE MATERIAL TURN IN CHINESE CINEMA
AND STREET SCENES OF GLOBALIZATION

Nostalgia implies a historical imagination that envisages a different present and points to a different future. The "historical imagination" is a useful term, because in its tentative, "artistic" way, it has not been formalized into "historical discourse."[1] This imagination manifests itself in the fresh endeavors to seek alternatives. It questions the assumptions of the free market model of social development as well as overly centralized socialism. It is an attempt to break out of the normative, mainstream historical narrative, to brush history against the grain, aligning itself with the various critiques of capitalist modernity.

Marx, Nietzsche, Benjamin, and Lukács could be called "material" critics of modernity. They proposed to break out of the idealistic encrustations of mainstream culture. Mainstream culture has become a venerated body of canonized texts, monuments, and norms. These critics sought to confront them with a disruptive awareness of the "unformed" reality in sociohistorical flux. It is helpful to take a new look at the notion of "material" and consider how memory functions in it. A material understanding of history has much to say to the notions of realism and documentary in filmmaking. Realistic and documentary practices ebbed and flowed since the 1980s through the advent of globalization in the late 1990s. Yet the material approach, as a broader rubric, could help us see why realism comes on and off along with the urgency of the times by inserting itself into the reified orbit of simulacra. Rather than simply register a chunk of reality out there, realism gestures toward an interactive, performative involvement with the material process of social reality, fraught as it is with contradictions, catastrophes, traumas, ambiguity, and uncertainty. When Benjamin attempted to bring photomontage into the reconstruction of history, he meant a "material" turn to traverse the unwieldy field of conflicting forces as they impinge on sensory and sensuous life, and he meant to present a contradictorily articulated space of experience.[2]

In the current cultural climate, marked by a hasty embrace of the digitized simulacrum, it is rather late in the day to bring up realism. *Realism* has been such a suspect term in modern China since the 1980s that few critics would use it without suspicion and qualms. Realism, one feels, is passé and has long been the most "unreal" illusions in historical narrative and film discourse.[3] It has been regarded as the mystifying rhetoric of the established powers in modern times in coaxing ordinary people to resign to whatever reality they can endure. Realism in this ossified sense, however, has already forgotten its initial realist earthiness and energy; it is but a form of enshrined classicism. As a preeminent form of artistic creativity in relation to history in the twentieth century, film has been recognized for its photographic and realistic potential. But how much of this potential has really played out—in what generic manifestations—is a question that needs to be kept alive as long as symbolic activity seeks to engage ongoing sociohistorical realities intransigent to free-floating signs. Gilberto Perez notes that classicism is classic because it reins in the rough edges of film's "naturalistic possibilities." A classic style is one that "settles comfortably within the norms and forms of its own artifice, a style that follows convention with confidence in the adequacy of its own conventions to express all that needs to be expressed."[4]

In this sense Hollywood is classicism, and so is the ossified realism of any kind. Socialist realism is so reified as to become a form of classicism, drained of its original edginess, earthiness, and engagement with sociohistorical reality and with lived experiences of ordinary people.

In the face of the global landscape steeped in simulacra and spectacle, reconsideration of realism would appear to be a feeble countermove. But for all its fluidity and novelties, the simulacrum of transnational or state-sponsored culture industry has become the new classicism of the day, with its overarching authority and infinitely variegated, superficial innovations. The classic veil needs to be pierced through with sharp realism.

This skepticism of the "classical" rigidity of the mass media may account for the urge, since the early 1990s, to reconsider a "realist" approach to the representation of Chinese reality. In documentary filmmaking, in the insistence on the literary and theatrical performance of the body as authentic experience, in the appropriations of Italian neorealism and the French new wave by the new directors, and in the grassroots fieldwork of engaged social scientists, one finds a strain of commitment and activity that insists on engaging with the neglected, marginalized, concealed strata of the real.[5]

In Chapter 2, I discussed briefly the way the trauma-ridden cinema of the 1930s confronted and documented the occurrences of war, poverty, disaster, and social injustice. The prominent use of the long take and montage implied a material turn at what the filmmakers thought to be real but was glossed over by the mainstream commercial cinema under the influence of Hollywood. This preoccupation with reality was brought up for discussion in the 1980s, notably through Li Tuo and Zhang Nuanxin's 1979 essay "On the Modernization of Film Language" (Tan dianying yuyan de xiandaihua). The debate on cinematic realism has continued intermittently since the late 1990s. This interest can be attributed to a rising skepticism against commercialization of culture and the tendency of the transnational culture industry to turn reality into simulacra.

The 1980s preoccupation with realism started off with a different agenda. In their manifesto-like essay Li and Zhang privileged the realist, antidramatic, antinarrative innovations of Italian neorealism and the French new wave. They saw in these innovations a source of inspiration for Chinese filmmakers. They favor the long take as an antidote to the classical editing style and dramatic narration of classical Hollywood as well as of the socialist cinema. Like André Bazin, they seek to credit cinema with the power to carry out an ever-intensified engagement with the real.[6] In the 1980s Bazinian realism was a running theme in the thinking of film critics and film practice. Since then, its vitality served as a countermemory in the face of the hegemonic narrative of history: first the master narrative embodied by the "classical" cinema of socialist realism, and then the newfangled glamorous history of globalization as celebrated by commercial cinema. To understand how such renewable realism is entwined with historical thinking, it is instructive to place this notion in the tradition of the radical, modernist discourse that articulates the disruptive potential of visual technology against the mainstream modern culture.

In the 1980s, in the endeavor to absorb modernist film theories, the most remarkable candidate for interpretation and translation is the French theorist André Bazin. Given the photographical nature of film, this should not come as a surprise. Bazin credits film with an innate capacity to penetrate physical reality. In his study of Chinese modernism, Xudong Zhang shows that theoretical interest in Bazin centers on the documentary, indexical power of cinema to refer to reality in flux. Through a mechanical and chemical process, the technology of film is capable of laying bare an uncoded and contingent reality. The realism of the 1980s, exemplified by fifth-generation filmmakers, seemed to be able to escape the established social and visual field overlaid with excessive meanings and coded perceptions endorsed by the dominant culture.[7] The realist clearing of the ground overgrown with cultural codes recalls Kracauer's notion of film as redemption of physical reality (see Chapter 2). It is interesting how this act of "remembering realism" has the function to disturb and challenge the established historical narrative.

Li Tuo and Zhang Nuanxin see Bazin's realism as a photographical, indexical disruption of the cinematic apparatus. They use this realism to critique the reified conventions of socialist realism and its teleological vision of history. Their discussion heralds the new film works by the fifth-generation filmmakers just five to six years after the debate. But the realist turn in the late 1990s had a different target. In the increasingly globalized trade and capital flows, the target was the aggressive image-repertoire of the transnational culture industry. The global image factory is hijacking the Bazinian, realist critique of socialist realism and is in the process of broadcasting its values, meaning, and images over the cultural landscape.

This concern brings back the historical conjuncture of the 1930s, when Chinese filmmakers both resisted and borrowed from Hollywood. In this light the realist turn can be placed in a larger context of capitalist modernity in twentieth-century China. The realist turn evinces a power to disrupt the hegemonic narrative nurtured by the capitalist culture industry. The expansion of capital is accompanied by cultural overreach. Transnational corporations aggressively promote visual products and their image production functions as the pedagogical wing of capital accumulation and expansion. Dissemination of imagery fulfills the mission of molding the subjectivity and docile competence of workers across the globe. As the visual regime of modern capitalism, Hollywood has been more successful than any other cultural sector in the visual constitution of proper subjectivity suited to the accumulation and expansion of capital. It instills a "universal" culture in terms of work ethic, morality, civil and liberal values, and normative lifestyle. This global context allows us to remember the critical potential in the visual theories of Bazin, Brecht, and Roland Barthes.

The Visual Regime of Capitalism and Its Dissidents

A political analysis of resistance to the visual regime of the dominant culture is now important in a "socialist" economy on its way to capitalism as well as in late capitalism in the west. This analysis is to bring politics into aesthetics. The worldwide appeal of Hollywood as America's cultural exports and "soft-power" invasion has been much commented on.[8] Chinese filmmakers, critics, and fans are also debating the pros and cons of Hollywood's blockbusters (*da pian*) in undermining the national film industry. The point here is not simply about economic competition, style, or taste, but about the promotion of an images-saturated belief and life form as linchpin to the operation of capital. Benjamin Barber rightly captures the ideological function of Hollywood by calling it "McWorld's Videology."[9] Critics of the media have also shed light on the intimate links between cinema and capital.[10]

The classical Hollywood cinema is an instance of dominant discourse in the service of capital. It promulgates notions of subjectivity, the body, sexuality, and pleasure within a simulacral circuit of socioeconomic reproduction and consumption. Its pedagogical function is wedded to the accumulation strategy of capital. Its image bank offers a kind of off-job training and socialization for the worker as consumer. As an ideological apparatus, Hollywood cinema aims at reproducing functional performers for commodity production, consumption, and world markets. The early history of classical Hollywood cinema demonstrated this unifying, "civilizing" power, the power of constituting the appropriate subject nourished in a coherent pattern of image and narrative. The classical Hollywood cinema's influence on Chinese cinema in the 1930s and 1940s has been much studied and is a familiar story.[11] But there is still the need to ascertain the ways in which Hollywood as an ideological apparatus promotes the formation of a homogeneous subjectivity of the middle class in tune with capitalism's worldwide expansion and colonization. To see what kind of subjectivity is brought to bear on the local audience, we may turn to the ideal spectatorship of Hollywood film, which has its own history of genesis and struggle before it was inscribed, although not completely, in the classical narration.

Miriam Hansen's study of the transition from the cinematic experience before the nickelodeon period (1905–6) to the classical narrative mode illustrates how a popular, grassroots form of moviegoing was turned into a gentrified spectatorship. This new spectatorship constituted an experience increasingly dependent on the register of the look and empathetic identification. Closely associated with middle-class values, the insular spectatorship works to foster the illusions of coherent and homogeneous subjectivity, overriding the diverse cultural constituencies of immigrants and working classes. Prenickelodeon moviegoing catered to a heterogeneous mass audience of recent immigrants and multiethnic urban residents. Located within the neighborhoods of this audience, the movie shows were part of the emergent public space of commercialized leisure. Moviegoing, in contrast with film viewing, included many nonfilm variety shows and performance repertoire: theme parks, vaudeville shows, acrobatics, road shows, magic shows, animal acts, and so on.[12] This theatrical environment fostered a casual, boisterous atmosphere and "made moviegoing an interactive rather than passive experience." Such practices lent moviegoing the immediacy and singularity of a one-time performance.[13] With its aesthetics of distraction and random disorientation, its "raw" collectivity, conviviality, and ethnic diversity, the cinema in this mode gestured toward a contradictory public space challenging the homogeneity of the dominant bourgeois culture.

The shift from this "primitive" to the classical cinema was made through the codification of a universal visual language to the exclusion of those unruly elements of popular, multiethnic entertainment. From the perspective of speech act, this emerging language aspires to a grammatical and constative status. It marked the development of a self-explanatory, unified narrative and visual pattern in which resources of cinematic discourse, such as framing, editing, and mise-en-scène, was deployed to facilitate a linear flow of images and scenarios. This pattern tells stories with clearly defined temporal and spatial boundaries, unfolds a cause-and-effect structure, and focuses on the psychological motivation and action of individual characters. Through privileging certain visual devices, such as continuity editing, cutting on movement, point-of-view shots, and the 180-degree rule, the classic mode encourages a "realist" drama, a "self-evident" style of verisimilitude. With this rarified vocabulary the classical cinema inserts the spectator seamlessly into the flow of narration and encourages an empathetic visual identification with private predicaments of the characters. The contrast with the earlier cinematic experience is striking. The participatory, interactive moviegoing practice, with its pantomimic acting and festival interaction between film and audience, was pregnant with heterogeneous possibilities of performative, communicative, and idiosyncratic gestures and utterances. But these rich possibilities, rooted in vibrant urban, multiethnic communities, inherited life forms, and embodied memories, were replaced by a narrow visual regime of the look, by the cultivation of a distanced yet empathetic spectator. As the ideal subject of gentrified social norms, the film viewer is compelled to have his or her gaze riveted on the flow of the event and consciousness inscribed into the narrative texture.[14]

Hollywood's film language works to fashion the imaginary coherence of the solitary bourgeois subject. It assembles the infinitely complex and lived body, embedded in historical and local conditions and ethnic memory, into an abstract item cleansed of traces of time. This item further corresponds to the image of a grammatical subject or a semantic entity. It thus becomes a lingua franca, which is able to be circulated and exchanged in the world market as a form of currency or commodity. The abstract subject cut loose from the sociopolitical reality harks back to its double as a grammatical entity. In this sense the universal language legitimates a normative grammar and syntax and maintains a vocabulary of semantic entities. It bolsters a universal subjectivity floating freely above a world of social, ethnic, and national differences and conceals the memory of its own accidental history of genesis, thus establishing itself as natural and self-evident by suppressing its heterogeneous other.

Resistance to this normative language has persisted in avant-garde cinema, independent filmmaking, and other subversive endeavors. In addition to Bazinian realism, the works of Brecht, Benjamin, and Barthes sought to rearticulate the performative, interactive power that marks alternative cinemas and exposes the constructed nature of the hegemonic discourse.

In his reading of Brecht's epic drama, Benjamin pits the epic form against the classical drama, which in its receptive mode is similar to the classical Hollywood cinema.[15] The spectatorship of classical drama is one of empathetic identification and presupposes a spectator "who, with every fiber of his being, is intently following a process." Empathetic identification has echoes of Aristotelian catharsis, the purging of the emotions through identifying with the hero's fate. The epic drama of Brecht, by contrast, calls for a relaxed, detached collective audience, who is ready to "take up an attitude toward what it sees."[16] Compelled to perform detective work on the tensions between what it sees and what it experiences, the mass audience is encouraged to see the "artistic armature," the productive process that turns out images and actions on stage.

The impulse to see the productive mechanism, the otherwise invisible, contrived aspects of drama or film, leads to the formulation of the well-known aesthetic of estrangement (*verfremden*). Benjamin compares epic drama to images on a strip of film. The epic form is similar to a montage sequence ripped asunder by conflicting shots, evoking "the forceful impact on one another of separate, sharply distinct situations in the play." The montage image destroys empathetic identification and jolts the audience into a sharpened awareness of a messy reality. The strategy of making strange is to uncover the social condition and blast it out of its "realist" illusion of common-sense continuum. One strategy is the quotable gesture, an interruptive performance in fits and starts. The actor must try to "act himself thinking." He must not only unmask the social circumstances by his interruption, but also quote himself so as to reveal himself as an alienated product of those circumstances.[17]

The strategy of estrangement still relies on a sovereign, reflective subject able to figure forth a scenario of demystification. Although it calls for the audience's participation, epic theater is weakened in its political effectiveness by resting contented with the act of detached contemplation, of seeing through the veil, as if mere "raising consciousness" were sufficient. Despite its revolutionary potential, the basic assumption of the self-referential aesthetic subject remains unchanged. Brecht's aesthetics of estrangement, however, can be expanded along with avant-garde, pop culture practices, independent filmmaking, and critical theory in a broader modernist project resisting the simulacrum. This is a strand of cultural rebellion going back to what Lukács called "romantic anti-capitalism."[18] The abstraction of discourses and pervasive simulacra have become the dominant grammar and the visual regime buttressed by the established power. Radical aesthetic practices have rebelled against this reified regime with repeated innovations. Thus, apart from estrangement, there is also a strategy of shock, which strives to pierce through the heart of the simulacrum—the imagistic regime of photography, cinema, and the digital media. Benjamin, Siegfried Kracauer, and Roland Barthes have discussed this strategy. Obviously, this recalls the traumatic visuality of Chinese cinema in the 1930s.

Instead of demystifying the contrived mechanism of the reified code, the aesthetic of shock turns the contrived reality onto the unformed, conflict-ridden, irruptive reality. The aesthetics of shock seeks to cut through the dreamy, triumphant façade of the visual regime and gets immersed in an unflinching, often melancholy, confrontation with the abysmal real. Roland Barthes speaks of the disruptive shock of *punctum* in photography. The *punctum*, a break or shock, is a puncture on a plane of culturally sanctified meaning (which is "un contrat passé entre les créateurs et les consommateurs," a contract reached between creators and consumers). The contract implies the contractual arrangement and regulation of bourgeois society. The *punctum* is a not a performance orchestrated by conscious will; we cannot invest its irreducible thingness with directing consciousness. "C'est lui qui part de la scène, comme une flèche, et vient me percer" (It is this that rises from the scene, shoots out of it like an arrow, and pierces me).[19] It resembles Lacan's definition of the real as repetition of trauma breaking through the precariously formed symbolic. The *punctum* renders glaringly visible the symbolic order's vulnerability and precariousness in political struggle. It seeks to touch the real in the unsymbolizable abyss of history and death. As Benjamin puts it, "death digs most deeply the jagged line of demarcation between physical nature and significance."[20]

The *punctum* is thus an irruption of the real within the sanitized visual regime, a piercing of the simulacrum that pretends to be the real. It is also this risky adventure against the mythical abstractions that prompted Benjamin to consider bringing photomontage into the reconstruction of history. In Benjamin's account of modernity, the dream world of capitalist culture, with its promise of progress, consumption, technological control of humans and nature, has frozen history into a vast mythology. The historical condition of capitalist production, for all its rationality and technical innovations, has regressed into primordial nature, a land of dinosaurs roaming the prehistorical wilderness, sleepwalking and acting on primal instincts. It lapses into homogeneous, empty time, a cyclical wheel of the perpetual return of the same. In the critical spirit of historical materialism, Benjamin's vision of history as photomontage of the "dialectical image" seeks to awaken historical momentum and to open up alternative horizons. This awakening from prehistory to history proper carries the force of Barthes's *punctum* or Brechtian *verfremden*. But Benjamin goes a step further in his conception of the historical movement as both the irruption of the real (Barthes) and a staging, mounting performance (Brecht and Eisenstein).

Benjamin suggests that the discovery of future horizons depends on our constant mindfulness of history as a state of emergency bordering on catastrophe, a conflicted array of options coming up for grabs. The materialist historian is bent on rescuing repressed and forgotten objects—ruins, trash, debris, memories, things of use value, and the oppressed and powerless—from the simulacral continuum of History. He or she seeks to scramble the reified continuum by inserting heterogeneous material objects. Montage, the yoking of disparate elements into a visual sequence, envisages the dialectic movement of history. It achieves this by blasting repressed material objects out of the frozen continuum. "It does so in the form of the historical confrontation that makes up the interior (and, as it were, the bowels) of the historical object, and into which all forces and interests of history enter on a reduced scale."[21] If historical representation is a performance in thinking and imagining, then it "involves not only the flow of thoughts, but their arrest as well":

Where thinking suddenly stops in a configuration pregnant with tensions, it gives that configuration a shock, by which it crystallizes into a monad. A historical materialist approaches a historical subject only where he encounters it as a monad. In this structure he recognizes the sign of a Messianic cessation of happening, or, put differently, a revolutionary chance in the fight for the oppressed past. He takes cognizance of it in order to blast a specific era out of the homogeneous course of history—blasting a specific life out of the era or a specific work out of the lifework.[22]

The pregnant moment is achieved by means of a "constructive principle." This performative act sinks its teeth into contradictions of history and then actively "mounts" (montage means mounting) a crisis-ridden mirror image of them. It plays on the dynamic tensions between the memory of unfulfilled, oppressed pasts and the mythologized present, between the prehistory of capitalist sleepwalking and the jump-start of revolutionary action for change, between authentic experience and simulacral images, between real labor and abstract labor. Through this montage of history, Benjamin stages a material turn in historical discourse. His dialectical vision seeks to traverse the unwieldy field of conflicting forces as they impinge on sensory and sensuous life and presents a contradictorily montaged experience of modernity.

The Realist Impulse and Cinematic Fragments of Globalization

This aesthetic of shock resonates with Bazinian or other versions of realism in contemporary Chinese cinema. The recall of this aesthetic strain shows how it is bound up with historical thinking. It helps us trace the realist motif from Li Tuo and Zhang Nuanxin's essay, to the formation of a new cinematic discourse and fifth-generation filmmakers, through what has emerged as the "urban generation" in the last decade.

The realist impulse cannot be traced by appeal to an insistence on the transcendental truth or a pristine reality untouched by narrative and image. Bazin's theory of realism and Li Tuo's call for a new cinematic language may give the impression of a naive confidence in the changeless essence of reality and intrinsic nature of the film medium. Yet to question the idea of raw reality "in itself" should not lead us to assume that all realities are representational and watertight symbolic constructs. Bazinian realism rests on a respect for the "prefilmic" material "put or found in front of the camera for filming" and eschews manipulation by the filmmaker to project overly subjective design on raw reality.[23]

The insistence on the photographical, indexical reality may be misleading in light of the overall contour of Bazin's analysis of Italian neorealism. Bazin's analysis derives its force from a historical awareness of the sociohistorical condition of postwar Italy, where the liberation did not end with the defeat of the Nazis, but transformed economic and political life

on a daily basis. The engagement with a volatile actuality through the documentary "reportage" of mundane scenes in the streets was motivated by a
transformative impulse. Bazin finds this realistic element exemplified not
only by a "naturalistic" realism but also by Eisenstein's dynamic realism.
Despite his criticism of montage editing, Bazin points to a common revolutionary fervor that informs the aesthetics of engaging contemporary reality. This realistic engagement was opposed to the official and Hollywood
cinematic portrayals of reality, in which lived reality is not seriously regarded, "loved" (*aimée*) for itself but is "rather rejected or defended as political sign."[24] The target of realism is the ideologically saturated narrative
and image repertoires. On this account, Li and Zhang's reading of Bazin
surely hits the right point. They pit Bazinian realism against the reified cinematic structures of stylized theater, overly melodramatic narratives, and
officially articulated messages.[25] We may note once again that their an-
titheatrical, antinarrative stance harks back to the theater debate in May
Fourth and the radical cinema of the 1930s.

    This attempt to make a clearing through realism can be traced in the
fifth-generation filmmakers. As critics have noted, film practice in the
1980s aimed at unraveling a hidden reality. Yet this laying bare of "reality"
has the political implication of challenging the habitual visual pattern and
prejudices of the dominant discourse. "By being transparent to the reality,"
by prioritizing the impersonal, photographical dimension of the film
medium, the subjective design of the filmmaker would be taken over by a
new visual field, which proves to be "raw" and "objective" in the sense of
political ambivalence and semantic multiplicity.[26]

    For some, this reading of Bazin in terms of political openness and se-
mantic ambiguity may be a misreading.[27] The assertion of an unadorned,
prediscursive reality, however, shows precisely the nodal point in Bazin's
theory between cinema and history and offers us clues to the realist impulse in the different generations of filmmakers. The suspicion of Bazinian
realism is symptomatic of the suspicion of socialist realism or any realist
project as a work of historical imagination. The bankruptcy of official re-
alisms should not liquidate the concept's initial realist potential and critical force. Apart from the political demystifying power, Bazinian realism
also contains a reflection on history as an open, unfinished process that
eludes and slips through arbitrary and cinematic imposition of meaning.
As Philip Rosen shows, Bazin's realism is entwined with an act of striving

to write history, an ongoing activity on the part of the historicizing subject in the unceasing reconstitution of the real. Bazin's documentary reality corresponds to a flexible, tension-filled notion of history writing and implies a conception of "filmic textuality as an ongoing, never-completed dialectical sequence of representational strategies attempting to move toward total flexibility and completeness in countering the real."[28]

In this light Bazinian realism is consonant with a dialectical notion of historicity charged with fluid temporality. Historicity is a moment of tension that combines two aspects. One is history writing as a discursive and visual construction, and the other is history, which is "the actual past" that history writing, if it is not sheer fictional representation, has to refer to. "Historiography always purports to be referential," Rosen writes, in spite of all its aesthetic, narrative procedures and structures.[29] Because a certain degree of reference is inevitable and necessary, it follows that there are different modes of history writing. At certain times, only a certain mode is considered legitimate. Reality is thus the site of contestation and struggle for legitimacy among the competing modes of history writing. The real is therefore not an absolutely concrete chunk of data or facts neutrally recorded by an impersonal camera. Rather, it reveals "a subjective striving, a subjective investment in the image precisely as objectivity."[30] I need to add that history cannot be a purely subjective projection of an intention to be realized in aesthetics. The realistic image is an intersubjective, shared project, one that links realism to praxis. It is a dynamic process of legitimating a new narrative by investing in "real" images and by working toward a different reality.

Yellow Earth (Huangtu di, 1986) illustrates how the tension between history writing and the "actual" past plays itself out. This film is a classical example of the fifth generation in its cinematic approach to history. The filmmakers fixed their gaze, frequently through the long take and long shot, the Bazinian favorites, on the nightmare, grotesqueries, and stagnation of China's past. In this iconic image and in the emergent film language, Lu Xun's vision of history as a field of nothingness (*wu wu zhi zhen*) bursts forth with powerful, startling realism, corresponding with Walter Benjamin's image of history as a death's head.[31] This cinematic method is also allegorical and signals an attempt to make piecemeal, moment-by-moment sense out of senseless ruins and traces, putting the received symbolic resources and preconceptions in suspense. In Dai Jinhua's accurate state-

ment, the fifth-generation filmmakers tried to find a narrative, a representation, to make sense of traumatic experiences. They did not succeed in
forging a new one, yet their stuttering or difficulty in grappling with the
stubborn reality turned out to be a success. In the risqué endeavor to present what eludes the received aesthetic mode, they staged a critique of representation in general and of the official historical narrative in particular.[32]
They were also stuck in a paradox. The impulse to demythologize official
representations gave rise to the refreshingly raw, "material" texture of physical reality, never before seen on the Chinese screen. One only has to recall
the crude earth and the peasant's indescribable face in *Yellow Earth*. Although approaching history realistically, they gradually withdrew from it,
as they repeatedly stage this anguished inability to come to terms with history. In so doing they turned their historical reflection into a canonized art,
into a posture of classicism. An anxiety about what to say and how to say
it led to a repeated staging of narrative angst by design. The fifth generation's initial material turn to history, in other words, is compromised by an
excessively modernist preference for the aporias of representation. A revolutionary desire to unsettle the inherited conventions seemed to get stuck
on its own track and risked becoming a narcissistic form of high art. For
many commentators the creativity of the fifth generation gave way to the
pursuit of the spectacular and dramatic in the 1990s. But it is still debat-
able whether the realist and transformative energy expired when the fifth
generation was no longer active in the representation of history.

The 1990s witnessed the massive commercialization of culture, in
which history and reality are dissolved into spectacle. It is in this context
that the realist impulse made a comeback. One salient feature of what is
often called the urban generation is documentary immersion in everyday
reality. Wu Wenguang, for many the foremost documentary filmmaker,
represents this principle. Wu speaks of his work as cultural ethnography,
which is undertaken on the basis of extensive fieldwork. The fieldwork focuses on the margins of society, on the disadvantaged, impoverished, and
downtrodden sections of the population. The documenting camera, says
Wu, should always keep recording these grassroots scenes. Some years ago
Wu was invited to collaborate with artists in Singapore in a project about
Chinese rickshaw pullers of a half-century before. From the ample data in
the archive—interviews, photos, and audio recordings dating as far back as
eighty years—Wu heard a recorded voice of a boy of seven or eight, a child

rickshaw puller. Although he did not understand the boy's dialect, he was shocked to realize how history endures and comes alive in a living voice. Lamenting the lack of such rich archives in China about the life of common folk, he urges that the documentary should fill the gap and act as witness to history.[33]

Wu's work represents a form of documentary filmmaking that has been gathering momentum since the early 1990s and reenergizing cinematic realism as a counterweight to the newfangled mystifications in the atmosphere of globalization. The official media join commercial enterprises in promoting the triumphant prospects of endless development, prosperity, and middle-class lifestyle. The mainstream cinema and TV turn the past into consumable spectacles and attempt to picture the current reality as nothing more than an endless stream of soaps and melodrama. For documentary filmmakers, the visual landscape is saturated with lies and illusions. On the other hand, fast-paced modernization has given rise to new traumas of disintegration, displacement, and loss, not to mention life-and-death social problems. This chaotic situation is constantly belied by the smooth, shining surface of the new narratives and images. Polemically, the documentary principle aims at cutting through the veneer of fantastic lies to get at the neglected and hidden strata of reality.

The documentary thus makes intervention into an overcrowded visual landscape. Wu Wenguang and others do not naively seek to deliver a transparent piece of reality in objective fashion. Lingering on the physical surface by means of the long take or heightening the collusion of dynamic forces are no longer their options. Rather, the documentary principle is one of interactive, collaborative involvement with subject matters and physical locations. In an interview Wu describes how he made the documentary *Jianghu* (The wide world). He befriended the members of a wandering pop theater troupe, erased his identity as a filmmaker, and became one of them. He ate, slept, and did everyday work and chores with the theater group as in a family. By using an inconspicuous, inexpensive digital video camera, he minimized the presence of the camera and ensured that nobody tried to act a part. The documentary in Wu's conception implies taking the camera into the thick of everyday acts and incidents, plunging it into a hundred and one random facts of moment-to-moment living, registering human interaction in real social settings.

This does not mean that the camera picks up particulars mindlessly.

The point is to create a confrontation, an encounter of mind with reality. Gilberto Perez uses the notion of documentary image to classify a whole string of directors who have exhibited this material turn, including Flaherty, Eisenstein, Rossellini, and De Sica. Although working in different realist modes, these directors sought "from reality something richer and stranger, of more potency and consequence." But this is also a reality "harder to deal with coherently, more resistant to articulate arrangement."[34] The closer the director tries to engage reality, the more difficult it is to shape and narrate it into a coherent form and meaning.

The documentary filmmakers are ready to take the risk of incoherence. They are prepared to meet the challenge of an unwieldy reality, in Perez's elegant words, "on a ground close enough to its own for its energies and resistance to come into play."[35] For Wu Wenguang, to record and confront reality is not just about making a film, but an experiment with living a different life and with its representation. He declares, "I record, therefore I am." But to record means to question and suspend received "-isms," conceptions, and conventions.

This documentary impulse finds its way into feature films. In what follows I will discuss briefly two films in light of the material turn. I examine Jia Zhangke's *Xiao Wu* (The pickpocket, 1998) and Lou Ye's *Suzhou he* (Suzhou River, 2000) to illustrate the new realism. I choose feature films instead of documentaries because the documentary strain is heightened if it is inserted within the established conventions of fictional drama and narrative. The documentary takes a radical epistemological stance to historical reality. It seeks to draw the unedited, unprocessed real into its own texture, thus preserving the disruptive "reality effect" that questions and challenges the run-of-the-mill dramatic fiction.

Xiao Wu is a radical departure from the contemporary films bent on depicting the Chinese city in drastic transition through modernization and commercialization. The film portrays Fenyang, a town in Shanxi Province far from the metropolitan centers, and pays special attention to people on the margin of society. The narrative follows Xiao Wu, a pickpocket, as he goes through frustration, misdemeanor, failures in relationships, and the final arrest by police. The film is short on dramatic action but long on documentary recording of the town's streets and the villages at their crudest. Instead of being the modernist *flâneur*, Xiao Wu is a listless drifter, serving as an observer of his native town in disorienting social transition. We might have his point of view to guide us around the town, but a disembodied camera always outweighs the potential point-of-view shots and is ready to look at ignored refuse, dregs, and mundane banalities hostile to pleasure-seeking eyes.

The film evokes documentary qualities by inserting TV cameras to cover the town's events. Reporters from the local TV station shoot the scenes they would like the public to see: the campaign against criminal acts, the marriage of the successful entrepreneur as the hero of our times, and the newsworthy arrest of the thief Xiao Wu. If the TV camera looks at the surface of the table, Jia Zhangke's camera looks beneath it. The film suggests that somebody is taking a camera right into the thick of things in the streets, shooting objects, looking into every nook and corner indiscriminately and casually, frequently from unusual, unnatural angles. The images come across, as it were, smeared with dust, dirt, smells, and sweat from the streets of an old town being twisted by modern changes. We may have at times a summary view, but we are often forced to stare at truncated parts of bodies or a fragment from a street peddler or eatery stand.

This slow film, with abundant long takes, blatantly ignores the time scheme integral to dramatic rhythm dictated by the forward movement of action. Its time is one that dwells on and delves into the space of the moment. This "suspensive" time is reminiscent of Italian neorealism, as in films by Michelangelo Antonioni. Time in Antonioni, writes Perez, "is not a time of the what next but a time of the what now, not a linear but a lingering time that views each moment as a point of intersection of many lines of actuality and possibility."[36] We may try to connect and classify these images, yet the content in each shot is not related to those of others by any thread of narrative, nor by any commercial, consumer, or other interests and activities. An enlarged context can provide a view for these shots: they are extended snapshots, resembling long and lingering stares, at the Chinese streets on ground zero.

This treatment of time slows us down into a suspended contemplation of a dense welter of material of a small town, in all its debased, opaque flux. It also draws us into characters caught in the frayed and breaking social fabric, who at once resist and invite sympathy. It is only fitting that the film's typical shot is the long take, which is often used to the extreme. It makes us share with the characters an unabridged, prolonged interval in their daily life and forces us to take a long, hard look at the space they move in, until the space's intrinsic, unredeemed, untold banality leaves an indelible imprint in our consciousness. Things and characters are left alone in their material density, not as a sign for something else, nor as a potential element for psychological motivation and narrative development.

Consider a shot in which Xiao Wu comes to comfort the singing girl sick and bedridden in her bedroom. They appear to be on the way to something of a relationship. The scene starts with Xiao Wu's return with a thermobag for the girl's ailment and ends with them leaning on each other intimately. It is done by an extreme long take through a stationary camera and lasts for more than seven minutes. In it the girl and boy talk about themselves for the first time, seated on the bed against the window, but the questions are not answered, and the answers do not quite follow the question. The girl sings a sentimental pop song, Xiao Wu responds to her request to sing by turning on a cigarette lighter that plays a shrill, metallic version of Beethoven's "Für Elise." This tune is both appropriate and kitschy. The scene is stripped relentlessly of its potential romance by the camera's long stare at the bareness of the room, the banality of the layout, the constant jarring sounds from the streets, the cheap, kitschy posters, the pop songs. Yet if this pitiless dragging through a down-and-out situation creates emotional distance, the couple's desperate clinging to each other in mutual pity serves on the other hand to draw us in. We know their "relationship" may not lead to anywhere and that they do not have much chance anyway. Indeed, this "suspensive" moment, intensified by the bareness, opacity, and the kitschy feel of the mise-en-scène, defies the clarity of judgment and ease of perception. A strong sense of depression and hopelessness creeps in through this prolonged shot.

I have used the term *kitsch* to describe a debased atmosphere that is rather pervasive in the film.[37] The kitschy atmosphere seems to flow directly from a debased reality and stems from the ubiquitous entrepreneurship that mocks the prevalent eulogies of elegant lifestyle of the west. Kitsch in this film is symptomatic of the unwieldy mix of the global modern and residually traditional. It is a sign of uneven development in a country scrambling to modernize in the shadow of global capital. Remarkably, in this small, crumbling town, there is a universal desire to imitate fads, styles, and lifeways of America or the west, yet every contrived object for this desire seems to be a debased, faked version, referring neither to native tradition nor to the west. Yet this inauthenticity is registered so faithfully and accurately as to become, by default, an authentic experience of the moment. The camera knows well what grotesque mixture to look at and what cheap, pseudotrends and fake art to evoke, through direct recording or editing reconstruction. The loud pop songs to evoke macho actions, the cheap posters in the makeshift hair salon or dancing parlor, or any business that looks makeshift; the vulgar, faddy, or fake-looking store-fronts and signs mingle with beat-up, noisy tractors and peddlers all over the place. The modern entertainment of karaoke drenched with tearful melodies runs matter-of-factly into a funeral store cramped with wreaths for mourning; the modern dancing "model" with nice legs mixes noncha-lantly with uncouth peasants in the street; the posters of western media and fashion stars cover the walls of the most squalid bedroom or hastily put-up stores.

Even in the village, where Xiao Wu's peasant parents live, the feel of a degraded or kitschy modernity is everywhere, debasing the agrarian land-scape and human relationships. The family gathering, chat, and meals—traditionally the most elemental form of communal life—are poisoned by money talk and calculation, by bickering over advantages, by the consumer desire for American goods. Sick of this poisoned atmosphere and driven out by his father, Xiao Wu is once again on his way back to town. The camera accompanies him and takes a prolonged look at the village land-scape. The lonely trees are endangered by electric poles and power lines, the industrial-looking, cheap buildings are taking up the rural space, and the air is filled with the noise of fuming motorcycles and of the village loudspeaker that announces current news together with sales of homemade goods within the village.

The kitschy feel, stemming from the degraded mishmash of tradi-tional and modern, local and global, is so ubiquitous and penetrating that it looms large and real as the inescapable experience of the day. The film registers this effectively, and in doing so goes along with pop and kitsch and all the grotesque signs of uneven development. The film itself takes on a kitschy quality and becomes a kind of pseudocinematic art. This is per-haps what it aims to do without apology: in the spirit of modernist avant-garde, it explodes the established art form and narratives and comes to an intense engagement with the real texture, emotional and visceral, of con-temporary China in unpredictable flux.

Suzhou River by Lou Ye, in its glossy look, apparently makes a sharp contrast with *Xiao Wu*. The documentary strain, if any, is of an explicitly contrived sort. The postmodern simulacrum and the mean streets of film noir are fitting descriptions for this cinematic registering of Chinese reality. Critics have noted the film's stylistic similarity to Wong Kar-wai's portrayal of shimmering city scenes and spiritual dislocations in Hong Kong.[38] The simulacral dissolving of the line between reality and fantasy is indeed integral to the film's structure. The "reality" is mostly filtered through the first-person narrator, who is a video-photographer, making a living by filming everything from weddings to lovemaking. Much of the narration and drama is provided by his conjecture. In what way can we take his video "documentation" of Shanghai streets as an approximation to the real?

A realist thrust counterbalances the whimsical camera of this idiosyncratic photographer. After an enigmatic conversation in the blank screen questioning the sincerity of love, "Would you look for me until death?" the film gives over to a long montage sequence, with shifting and quick panning shots over the scenes on and off the Suzhou River, which is located in the middle of Shanghai. The montage sequence recalls that in *Street Angel*, whose low shots are also of the Suzhou River. In Lou Ye the montage is much more compelling in its vigorous, fast-paced searching for images of the common people living for generations on the river—in the boats, in huts, on the riverbank—with blocks of half-demolished buildings and dilapidated housing. It hints at the normally slighted subculture of the boat people, who are endowed with a history and a past of their own, and confers on them serious attention, even dignity. This attention to a subculture of migrant laborers in Shanghai is evident through the striking absence of the glamorous icons of the city, the Bund and the Pudong development zone with the sky-scraping TV tower. These are consigned to the vague horizon while the fast-paced, searching, ethnographic montage thrusts a dirty river block onto the foreground.

Although the film does not directly address the boat people, it focuses on a number of young people caught in a drastic social transition. The streets are clearly penetrated and twisted by the forces of commercialization and global flow of goods. The riverbank is practically dominated by networks of reckless gangsters and entrepreneurs. The narrator-videographer, because of the nature of his odd jobs, has access to the various aspects and strata of business and transactions. For young people, there was little chance to keep pace with a global modernity symbolized by the new development zone. The riverbank life, just like the dusty little town of *Xiao Wu*, is as lacking in opportunities for personal fulfillment as it is damaged by forces of modernization.

Yet despite its postmodern look, its urban simulacra, and the shopworn sensibility of alienation and loneliness; despite its film noir elements of mean streets and cynicism (the narrator, before breaking up with his girlfriend Mei Mei, asks when they should make love, before or after saying goodbye), *Suzhou River* does not simply replicate the postmodern techniques of Wong Kar-wai. On the other hand it differs from *Xiao Wu* in one aspect: in its ability to hope. Instead of recording an elusive, degraded reality, Lou Ye's film dares to tell a story, a "love story" with fairy-tale flavor, in a barren urban neighborhood, threatened by demolition and forces of globalization.

This fairy tale comes from a conjecture by the narrator from a newspaper story about a girl who has thrown herself into the river. The narrative revolves on the conflict of money and love. Ma Da, the delivery boy on a motorcycle, becomes attached to Mu Dan, the daughter of a rich liquor smuggler. Caught against his will in the gangster network, Ma Da is ordered by the gangster chief to kidnap Mu Dan so as to secure a huge ransom from her father. Mu Dan, shocked to find her personal worth put up for sale by her boyfriend, throws herself into the river. Held responsible for the incident, Ma Da is imprisoned for a couple of years. In his desperate search for Mu Dan after his release from prison, he finds a substitute in Mei Mei, a Mu Dan look-alike, who swims as mermaid in a big fish tank in a nightclub. Ma Da tells his story to Mei Mei. While savoring Mei Mei's growing attachment to him, Ma Da runs into Mu Dan, still alive. They unite in their love for a brief moment, only to be drowned in the river in a motorcycle incident.

Crucial to the whole story is the image of the mermaid, which is Mu Dan's symbolic accessory, a Barbie from Ma Da, and which also signals Mei Mei's erotic, entertaining role in the club. One is pure, and other commercial. As a symbol from the west, the mermaid also implies the poverty of local cultural resources and the preference for things global. The happiest, the most innocent moment between Ma Da and Mu Dan is the birthday get-together, fitted out with the mermaid Barbie, a fast motorcycle ride on the river bank à la Schwarzenegger, and vodka drinking. There seems to be nothing homegrown on the Suzhou River.

Yet what allows the film to tell a mermaidlike fairy tale, dressed up with all the foreign or global cultural trappings, and to tell it with authentic conviction and a large dose of realism, is the persistent quest for a livable space, for emotional support in a culturally and economically impoverished setting. Mermaid or not, people need to live on. The young people try to live a life as best they can in the limited, threatened locale of the river. Thus the hints of the impoverished yet vital life of the boat people run parallel with that of the young people, who are desolate on a psychic level. The boats and the river do not seem to be a space for a fulfilling, happy life, falling far short of the global standards of consumption and material goods. Yet on the river, the narrator reminds us, there has accumulated all the history, memory, and stories of the boat people, through hazards of the ages. Many people live their whole lives on the river.

As a video maker with an ethnographic interest, the narrator has videotaped the life cycle of boat people: their weddings, births, and deaths on the boats. Mu Dan's plunge into the river from the bridge is as much part of the river culture as the birth of a new baby. After the incident, the narrator interviews many boat people, and all of them admit witnessing not only the plunge, but also the reappearance of the girl in the shape of a mermaid. Is this a fairy tale, or is it a sign of inexhaustible hope, even among people who may not have heard about the mermaid before? This question allows the initial montage of the river to come back with a strong assertion of a popular, grassroots culture. It is a way of life that, for all its limitations, shabbiness, and poverty, remains resilient and alive. There is no fulfillment and glamor, but this life is dignified and hopeful.

Thus it misses the point to play up the postmodern gloss of the film. The film is a study of the material condition of the local culture ravaged and transformed by aggressive forces of global capital. The mermaid may be a legacy of Europe or a reinvention of Disney, but as an emblem of hope, it matters much to the Suzhou River now, to the young people, as well as the boat people. They must make do with whatever is still available. People on the river must build their life as it grows out of the local conditions, yet still hope for better things to come. The mermaid is a symbol reappropriated by the locals for their own use and seems to have come to stay as part of their own cultural resources. "When you cannot have what you want," quotes Michel de Certeau from a writer, "you must want what you have."[39] This desire for sustaining a down-to-earth, resilient life is what makes this seemingly fairy-tale film paradoxically a realist film. In spite of its closeness to the simulacral, inauthentic urban experience of alienation, purposelessness, and loneliness, a hint of hope is woven into the material, lowly texture of ordinary people's life, a life maintained and made vital with human ingenuity, dignity, and imagination, including the mermaid.

Rather than fascinate and mesmerize as commodified simulacra, the documentary and realist images scramble the viewing habit schooled in the conventional coordinates of space and time and challenge the continuity of common-sense assumptions. They throw the spectator into an experience of constantly living on edge, the experience of crisis-ridden modern life in the shadow of globalization. Although they are fraught with grotesque contradictions between China's past and new global elements, they call into question the abstract subject embodied in the Hollywood story of individual psychological development. They also challenge the image of the citizen of the world riding on the bandwagon of the free market. The universal visual language of globalization is in the service of capital accumulation and expansion. Against this language, the realist image brings to the screen the contradictions of history that give the lie to the abstract subject and the myth of free markets. Realism explodes a history under the sign of simulacra but also performs an act of imagining a wider horizon of history fraught with possibilities. On the one hand it plunges the spectator into a "kaleidoscope with consciousness," unable to find an anchor. On the other hand, it calls forth the collective desire and energy for social change.[40]

Notes

INTRODUCTION

1. Hardt and Negri, *Empire*, 8. Also see Harvey, *New Imperialism*.
2. Hardt and Negri, *Empire*, 9.
3. Steinmetz understands Empire as "a historical reflection on the post-Fordist formation that crystallized in the 1990s . . . rather than a consideration of the present and the future." My argument is that the ethical dimensions of globalization or Empire need to be maintained when a new imperialism is rising. See Seinmetz, "State of Emergency," 324.
4. Ibid., 19–20.
5. Jean and John Comaroff call this "millennial capitalism" in their edited volume of essays on global capitalism.
6. By "historical imagination," I refer to Castoriadis's notion of "work of the social imaginary, of instituting society." "Society," as Castoriadis puts it, "is self-creation deployed as history." See his *World in Fragments*, 3–18.
7. See Dirlik, "Reversals, Ironies, Hegemonies."
8. Richard Terdiman's book *Present Past* comprehensively theorizes the intellectual legacy concerning the relation of memory and history. Also see Halbwachs, *Cadres sociaux de la mémoire*.
9. Nora, "General Introduction," 1. See also Harvey, *Justice, Nature*, 29.
10. Nora, "General Introduction," 1–2.
11. Ibid., 3, 6.
12. See Hegel's *Philosophy of History* for an elaboration on historical consciousness. Also see Habermas, *Philosophical Discourse of Modernity*, 1–44.
13. Terdiman, *Present Past*.
14. Dirlik, "Reversals, Ironies, Hegemonies," 127. Dirlik writes that Confucianism was earlier regarded as an obstacle to China's development, along with imperialism. In the newly triumphant narrative of global capitalism, however, Confucianism "has reemerged from the museum 'to advance toward the twenty-first century with a smile on his lips,' to quote a recent article in the *Renmin ribao*."

15. This invention of the past, as Eric Hobsbawm terms it, is indeed a hallmark of modern historiography in the process of legitimating the nation-state. See Hobsbawm and Ranger, *Invention of Tradition.*

16. Hutton, *History as an Art of Memory*, xxiv.

17. For a discussion of history as the domain of the possible, see Castoriadis, *World in Fragments*, 76–77.

18. Benjamin, *Arcades Project*, 471.

19. Wang Xiaoming and a group of critics have dubbed this new myth the "new ideology." For an analysis and criticism of this new historical narrative, see Wang Xiaoming, *Zai xin yishi xingtai de longzhao xia.*

20. See Caruth, *Trauma.* Also see Herman, *Trauma and Recovery*; Farrell, *Post-Traumatic Culture*; and Leys, *Trauma.*

21. See Caruth, *Trauma*; and Leys, *Trauma.* For a discussion of the shift from the psyche to the social field, see Ban Wang, "Historical Trauma"; and Ban Wang, "Introduction."

22. Wang Xiaoming, *Zai xin yishi xingtai de longzhao xia*, 238–42.

23. Jameson, *Seeds of Time*, 102–3.

24. Nietzsche, *Use and Abuse*, 9.

25. Ibid., 21.

26. Gu Xin, *Zhongguo qimeng de lishi tujing*; Rubie S. Watson, *Memory, History, and Opposition*; and Meng Yue, "Ye tan bashi niandai wenxue de xihua."

27. Vera Schwarcz, *Bridges Across Broken Time.*

28. Watson, *Memory, History, and Opposition.*

CHAPTER I

1. David Wang, *Fin-de-Siècle Splendor.* Yu Yingshi, *Shixue yu chuantong*, 93–107. In the growing body of literature on tradition and modernity, the local and global, one can get a sense of the urgency of the debate by reading works that deal with general intellectual trends. See Lin Yusheng, *Zhongguo chuantong de chuangzaoxing zhuanhua.*

2. Vera Schwarcz, *Chinese Enlightenment.*

3. Li Zehou, *Zhongguo xiandai sixiangshi lun.*

4. For a collection of essays by a prominent group of scholars on this topic, see Lin Yusheng et al., *Wusi.*

5. Dirlik makes this quite clear. See "Reversals, Ironies, Hegemonies."

6. See Duara's critique of nationalism in his *Rescuing History from the Nation.*

7. Lydia Liu's work on translingual practice helps us understand the process of borrowing. See Liu, *Translingual Practice.*

8. See Duara, *Rescuing History from the Nation.*

9. Karl, *Staging the World*, 17–18.

10. Arendt, *On Revolution*, 232.

11. Meisner, *Mao's China*, 55.

12. Foucault, "Nietzsche, Genealogy, History," in *Language, Counter-Memory, Practice*, 160.

13. Ibid., 154. Also see Foucault, *Archéologie du savoir*, 172–73. In the chapter on "L'a priori historique et l'archive," Foucault elaborates on the gap between our discursive and the endless mass of the archive, a gap that prevents a narcissistic identification of history with preconceived narrative.

14. Foucault, "Nietzsche, Genealogy, History," 154.

15. Bernstein, "Foucault," 295.

16. Roth, *Ironist's Cage*, 72.

17. Ibid., 78.

18. Ibid., 76.

19. The "TINA" (There is no alternative) talk resonates with the neoliberal end of history thesis. See Francis Fukuyama, *End of History*.

20. For a more specific understanding of modern historical discourse, see Hutton, *History as an Art of Memory*, chap. 7, "The Role of Memory in the Historiography of the French Revolution." Habermas writes, "Modernity can and will no longer borrow the criteria by which it takes its orientation from the models supplied by another epoch; *it has to create its normativity out of itself.* Modernity sees itself cast back upon itself without any possibility of escape. This explains the sensitiveness of its self-understanding, the dynamism of the attempt, carried forward incessantly down to our time, to 'pin itself down'" (*Philosophical Discourse of Modernity*, 7; italics in original).

21. Q. Edward Wang, *Inventing China Through History*, 44–45.

22. Ibid., 28.

23. Xiaobing Tang, *Global Space*, 36.

24. Liang Qichao, *Zhongguo lishi yanjiu fa*, 36.

25. Lu Xun, *Lu Xun quanji*, 6:39; hereafter cited as LXQJ.

26. Dipesh Chakrabarty insists on the inescapable European framework in the subaltern history, yet tries to insert newly created figurations of native cultural memory in rewriting the imposed European history. Apart from the indigenous rewriting, the presumed identity of the European historical narrative needs to be shown to be full of cracks and opportunities. This is Lu Xun's way of treating the "master narrative." See Chakrabarty, *Provincializing Europe*.

27. Shu-mei Shih, *Lure of the Modern*, 73–84.

28. Pusey, *Lu Xun and Evolution*, 1–28.

29. Gould, *Full House*, 41.

30. Buck-Morss, *Dialectics of Seeing*, 58.

31. See Duara, *Rescuing History from the Nation*; Lee, "Modernity and Its Discontents."

32. Spence, *Search for Modern China*, 301.

33. Lee, "Modernity and Its Discontents," 161.
34. Benjamin Schwartz, *In Search of Wealth and Power*, 46.
35. Adam Cohen, "What the Monkeys can Teach Humans about Making America Fair," *New York Times*, editorial/op-ed, September 21, 2003, section 4, p. 10.
36. See Zhu Weizheng, *Zhongguo xiandai sixiang shi ziliao jianbian*, 387–90.
37. Li Zehou, *Zhongguo xiandai sixiangshi lun*, 14.
38. Pinkard, *Hegel*, 471.
39. "History" encompasses both the sense of antitraditionalism, exemplified by modern, forward history, and the idea of the continuity of tradition. It is in the latter sense that one may see Enlightenment history as antihistorical because it assumes a rupture with sedimented historical time. See Collingwood's discussion of the ahistorical tendencies in European Enlightenment thinkers in *The Idea of History*, 76–77.
40. Lyell, *Lu Hsün's Vision of Reality*, 161. Wang Hui, *Fankang juewang*, 134.
41. Between despair and hope, we can trace a whole series of historical reflection and aesthetic innovations in Lu Xun. This duality has been indeed extended to explain the aesthetic and literary practice marked by irony. Critics have much to say about the typical Lu Xun narrator caught in an ironical bind between criticism of traditional life forms and the guilt-ridden complicity with those very forms under assault. See Hanan, "Technique of Lu Xun's Fiction," 53–96.
42. See Terdiman, *Present Past*; and Nora, "General Introduction."
43. Marx and Engels, *Marx-Engels Reader*, 437.
44. For an account of Hegel's link to tradition, see Taylor, *Hegel and Modern Society*. Marx's theory of history offers the utopian imagination as the link to the past dream awaiting future fulfillment. See Marx and Engels, *Marx-Engels Reader*, 10.
45. For an engaging summary of the situation, see part 2 of Spence, *Search for Modern China*. For Roth, see note 14.
46. In "Kexue shi jiaopian (Notes on brief history of science)," Lu Xun mentions the name of Ranke, the father of historicist thinking, and uses a historicist approach to analyze scientific achievements relative to an epoch. See LXQJ 1:26, 29–30.
47. I am fortunate to use Jon Kowallis's precise and elegant translation of Lu Xun's early essays in this book. See Kowallis's forthcoming book of translation and his introduction of Lu Xun.
48. For the English translation, see Kowallis, *Warriors of the Spirit*, 137.
49. See Kowallis, "Mara Poetry," in *Warriors of the Spirit*, 17.
50. Benjamin Schwartz, *China and Other Matters*, 208–26.
51. Denton, *Problematic of Self*, 6, 68.
52. Lydia Liu, *Translingual Practice*, 82–112.
53. See the Introduction to this book.

54. Wang Hui's research on Lu Xun's connection with modernist and anarchist strands of the western intellectual tradition has illuminated the subjective and antihistorical aspects of Lu Xun. I would argue, however, that Lu Xun leans much more on the best parts of classical notions of the Enlightenment, which makes history a temporal and empirical process of realizing human freedom and unique personality. See Wang Hui, *Fankang juewang*.

55. Taylor, *Hegel and Modern Society*, 112.

56. Lu Xun did not use *alienate*, but his Schillerian concept of man allows him to talk about the estrangement of the individual from society, the state, and his sensibility in the sense of the alienated individual. Marx's idea of alienation stemmed from Schiller's notion of an ideal, aesthetically fulfilled personality and its extension, the society of harmony and freedom.

57. Lu Xun said that Napoleon was the highest poetry. In "Moluo shili shuo," LXQJ 1:93.

58. LXQJ 1:63–115.

59. Leo Ou-fan Lee has provided a succinct account of prior research and offered an insightful analysis on lineal historical consciousness. See Lee, "Modernity and Its Discontents," 158–77.

60. Lee, *Voices from the Iron House*, 106.

61. Yang, *Chinese Postmodern*. See Chapter 3. Commenting on Freud's reflection on "war neuroses" from World War I, Caruth writes that "the returning traumatic dream startles Freud" because it is not about wish fulfillment in dream, but is "purely and inexplicably, the literal return of the event against the will of the one it inhabits." Caruth, *Trauma*, 5.

62. Scarry, *Body in Pain*, 162, 164.

63. "Yesong" (Ode to the night), LXQJ 5:193.

64. Quoted in Hannah Arendt's introduction to Walter Benjamin, *Illuminations*, 19.

65. Wang Hui, *Wudi panghuang*, 336.

66. Jian Xu, "The Will to the Transaesthetic," 61–92.

67. Adorno et al., *Aesthetics and Politics*, 194.

68. Adorno, *Aesthetic Theory*, 33.

69. Lee, *Voices from the Iron House*, 80–81. Xiaobing Tang, *Chinese Modern*, 74–96.

70. I use Yang Xianyi and Gladys Yang's English translation of this passage in *Lu Hsun: Selected Stories*, 55. Further references will appear with page numbers together with the page number of the translation.

CHAPTER 2

1. Lee, "Modernity and Its Discontents," 158.

2. Ibid., 159–60.

3. See Duara, *Rescuing History from the Nation.* Gu Xin, *Zhongguo qimeng de lishi tujing.* Also see Shu-mei Shih, *Lure of the Modern*, 49–68.

4. Raymond Williams, *Modern Tragedy*, 64.

5. White, *Metahistory*, 1–42.

6. Marx and Engels, *Marx-Engels Reader*, 436.

7. In Chapter 5, I discuss a new aesthetics of representing history on the screen. In the 1980s one popular way of prettifying history is the melodramatic film that aims to achieve cathartic effects. This runs counter to the realistic "tragic vision," much needed in rethinking modern Chinese history and the traumas of political victimization.

8. Jiao Shangzhi, *Zhongguo xiandai xiju meixue sixiang fazhan shi*, 40–91.

9. Zhu Guangqian, the prominent Chinese aesthetician, discussed this topic at length. See Zhu Guangqian, *Beiju xinli xue.*

10. Steiner, *Death of Tragedy*, 5.

11. Krieger, *Tragic Vision*, 10–21.

12. Benjamin, *Illuminations*, 71.

13. Yinque Chen, *Chen Yinque xiansheng lunwen ji*, 173.

14. In the collection of articles contributed to the debate on the National Theater Movement, critics like Liang Shiqiu, Yu Shangyuan, and others repeatedly refer to Aristotle and Greek tragedy. See Yu Shangyuan, *Guoju yundong.*

15. Wang Guowei, *Wang Guowei wenxue meixue lunzhu ji*, 1–23. Further references to Wang Guowei's essays will be in the text.

16. Ibid., 11. For a detailed discussion of Wang Guowei's notion of the sublime, see Ban Wang, *Sublime Figure of History*, 17–54.

17. Jiao Shangzhi, *Zhongguo xiandai xiju meixue sixiang fazhan shi*, 14.

18. Chen Mingshu et al., *Ershi shiji zhongguo wenxue dadian*, 145.

19. Ibid., 35.

20. Shangyuan Yu, *Guoju yundong*, 14.

21. Jiao Shangzhi, *Zhongguo xiandai xiju meixue sixiang fazhan shi*, 15. In her recent study of contemporary Chinese drama, Chen Xiaomei also brings up the realist function of spoken drama as opposed to traditional conventionalism. See her *Acting the Right Part*, 17–18.

22. Hu Shi, *Wenxue gailiang zhouyi*, 155.

23. Ibid., 155–56.

24. Ibid., 164.

25. Ibid., 162–63.

26. Liu Zaifu, *Lu Xun meixue sixiang lungao*, 98–99.

27. Lu Xun, *Lu Xun quanji*, 1:237–41. Further references to this text will be cited as LXQJ.

28. Hui Wang, *Fankang juewang*, p. 238.

29. Just about every book to do with Lu Xun has to perform a de rigueur discussion of this episode of slide watching. See Lyell, *Lu Hsun's Vision of Reality,*

74–75. Lee, *Voices from the Iron House*, 17–19. Lydia Liu, *Translingual Practice*, 61–64.

30. Rey Chow, *Primitive Passions*, 6. See Part 1 of Chow's book.

31. Rey Chow, *Primitive Passions*, 14.

32. Ibid., 15.

33. Paul G. Pickowicz, "Melodramatic Representation."

34. Hu Shi, *Wenxue gailiang zhouyi*, 155–69. Jiao Shangzhi, *Zhongguo xiandai xiju meixue sixiang fazhan shi*, 40–57.

35. Wang Chenwu, "Road of the Chinese Cinema," 1:137. Also see Pickowicz, "Melodramatic Representation," 298–99.

36. Leo Ou-fan Lee, *Shanghai Modern*, 93–119. The quote is from Hansen, *Babel and Babylon*, 141.

37. This scenario is evoked by Kracauer in *Theory of Film*, 14.

38. Benjamin, *Illuminations*, 226.

39. Hansen, Introduction to Kracauer, *Theory of Film*, xxv.

40. Luo Yijun et al., *Zhongguo dianying lilun wenxuan*, 151.

41. Adorno, *Aesthetic Theory*, 6.

42. Williams, *Politics of Modernism*, 113.

43. Ma Ning, "Textual and Critical Difference," 22–31.

44. Jameson, "Third World Literature," 65–88.

45. For a fuller discussion of the dialectic relation between allegory and symbol, see Benjamin, *Origin of German Tragic Drama*, 159–89. Also see Ban Wang, *Sublime Figure of History*, 70–79.

46. Wood, "Ideology, Genre, Auteur," 476–77.

47. Jameson, *Political Unconscious*, 79.

48. Ma Ning, "Textual and Critical Difference," 29.

49. For an assessment of Chinese appropriation of montage theories, see Luo Yijun et al., *Zhongguo dianying lilun wenxuan*, 15–19.

50. Perez, *Material Ghost*, 160.

51. Eisenstein, *Film Form*, 45–63.

52. Ibid., 47.

53. Quoted in Perez, *Material Ghost*, 152.

54. I sketch Benjamin's notion here. For a fuller appreciation of Benjamin's ideas of history and its potential links to Eisenstein's montage, see *Illuminations*, 253–64.

55. Leo Ou-fan Lee, *Shanghai Modern*, 106–7; Also see Ma Ning, "Textual and Critical Difference."

56. Ma Ning, "Textual and Critical Difference," 24.

57. "A kaleidoscope equipped with consciousness" is a phrase used by Walter Benjamin to describe the disorienting impact of urban life on human perception and consciousness. Here I go further to see consciousness dissolved in a mess of images. See *Illuminations*, 175.

58. Ma Ning, "Textual and Critical Difference," 24–25.
59. Luo Yijun et al., *Zhongguo dianying lilun wenxuan*, 149–55.
60. Quoted by Leo Ou-fan Lee, *Shanghai Modern*, 109.
61. Rosen, *Change Mummified*, 20–21.

CHAPTER 3

1. See Dai Jinhua, *Dianyin lilun yu piping shouce*, 5. Also see Zhang Xudong's discussion of the "Cultural Fever" in *Chinese Modernism*, 35–99.

2. Among numerous and growing publications on Benjamin, it is hard to give a manageable body of works for reference. For insightful and convenient reference, see Susan Buck-Morss, *Dialectics of Seeing*; and Richard Wolin, *Walter Benjamin*.

3. Zhang Xudong of New York University has been a major translator and interpreter of Benjamin's writing in China. Zhang's work has much influence among Chinese critics. Zhang told me a few years ago that his Chinese translation of Benjamin's *Charles Baudelaire*, published in 1989, has had 25,000 copies in print. He and I also translated Benjamin's *Illuminations* into Chinese (Oxford University Press, 1998). Benjamin's work has inspired Chinese critics Dai Jinhua and Meng Yue. According to Li Tuo, there is a project under way to translate the complete works of Benjamin into Chinese. It is safe to say that China has a large audience, and a Benjamin cottage industry is booming.

4. Benjamin, *Origin*, 162. Further references to this book will appear with page numbers in the text.

5. Wolin, *Walter Benjamin*, 66–67.

6. Buck-Morss, *Dialectics of Seeing*, 168–69.

7. "Posttraumatic" is derived from the term "posttraumatic stress disorder," which the American Psychiatric Association coined in 1980 to acknowledge a long-recognized but ignored mental condition. Yet many studies of trauma for decades before this naming, since World War I, have stressed the breakdown of life-sustaining collective and personal meanings and its lasting psychic wounds. This line of inquiry has been increasingly explored by cultural critics and seems to me very pointed in describing the effects of the Chinese Cultural Revolution. Herman's definition of trauma in terms of social, cultural, and emotional damage is useful here. She says that external damage to communal life is not secondary to trauma: "Traumatic events have primary effects not only on the psychological structures of the self but also on the system of attachment and meaning that link individual and community. . . . Traumatic events destroy the victim's fundamental assumption about the safety of the world, the positive value of the self, and the meaningful order of creation." It is this traumatic destruction of the shared symbols, attitudes, and emotions that Chinese intellectuals were grappling with. See Herman, *Trauma and Recovery*, 51.

8. Yang, *Chinese Postmodern*; Braester, *Witness Against History*.

9. Benjamin, *Illuminations*, 257–58.

10. Chow, *Primitive Passions*, 4–12.

11. Meng Yue, *Lishi yu xushu*, 25.

12. Benjamin, *Origin*, 177–78. I use John McCole's translation of this sentence, which is more precise than that of John Osborne in the Verso edition I use here. See John McCole, *Walter Benjamin*, 141.

13. Dai Jinhua, *Dianyin lilun yu piping shouce*, 25.

14. Meng Yue, *Lishi yu xushu*, 26.

15. Benjamin, *Origin*, 164.

16. Ibid., 166.

17. Ibid., 166.

18. Meng Yue, *Lishi yu xushu*, 166.

19. Dai Jinhua, *Dianyin lilun yu piping shouce*, 183.

20. See Lyotard, "Réponse à la question," 357–67.

21. Benjamin, *Illuminations*, 161.

22. Ibid., 232, 235–42.

23. Ibid., 83–109.

24. Zhang Xudong, *Huanxiang de zhixu*, 157–58. Peter Bürger may be the most reliable authority on the subject of allegory and symbol in Benjamin's theory. See Bürger, "Art and Rationality" and *Theory of the Avant-Garde*.

25. Li Zehou, *Meixue sijiang*, 110–25.

26. Benjamin, *Illuminations*, 158.

27. Caruth, *Trauma*, 5.

28. Meng Yue, "Ye tan bashi niandai wenxue xiandai xing," 37.

29. Li Tuo, "1986," 59–73.

30. See Zhang Xudong, *Chinese Modernism*, 19.

31. Ibid., 61.

32. This is a fruitful line of scholarship conducted by a group of social scientists, who have shown oppositional politics at the grassroots through practices of remembrances. See Rubie S. Watson, *Memory, History*.

33. Benjamin, *Illuminations*, 83.

34. Han Shaogong, "Da renmin ribao haiwaiban jizhe wen." Also see Wang Yichuan, "Chuantong yu xiandai de weiji."

35. Benjamin, *Illuminations*, 57.

36. Han Shaogong, *Xie pi*, 29. I use and modify Alice Childs's English-language translation of "Return."

37. Han Shaogong, *Xie pi*, 33.

38. Benjamin, *Illuminations*, 185.

39. Much scholarship has been done on the literature of the search-for-roots movement. For references, see Ji Hongzhen, *Youyu de linghun*. I will place this cultural phenomenon in a larger context, namely the reconstruction of history and memory.

40. See Caruth, *Trauma*; Lifton, *Broken Connection*; Herman, *Trauma and Recovery*; and Farrell, *Post-traumatic Culture*.

41. The Chinese word for "trauma," *chuangshang*, was used as a clinical and psychological term until the mid-1980s. In the atmosphere of intensive cultural reflection, *chuangshang* gained wide currency as a term referring to the "ruptures" in culture and shock experience stemming from a whole series of catastrophic events in modern Chinese history. The introduction of Benjamin's theory on shock experience in the modern age of industrialization contributed to the use of this term as a culturally oriented concept in film studies, literary criticism, and philosophical discourse. See Meng Yue, *Lishi yu xushu*; Dai Jinhua, *Dianyin lilun yu piping shouce*, 15–44; and Zhang Xudong, *Chinese Modernism*, 232–46.

42. Caruth, in her introduction to the edited volume *Trauma*, sums up various findings in trauma studies (4–5).

43. Shoshana Felman, "Education and Crisis."

44. Lin Jinlan, *Shi nian shi yi*, 4. See also Kleinman, *Social Origins of Distress and Disease*, for a focused psychiatric description of the relation of social experience to trauma in China. Kleinman also discusses the trauma of the Cultural Revolution.

45. Meng Yue, "Ye tan bashi niandai wenxue xiandai xing," 38.

46. Zhang Xudong, *Chinese Modernism*, 251.

47. E. Ann Kaplan, "Problematising Cross-Cultural Analysis."

48. Boym, *Common Places*, 285.

49. Ibid., 285.

CHAPTER 4

1. See Jean and John Comaroff, *Millennial Capitalism*.

2. Heller, *Theory of Modernity*, 176.

3. Benjamin, *Illuminations*, 159.

4. Teng Wei, "Yingxiong yinqu chu zhongcan jieji de ziwo shuxie."

5. Heller, *Theory of Modernity*, 177, 182.

6. Ibid., 182.

7. Benjamin, *Illuminations*, 159–60. I paraphrase Benjamin's remarks here into plainer sentences.

8. Philosophers of modernity, such as Hegel, Marx, Lukács, Walter Benjamin, and Max Weber have linked modernity to history and tradition to memory, even when they do not discuss memory per se. This distinction is not fixed, of course, but is dialectically conceived to open up multiple temporal lines within both modernity and residual tradition. For a useful summary of this line of interpretation, see Pierre Nora, "General Introduction."

9. Wang Hui, *Sihuo chongwen*. Also see Duara, *Rescuing History*.

10. The invention of the past, as Eric Hobsbawm terms it, is indeed a hallmark

of modern historiography in the process of legitimating the nation-state. See Hobsbawm and Ranger, *Invention of Tradition*.

11. Eric Hobsbawm, *Age of Extremes*, 334–35.

12. For a fuller discussion of this displacement, see Chapter 8 of this book.

13. See Wu Liang and Wang Anyi, "Guanyu jishi yu xugou de duihua."

14. Lukács, *Theory of the Novel*, 77–78.

15. Nora, "General Introduction," 10.

16. Lukács, *Theory of the Novel*, 77–78.

17. For a discussion of testimonies derived from the Holocaust experience, see Ernst van Alphen, *Caught by History*.

18. See Horkheimer and Adorno, *Dialectic of Enlightenment*.

19. Wang Anyi, *Jishi yu xugou*, 327. Further references to this novel will be given in the text.

20. Benjamin, *Reflections*, 155.

21. Benjamin, *Illuminations*, 185.

22. Wang Anyi, *Yinju de shidai*, 23.

23. Ibid., 27.

24. Giddens, *Consequences of Modernity*, 105.

25. Ibid., 105.

26. Wang Anyi, *Yinju de shidai*, 24.

CHAPTER 5

1. Gu Xin, *Zhongguo qimeng de lishi tujing*. This book provides a useful survey of the major statements on morally informed history writing in both China and the West.

2. These are the major outlines that underlie the conception of history and inform history writing. The Enlightenment narrative of progress and emancipation, as Duara has argued, is the key narrative that spawned other historical narratives in modern China. The most important feature of this narrative is a teleological narrowing down of historical horizons that assembles and mobilizes all social forces and tendencies for nation building, to the exclusion of other historical visions. Although Duara overlooks the historical emergent and radical elements in the nationalistic discourse, his portrayal of the abstract nature of the narrative, especially when applied to the political calamities of the Mao age, is accurate and convincing. See Duara, *Rescuing History*, 4–50.

3. Meng Yue, *Lishi yu xushu*, 52.

4. See Ma Ning, "Spatiality and Subjectivity." Also see Nick Browne, "Society and Subjectivity."

5. Zhu Dake, "Xiejin dianying moshi de quexian."

6. Rosenstone, *Visions of the Past*, 59

7. Pickowicz, "Melodramatic Representation," 320–21.

8. The fifth-generation filmmakers are the first group of graduates from the Bejing Film Academy, who launched their diverse careers in the early 1980s and established their reputation in the mid- through late 1980s. The prominent members include Chen Kaige, Zhang Yimou, Tian Zhuangzhuang, Hu Mei, Wu Ziniu, Huang Jianxin, and Zhou Juntao. It is often noted that the first significant achievement was *Yellow Earth*, directed by Chen Kaige; the film that marked the end of this searching, reflective style is *Red Sorghum*. The films I discuss here are the post-fifth-generation films. Their production was mostly funded by multinational corporations, and their styles are diverse. Although they lack the obstinate questioning of the earlier phases of cinema, these works still share an intense preoccupation with history and trauma.

9. Caruth, *Trauma*, 4–5.

10. Wang Bin, *Huo zhe*, 34–35.

11. Wang Xiyan, *Fen xin zhu gu de rizi*, 137.

12. Dai Jinhua, *Dianyin lilun yu piping shouce*, 126–42.

13. Critics have noted a new brand of humanism in Xie Jin's films—a socialist humanism. Drawing on Confucian notions about the status of the human and the popular nostalgia of the earlier, more "congenial" environment, this humanism stages a critique of the deprivation and destruction of what is crucial to the basic well-being of a human being during the Cultural Revolution. See Nick Browne, "Society and Subjectivity." The favorite themes of this humanism are love, sexual relationship, beauty, life, and modern scientific knowledge. Under the aegis of benign and watchful history, a believer in "human nature" would hold on to these good things in life, and the good things will eventually prevail over the bad and help us leap over the abyss of history. These elements are well illustrated by Xie Jin's films.

14. Wu Wenguang, *Geming xianchang*, 142.

15. For a perceptive discussion of testimonial memory, see Yomi Braester, *Witness Against History*, 6–10.

16. Kundera, *The Art of the Novel*, 36–37.

17. Dai Jinhua, *Dianyin lilun yu piping shouce*, 127–28.

CHAPTER 6

1. Lukács, *Historical Novel*, 19–88.

2. Realism in Chinese fiction from 1949 to the new era of the 1980s is more transcendent and idealistic than realistic. See Ban Wang, "Revolutionary Realism and Revolutionary Romanticism."

3. Ibid., 29.

4. Critics have noted that in the 1980s thought liberation movement (*sixiang jiefang*), the fundamental literary mode and historical consciousness were derived from a Hegelian-Marxist version of the unity of subject and object, the individual

and history. So the self that was upheld was not an autonomous self cut off from the collectivity of social processes but was assimilated and modeled by the requirements of the modernization drive. See Qi Shuyu, *Shichang jingji xia de zhongguo wenxue yishu,* 103–4.

5. This view of Hegel's on art is evoked by Lukács in his preface to *Theory of the Novel,* 11–23. Also see Hegel, *Philosophy of History,* 53–54.

6. Ibid., 17.

7. Eileen Chang, *Liuyan,* 7. Further references to this collection will be given with page numbers in the text.

8. In his *Shanghai Modern,* Leo Ou-fan Lee has traced Eileen Chang's writing and the commercial urban culture she was immersed in. See the chapter entitled "Eileen Chang: Romances in a Fallen City," 267–303.

9. Wang Anyi, *Piaopo de yuyan,* 427–31.

10. Benjamin, "The Storyteller," in *Illuminations,* 83–109.

11. Tang Xiaobing, *Chinese Modern,* 320–21.

12. Ibid., 322.

13. See Wu Liang and Wang Anyi, "A Conversation on *Reality and Fiction,*" in Wang Anyi, *Jishi yu xugou,* 325.

14. Wang Anyi, *Shushu de gushi,* 2.

15. Adorno, "Essay as Form," 3–23.

16. Ibid., 17.

17. Ibid., 16.

18. Wang Anyi, *Shushu de gushi,* 39. Further references to this novella will be cited in the text.

CHAPTER 7

1. See Neil Smith, "Satanic Geographies"; and Bauman, *Globalization.*

2. Appadurai, *Modernity at Large,* 188–99.

3. Benjamin, *Illuminations,* 180–92. Also see Tönnies, *Community and Society.*

4. Lukács, *History and Class Consciousness,* 88.

5. Academic criticism of Zhu Tianwen's writing often emphasizes its literary or aesthetic aspect. The social environment, the metropolis of Taipei, is especially seen as a background that her writing responds to. I describe contextual elements of globalization as built into the very texture of her writing. For a good example of such criticism, see Huang Jinshu, "Shenju zhi wu."

6. Wang Dewei, "Chong kuangren riji dao huangren shouji," 8.

7. Terdiman, *Present Past,* 12.

8. One may claim, following Michel de Certeau, that the consumer can exercise the will to choose and resist the glut of images. Like many optimistic theorists trying to defy consumer trends, de Certeau recommends the tactics of resistance, the making do, *bricolage.* He stakes out a theoretical space where consumption is

not passive and mindless, but active and self-serving. The individual consumer can construct his or her own unique sentences, to use a linguistic metaphor, with and within "an established vocabulary and syntax," i.e., the centralized, clamorous media and consumer trends. But de Certeau's consumer is very much an independent, artistic, and not to say idealized person of intellectual discretion, capable of waging a guerrilla war against all-consuming practices. Unfortunately, one has yet to encounter such a guerrilla fighter in the shopping mall. The possibility of choice is an illusion if it is fed on media-bound images on a daily basis. One can think of the possibility of choice and resistance if one resorts to alternative sets of images. This set of images may be retrieved from cultural memory or tradition, which I discuss in Chapter 8 of this book. See Michel de Certeau, xi–xxiv.

9. Zhu Tianwen, "Shiji mo de huali," in *Hua yi qianshen*, 201. Further references to this story and to "Eden No More" are from this edition of Zhu Tianwen's works and will be given with page numbers in the text.

10. Yvonne Chang, *Modernism and the Nativist Resistance*, 207.

11. Stewart, *On Longing*, 136.

12. Zhu Tianwen, *Huangren shouji*, 54. Further references to this novella will be given in the text. I use my own English translation to suit the purpose of the argument, but for a good English-language translation, see *Notes of a Desolate Man*, translated by Gloldblatt and Lin.

13. Zhan Hongzhi, "Yizhong laoqu de shengyin," 259–64. Also see Huang Jinshu, "Shenju zhi wu."

14. Benjamin's distinction between the aura-filled cult object and the exhibition value of consumer goods derives from the Marxist opposition between use value and exchange value. This pair of ideas helps illuminate my implicit distinction here between a sensibility grounded in memory and history and a sheer consumerist hankering after depthless thrills for any object, exotic or not, on display. This may include memorabilia collected and displayed as a "feast for the eyes." We may note, in connection with the theme in Zhu's "Shiji mo de huali," that the charm of the commodity is double edged. On the one hand, it delivers an impression of "use value" disguised as seductive illusions of fulfillment. On the other hand, the commodity can have real use value by being appropriated and invested with the aura of desire and yearning by the consumer. I argue this point through an analysis of Wang Anyi's *Changhen ge* in Chapter 8. This duality also marks Benjamin's discussion of mechanically produced commodities. See Walter Benjamin's "The Work of Art in the Age of Mechanical Reproduction," in *Illuminations*, 224–25.

15. Zhu Tianwen, "Shiji mo de huali," in *Huayi qianshen*, 201–17.

16. Benjamin, *Illuminations*, 186.

17. Stewart, *On Longing*, 14–15.

18. Chow, *Ethics after Idealism*, 153.

19. Ibid., 151–58.

20. Ibid., 157.
21. Xu Baoqiang, "Shijie zibenzhuyi xia de beijin xiangxiang."
22. Chow, *Ethics after Idealism*, 176.
23. Arnold, *Culture and Anarchy*, 204.
24. Masao Miyoshi, "Globalization and the University."
25. Harvey, *Condition of Postmodernity*, 240.
26. Michelle Huang, *Walking Between Slums and Skyscrapers*, 15–17.
27. Harvey, *Condition of Postmodernity*, 284–85.
28. Abbas, *Hong Kong*, 26.
29. Ibid., 26.
30. Ibid., 27.
31. The category "affect" makes sense only to a conception of the human psyche as a multilayered, finely engineered machine, amenable to analysis by the method of clinical psychoanalysis, psychiatry, and therapy. In a TV commercial for Staples, an office-supply store, for example, a robot can experience "romantic" affect for a printer.
32. Esther Yao, *At Full Speed*.
33. Bauman, *Globalization*, 85.
34. Santner, *Stranded Objects*, 2–3.
35. Adorno, *Aesthetic Theory*, 64.
36. Ibid., 68.

CHAPTER 8

1. For a broad analysis of the liberal embrace of the market in conflict with other current discourses in China, see Wang Hui, *Sihuo chongwen*, 42–94.
2. Zhang Xudong. "Shanghai Nostalgia."
3. Marx and Engels, *Capital*, 84.
4. Adorno, *Critical Models*, 339.
5. Ibid., 339.
6. Chakrabarty, *Provincializing Europe*, 92.
7. Marx and Engels, *Capital*, 84.
8. See Eagleton, "Nationalism." Arguing against the postmodern misconception of universal assumptions, Eagleton makes clear the dialectic interplay of universal and particular. Speaking of oppressed groups struggling for their right to be different, Eagleton says, "For the freedom in question is not the freedom to 'be Irish' or 'be a woman' . . . but simply the freedom now enjoyed by certain other groups to determine their identity as they may wish. Ironically, then, a politics of differences or specificity is in the first place in the cause of sameness and universal identity—the right of a group victimized in its particularity to be on equal terms with others as far as their self-determination is concerned. This is the kernel of truth of bourgeois Enlightenment: the abstract universal right of all to be free, the

shared essence or identity of all human subjects to be autonomous." But this universal equality does not mean the leveling out of differences. On the contrary, "the only point of enjoying such universal abstract equality is to discover and live one's own particular difference" (363). Without abstract rights and universal freedom that every individual is entitled to, one cannot even have the opportunity to act out a private, individual trajectory and imagine an alternative horizon.

9. I situate memory, as most critics of modernity do, within the problematic of modernity and tradition, in the tension between society and community. This has a long line of tradition in the West, including Ferdinand Tönnies with his influential distinction between *Gemeinschaft* and *Gesellschaft*; Durkheim; Weber; Lukács; and Benjamin. With the advent of the market and capitalist modernity in China, this analysis becomes pointedly relevant and illuminating. One needs to be cautious, of course, about the rigid polarity of the distinction, and one should approach the modern and the traditional more as interwoven, and still interweaving, conflictual strands. For an elaborate discussion of this problematic, see Maurice Halbwachs, *Les cadres sociaux de la mémoire.*

10. Marx and Engels, *Capital,* 83. Guy Debord, *Société du spectacle.* Fredric Jameson, *Postmodernism,* 18.

11. Baudrillard, *Simulacra and Simulation,* 3. For a classical Marxist statement of commodity aesthetics, see Haug, *Critique of Commodity Aesthetics.*

12. Ibid., 1.

13. For an analysis of the revolution-inspired spectacle, see Ban Wang, *Sublime Figure of History.* See in particular the chapters entitled "Desire and Pleasure in Revolutionary Cinema" and "The Cultural Revolution: A Terrible Beauty is Born."

14. Leo Ou-fan Lee, in his recent work, describes in detail the formation of this urban culture based on consumption and civil society. See Lee, *Shanghai Modern.*

15. Perry Link, "Traditional-Style Popular Urban Fiction."

16. For a record of contributions to this extended debate on humanist spirit, see Xiaoming Wang, *Renwen jingshen xunsi lu.*

17. For a sample of these two styles of writing, see Wang Biao, *Xin lishi zhuyi xiaoshuo xuan*; and Chen Xiaoming, *Zhongguo xin xieshi xiaoshuo jingxuan.*

18. Benjamin, *Illuminations,* 263.

19. Wang Anyi, *Changhen ge,* 38. Further references to this novel will be given in the text.

20. Zhang Xudong, "Shanghai Nostalgia," 24.

21. Buck-Morss, *Origin of Negative Dialectics,* 55.

22. De Certeau, *Practice of Everyday Life,* 1–29.

23. In Tang Xiaobing's analysis of anxiety over quotidian amenities and enjoyment of commodities in everyday life under socialism, we find some instances of

the persistence of exchange relations within a homogeneous ideology of production and efficiency. Elements of everyday life, of course, are what the dominant ideological practice sets out to eliminate. The constant ideological indoctrination implies symptomatically the impossibility of eliminating the commodity and its related desire and consumption. The analysis of the commodity can also lead to a similar account of submerged sexual desire within a "desexualized," politicized frame of sexuality. See Tang Xiaobing, *Zai jiedu*, 184–95. Also see Ma Junxiang, "*Shanghai guniang* yu guankan wenti." The distinction between the disembodied male discourse of modernity and embodied female experience in a more "natural" strata provides another insight into the lived experience of commodities, especially when the commercial culture of *Changhen ge* is embodied by a feminized Shanghai. For a discussion of the gendered position in Chinese modernity, see Zhong, *Masculinity Besieged?*

24. Benjamin, *Illuminations*, 224.

CHAPTER 9

1. See note 2 in the Introduction for a definition of historical imagination.
2. Benjamin, *Arcades Project*, 460.
3. Zhang, *Chinese Modernism*, 236.
4. Perez, *Material Ghost*, 262.
5. The realist spirit can be seen in Wu Wenguang's reflection on his documentary filmmaking. See his *Jianghu baogao*. Jia Zhangke, Zhang Yuan, and others of the "urban" or sixth generation also display a realist tendency in filmmaking.
6. Li Tuo and Zhang Nuanxin, "Tan dianying yuyan de xiandai hua," 18–22.
7. Ibid., 241.
8. The analysis of a political scientist on this issue may be more penetrating, especially in the post–September 11 world. See Benjamin Barber, *Jihad vs. McWorld*, 88–99.
9. Ibid., 88.
10. Beller, "Capital/Cinema."
11. See Zhang Yingjin, *Cinema and Urban Culture*.
12. Hansen, *Babel and Babylon*, 29.
13. Ibid., 61, 94.
14. Ibid., 79. Mary Ann Doane, in her recent work on cinema and time, sees the rise of a standardized grammar of time in cinema. Time, as in cinematic language, is also a component of the subjective experience and the operations of capital in capitalist culture. See Doane, *Emergence of Cinematic Time*, 1–32.
15. The epic here seems to have little to do with the Lukácsian epic I discuss in Chapter 6. But one can still see that in promoting a reflective attitude in the audience, Brecht is thinking in terms of history that involves multitudes as participants.

16. Benjamin, *Understanding Brecht*, 15.

17. Ibid., 19–21.

18. Lukács, *Theory of the Novel*, 19.

19. Barthes, *La chambre claire*, 1126–27.

20. Benjamin, *Origin*, 166.

21. Benjamin, *Arcades Project*, 475.

22. Benjamin, *Illuminations*, 262–63.

23. Philip Rosen, *Change Mummified*, 3. Also see André Bazin's analysis of cinematic ontology in *Qu'est-ce que le cinéma?*, 1:10–19.

24. Bazin, *Qu'est-ce que le cinéma?*, 4: 15.

25. Li Tuo and Zhang Nuanxin, "Tan dianying yuyan de xiandai hua," 20–21.

26. Zhang, *Chinese Modernism*, 241.

27. See Dai Jinhua, *Dianyin lilun yu piping shouce*, 6.

28. Rosen, *Change Mummified*, 6.

29. Ibid., 7.

30. Ibid., 14.

31. Benjamin, *Origin*, 166.

32. Ibid., 24–25.

33. Lü Xinyu, *Jilu zhongguo*, 3–34. For more information about Wu Wenguang and documentary filmmaking, see the Beijing University Web site, available at: http://movie.newyouth.beida-online.com/.

34. Perez, *Material Ghost*, 40.

35. Ibid., 40.

36. Ibid., 370.

37. For a theoretical elaboration of kitsch, see Matei Calinescu, *Five Faces*, 225–62.

38. An anonymous critic, "How I see *Suzhou River*," available at: http://movie.newyouth.beida-online.com/.

39. De Certeau, *Practice of Everyday Life*, xxiv.

40. "A kaleidoscope equipped with consciousness" is a phrase used by Walter Benjamin to describe the disorienting impact of urban life on human perception and consciousness. See *Illuminations*, 175.

Chinese Names and Terms

Ai zai caoyuan	爱在草原
"Ban zhuren"	班主任
Bawang bieji	霸王别姬
beiju	悲剧
beiju yishi	悲剧意识
"Bing hou zatan"	病后杂谈
"Bing hou zatan zhi yu"	病后杂谈之余
Changhen ge	长恨歌
Changsheng dian	长生殿
Chen Dabei	陈大悲
Chen Duxiu	陈独秀
Chen Kaige	陈凯歌
Chen Yinque	陈寅恪
"Chengshi wu gushi"	城市无故事
Chengshi zhi ye	城市之夜
Chun chan	春蚕
Chunliu she	春柳社
cong xuepo zhong xunchu xianshi lai	从血泊中寻出闲适来
da huanxi	大欢喜
da pian	大片
"Duosuo"	哆嗦
fansi	反思
Feng Qinglan	冯晴岚
Fu Pin	富萍
Fu Sinian	傅斯年
Fukan	副刊
Furong zhen	芙蓉镇

gaizao guomin xing	改造国民性
ganjue	感觉
Genzhe ganjue zou	跟着感觉走
geren hua xiezou	个人化写作
gexing	个性
gongli	公理
"Gudu zhe"	孤独者
"Gui qu lai"	归去来
guo ba yin jiu si	过把瘾就死
Guo Moruo	郭沫若
"Guxiang"	故乡
haipai	海派
Hei junma	黑骏马
Heinu yu tian lu	黑奴吁天录
"Honglou meng pinglun"	红楼梦评论
Honglou yuan meng	红楼圆梦
Hou shitou ji	后石头记
Hu Mei	胡玫
huaigu	怀古
huaju	话剧
Huang Lingshuang	黄凌霜
huangjin shijie	黄金世界
Huangren shouji	荒人手记
Hulan he zhuang	呼兰河传
Huozhe	活着
Hushing shuyuan	沪上淑媛
Jia Zhangke	贾樟柯
Jiang Guanyun	蒋观云
Jianghu	江湖
Jin Yong	金庸
Jing Qing	景清
Jingpai	京派
jingyan	经验
Jishi yu xugou	纪实与虚构
juan cun	眷村
"Kexue shi jiaopian"	科学史教篇
Kuangliu	狂流

Lan fengzheng	蓝风筝
Lao She	老舍
letian	乐天
Li Shutong	李叔同
Lin Jinlan	林斤澜
liangxiao wucai	两小无猜
Lishi yu xushu	历史与叙述
Liu yan	流言
longtang	弄堂
Malu tianshi	马路天使
maoxianjia de leyuan	冒险家的乐园
mobei caoyuan	漠北草原
"Moluo shili shuo"	魔罗诗力说
Muma ren	牧马人
neiyao	内耀
Nüer lou	女儿楼
Ouyang Yuqian	欧阳予倩
"Pipa xing"	琵琶行
Qian Xuantong	钱玄同
Qin Hui	秦桧
Qingchun ji	青春祭
Qiuyue	秋月
quzhong zhouya	曲终奏雅
"Ren zhi lishi"	人之历史
ru	茹
Ruan Lingyu	阮玲玉
San ge moden nüxing	三个摩登女性
Shanghai ershisi xiaoshi	上海二十四小时
Shengsi chang	生死场
Shennü	神女
"Shiji mo de huali"	世纪末的华丽
shili yangchang	十里洋场
shimin wenhua	市民文化
Shu guijian	蜀龟鉴
Shuo Yue zhuan	说岳传

Shushu de gushi	叔叔的故事
Suzhou he	苏州河
"Tan dianying yuyan de xiandaihua"	谈电影语言的现代化
Tian Han	田汉
Tian Zhuangzhuang	田壮壮
"Tianxian pei"	天仙配
Tianyunshan chuanqi	天云山传奇
Tie Xuan	铁铉
"Tongyan wuji"	童言无忌
tuanyuan zhuyi	团圆主义
wali zhong xiubu laoli	瓦砾中修补老例
wan de jiu shi xintiao	玩的就是心跳
Wang Qiyao	王琦瑶
Wang Shuo	王朔
wangguo miezhong	亡国灭种
Wei Hui	卫慧
weilu yehua	围炉夜话
"Wenhua pianzhi lun"	文化偏至论
Wenhui bao	文汇报
"Wenxue jinhua guannian yu xiju gailiang"	文学进化观念与戏剧改良
Wu Wenguang	吴文光
wu wu zhi zhen	无物之阵
Wu Yonggang	吴永刚
Xia Yan	夏衍
Xiao baozhuang	小鲍庄
xiao shimin	小市民
Xiao Wu	小武
Xie Jin	谢晋
xin ganxing	新感性
Xin shiqi	新时期
xinqu	新区
Xinmin congbao	新民丛报
ye shi	野史
yi	瘾
"Yidian bu zai"	伊甸不再
Yiku sitian	忆苦思甜
Yongle	永乐
Yue Fei	岳飞

zai bian	灾变
"Zai chuangshang jiyi de huaibao zhong"	在创伤记忆的怀抱中
"Zai lun leifengta de daota"	再论雷峰塔的倒塌
zawen	杂文
Zhang Chengzhi	张承志
Zhang Nuanxin	张暖忻
Zhang Yimou	张艺谋
Zhongguo lish yanjiu fa	中国历史研究法
zhongjian wu	中间物
zhuangmei	壮美
zijue	自觉

Bibliography

Abbas, Ackbar. *Hong Kong: Culture and the Politics of Disappearance.* Minneapolis: Minnesota University Press, 1997.

Adorno, Theodor W. *Aesthetic Theory.* Edited and translated by G. Adorno and R. Tiedemann. Minneapolis: University of Minnesota Press, 1997.

———. *Critical Models: Interventions and Catchwords.* New York: Columbia University Press, 1998.

———. "The Essay as Form." In *Notes to Literature,* edited by Rolf Tiedemann and translated by Shierry W. Nicholsen, 1:3–23. New York: Columbia University Press, 1991.

Adorno, Theodor, et al. *Aesthetics and Politics.* Edited by Fredric Jameson. London: Verso, 1977.

Alphen, Ernest van. *Caught by History.* Stanford, CA: Stanford University Press, 1997.

Appadurai, Arjun. *Modernity at Large: Cultural Dimensions of Globalization.* Minneapolis: University of Minnesota Press, 1996.

Arendt, Hannah. *On Revolution.* New York: Penguin, 1965.

Arnold, Matthew. *Culture and Anarchy.* New Haven: Yale University Press, 1994.

Barber, Benjamin. *Jihad vs. McWorld: How Globalism and Tribalism are Reshaping the World.* New York: Ballantine Books, 1995.

Barthes, Roland. *La chambre claire: Note sur la photographie.* In *Oeuvres Complètes,* 1105–97. Paris: Editions du Seuil, 1995.

Baudrillard, Jean. *Simulacra and Simulation.* Translated by Sheila F. Glaser. Ann Arbor: University of Michigan Press, 1994.

Bauman, Zygmunt. *Globalization: The Human Consequences.* New York: Columbia University Press, 1998.

Bazin, André. *Qu'est-ce que le cinéma? Ontologie et langage.* Vol. 1. Paris: Éditions du Cerf, 1958.

———. *Qu'est-ce que le cinéma? Une esthétique de la réalité: Le néo-réalisme.* Vol. 4 Paris: Éditions du Cerf, 1962.

Beller, Jonathan L. "Capital/Cinema." In *Deleuze and Guattari: New Mappings in*

Politics, Philosophy, and Culture, edited by Eleanor Kaufman and Kevin Heller, 77–95. Minneapolis: University of Minnesota Press, 1998.

Benjamin, Walter. *The Arcades Project.* Translated by Howard Eiland and Kevin McLaughlin. Cambridge, MA: Belknap Press of Harvard University Press, 1999.

———. *Illuminations.* Translated by Harry Zohn. Introduction by Hannah Arendt. New York: Schocken Books, 1969.

———. *The Origin of German Tragic Drama.* Translated by John Osborne. London: Verso, 1977.

———. *Understanding Brecht.* Translated by Anna Bostock. Introduction by Stanley Mitchell. London: Verso, 1998.

———. *Reflections.* Translated by Edmund Jephcott. New York: Schocken Books, 1986.

Bernstein, Richard. "Foucault: Critique as a Philosophical Ethos." In *Philosophical Interventions in the Unfinished Project of Enlightenment*, edited by Axel Honnett et al., 280–310. Cambridge, MA: MIT Press, 1992.

Boym, Svetlana. *Common Places: Mythologies of Everyday Life in Russia.* Cambridge, MA: Harvard University Press, 1994.

Braester, Yomi. *Witness against History: Literaure, Film, and Public Discourse in Twentieth-Century China.* Stanford, CA: Stanford University Press, 2003.

Browne, Nick. "Society and Subjectivity." In Nick Browne et al., *New Chinese Cinemas*, 40–56.

Browne, Nick, et al., eds. *New Chinese Cinemas: Forms, Identities, Politics.* New York: Cambridge University Press, 1994.

Buck-Morss, Susan. *The Dialectics of Seeing: Walter Benjamin and the Arcades Project.* Cambridge, MA: MIT Press, 1989.

———. *The Origin of Negative Dialectics.* New York: Free Press, 1977.

Bürger, Peter. "Art and Rationality." In *Philosophical Interventions in the Unfinished Project of Enlightenment*, edited by Axel Honneth et al., 220–34. Cambridge, MA: MIT Press, 1992.

———. *Theory of the Avant-Garde.* Minneapolis: University of Minnesota Press, 1984.

Calinescu, Matei. *Five Faces of Modernity.* Durham, NC: Duke University Press, 1987.

Caruth, Cathy, ed. *Trauma: Explorations in Memory.* Baltimore: Johns Hopkins University Press, 1995.

Castoriadis, Cornelius. *World in Fragments: Writings on Politics, Society, Psychoanalysis, and the Imagination.* Edited and translated by David Curtis. Stanford, CA: Stanford University Press, 1997.

Chakrabarty, Dipesh. *Provincializing Europe: Postcolonial Thought and Historical Difference.* Princeton, NJ: Princeton University Press, 2000.

Chang, Eileen. *Liuyan* (Floating words). Taipei: Crown Press, 1984.

Chang, Yvonne. *Modernism and the Nativist Resistance: Contemporary Chinese Fiction from Taiwan.* Durham, NC: Duke University Press, 1993.

Chen Mingshu, et al., eds. *Ershi shiji zhongguo wenxue dadian: 1897–1929* (Compendium of twentieth-century Chinese literature: 1897–1929). Shanghai: Shanghai Education Press, 1994.

Chen Qingqiao, ed. *Wenhua xiangxiang yu yishi xingtai* (Cultural imaginary and ideology). Hong Kong: Oxford University Press, 1997.

Chen Xiaomei. *Acting the Right Part: Political Theater and Popular Drama in Contemporary China.* Honolulu: University of Hawaii Press, 2002.

Chen Xiaoming, ed. *Zhongguo xin xieshi xiaoshuo jingxuan* (Selected works of Chinese neorealism). Lanzhou: Gansu renmin chubanshe, 1993.

Chen Yinque. *Chen Yinque xiansheng lunwen ji* (Scholarly essays by Chen Yinque). Vol. 2. Taipai: Sanrenxing chubanshe, 1974.

Wang Chenwu. "The Road of the Chinese Cinema." In Luo Yijun et al., *Zhongguo dianying lilun wenxuan,* 1:134–43.

Chinese Literature Magazine, ed. *Best Chinese Short Stories: 1949–1989.* Beijing: Panda Books, 1989.

Chow, Rey. *Ethics After Idealism: Theory-Culture-Ethnicity-Reading.* Bloomington and Indianapolis: Indiana University Press, 1998.

———. *Primitive Passions: Visuality, Sexuality, Ethnography, and Contemporary Chinese Cinema.* New York: Columbia University Press, 1995.

Cohen, Adam. "What the Monkeys can Teach Humans about Making America Fair." *New York Times.* Editorial/Op-Ed, September 21, 2003.

Collingwood, R. G. *The Idea of History.* New York: Oxford University Press, 1956.

Comaroff, Jean and John, ed. *Millennial Capitalism and the Culture of Neoliberalism.* Durham, NC: Duke University Press, 2001.

Dai Jinhua. *Dianyin lilun yu piping shouce* (Handbook to film theory and criticism). Beijing: Science and Technology Document Press, 1993.

Dai Jinhua, ed. *Shuxie wenhua yingxiong* (Writing cultural heroes). Nanjing: Jiangsu renmin chubanshe, 1999.

De Certeau, Michel. *The Practice of Everyday Life.* Berkeley: University of California Press, 1984.

Denton, Kirk. *The Problematic of Self in Modern Chinese Literature: Hu Feng and Lu Ling.* Stanford, CA: Stanford University Press, 1998.

Debord, Guy. *La société du spectacle.* Paris: Buchet-Chastel, 1967.

Dirlik, Arif. "Reversals, Ironies, Hegemonies: Notes on the Contemporary Historiography of Modern China." In *History after the Three Worlds: Post-Eurocentric Historiographies,* edited by Arif Dirlik, Vinay Bahl, and Peter Gran, 125–56. New York: Rowman and Littlefield, 2000.

Dirlik, Arif, Vinay Bahl, and Peter Gran, eds. *History after the Three Worlds: Post-Eurocentric Historiographies.* New York: Rowman and Littlefield, 2000.

Doane, Mary Ann. *The Emergence of Cinematic Time: Modernity, Contingency, and the Archive*. Cambridge, MA: Harvard University Press, 2002.

Duara, Prasenjit. *Rescuing History from the Nation: Questioning Narratives of Modern China*. Chicago: University of Chicago Press, 1995.

Eagleton, Terry. "Nationalism: Irony and Commitment." In *The Eagleton Reader*, edited by Stephen Regan, 359–69. Oxford, UK: Blackwell, 1998.

Eisenstein, Sergei. *Film Form: Essays in Film Theory*. Edited and translated by Jay Leyda. New York: Meridian Books, 1957.

Farrell, Kirby. *Post-traumatic Culture: Injury and Interpretation in the Nineties*. Baltimore: Johns Hopkins University Press, 1998.

Felman, Shoshana. "Education and Crisis, or the Vicissitudes of Teaching." In *Trauma: Explorations in Memory*, edited by Cathy Caruth, 13–60. Baltimore: Johns Hopkins University Press, 1995.

Foucault, Michel. *L'archéologie du savoir*. Paris: Éditions Gallimard, 1969.

———. *Language, Counter-Memory, Practice*. Edited and with an introduction by Donald Bourchard. Ithaca, NY: Cornell University Press, 1977.

Fukuyama, Francis. *The End of History and the Last Man*. New York: Free Press, 1992.

Furth, Charlotte, ed. *The Limits of Change: Essays on Conservative Alternatives in Republican China*. Cambridge, MA: Harvard University Press, 1976.

Giddens, Anthony. *The Consequences of Modernity*. Stanford, CA: Stanford University Press, 1990.

Gould, Stephen J. *Full House: The Spread of Excellence from Plato to Darwin*. New York: Three Rivers Press, 1996.

Gu Xin. *Zhongguo qimeng de lishi tujing* (The historical visions of Chinese enlightenment). Hong Kong: Oxford University Press, 1992.

Habermas, Jürgen. *The Philosophical Discourse of Modernity*. Translated by Frederick G. Lawrence. Cambridge, MA: MIT Press, 1990.

Halbwachs, Maurice. *Les cadres sociaux de la mémoire*. New York: Arno Press, 1975.

Han Shaogong. "Da renmin ribao haiwaiban jizhe wen" (Answers to the questions by the reporter of *Overseas Chinese Daily*). In *Zhongshan* (Mount Zhong literary magazine) 5 (1987): 12–15.

———. "Return." Translated by Alice Childs. In *Best Chinese Short Stories: 1949–1989*, edited by Chinese Literature Magazine, 432–48. Beijing: Panda Books, 1989.

———. *Xie pi* (Obsession with shoes). Wuhan: Changjiang wenyi chubanshe, 1994.

Hanan, Patrick. "The Technique of Lu Xun's Fiction." *Harvard Journal of Asiatic Studies* 34 (1981): 53–96.

Hansen, Miriam. *Babel and Babylon: Spectatorship in American Silent Film*. Cambridge, MA: Harvard University Press, 1991.

———. Introduction to Siegfried Kracauer, *Theory of Film*, vii–xiv. Princeton, NJ: Princeton University Press, 1997.

Hardt, Michael, and Antonio Negri. *Empire*. Cambridge, MA: Harvard University Press, 2000.

Harvey, David. *The Condition of Postmodernity*. Cambridge, MA: Blackwell, 1990.

———. *Justice, Nature and the Geography of Difference*. Oxford, UK: Blackwell, 1996.

———. *The New Imperialism*. Oxford: Oxford University Press, 2003.

Haug, Wolfgang Fritz. *Critique of Commodity Aesthetics: Appearance, Sexuality and Advertising in Capitalist Society*. Translated by Robert Bock. Minneapolis: University of Minnesota Press, 1986.

Hegel, Georg William Friedrich. *The Philosophy of History*. Translated by J. Sibree. New York: Prometheus Books, 1991.

Heller, Agnes. *A Theory of Modernity*. Oxford, UK: Blackwell, 1999.

Herman, Judith L. *Trauma and Recovery*. New York: Basic Books, 1992.

Hobsbawm, Eric. *The Age of Extremes: A History of the World, 1914–1991*. New York: Pantheon Books, 1994.

Hobsbawm, Eric, and T. Ranger, eds. *The Invention of Tradition*. New York: Cambridge University Press, 1984.

Horkheimer, Max, and Theordor Adorno. *Dialectic of Enlightenment*. New York: Continuum, 1999.

Hu Shi. *Wenxue gailiang zhouyi* (Discussions on reform of literature). Hong Kong: Yuanliu Press, 1986.

Huang Jinshu. "Shenju zhi wu" (Dances of the Goddess). In Zhu Tianwen, *Hua yi qianshen*, 265–312.

Huang, Tsung-Yi Michelle. *Walking Between Slums and Skyscrapers: Illusions of Open Space in Hong Kong, Tokyo, and Shanghai*. Hong Kong: Hong Kong University Press, 2004.

Hutton, Patrick H. *History as an Art of Memory*. Hanover: University Press of New England, 1993.

Jameson, Fredric. *The Political Unconscious*. Ithaca, NY: Cornell University Press, 1981.

———. *Postmodernism, or, The Cultural Logic of Late Capitalism*. Durham: Duke University Press, 1991.

———. *The Seeds of Time*. New York: Columbia University Press, 1994.

———. "Third World Literature in the Era of Multinational Capitalism." *Social Text* 15 (1986): 65–88.

Ji Hongzhen. *Youyu de linghun* (The melancholy soul). Changchun: Shidai yishu chubanshe, 1992.

Jiao Shangzhi. *Zhongguo xiandai xiju meixue sixiang fazhan shi* (Aesthetic history of modern Chinese drama). Beijing: Dongfang chubanshe, 1995.

Kaplan, E. Ann. "Problematising Cross-Cultural Analysis: The Case of Women in the Recent Chinese Cinema." In *Perspectives on Chinese Cinema,* edited by Chris Berry, 146–47. London: British Film Institute, 1992.

Kaplan, E. Ann, and Ban Wang, eds. *Trauma and Cinema: Cross-Cultural Explorations.* Hong Kong: Hong Kong University Press, 2004.

Karl, Rebecca. *Staging the World: Chinese Nationalism at the Turn of the Twentieth Century.* Durham, NC: Duke University Press, 2002.

Kleinman, Arthur. *Social Origins of Distress and Disease.* New Haven: Yale University Press, 1986.

Kowallis, Jon E. *Warriors of the Spirit: Mara and Other Turn-of-the-Century Wenyan Essays by Lu Xun.* Berkeley, CA: East Asian Institute Monograph Series. Forthcoming.

Kracauer, Siegfried. *Theory of Film: The Redemption of Physical Reality.* New York: Oxford University Press, 1960. Introduction by Miriam Hansen. Reprint, Princeton, NJ: Princeton University Press, 1997.

Krieger, Murray. *The Tragic Vision.* Chicago: University of Chicago Press, 1960.

Kundera, Milan. *The Art of the Novel.* New York: Harper and Row, 1986.

Lee, Leo Ou-fan. "Modernity and Its Discontents: The Cultural Agenda of the May Fourth Movement." In *Perspectives on Modern China,* edited by Kenneth Lieberthal et al., 158–77. Armonk, NY: M. E. Sharpe, 1991.

———. *Shanghai Modern: The Flowering of a New Urban Culture in China, 1930–1945.* Cambridge, MA: Harvard University Press, 1999.

———. *Voices from the Iron House: A Study of Lu Xun.* Bloomington: Indiana University Press, 1987.

Leys, Ruth. *Trauma: A Genealogy.* Chicago: University of Chicago Press, 2000.

Li Tuo. "1986." *Jintian* (Today) 3/4 (1991): 59–73.

Li Tuo and Zhang Nuanxin. "Tan dianying yuyan de xiandai hua" (On the modernization of film language). In Luo Yijun et al., *Zhongguo dianying lilun wenxuan,* 2:9–34.

Li Zehou. *Meixue sijiang* (Four talks on aesthetics). Beijing: Sanlian shudian, 1989.

———. *Zhongguo xiandai sixiangshi lun* (Essays on intellectual history of modern China). Beijing: Dongfang chubanshe, 1987.

Liang Qichao. *Zhongguo lish yanjiu fa* (Methodology on the study of Chinese history). Beijing: Dongfang chubanshe, 1996.

Lifton, Robert J. *The Broken Connection.* New York: Simon and Schuster, 1979.

Lin Jinlan. *Shi nian shi yi* (Ten years, ten cases of madness). Beijing: Zhongguo huaqiao chubanshe, 1996.

Lin Yusheng. *Zhongguo chuantong de chuangzaoxing zhuanhua* (Creative transformation of the Chinese tradition). Beijing: Sanlian shudian, 1988.

Lin, Yusheng et al., ed. *Wusi: Duoyuan de fansi* (May Fourth: Multiple reflections). Hong Kong: Sanlian shudian, 1989.

Link, Perry. "Traditional-Style Popular Urban Fiction in the Teens and Twenties." In *Modern Chinese Literature in the May Fourth Era*, edited by Merle Goldman, 327–49. Cambridge, MA: Harvard University Press, 1977.

Liu, Lydia. *Translingual Practice: Literature, National Culture, and Translated Modernity, China, 1900–1937*. Stanford, CA: Stanford University Press, 1995.

Liu Zaifu. *Lu Xun meixue sixiang lungao* (Essays on Lu Xun's aesthetic thoughts). Taipei: Mingjing wenhua shiye, 1988.

Lü Xinyu. *Jilu zhongguo: dangdai zhongguo xin jilu yundong* (Recording China: the new documentary movement in contemporary China). Beijing: Sanlian, 2003.

Lu Xun. *Lu Xun quanji* (Complete works). 16 vols. Beijing: People's Literature Press, 1980.

Lukács, Georg. *The Historical Novel*. Lincoln: University of Nebraska Press, 1962.

———. *History and Class Consciousness: Studies in Marxist Dialectics*. Translated by Rodney Livingstone. Cambridge, MA: MIT Press, 1971.

———. *The Theory of the Novel*. Cambridge, MA: MIT Press, 1971.

Luo Yijun et al., eds. *Zhongguo dianying lilun wenxuan* (Chinese film theory: An anthology). 2 vols. Beijing: Wenhua yishu chubanshe, 1992.

Lyell, Williams, Jr. *Lu Hsun's Vision of Reality*. Berkeley and Los Angles: University of California Press, 1976.

Lyotard, Jean-Francois. "Réponse à la question: Qu'est-ce le postmoderne?" *Critique* 419 (1982): 357–67.

Ma Junxiang. "*Shanghai guniang* yu guankan wenti" (The film *Shanghai Girl* and the question of the gaze). In Tang Xiaobing, ed. *Zai jiedu* (Reinterpretations). Hong Kong: Oxford University Press, 1993, 127–46.

Ma Ning. "The Textual and Critical Difference of Being Radical: Reconstructing Chinese Leftist Films of the 1930s." *Wide Angle* 11, no. 2 (1989): 22–31.

———. "Spatiality and Subjectivity in Xie Jin's Film of Melodrama of the New Period." In Nick Browne et al., *New Chinese Cinemas*, 15–39.

Marx, Karl. *Capital: A Critique of Political Economy*. New York: Charles H. Kerr, 1906.

Marx, Karl, and Friedrich Engels. *The Marx-Engels Reader*. Edited by Robert Tucker. New York: Norton, 1972.

McCole, John. *Walter Benjamin and the Antinomies of Tradition*. Ithaca, NY: Cornell University Press, 1993.

Meisner, Maurice. *Mao's China: A History of the People's Republic*. New York: Free Press, 1977.

Meng Yue. *Lishi yu xushu* (History and narrative). Taiyuan: Shaanxi People's Press, 1991.

———. "Ye tan bashi niandai wenxuede xihua" (Further talk about westernization of literature in the 1980s). In *Jintian* (Today) 3/4 (1991): 30–42.

Miyoshi, Masao. "'Globalization,' Culture, and the University." In *The Cultures of Globalization*, edited by Fredric Jameson and Masao Miyoshi, 247–70. Durham, NC: Duke University Press, 1998.

Nietzsche, Friedrich. *The Use and Abuse of History*. Translated by Adrian Collins. Introduction by Julius Kraft. New York: Liberal Arts Press, 1957.

Nora, Pierre. "General Introduction: Between Memory and History." In *Realms of Memory*, edited by Pierre Nora et al., 1:1–20. New York: Columbia University Press, 1996.

Perez, Gilberto. *The Material Ghost: Films and Their Medium*. Baltimore: Johns Hopkins University Press, 1998.

Pickowicz, Paul G. "Melodramatic Representation and the 'May Fourth' Tradition of Chinese Cinema." In Ellen Widmer and David Wang, *From May Fourth to June Fourth*, 295–326.

Pinkard, Terry. *Hegel: A Biography*. New York: Cambridge University Press, 2000.

Pusey, James R. *Lu Xun and Evolution*. Albany: State University of New York Press, 1998.

Qi Shuyu. *Shichang jingji xia de zhongguo wenxue yishu* (Chinese literature and art in market economy). Beijing: Beijing University Press, 1998.

Rosen, Philip. *Change Mummified: Cinema, Historicity, Theory*. Minneapolis: University of Minnesota Press, 2001.

Rosenstone, Robert A. *Visions of the Past: The Challenge of Film to our Idea of History*. Cambridge, MA: Harvard University Press, 1995.

Roth, Michael. *The Ironist's Cage: Memory, Trauma, and the Construction of History*. New York: Columbia University Press, 1995.

Santner, Eric. *Stranded Objects: Mourning, Memory, and Film in Postwar Germany*. Ithaca, NY: Cornell University Press, 1990.

Scarry, Elaine. *The Body in Pain: The Making and Unmaking of the World*. New York: Oxford University Press, 1985.

Schwarcz, Vera. *Bridges Across Broken Time: Chinese and Jewish Cultural Memory*. New Haven: Yale University Press, 1998.

———. *The Chinese Enlightenment: Intellectuals and the Legacy of the May Fourth Movement of 1919*. Berkeley: University of California Press, 1986.

Schwartz, Benjamin. *China and Other Matters*. Cambridge, MA: Harvard University Press, 1996.

———. *In Search of Wealth and Power: Yen Fu and the West*. Cambridge, MA: Belknap Press of Harvard University Press, 1964.

Shih, Shu-mei. *The Lure of the Modern: Writing Modernism in Semicolonial China, 1917–1937*. Berkeley: University of California Press, 2001.

Smith, Neil. "The Satanic Geographies of Globalization: Uneven Development in the 1990s." *Public Culture* 10, no. 1 (Fall 1997): 169–89.

Spence, Jonathan. *The Search for Modern China*. New York: Norton, 1990.

Steiner, George. *Death of Tragedy.* New York: Oxford University Press, 1961.

Steinmetz, George. "The State of Emergency and the Revival of American Imperialism: Toward an Authoritarian Post-Fordism." *Public Culture* 15, no. 2 (2003): 323–45.

Stewart, Susan. *On Longing.* Durham, NC: Duke University Press, 1993.

Tang Xiaobing. *Chinese Modern: The Heroic and the Quotidian.* Durham, NC: Duke University Press, 2000.

———. *Global Space and the Nationalist Discourse of Modernity: The Historical Thinking of Liang Qichao.* Stanford, CA: Stanford University Press, 1996.

Tang Xiaobing, ed. *Zai jiedu* (Reinterpretations). Hong Kong: Oxford University Press, 1993.

Taylor, Charles. *Hegel and Modern Society.* New York: Cambridge University Press, 1979.

Teng Wei. "Yingxiong yinqu chu zhongchan jieji de ziwo shuxie" (Middle-class self-writing where the hero disappears). In *Shuxie wenhua yingxiong* (Writing cultural heroes), edited by Dai Jinhua, 292–324. Nanjing: Jiangsu renmin chubanshe, 1999.

Terdiman, Richard. *Present Past: Modernity and the Memory Crisis.* Ithaca, NY: Cornell University Press, 1993.

Tönnies, Ferdinand. *Community and Society.* Translated by Charles P. Loomis. New York: Harper and Row, 1963.

Wang Anyi. *Changhen ge* (Song of unending sorrow). Beijing: Zuojia chubanshe, 1996.

———. *Jishi yu xugou* (Reality and fiction). Taipei: Rye Field, 1996.

———. *Piaopo de yuyan* (Free-floating languages). Beijing: Zhuojia chubanshe, 1996.

———. *Shushu de gushi* (The story of our uncle). In *Xianggang de qing yu ai* (Feelings and love in Hong Kong), 1–77. Beijing: Zuojia chubanshe, 1996.

———. *Yinju de shidai* (The age of hermitage). Shanghai: Shanghai wenyi chubanshe, 1999.

Wang Ban. "Introduction: From Traumatic Paralysis to the Force Field of Modernity." In *Trauma and Cinema: Cross-Cultural Explorations,* edited by E. Ann Kaplan and Ban Wang, 1–22. Hong Kong: Hong Kong University Press, 2004.

———. "Historical Trauma in Multi-National Cinemas: Rethinking History with Trauma." *Tamkang Review* 31, no. 1 (Autumn 2000): 23–48.

———. "Revolutionary Realism and Revolutionary Romanticism: *The Song of Youth.*" In *Columbia Companion to Modern East Asian Literature,* edited by Joshua Mostow, 251–59. New York: Columbia University Press, 2003.

———. *The Sublime Figure of History: Aesthetics and Politics in Twentieth-Century China.* Stanford, CA: Stanford University Press, 1997.

Wang Biao, ed. *Xin lishi zhuyi xiaoshuo xuan* (An anthology of new historical fiction). Hangzhou: Zhejian wenyi, 1993.

Wang Bin. *Huo zhe: Yibu dianying de dansheng* (*To Live*: The birth of a film). Taipei: Guoji chun wenku shudian, 1994.

Wang, David Der-wei. *Fin-de-Siècle Splendor: Repressed Modernities of Late Qing Fiction, 1848–1911*. Stanford, CA: Stanford University Press, 1997.

Wang Dewei. "Chong kuangren riji dao huangren shouji" (From "Diary of a Madman" to "Handwritten Notes of a Desolate Man": An introduction). In Zhu Tianwen, *Hua yi qianshen*, 7–23.

Wang Guowei. *Wang Guowei wenxue meixue lunzhu ji* (Selected essays on literature and aesthetics). Edited by Luo Xishan. Taiyuan: Beiyue wenyi chubanshe, 1987.

Wang Hui. *Fankang juewang* (Combating despair). Shanghai: Shanghai remin chubanshe, 1991.

———. *Sihuo chongwen* (Dead ashes rekindled). Beijing: Remin wenxue, 2000.

———. *Wudi panghuang* (Wandering in no-man's-land). Hangzhou: Zhejiang wenyi, 1994.

Wang, Q. Edward. *Inventing China Through History: The May Fourth Approach to Historiography*. Albany: State University of New York Press, 2001.

Wang Xiaoming. *Renwen jingshen xunsi lu* (The search for humanist spirit). Shanghai: Wenhui chubanshe, 1996.

———. *Zai xin yishi xingtai de longzhao xia* (In the shadow of the new ideology). Nanjing: Jiangsu renmin chubanshe, 2000.

Wang Xiyan. *Fen xin zhu gu de rizi* (Days when the heart was wrenched and the body mutilated). Hong Kong: Kunlun zhizhuo gongsi, 1991.

Wang Yichuan. "Chuantong yu xiandai de weiji" (Crisis in tradition and modernity: The Chinese myth in search-for-roots literature). *Wenxue pinglun* (Literary reviews) 4 (1995): 97–108.

Watson, Rubie S., ed. *Memory, History, and Opposition*. Santa Fe, NM: School of American Research Press, 1994.

White, Hayden. *Metahistory: The Historical Imagination in Nineteenth-Century Europe*. Baltimore: Johns Hopkins University Press, 1973.

Widmer, Ellen, and David Der-wei Wang. *From May Fourth to June Fourth: Fiction and Film in Twentieth-Century China*. Cambridge, MA: Harvard University Press, 1993.

Williams, Raymond. *Modern Tragedy*. Stanford, CA: Stanford University Press, 1966.

———. *The Politics of Modernism*. London: Verso, 1989.

Wolin, Richard. *Walter Benjamin: An Aesthetic of Redemption*. Berkeley: University of California Press, 1994.

Wood, Robin. "Ideology, Genre, Auteur." In *Film Theory and Criticism*, 4th ed., edited by Gerald Mast, Marshal Cohen, and Leo Braudy, 475–85. New York: Oxford University Press, 1992.

Wu Liang and Wang Anyi. "Guanyu *Jishi yu xugou* de duihua" (Conversation on *Reality and Fiction*). In Wang Anyi, *Jishi yu xugou*, 325.

Wu Wenguang. *Geming xianchang: 1966* (Revolutionary scenes: 1966). Taipei: Shibao wenhua, 1994.

———. *Jianghu baogao*. Beijing: Zhongguo qingnian, 2001.

Xu Baoqiang. "Shijie zibenzhuyi xia de beijin xiangxiang" (The northward imaginary under global capitalism). In Chen Qingqiao, *Wenhua xiangxiang yu yishi xingtai* (Cultural imaginary and ideology), 115–25. Hong Kong: Oxford University Press, 1997.

Xu Jian. "The Will to the Transaesthetic: The Truth Content of Lu Xun's Fiction." *Modern Chinese Literature and Culture* 11, no. 1 (1999): 61–92.

Yang Xianyi, and Gladys Yang. *Lu Hsun: Selected Stories*. New York: Norton, 1977.

Yang Xiaobin. *The Chinese Postmodern: Trauma and Irony in Chinese Avant-garde Fiction*. Ann Arbor: University of Michigan Press, 2002.

Yao, Esther, ed. *At Full Speed: Hong Kong Cinema in a Borderless World*. Minneapolis: University of Minnesota Press, 2001.

Yu Shangyuan, ed. *Guoju yundong* (National theater movement). Shanghai: Xinyue shudian, 1929. Reprint, 1992.

Yu Yingshi. *Shixue yu chuantong* (Historiography and tradition). Taipei: Shibao wenhua, 1982.

Zhan Hongzhi. "Yizhong laoqu de shengyin" (An aging voice). In Zhu Tianwen, *Hua yi qianshen*, 259–64.

Zhang Xudong. *Chinese Modernism in the Era of Reforms*. Durham, NC: Duke University Press, 1997.

———. *Huanxiang de zhixu* (The order of the imaginary). Hong Kong: Oxford University Press, 1997.

———. "Shanghai Nostalgia: Postrevolutionary Allegories in Wang Anyi's Literary Production in the 1990s." *positions* 8, no. 2 (2000): 349–87.

Zhang Yingjin, ed. *Cinema and Urban Culture in Shanghai, 1922–1943*. Stanford, CA: Stanford University Press, 1999.

Zhong Xueping. *Masculinity Besieged?: Issues of Modernity and Male Subjectivity in Chinese Literature of the Late Twentieth Century*. Durham, NC: Duke University Press, 2000.

Zhu Dake. "Xiejin dianying moshi de quexian." In Luo Yijun et al., *Zhongguo dianying lilun wenxuan*, 493–95.

Zhu Guangqian. *Beiju xinli xue* (The psychology of tragedy). Hefei: Anhui jiaoyu chubanshe, 1989.

Zhu Tianwen. *Huangren shouji* (Handwritten notes of a desolate man). Taipei: Shibao wenhua, 1997.

————. *Hua yi qianshen* (The flower remembers her previous life). Edited by David Wang. Taipei: Rye Field, 1996.

————. *Notes of a Desolate Man.* Translated by Howard Goldblatt and Sylvia Li-chun Lin. New York: Columbia University Press, 1999.

Zhu Weizheng, ed. *Zhongguo xiandai sixiang shi ziliao jianbian* (A short anthology of writings on the intellectual history of modern China). Vol. 1. Hangzhou: Zhejiang remin, 1982.

Index

A la recherche du temps perdu (Proust), 109, 125
Abbas, Ackbar, 204–6
Adorno, Theodor, 54–55, 82, 132, 173–74, 183, 186–87, 210, 215
Aeschylus, 70
aesthetics: and commercialization, 177–78, 188; of estrangement (*verfremden*), 242–44; and experience, 103–4, 107–12; in film, 78, 82, 264n7; and history, 59–60, 107–12, 247; of Hong Kong, 206; material, 82; and mechanical reproduction, 102; modern *vs.* traditional, 224–25; and politics, 239; and sexuality, 193–94; of shock, 243; and spiritual crisis, 107; western, 60, 224–25; in Zhu Tianwen, 185, 194
affectivity, 205–6, 273n31
agency, 23, 42–43, 47, 221; and history, 11, 41, 45, 51, 130, 165
Ah Q, 33
alienation, 103–4, 129, 183–85, 189–91, 255, 257, 263n56
allegory, 94–96, 103, 176, 198; in film, 83–84, 156, 247; and historical narrative, 98–99; history writing as, 100–101; national, 83–84, 165; *vs.* symbolism, 100
Amadeus (film), 188
anarchism, 29–30, 44, 46, 263n54
"Angelus Novus," 96
Antirightist Campaign, 159–60

Antonioni, Michelangelo, 251
Appadurai, Arjun, 182
Arendt, Hannah, 21
Aristotle, 62–64, 242
Army Nurse (Nüer lou; film), 118–19
Arnold, Matthew, 203
At Full Speed (Yao), 206
aura, 196–98, 227, 230, 272n14
authoritarianism, 8, 23, 103, 159, 192, 201; and nationalism, 19, 21–22
autobiography, 11, 113, 127, 130–31, 168
Autumn Moon (Qiuyue; film), 199, 206–11

Ba Jin, 148–49
Bai Juyi, 66, 70
Barber, Benjamin, 239
Barthes, Roland, 239, 242–44
Baudelaire, Charles, 102–3, 132
Baudrillard, Jean, 218–19
Bauman, Zygmunt, 206
Bazin, André, 237–39, 242, 245–47
Beijing style (*jingpai*), 220
beiju (tragedy), 61–63
beiju yishi (tragic consciousness), 69, 72–76, 78
Benjamin, Walter, 3–4, 7, 63, 99, 118, 183; on Adorno, 187; on aura, 196, 230, 272n14; on Baudelaire, 102; on Brecht, 242; in China, 13, 94–96, 266n3; on commodity exchange, 215–16; on consciousness, 265n55,

276n40; on experience, 103–4, 107, 111; on history, 96–98, 101, 247; on imaging, 96–98, 100; on Kafka, 54; on material turn, 236; on modernity, 94, 235, 268n8, 274n9; on montage, 87, 236, 243–45; on photography, 80–81; on politics of difference, 219; on Proust, 125–26; on reification, 185; and searching for roots, 106; on shock, 94, 243, 268n41; on story-telling, 171; on trauma, 77; and Wang Anyi, 133

Bense, Max, 173
Bergson, Henri, 5, 108
Berlin Wall, fall of, 1, 24
Bernstein, Richard, 23
The Black Steed (Hei junma; Zhang Chengzhi), 120–21
Blue Kite (Lan fengzheng; film), 145–48, 154–62
boat people, 254, 256
the body, 131, 194, 196, 198, 215, 237, 239
Borges, Jorge Luis, 219
bourgeoisie, 10, 130–31, 214, 217, 221; culture of, 81–84, 87; and film, 83–84, 240, 243, 249
Boym, Svetlana, 122
Braester, Yomi, 95
Brecht, Bertolt, 239, 242–44, 275n15
Britain, 200–202
Brooks, Peter, 145
Browne, Nick, 144
Buck-Morss, Susan, 95
Bürger, Peter, 267n24
Byron, George Gordon, Lord, 47

Cao Xueqin, 63, 65
Capital (Marx), 215
capitalism: and commodity, 217; and film, 78, 84, 238–42; global, 6, 17, 78, 119–20, 181–82, 259n14; and history, 13, 127, 214; and images, 238–39; and immigration, 204–5; and imperialism, 1–2, 214; Lu Xun on, 40; millennial, 124, 259n5; and moder-

nity, 3, 39, 41, 47, 84, 129, 131–32, 214, 235, 238; and modernization, 2, 131–32, 239; and montage, 244–45; and myth, 135; and nationalism, 122; and nostalgia, 119–20; and socialism, 2, 131–32, 239; and spectacle, 218; and time, 203–4, 275n14; trauma of, 135, 181–82; and urbanization, 183; visual regime of, 239–45; in Wang Anyi, 226, 228
Caruth, Cathy, 105, 147
Chakrabarty, Dipesh, 216, 261n26
Chang, Eileen, 134, 164, 167–70, 173, 225
Chen Dabei, 61
Chen Duxiu, 31, 69
Chen Kaige, 118, 146, 157, 270n8
Chen Ran, 125
Chen Xiaomei, 264n21
Chen Yinque, 63
"The Child Utters His Words Without Constraints" (Tongyan wuji; Chang), 168
China, mainland: Benjamin in, 13, 94–96, 266n3; cultural crisis in, 5; and evolutionism, 28–32; examination system in, 38; and genealogy, 24; history in, 3, 6, 11; and Hong Kong, 199–202, 207; and imperialism, 31, 61; intellectuals in, 33, 36, 94–96, 103, 106, 174–76, 216, 266n7; and Japan, 37, 51, 61, 78, 83; modernity in, 2, 6, 9–10, 13, 20, 31, 200, 202; nationalism in, 19–22; nostalgia for, 189; reification in, 187; and the West, 32–34, 38–46, 68, 97. *See also* Hong Kong; Taiwan
Chinese Communist Party (CCP), 159–60; self-correction by, 149–50, 161; Third Plenum, Eleventh Central Committee (1979), of, 93
Chinese language, 132; classical, 36, 38, 115
Chow, Rey, 77, 200–201
Christianity, 50, 62

chuangshang (trauma), 268n41
"The City Has No Story to Tell"
  (Chengshi wu gushi; Wang Anyi),
  170
classicism, 236–37, 239, 241–42, 248
collectivism, 10, 43, 106, 127, 165; and individual, 44, 46, 105, 107, 124–26
colonialism, 8–9, 11, 34, 61, 214; and
  evolutionism, 28, 30; and film, 78–
  79, 82; in Hong Kong, 200–202; and
  nationalism, 19–21; and universalism,
  27, 31, 127
commercialization: and aesthetics, 177–
  78, 188; of culture, 232–33, 248; and
  essay, 167, 170–71; in film, 250, 254–
  55; of leisure, 240; and New Period
  literature, 175–76; and nostalgia,
  119–20
commodification: and consciousness,
  191–92, 224; and consumer choice,
  271n8b; of culture, 13, 167, 191–92,
  223–26, 229, 237; and ideology, 220,
  230, 275n23; of language, 241; and
  liberalism, 128, 221–22; of literature,
  220–23; and nostalgia, 197–98, 212–
  34; and reification, 184–88; of sexuality, 191–96, 275n23; of social relations, 8, 229; and socialism, 221, 230,
  274n23; and subjectivity, 191–92, 218;
  and universal history, 13, 214–20; and
  Wang Anyi, 226–34. *See also* consumerism
commodity, 212–34; exchange *vs.* use
  value of, 215–16, 229–30, 232,
  272n14; mechanically reproduced,
  102, 272n14
communism, 24, 43, 106, 122, 226; and
  commodified literature, 221–22; in
  film, 143–44; utopian, 166–67, 214,
  222
community, 14, 56, 83, 128, 182; and experience, 102, 104–5; and globalization, 201, 206; and history, 25, 126,
  130; and individual, 8, 41–46, 112,
  131–35; of meaning, 104; and mem-

ory, 6, 218; and nationalism, 122; and
  reenchantment, 198; and searching
  for roots, 106; and third world film,
  84–85; traditional village, 35–36, 136,
  188–91, 212, 227; and trauma, 9, 95,
  113–14, 147, 266n7; and urbanization,
  170–71; in Xie Jin, 152, 154, 157
Confucianism, 5, 53, 259n14, 270n13; and
  drama, 78–79; *vs.* individualism, 44–
  45; late Qing, 38–39; and May
  Fourth, 18, 33; revivals of, 127–28
consciousness, 101, 193, 195, 210; Benjamin on, 243, 265n55, 276n40; and
  commodification, 191–92, 224; false,
  81, 141, 229; and film, 81, 241; kaleidoscope with, 257, 265n55, 276n40;
  modern, 34–35; and nation-state,
  166–67; tragic *(beiju yishi)*, 69, 72–
  76, 78; and trauma, 114, 147, 213; *vs.*
  unconscious, 109; and urbanization,
  265n55, 276n40. *See also* historical
  consciousness
consumerism, 9, 81, 125, 129, 134,
  272n14; and choice, 271n8b; culture
  of, 128, 164, 167–71, 224, 228–29,
  274n14; and essay, 164, 166–67, 172;
  and historical consciousness, 12, 195–
  96; *vs.* ideology, 177; and immigration, 204–5; media-induced, 187–88;
  vs. memory, 195–96; *vs.* nostalgia,
  195–96; and reification, 186–88; and
  trauma, 213
continuity, 6, 50, 94, 136, 139, 152; cultural, 8–9, 147, 171; and genealogy,
  22; historical, 18, 24, 127–28, 133; and
  memory, 109; and montage, 86, 88;
  and nostalgia, 213; of tradition,
  262n39; and trauma, 114, 147
countermemory, 22, 237
"Critique of *The Dream of Red
  Chamber*" (Hongloumeng pinglun;
  Wang Guowei), 63–66
Cultural Revolution, 100, 174, 270n13;
  in film, 12, 146–48, 154–62; and history writing, 12–13, 142–43; posttrau-

matic aftermath of, 94–98, 142; and traumatic memory, 93, 112–19, 266n7; Xie Jin on, 148, 151–54

culture: Benjamin on, 94; bourgeois, 81–84, 87; commodification of, 13, 167, 191–92, 223–26, 229, 232–33, 237, 248; communist, 24; consumer, 128, 164, 167–71, 224, 228–29, 274n14; continuity of, 8–9, 50, 147, 171; and Disney, 204; and experience, 103; and film, 77, 80, 82–84; folk, 12, 36; and globalization, 201, 256; Hellenic, 62–63; and history, 13, 59–60, 143, 229; as industry, 3, 119–20, 236, 238; Judeo-Christian, 62; local *vs.* global, 2–3, 14, 17, 27, 31–32, 256; Lu Xun on, 39–40; mainstream, 235; and memory, 4, 6, 53; minority, 27, 200; and modernization, 6, 182; myth of commercial, 232–33; and nation-state, 202–3; *vs.* nature, 100–101, 118; out-of-joint, 167; popular, 11, 73, 77, 80, 82–83, 172, 202, 243; primordial, 108–11; and the tragic, 59; traumatized, 52, 113–14, 146–47; uniform mass, 182, 239; universal, 13, 31–32; and urbanization, 171; western, 34, 39–40; in Zhu Tianwen, 191–92, 194

culture, Chinese, 17, 63; historical consciousness in, 26–27, 113; in Hong Kong, 199–203; late Qing, 38; May Fourth, 37; modern, 3, 101, 125, 127; and realism, 65–66; in Shanghai, 231–32; traditional, 5–6, 79, 97; and tragedy, 61–62, 65–66; visuality in, 77

Dai Jinhua, 99, 101, 150, 161, 247, 266n3
Darwin, Charles, 28, 32
De Certeau, Michel, 219, 229, 256, 271n8b
De Sica, Vittorio, 250
Debord, Guy, 218, 224
democracy, 39, 41, 217, 222; and discipline, 193; and evolutionism, 29; in film, 83–84; and globalization, 206; in Hong Kong, 200, 202; and individual, 232; liberal, 7, 10, 18, 24; Lu Xun on, 49; and May Fourth, 32, 59; and mechanical reproduction, 102; one-sidedness of, 40; parliamentary, 45–46; and universalism, 125

Deng Xiaoping, 93
Denton, Kirk, 43
determinism: and evolutionism, 28–29, 32, 72; historical, 42–43, 48–51, 98–99, 167, 169, 173, 175, 214, 238, 269n2
"Diary of a Madman" (Lu Xun), 33–34, 54, 74
Dirlik, Arif, 2, 259n14
Disney (Hong Kong), 203–4, 206
Doane, Mary Ann, 275n14
Dostoevesky, Fyodor, 174
drama. *See* theater
Dream of the Red Chamber (*Hongloumeng*; Cao Xueqin), 63–66, 69–70, 72, 225–26
Duara, Prasenjit, 20, 269n2
Durkheim, Emile, 4, 274n9

Eagleton, Terry, 273n8
Eastern Europe, 30
Economic and Philosophic Manuscripts (Marx), 215
economic development, 93, 128, 135, 172, 182, 217; in China, 2, 6, 18; in Shanghai, 232–33; in Taiwan, 183. *See also* industrialization; modernization
"Eden No More" (Yidian bu zai; Zhu Tianwen), 189–91, 197
Educated Youth, 122
Eisenstein, Sergei, 86–88, 102, 244, 246, 250
elites, 26, 75–77. *See also* bourgeoisie
the Enlightenment, 2, 7, 31–32, 94, 131, 214, 262n39; and Chinese historical consciousness, 26–27; and history writing, 142, 269n2; and literature, 173, 221; and Lu Xun, 34, 40–41, 43,

45, 50, 263n54; and May Fourth, 11–12, 18–25, 59; and the nation-state, 19–20, 45; and politics of difference, 273n8; and subjectivity, 46; and tradition, 33, 37

ennui, 135–36

essay, personal, 11, 163–78; and commercialization, 167, 170–71; *vs.* novel, 163–67

"The Essay as Form" (Adorno), 173

Euripides, 70

Evolution and Ethics (Huxley), 29

evolutionism: and determinism, 28–29, 32, 72; humanitarian, 29–30; late Qing, 40; in May Fourth thought, 28–32, 48–49; and theater reform, 69

experience: and aesthetics, 102–4, 107–12; atrophy of, 108–9; and aura, 197–98; authentic, 184–85, 188–89, 195–98, 224, 230, 237, 245; childhood, 125, 155; everyday, 182, 223, 229–30, 274n23; lived, 124–26, 135, 188, 195–96, 206; and memory, 102, 105; personal, 10, 104–5, 124–27, 150, 152, 154, 163; public, 125; and reification, 186; shock as historical, 156, 268n41; terms for, 103; traumatic, 101–6, 114, 135

family, 144, 188, 206, 218; in *Autumn Moon*, 207–11; and urbanization, 171, 183; in Xie Jin, 150–54, 157

fansi (self-reflective) movement, 143

Farewell My Concubine (Bawang bieji; film), 146, 157, 159

"Father, father, father" (Bababa; Han Shaogong), 109

Felman, Shoshana, 115

fiction, 11–12, 60, 68, 108; bourgeois, 131; epic, 275n15; essayistic, 172–76; experimental, 93, 107; late Qing, 17–18; Mandarin Duck and Butterfly, 220, 225–26; narrative, 170, 172, 174; realism in, 65–66, 270n2; and roundism, 69–70; and search for roots, 113

The Field of Life and Death (Shengsi chang; Xiao Hong), 98

film: aesthetics in, 78, 82, 264n7; allegory in, 83–84, 156, 247; avant-garde, 241, 243, 253; bourgeois, 83–84, 240, 243, 249; and capitalism, 78, 84, 238–42; classicism in, 236–37; communism in, 143–44; Cultural Revolution in, 12, 146–48, 154–62; and culture, 77, 80, 82–84; documentary, 77, 79, 81–82, 89–90, 235, 237–38, 245–50, 257; documentary impulse in feature, 250–57; and globalization, 206, 238, 245–57; and history, 76–85, 90, 143–46, 246–47; in Hong Kong, 205–11, 254; ideology in, 81–84; kitsch in, 252–53; language of, 117–18, 237, 245; and literature, 78, 220; material turn in, 78, 82, 235–57; and mechanical reproduction, 102; and memory, 11, 117–18, 241; and moviegoing, 240–41; and nostalgia, 212; and photography, 80–81, 236, 238, 245–46; post-traumatic, 95; radical (1930s), 78–85, 238, 240, 246; realism in, 58, 76–85, 90, 237, 245–57; search-for-roots movement in, 107–8, 113, 146; and theater, 80; third world, 84–85; time in, 247, 275n14; and the tragic, 13, 59; trauma in, 94, 118, 146–48, 237, 248, 270n8; and traumatic visuality, 12, 77–78; women in, 82–83

filmmakers: fourth generation, 13, 93, 163; fifth generation, 13, 93, 99, 107, 117–18, 145, 154–55, 157, 163, 238, 245–48, 270n8; independent, 241, 243; and search for roots, 107–8, 113; urban (sixth) generation, 245, 248, 275n5

"Fin de Siècle Splendor" (Shiji mo de huali; Zhu Tianwen), 187–88, 196–98

Flaherty, Robert, 250

"Floating Words" (Liu yan; Chang), 168

Foucault, Michel, 7, 101, 132, 192–93,

261n13; genealogy of, 18, 20, 22–25, 44
French Revolution, 39, 59
Freud, Sigmund, 5, 263n61
frontier, American myth of, 46
Fu Ping (Wang Anyi), 129
Fu Sinian, 69

gaizao guomin xing (transforming the national character), 42–43, 45
the gaze, 118, 135
Ge Fei, 108
genealogy, 18, 20, 22–25, 44, 132–34, 136
geren hua xiezou (individualistic writing), 125
Germany, 30, 39, 95
gexing (individual authenticity), 48
Giddens, Anthony, 139
globalization: and abstract labor, 216; and capitalism, 6, 17, 78, 119–20, 181–82, 259n14; and Confucianism, 259n14; and culture, 2–3, 14, 17, 27, 31–32, 201, 256; and film, 206, 238, 245–57; and history, 1–14, 25, 143; and Hong Kong, 14, 199–202; and immigration, 182, 206; and individual, 112, 131; and kitsch, 252; and literature, 167, 181–211; and memory, 1–14, 182; and myth, 135; and nostalgia, 14, 123, 182, 209–11, 213–14; and realism, 235–57; and reenchantment, 198; and reification, 186; and spectacle, 232; and time-space compression, 203–4, 206; and trauma, 203; trauma of, 9, 181–82, 210; universal visual language of, 240–41, 257; and Wang Anyi, 129, 133, 217, 219–20, 228, 234; and Zhu Tianwen, 185, 192
Goddess (Shennü; film), 77
gongli (universal principle), 30–31
Gould, Stephen J., 28–29
Gramsci, Antonio, 175
Great Leap Forward, 135
Greece, 62–63
Guangxu, Emperor, 38

The Guermantes Way (Proust), 80
Guo Moruo, 61

Habermas, Jürgen, 23, 261n20
haipai (Shanghai style), 220
Han Shaogong, 108–11
Hansen, Miriam, 79–80, 240
Hardt, Michael, 1–2
Harvey, David, 219
"The head teacher" (Ban zhuren; Liu Xinwu), 143
Hegel, G.W.F., 29, 33, 37, 42, 45, 268n8; and personal essay, 166–67; and thought liberation movement, 270n4
Heidegger, Martin, 77, 126
Heinu yu tian lu (Uncle Tom's Cabin), 67
Heller, Agnes, 124–26, 130, 164
Herder, Johann, 45
The Herdsman (Muma ren; film), 149–51
Herman, Judith L., 266n7
Hibiscus Town (Furong zhen; film), 145, 149–54, 161
historical consciousness, 4, 17–57; and Chinese culture, 26–27, 113; and commodification, 218, 221; and consumerism, 12, 195–96; critical, 5, 10–11, 37–48, 58, 89, 120, 143, 145, 163–64; and Eileen Chang, 169–70; in film, 89, 146, 154, 162; in Hong Kong, 199; linear, 25–32, 37; of Lu Xun, 53, 72–76, 78; of May Fourth era, 25, 35–37, 48–49, 58–59; morality in, 142; *vs.* personal essay, 163–64; and thought liberation movement, 270n4; tragic, 58–61, 68–76; tragic-realist, 72; and Wang Anyi, 129, 175; and Zhu Tianwen, 194
historical imagination, 2, 235, 246, 259n6
historical materialism, 72, 112, 137, 140, 143, 244
historicism, 247, 262n46
historiography, 7, 12–13, 23, 26, 269n10; *vs.* history writing, 18, 142; and trauma, 8–11; western *vs.* native, 200, 261n26

history: angel of, 96–97; and art, 82; authentic, 234; as catastrophe, 96–100; crisis-ridden, 49; end of, 42, 112, 166, 184, 216, 222, 232, 261n19; Eurocentric model of, 26–27; homogenous, 214–20; hope and despair in, 51–57; impossible, 116, 147; intellectual, 58; justice of, 148–49; life as *vs.* in, 125, 164; linear, 25–32, 37, 49, 127–28; linear *vs.* cyclical, 59; lived, 124–27, 130; local *vs.* global, 2–3; lost, 130; and memory, 1–14, 37–48, 76, 90, 93–94, 109–10, 126; *vs.* memory, 4–5; of minorities, 130; modern, 5–6, 26, 51–52; natural, 214; official, 113, 134, 218, 248; official *vs.* unofficial (*ye shi*), 74–75, 214; pendulum swings in, 9–10, 39–40, 49; postrevolutionary, 93–123; reconstruction of, 13; sense of, 26, 38, 43, 58–59, 106–7; sense of, *vs.* historical sense, 23–25; strategic approach to, 38–39; teleological, 42–43, 48–51, 98–99, 167, 169, 173, 175, 214, 238, 269n2; traditional dynastic, 25–26; tragic-realist approach to, 67, 72–76, 78; traumatic, 12, 53, 93–123, 142–62; universal, 2, 13–14, 26, 124–25, 127–28; utopian, 48–49, 53, 55; western, 39–40, 49
History and Narrative (Lishi yu xushu; Meng Yue), 98
"The history of mankind" (Ren zhi lishi; Lu Xun), 37
history writing: as allegory, 100–101; and Cultural Revolution, 12–13, 142–43; and the Enlightenment, 142, 269n2; and film, 247; *vs.* historiography, 18, 142; and hope and despair, 51–57; and language, 117; and memory, 3, 107–8, 112–19; and modernity, 127–28; morality in, 142, 269n1; and myth, 134; and politics, 25, 112–13; and progress, 142, 269n2; and search for roots, 107–8, 113; traditional dynastic, 25–26; and tragedy, 73
Hobsbawm, Eric, 128, 260n15, 268n10
Hollywood, 246, 257; and capitalism, 239–42; and Chinese drama, 80; and Chinese film, 78–80, 144, 238, 240, 255; and classicism, 236–37, 239; and Hong Kong, 206; and ideology in film, 81–84, 239–40; and montage, 86, 88–89; and Zhu Tianwen, 188
Holocaust, 269n17
homosexuality, 192–94
Hong Kong: culture of, 199–203; and Eileen Chang, 168; film in, 205–11, 254; and globalization, 14, 199–202; literature of, 182–83, 223; and mainland China, 199–202, 207; memory in, 183, 199, 202; modernization in, 182–83; nostalgia in, 203–12
Hongloumeng. See *Dream of the Red Chamber*
Hu Feng, 43
Hu Mei, 118, 270n8
Hu Shi, 31, 60; on roundism, 68–71; on tragedy, 61, 70–73, 76
huaigu (nostalgia for the past), 48
huaju (spoken drama), 68
Huang, Michelle, 203–4
Huang Ailing, 89
Huang Jianxin, 270n8
Huang Lingshuang, 29–30
humanism, 2, 13, 216, 221; *vs.* collectivism, 106; in Marx, 104; socialist, 270n13; in Xie Jin, 150, 152–53, 270n13
Hutton, Patrick, 7
Huxley, Thomas, 29
hysteria (*yi*), 115–16

"The Idea of Literary Evolution and Reform of Theater" (Wenxue jinhua guannian yu xiju gailiang; Hu Shi), 69
identity: and genealogy, 23, 130; of Hong Kong, 199–200, 202; individual,

104–5; and memory, 14, 108–9, 196, 218; and modernity, 35, 132; and modernization, 14, 182; and myth, 134, 136; national, 108; and nostalgia, 190; and politics of difference, 273n8; and trauma, 9, 114; in Wang Anyi, 227

ideology, 56, 125, 145, 150, 172, 177, 260n19; American, 84; and commodification, 220, 230, 275n23; communist, 122; in film, 81–84, 239–40; and literature, 165, 176; loss of, 213; and realism, 164, 246

images, 99, 206, 271n8b, 276n40; Benjamin on, 96–98, 100; and capitalism, 238–39; as commodity, 219; and history, 96–98, 143; and trauma, 52–53; and visual technology, 224; in Zhu Tianwen, 187–88. *See also* visuality

immigration, 182, 199, 204–7, 240

imperial paradigm, 1–2

imperialism, 8–9, 11, 34, 259n3; and capital, 1–2, 214; in China, 31, 61; and evolutionism, 28, 30; and film, 78–79, 81–82; and history, 2, 127; and Hong Kong, 200–201; ideology of, 84; and nationalism, 19–21; and universalism, 27, 31, 127

in-betweenness (thing in between, *zhongjian wu*), 34–35

India, 30, 38

individual: and abstract labor, 215–17; as agent of history, 11, 41, 45, 51, 130, 165; and allegory, 83; and art, 46–47; *vs.* collective, 44, 46, 105, 107, 124–26; and community, 8, 41–46, 112, 131–35; and consumer choice, 271n8b; discipline of, 191–92; as ethical agent, 42–43; and experience, 102–4, 188; in film, 156, 162; and genealogy, 23; and globalization, 2, 112, 131; and history, 72–73, 96, 155; idealized, 42–43; identity of, 104–5; and literature, 46–47, 165, 221–22; and

Lu Xun, 263n56; and memory, 47, 154, 218; and nation-state, 46, 232; and new historicism, 223; and nostalgia, 120; and reenchantment, 198; and reification, 186; and search for roots, 113; and sexuality, 118–19; and socialist realism, 164–65; and society, 46–48, 76, 128, 263n56; subjectivity of, 47, 104, 165; and third world film, 84–85; and thought liberation movement, 270n4; and tragedy, 63–64, 71; and trauma, 8, 95, 113–14, 147, 266n7; and urbanization, 171, 184; in Wang Anyi, 133, 174

individualism, 33, 40, 120, 122, 130; *vs.* collectivism, 106; *vs.* Confucianism, 44–45; and Eileen Chang, 169; in film, 82–84; *vs.* history, 124–26; Lu Xun on, 41–48; in May Fourth era, 28, 44; and overreaction, 9–10; in Republican period, 43–44; retreat to, 125

individualistic writing *(geren hua xiezou)*, 125

industrialization, 5, 101, 103, 131, 183–84, 268n41

Inner Mongolia, 121

intellectuals, 13, 94–96, 177; and Chinese tradition, 33, 36; and commodity, 216; May Fourth, 33–35, 49, 53; post-Mao, 103, 174–76; public, 164; and searching for roots, 106; and trauma, 51–52, 266n7; western-educated, 40

Jacobinism, 46

Jameson, Fredric, 10, 83, 85, 165, 218

Japan, 31, 83; Lu Xun in, 77, 97; theater in, 66–67; war with, 37, 51, 61, 78–79

Jia Pingwa, 113, 117

Jia Zhangke, 250–53, 275n5

Jiang Guanyun, 66

Jianghu (The wide world; film), 249

Jin Yong, 223

Jing Qing, 75
Jinhua (Evolution; magazine), 29–30
The Joke (Kundera), 160–61
Jung, Carl, 5

Kafka, Franz, 54
Kang Youwei, 38
Kant, Immanuel, 64
Kaplan, E. Ann, 119
Karl, Rebecca, 21
Kierkegaard, Søren, 45, 62
Klee, Paul, 96
Kracauer, Siegfried, 80–81, 87, 238, 243
Krieger, Murray, 62–63, 70
Kundera, Milan, 160–61

labor, abstract, 214–20; *vs.* real, 216, 245
Lacan, Jacques, 243
language, 95, 107; in film, 117–18, 237,
    245; resistance to normative, 241–42;
    of sexuality, 119; and trauma, 115–16;
    universal visual, 240–41, 257
Lao She, 99–100
Law, Clara, 183, 199, 206–11
Lee, Leo Ou-fan, 58–59, 79, 274n14
Lefebvre, Henri, 183
Legend of Hulan River (Hulan he
    zhuang; Xiao Hong), 98
The Legend of Tianyun Mountain
    (Tianyunshan chuanqi; film), 149, 151
legitimation, 20–21, 127, 225, 247; and
    genealogy, 23–24; of nation-state,
    260n15, 269n10
Leskov, Nikolay, 102
"A Lesson on the History of Science" (Ke-
    xue shi jiaopian; Lu Xun), 37, 49–51
Levi-Strauss, Claude, 192
Li Rui, 125
Li Shutong, 66–67
Li Tuo, 105–6, 237–38, 245, 266n3
Li Zehou, 104
Liang Qichao, 26, 38, 60
liberalism, 43, 45, 84, 104; and commod-
    ification, 128, 221–22; and democ-
    racy, 7, 10, 18, 24; and May Fourth,

18–19; and overreaction, 9–10. *See
    also* neoliberalism
Lin Jinlan, 115–17
Lin Shu, 67
literature: and alienation, 183–85; classi-
    cal Chinese, 36; commodification of,
    176–77, 223; of consumption *vs.*
    commitment, 220–22; and Cultural
    Revolution, 12; and the Enlighten-
    ment, 173, 221; and evolution, 69;
    and film, 78, 220; generational differ-
    ences in, 175–76; and globalization,
    181–211; and history, 175–78; of
    Hong Kong, 182–83, 223; and indi-
    vidual, 46–47, 165, 221–22; Maoist,
    105–6; and modernization, 170, 172;
    New Period, 175–76; new wave, 134;
    realism in, 58, 65–66, 173, 270n2;
    and the self, 42; Taiwanese, 182–83,
    185, 188–91, 223; and the tragic, 59;
    and trauma, 52–54, 77, 94; wound,
    13, 93, 143. *See also* essay, personal; fic-
    tion; poetry
Little Bao Village (Xiaobaozhuang; Wang
    Anyi), 136
Liu, Lydia, 43–44
Liu Xinwu, 143
Liu Zaifu, 72
"The Loner" (Gudu zhe; Lu Xun), 54
the long take, 85–86, 89, 237, 247, 249,
    251–52
Lou Ye, 250, 253–57
Lu Ling, 43
Lu Xun, 12–13, 17–57, 60, 261n26,
    262n41; darkness in, 53–57; essays of,
    37, 39, 48–51, 73–74, 169; experience
    of, 103; and film, 247; on history and
    memory, 36–48; hope in, 51–57;
    modernity *vs.* tradition in, 33–36;
    newsreel watched by, 77, 97–98;
    strategic approach of, 38–39, 47; on
    teleological history, 48–51, 99;
    tragedy in, 53, 61, 72–76, 78; and
    traumatic visuality, 77; and universal-
    ism, 27, 31

Lukács, George, 130, 163, 166, 175, 183, 243, 275n15; on modernity, 235, 268n8, 274n9; on reification, 184–85, 229

Lyell, William, 34

Lyotard, Jean-François, 102

Ma Ning, 82–83, 85, 88, 144

Manchuria, 79

Mandarin Duck and Butterfly fiction, 220, 225–26

manifest destiny, 84

Mao Dun, 77

Mao Zedong, 112, 116–17, 120, 122

Maoism, 6, 9, 24, 93, 128, 159; in literature, 105–6

Maoist period, 142, 213, 218, 270n13; commodity in, 229–30; socialist realism in, 164–65; Wang Anyi on, 224, 226, 231. *See also* Cultural Revolution

Marcuse, Herbert, 193

market forces, 128, 130, 135, 212–13; and history, 8, 12–13, 42; and Hong Kong, 199–200; and reform, 12, 93. *See also* capitalism; economic development

"Marriage of the Fairies" (Tianxian pei; Wang Anyi), 135–41

Marx, Karl, 4, 32, 262n44, 270n4; and abstract labor, 217; on alienation, 183, 263n56; on commodity, 214–15, 218; on history as tragedy, 60; humanistic writings of, 104; on modernity, 36, 235, 268n8

Marxism: and essay, 166–67, 173; and evolutionism, 28–29; exchange *vs.* use value in, 272n14; on history, 37, 112, 128, 229; on individual and society, 46; and literature, 165, 221; and May Fourth, 18, 59; and tragedy, 72

Masao Miyoshi, 203

material turn, 79, 235–57; in film, 78, 82, 237, 248, 250; to history, 85–86; and montage, 236, 245

May Fourth era, 6, 17–57; and aesthetic

history, 59–60; and Beijing style, 220; and commodified literature, 221; and Eileen Chang, 168, 170; and the Enlightenment, 11–12, 18–25, 59; evolutionism in, 28–32, 48–49; and filmmaking, 78; historical consciousness in, 25, 35–37, 48–49, 58–59; history writing in, 8, 142; hysteria in, 115–16; individualism in, 28, 44; intellectuals of, 33–35, 49, 53; and modernity, 12, 17–18, 32–37, 53; nationalism in, 19–22, 24, 59; and postrevolutionary period, 94, 175, 217; and progress, 19, 28, 49, 59; and realism, 246; and revolution, 18–19, 24; and theater reform, 69; and tradition, 11, 18–19, 24, 28; and tradition *vs.* modernity, 32–37, 53; the tragic in, 12, 58–90

mechanical reproduction, 102, 272n14

media, 103, 167, 176, 186, 249; classicism of, 237; and commodification, 224; and community, 128; and consumerism, 187–88, 271n8b; in Hong Kong, 205; and nostalgia, 189–91; and trauma, 77

Meisner, Maurice, 21

melodrama, 142–62, 246, 264n7; and *Blue Kite*, 158–59, 162; in Xie Jin's films, 144–46, 157

memory: childhood, 125, 129–30, 133, 208; collective, 7, 9, 14, 35, 102–3, 136–38, 140–41, 171, 182, 184; collective *vs.* personal, 6, 154; cultural, 4, 6, 53; definition of, 4; and globalization, 1–14, 182; and history, 1–14, 37–48, 76, 90, 93–94, 109–10, 126; *vs.* history, 4–5; and history writing, 3, 107–8, 112–19; and immigration, 205; involuntary, 187; involuntary *vs.* voluntary, 108–11, 125–26, 133; *milieux* of, 4–5, 14, 184; and modernity *vs.* tradition, 35–36, 274n9; personal, 6, 124–27, 150, 154; private, 163; rearticulation of, 3; repressed, 11; testimonial, 154–55; tradition as, 32–37; and trauma, 13; traumatic, 3, 36, 51, 53, 97, 112–19; unconscious, 147

Meng Yue, 98–101, 105, 107, 117, 143, 266n3

Methodology in the Study of Chinese History (Zhongguo lishi yanjiu fa; Liang Qichao), 26

Michelangelo, 194

Michels, Robert, 21

Mickiewicz, Adam, 47

middle class. *See* bourgeoisie

Mirrors of Sichuan (Shu guijian), 74

Mo Yan, 108, 113, 117

Modern Tragedy (Williams), 59

modernism, 60, 238, 263n54. *See also* postmodernism

modernity: Benjamin on, 94, 235, 268n8, 274n9; capitalist, 3, 39, 41, 47, 84, 132, 214, 235, 238; Chinese, 9–10, 13, 20, 200, 202; and commodified literature, 221; critiques of, 45, 184, 235; and Eileen Chang, 169; and evolutionism, 29; and experience, 101; and film, 82–84; gendered, 275n23; and genealogy, 23; Habermas on, 261n20; and history, 25, 36, 59, 99, 127–28, 214, 268n8; history of, 226; and history writing, 7, 127–28; and Hong Kong, 199–200, 202; and immigration, 207; and kitsch, 252–53; Lu Xun on, 12–13, 41, 53; and materialism, 40, 45; and May Fourth, 12, 17–18, 32–37, 53; and memory, 2, 4, 94, 135–41; and modernization, 212; and montage, 87, 244–45; and myth, 128, 135–41; and nature, 229; and nostalgia, 124; revolutionary, 214; socialist, 131–32; in Taiwan, 183, 185; and tradition, 135–41, 253; *vs.* tradition, 4, 17–19, 32–37, 39, 53, 76, 126, 205–6, 274n9; and the tragic, 63; trauma of, 94, 135, 181, 213; Wang Anyi on, 129, 133; western, 13, 25, 38–46

modernization: and capitalism, 2, 131–

32, 239; in China, 6, 31, 38; and culture, 6, 182; in film, 250, 254–55; and historiography, 7–8; and history, 127–28; in Hong Kong, 182–83; and identity, 14, 182; and literature, 165, 170, 172, 175; and memory, 132, 182, 229; and modernity, 212; and myth, 8, 137; and nostalgia, 124; and revolution, 97; and searching for roots, 106; in Shanghai, 228; socialist, 132, 214; and storytelling, 171; in Taiwan, 182–85; and thought liberation movement, 271n4; *vs.* tradition, 143, 182; trauma of, 9–10, 181–82, 212–13, 249; Wang Anyi on, 217

Monet, Claude, 188

Mongolia, 121, 133–34

Mongolian language, 121

A Mongolian Tale (Ai zai caoyuan; film), 120–22

montage, 85–90, 237, 246, 254, 256; and aesthetics of estrangement, 242–43; Benjamin on, 87, 236, 243–45; and history, 87, 243–45; and memory, 245; and modernity, 87, 244–45

morality, 142, 144, 269n1

"More Random Remarks after Illness" (Bing hou zatan zhi yu; Lu Xun), 74

"More Talk about the Collapse of the Tower of Leifeng" (Zai lun Leifengta de daota; Lu Xun), 73

moviegoing, 240–41. *See also* film

"My Old Home" (Guxiang; Lu Xun), 55–57

myth: of commercial culture, 232–33; and experience, 102; and history, 101, 127–35; history as, 133–35, 222; and identity, 134, 136; and modernization, 8, 137; and montage, 244; and nationalism, 122–23; and temporality, 124–41; and tradition *vs.* modernity, 128, 135–41; in Wang Anyi, 130, 133–35

Napoleon Bonaparte, 47

national essence, school of (*guocui*), 5

nationalism: and authoritarianism, 19, 21–22; and collectivism, 44; and film, 82; and history, 25–26, 127–28; and history writing, 269n2; and Hong Kong, 200, 202; May Fourth, 19–22, 24, 59; and modernity, 129; and myth, 122–23; and national character, 42–43, 45; and nativism, 200; *vs.* statism, 21; third-world, 19; and trauma, 77; and universalism, 31, 127–28

nation-state, 6–7, 17, 30–31; and allegory, 83–84, 165; and commodified literature, 221; and consciousness, 166–67; and culture, 202–3; and the Enlightenment, 19–20, 45; and globalization, 206; Hegel on, 166–67; and history, 26, 36, 127–28; and Hong Kong, 199–200, 202; and individual, 46, 232; legitimation of, 260n15, 269n10; *vs.* myth, 138

nature, 111, 214, 229, 246; *vs.* culture, 100–101, 118

Negri, Antonio, 1–2

neiyao (inner life), 41

neoliberalism, 5, 201, 206, 213, 261n19

neorealism, 90, 223, 250; Italian, 237, 245–46, 251

new historicism, 223

New Period *(Xin shiqi)*, 161; literature of, 175–76

New Period (x*in shiqi*): socialist realism in, 164–65

New School Theater (Japan), 66

new wave, French, 237

New Youth (magazine), 69, 78

Nietzsche, Friedrich, 10, 45, 62, 125, 235

The Night of the City (Chengshi zhi ye; film), 81, 88

"1985" (Li Tuo), 105–6

Nora, Pierre, 4–5, 130

norms, 1–2, 25, 241–42

nostalgia, 6, 48, 102, 109, 124, 129, 172; and capitalism, 119–20; and commodification, 197–98, 212–34; *vs.*

consumerism, 195–96; and globalization, 14, 123, 182, 209–11, 213–14; and history, 12, 120, 235; in Hong Kong, 203–12; and humanism, 270n13; for mainland China, 189; and media, 189–91; and memory, 120, 209; for old Shanghai, 222–26, 228, 231–33; as resistance, 213; for socialism, 10, 213, 219; in Taiwan, 188–91, 212; and utopianism, 119–23, 198; in Wang Anyi, 132–33, 136, 222–26, 228, 231–33; and women, 122; in Zhu Tianwen, 188–91, 197–98

nostalgic mode, 187–88, 197

Notes of a Desolate Man (Huangren shouji; Zhu Tianwen), 192–96

novel, 163–67, 170. *See also* fiction

"On One-Sidedness of Cultural Development" (Wenhua pianzhi lun; Lu Xun), 37, 39, 49

"On the Chinese Theater" (Jiang Guanyun), 66

"On the Modernization of Film Language" (Tan dianying yuyan de xiandaihua; Li Tuo and Zhang Nuanxin), 237

"On the Power of *Mara* Poetry" (Moluo shili shuo; Lu Xun), 37, 48

Opium War (1840s), 97–98

The Origin of German Tragic Drama (Benjamin), 98

Ouyang Yuqian, 69

Palace of Eternal Youth (Changsheng dian; play), 66

Perez, Gilberto, 236, 250–51

photography, 87, 212; and film, 80–81, 236, 238, 245–46; *punctum* in, 243–44

Pickowicz, Paul, 78, 144–45

Plato, 28

Plunder of Peach and Plum (Tao li jie; film), 89

Poetics (Aristotle), 63

poetry, 37, 46–48, 69–70, 102–3, 106
Poland, 38
political campaigns, 107, 110, 157–60.
    See also Cultural Revolution
politics, 1, 36, 48, 108, 172; and aesthet-
    ics, 239; of difference, 214, 219,
    273n8; and Eileen Chang, 169; and
    film, 81; and history writing, 25, 112–
    13; and May Fourth, 11–12; and
    trauma, 116–17; and victimization,
    144, 149–54, 264n7; in Wang Anyi,
    136, 174. *See also* Chinese Communist
    Party; Maoism
positivism, 173
post-Mao period, 103, 108, 143, 174–76,
    224. *See also* New Period
postmodernism, 7–8, 60, 94, 143, 254
Postscript to the Story of the Stone (Hou
    shitou ji), 69
poststructuralism, 9, 94
progress: and history, 96, 127–28; and
    history writing, 7, 142, 269n2; in
    May Fourth thought, 19, 28, 49, 59;
    mindless, 233; and nostalgia, 210;
    technological, 3, 7, 11; *vs.* tradition,
    140; and tragedy, 71–72; and trauma,
    96, 99, 181–82; and universalism,
    124–25, 127–28
prose, 166. *See also* essay, personal
Protestant Reformation, 39
Proust, Marcel, 5, 36, 55, 80, 102, 132, 189;
    Benjamin on, 125–26; involuntary
    memory of, 108–9, 125; and Wang
    Anyi, 133; and Zhu Tianwen, 187
public sphere, 106, 125, 164
Pudovkin, Vsevolod, 86
Pusey, James, 28

Qian Xuantong, 69
Qin Hui, 70
Qing period, 17–18, 37–40, 51

race, 28, 67, 84
"Random Remarks after Illness" (Bing
    hou zatan; Lu Xun), 74

Ranke, Leopold von, 39, 262n46
realism, 235–57; and aesthetic history,
    60; Bazinian, 237, 242, 245–47; in
    drama, 65–68, 71, 241; and experi-
    ence, 105; in fiction, 65–66, 270n2;
    in film, 76–85, 89–90, 245–57; and
    history, 58, 76–85, 175; in literature,
    58, 65–66, 173, 270n2; and montage,
    86; neo-, 90, 223, 237, 245–46, 250–
    51; and new historicism, 223; revolu-
    tionary, 163, 173; *vs.* simulacra, 235–
    37; socialist, 164–65, 236–37, 246; *vs.*
    spectacle, 236, 248–49; tragic, 13, 61–
    66, 68–72; and trauma, 236, 264n7
Reality and Fiction (Jishi yu xugou;
    Wang Anyi), 129–35
The Red Chamber Dream Come True
    (Honglou yuan meng), 69
Red Guards, 6, 116, 120, 151, 155–56
Red Sorghum (film), 270n8
red *vs.* expert, 42–43
reenchantment, 196–98
reform, 6, 26, 99, 226, 232; economic,
    12, 93, 217; late Qing, 38; and myth,
    134; political, 112; technological ap-
    proach to, 42–43; of theater, 69, 71,
    76, 78–79
reification, 182, 184–88, 198, 229; and
    disenchantment, 186–88; and sexual-
    ity, 193–94
the Renaissance, 50
Republican period, 43–44, 51, 129, 220,
    224. *See also* May Fourth era
Rescuing History from the Nation
    (Duara), 20
"Return" (Gui qu lai; Han Shaogong),
    109–11
revolution, 36, 43, 99, 202; and aesthet-
    ics of estrangement, 242–43; and
    Eileen Chang, 168; and film, 156, 158;
    history of, 59, 222, 228, 232; and liter-
    ature, 221; and May Fourth, 18–19,
    24; memory of, 2, 9; and modernity,
    97, 214; and montage, 87, 245; *vs.*
    myth, 138; permanent, 49; and real-

ism, 163, 173; and retreat to individualism, 125; in Shanghai, 226, 228; and spectacle, 219, 274n13; and statism, 21–22; and tragedy, 59, 72; in Wang Anyi, 132–33, 226, 234. *See also* Cultural Revolution

rights, 2, 10, 27, 217, 221; of nation-states, 30; and politics of difference, 273n8; and universalism, 124–25

ritual, 11, 132, 184, 200, 203, 208; everyday, 230–31; and tradition *vs.* modernity, 126, 136–41

Rosen, Philip, 90, 246–47

Rosenstone, Robert, 144

Rossellini, Roberto, 250

Roth, Michael, 23, 38

roundism *(tuanyuan zhuyi)*, 68–71, 78; and *Dream of the Red Chamber*, 69–70, 72

Rousseau, Jean-Jacques, 42, 45

Russia, 10, 122

Sacrificed Youth (Qingchun ji; film), 146

Saga of the Yue Family (Shuo Yue zhuan), 70

Scarry, Elaine, 52–53

Schiller, Johan Christoph Friedrich von, 42, 45, 47, 263n56

Schopenhauer, Arthur, 64

Schwartz, Benjamin, 42

science, 39–41, 59; Lu Xun on, 37, 49–51. *See also* technology

search-for-roots movement, 6, 13, 93, 105–13, 121, 143, 267n39; in film, 107–8, 113, 146; and spiritual crisis, 105–6; and Wang Anyi, 132, 136

the self, 6, 41–42, 46, 52–53, 271n4

self-awareness *(zijue)*, 41, 48

self-reflective *(fansi)* movement, 143

September 11, 2001, attacks, 1

sexuality: and aesthetics, 193–94; commodification of, 191–96, 275n23; in film, 118–19, 239; and memory, 229; in Zhu Tianwen, 185, 191–96

Shakespeare, William, 66–67

Shandong Province, 30

Shanghai, 79, 88, 168, 214, 220; and globalization, 232–33; nostalgia for old, 222–26, 228, 231–33; and Wang Anyi, 222–34

Shanghai style *(haipai)*, 220

Shanghai Triad (film), 148

Shelley, Percy Bysshe, 47

Shen Congwen, 77

simulacra, 243, 245; in film, 239, 254–55, 257; *vs.* realism, 235–37; and spectacle, 218–19

Sino-Japanese War (1894–95), 37, 51, 61

sixiang jiefang (thought liberation movement), 270n4

social Darwinism, 28–29, 59

social relations, 8, 217, 222, 226, 229

socialism, 6, 21, 202, 228; and capitalist modernization, 2, 131–32, 214, 239; and commodification, 221, 230, 274n23; and film, 237; and history, 8, 127, 214, 235; humanistic, 270n13; and May Fourth, 24; and modernity, 129, 131; nostalgia for, 10, 213, 219; and realism, 164–65, 236–37, 246; and universalism, 127, 214

society, 83–85; civil, 2, 125, 183, 221; and individual, 46–48, 76, 128, 263n56

The Society of Spectacle (Debord), 224

"Song of the Pipa" (Pipa xing; Bai Juyi), 70

Song of Unending Sorrow (Changhen ge; Wang Anyi), 129, 136, 223–34

"Song of Unending Sorrows" (Changhen ge; Bai Juyi), 66

Sophocles, 70

Soviet Union, 10, 122

spectacle, 12, 221, 232–33; history as, 205, 210; *vs.* realism, 236, 248–49; revolutionary, 219, 274n13; and Shanghai, 226, 228; and simulacra, 218–19; and use value, 230; and Wang Anyi, 218–19, 222–26, 228–29

spectatorship, 240, 242

Spencer, Herbert, 29, 32

Spring Silkworm (Chun chan; film), 81
Spring Willow Society (Chunliu she), 66–67
Stalin, Joseph, 158
Steinmetz, George, 259n3
Stewart, Susan, 189, 197
Stirner, Max, 45
The Story of Our Uncle (Shushu de gushi; Wang Anyi), 13, 164, 172–78
storytelling, 107, 125, 143, 170–71
Stowe, Harriet Beecher, 67
Street Angel (Malu tianshi; film), 82–83, 87–88, 254
Su Tong, 108, 117, 125
subjective turn, 108
subjectivity, 41, 46, 88, 173, 215; *vs.* collectivism, 106; and commodification, 191–92, 218; and Hollywood, 239–40; individual, 47, 104, 165; universal, 240–41
"Surrounded by Traumatic Memory" (Wang Xiaoming), 9
Suzhou River (Suzhou he; film), 250, 253–57

Taiwan, 14, 187, 199, 203; literature of, 182–83, 185, 188–91, 223; modernization of, 182–85; nostalgia in, 188–91, 212
Tang Xiaobing, 26, 172, 274n23
Tao Qian, 109
Taylor, Charles, 46–47
Tea House (Lao She), 99–100
technology, 40–43, 122, 135, 244; Lu Xun on, 43, 49–51; and mechanical reproduction, 102; of power, 132; and progress, 3, 7, 11; and realism, 81; and reform, 42–43; and socialism, 131–32; and trauma, 77; visual, 224, 238
television, 181, 251
temporality, 58, 124–41; alternative, 214; in film, 247, 275n14; homogenous, 218, 223; instrumental, 135; suspensive, 251; uniform, 216; in Wang Anyi, 228–29

Terdiman, Richard, 186, 259n8
testimonial, 131, 154–55, 269n17
theater: and aesthetic history, 59–60; and Confucianism, 78–79; epic *vs.* classical, 242; Japanese, 66–67; and May Fourth, 12; realist, 65–68, 71, 78, 241; reform of, 69, 71, 76, 78–79; spoken *(huaju)*, 68; traditional *vs.* modern, 66–69, 71, 78–79, 89; tragic, 13, 59–64, 68–69; western, 71
Theory of Film (Kracauer), 80
"Theses on the Philosophy of History" (Benjamin), 96
third world, 19, 84–85
thought liberation movement *(sixiang jiefang)*, 270n4
Three Modern Women (San ge moden nüxing; film), 81
Tian Han, 61
Tian Zhuangzhuang, 118, 154–62, 270n8; *vs.* Xie Jin, 145–46; *vs.* Zhang Yimou, 147–48
Tie Xuan, 75
To Live (Huozhe; film), 146–48, 157, 159
Tönnies, Ferdinand, 4, 183, 274n9
The Torrents (Kuangliu; film), 81
totalitarianism, 45, 193. *See also* authoritarianism
tradition: in *Autumn Moon*, 207–11; *vs.* colonialism, 200; and commodity, 225, 272n8; continuity of, 262n39; cultural, 5–6, 79, 97; and Cultural Revolution, 12; in drama, 66–69, 71, 78–79, 89; and Eileen Chang, 170; and the Enlightenment, 33, 37; and evolutionism, 29; and experience, 102; and history, 5, 32–37, 127–28, 143, 262n39; in Hong Kong, 203; and ideology, 81; and kitsch, 252–53; and Lu Xun, 12–13, 37–48, 53–54; in May Fourth thought, 11, 18–19, 24, 28, 32–37, 53; and memory, 6, 135–41, 218, 268n8; as memory, 32–37; and modernity, 135–41, 182, 253; *vs.* modernity, 4–5, 17–19, 32–37, 39, 53,

76, 143, 205–6, 274n9; and montage, 89; and nostalgia, 10, 122; and ritual, 126; and search for roots, 113; and tragedy, 68, 71–73, 76; and urbanization, 171, 184; and Wang Anyi, 13, 132, 217
tragedy: and Chinese culture, 61–62, 65–66; and existentialism, 62, 71; and historical consciousness, 68–76; Hu Shi on, 61, 70–73, 76; Lu Xun on, 53, 61, 72–76, 78; and realism, 61–66, 68–72; and the sublime, 64–65; in theater, 13, 59–64, 68–69; and tradition, 68, 71–73, 76; *vs.* the tragic, 62–63; in the West, 59, 61–63, 68, 70–72
the tragic: and consciousness, 69, 72–76, 78; and film, 13, 59, 89; and history, 58–90; and May Fourth, 12, 58–90; *vs.* tragedy, 62–63; and visuality, 76–77
trauma: and aesthetics of shock, 243; and allegory, 83; of capitalism, 135, 181–82; Chinese term for, 268n41; and community, 9, 95, 113–14, 147, 266n7; and consciousness, 114, 147, 213; of Cultural Revolution, 93–98, 112–19, 142, 146–48, 266n7; and culture, 52, 113–14, 146–47; and experience, 101–6, 114, 135; in film, 12, 77–78, 94–95, 118, 146–48, 237, 248, 270n8; Freud on, 263n61; of globalization, 9, 181–82, 203, 210; and historiography, 8–11; and history, 12, 51–53, 93–123, 142–62, 175, 270n8; of immigration, 204; and individual, 8, 95, 113–14, 147, 266n7; and language, 115–16; and literature, 52–54, 77, 94; and memory, 3, 13, 36, 51, 53, 97, 112–19, 124; of modernity, 94, 135, 181, 213; of modernization, 9–10, 181–82, 212–13, 249; and realism, 236, 264n7; and reification, 184–85; and time-space compression, 203–4; visual, 12, 58–90, 243; in Wang Anyi, 227; in Xie Jin, 148–54

trauma studies, 94
"Trembling" (Duosuo; Lin Jinlan), 116–17
tuanyuan zhuyi (roundism), 68–72, 78
Turkey, 38
24 Hours of Shanghai (Shanghai ershisi xiaoshi; film), 88

Uncle Tom's Cabin (Stowe), 67
unconscious, 108–11, 147. *See also* consciousness
United States (U.S.), 10, 30, 46, 84, 94, 131
universal principle *(gongli)*, 30–31
universalism: and colonialism, 27, 31, 127; and commodification, 13, 214–20; cultural, 13, 31–32; ethical, 27–28, 31; in history, 2, 13–14, 26, 124–25, 127–28; of Hollywood, 239; in language, 240–41, 257
urbanization: and commodified literature, 220; and consciousness, 265n55, 276n40; and consumer culture, 164, 167–71, 228–29, 274n14; and essayistic mode, 170–71; and experience, 101, 103; and film, 245, 248, 275n5; and memory, 5, 184; in Taiwan, 183–84; and tradition, 171, 184
utopianism, 51, 56, 87, 262n44; communist, 166–67, 214, 222; and consumerism, 195–96; and history, 48–49, 53, 55; in literature, 54–55, 163, 166, 173; of Marxism, 165; and nostalgia, 119–23, 198; and trauma, 53–54

Versailles conference (1919), 30–31
Vertov, Dziga, 87
victimization, political, 144, 149–54, 157–60, 264n7
village, traditional, 35–36, 136, 227; nostalgia for, 188–91, 212. *See also* community
visuality, 13, 239–45; technology of, 224, 238; and the tragic, 76–77; traumatic, 12, 58–90, 243; universal, 240–41, 257

Wang, David, 17, 185
Wang, Edward, 26
Wang Anyi, 13, 124–41, 164, 168, 170, 214, 217; essayistic fiction of, 172–76; essays of, 167; history in, 226–34; on memory, 231–32; and spectacle, 218–19, 222–26, 228–29; and Zhu Tianwen, 198
Wang Guowei, 60, 69, 100; and tragedy, 61, 63–66, 72–73, 76
Wang Hui, 32–35, 54, 73, 263n54
Wang Xiaoming, 9, 260n19
Weber, Max, 4, 132, 183, 213, 216, 268n8, 274n9
Wenhui bao (Assembly of writings; newspaper), 144
the West: aesthetics in, 60, 224–25; and Beijing style, 220; and China, 32–34, 38–46, 97; and Chinese drama, 68–69, 71; culture of, 34, 39–40; history in, 39–40, 49, 200, 261n26; and Hong Kong, 200, 203; and kitsch, 252–53; and Lu Xun, 34; and May Fourth, 18–19; melodrama in, 145; and modernity, 13, 25, 38–46; and modernization, 212; philosophy in, 173; rejection of, 10, 219; and searching for roots, 106; tragedy in, 59, 61–63, 68, 70–72. *See also* Hollywood
"What the Monkeys Can Teach Humans About Making America Fair" (*New York Times* editorial), 30
White, Hayden, 60
Wild Grass (*Yecao*; Lu Xun), 51
Will as Representation (Schopenhauer), 64
Williams, Raymond, 59, 82
Wolin, Rich, 94
Wong Kar-wai, 254–55
Wood, Robin, 84
World Trade Organization (WTO), 30
World War I, 71
wound literature, 13, 93, 143
Wu Wenguang, 155, 248–50
Wu Yonggang, 77
Wu Ziniu, 270n8

Xia Yan, 81, 88–89
Xiao Hong, 98–99
Xiao Wu (The pickpocket; film), 250–55
Xie Fei, 120
Xie Jin, 13, 148–54, 270n13; melodrama in, 144–46, 157; *vs.* Tian Zhuangzhuang, 155, 157, 159, 161–62
xin ganxing (new sensibility), 104
Xinmin congbao (Magazine of the new people), 66
xinqu (new zone of development), 233, 254–55
Xu Jian, 54

Yan Fu, 29
Yan'an, 137
Yang Xiaobin, 52, 95
Yao, Esther, 206
Yellow Earth (Huangtu di; film), 99, 247–48, 270n8
yi (hysteria), 115–16
Yongle, Emperor, 75
Yu Yingshi, 18
Yue Fei, 70

zawen (occasional essays), 169
Zhang Chengzhi, 120–22
Zhang Nuanxin, 146, 237–38, 245
Zhang Wei, 113, 117
Zhang Xianzhong, 74
Zhang Xudong, 103, 117–18, 214, 229, 238, 266n3
Zhang Yimou, 118, 146–48, 157, 270n8
Zhang Yuan, 275n5
Zhaxi Dawa, 108, 117
zhongjian wu (thing in between), 34–35
Zhou Juntao, 270n8
Zhu Tianwen, 183, 185–98, 271n5b; reenchantment in, 196–98; reification in, 186–88; sexuality in, 191–96
zhuangmei (gigantic beauty), 64
zhuanxing qi (period of transition), 216
zijue (self-awareness), 41, 48